U.S. LABOR AND EMPLOYMENT LAWS

1987 Edition

Edited by
Ruth C. Trussell
Senior Legal Editor
BNA's *Labor Relations Reporter*

The Bureau of National Affairs, Inc. Washington, D.C.

Copyright © 1987

The Bureau of National Affairs, Inc.
Washington, D.C. 20037

Library of Congress Cataloging-in-Publication Data

United States.
    U.S. labor and employment laws.

    Rev. ed. of: Federal labor and employment laws / prepared by the BNA editorial staff.
    1. Labor laws and legislation—United States.
I. Trussell, Ruth C. II. United States. Federal labor and employment laws. III. Title IV.
Title: US labor and employment laws.
KF3306   1987   344.73'01   87-18841
ISBN 0-87179-560-4   347.3041

Printed in the United States of America
International Standard Book Number: 0-87179-560-4

PREFACE

U.S. Labor and Employment Laws is a compilation of selected statutes that set forth the basic rights and obligations of employers and employees in both the government and the private sectors. It is an updated and greatly expanded version of *Federal Labor and Employment Laws,* published by BNA Books in 1985. All the statutes that appeared in the earlier work have been retained, and there are several important additions reflecting not only statutory changes but also increased interest in certain areas of labor law, such as the employment of aliens, the rights and opportunities of handicapped workers, and workplace safety.

Laws that were in the earlier work are reprinted as amended through January 1987. Where the amendments are extensive — most notably the Fair Labor Standards Act Amendments of 1985 and the Age Discrimination in Employment Amendments of 1986 — selected portions of the amending Act are printed after the basic statute. These "unincorporated" sections provide useful information concerning the implementation of the amendments, such as effective dates, applicability, or deadlines for the issuance of regulations and guidelines; some contain other congressional mandates, such as directions for studies on the effects of the changes.

The most significant addition in this 1987 edition is the new Part 8, "Alien Employment Laws." It contains all the Immigration and Nationality Act's labor and employment provisions, as amended or added by the Immigration Reform and Control Act of 1986. The changes are published as U.S. Code sections of the basic statute (principally, 8 U.S.C. §§1255a, 1324a, and 1324b). All sections of the law and the amending Act that even remotely deal with the employment of aliens are included, in order to give as much help as possible not only to employers, employees, and potential employees, but also to immigration lawyers, ethnic groups, unions, employer organizations, and others concerned with aliens' status in relation to employment. As with the ADEA and FLSA, relevant "unincorporated" provisions of the 1986 Act appear after the basic statute.

The Migrant and Seasonal Agricultural Worker Protection Act complements the alien employment laws section and appears in its entirety as new Part 9, "Agricultural Worker Protection Laws." First promulgated in 1983 to replace the Farm Labor Contractor Registration Act, it also was amended by the Immigration Reform and Control Act of 1986.

The Rehabilitation Act of 1973 has been updated to reflect major changes and additions effected by the Rehabilitation Act Amendments of 1986. This is followed by the text of an unincorporated "technical amendment" that provides an important clarification concerning an individual's right to sue a state under section 504 of the basic statute.

Finally, the Contract Work Hours and Safety Standards Act, as amended in 1986, has been added to round out the section on government contracting laws.

As in the earlier edition, the Finding List provides the appropriate official U.S. Code title and section numbers of all statutes in the book. The original public law section numbers appear in brackets at the beginning of the relevant paragraphs in the text of each statute.

An updated Appendix, now Part 10, provides references to relevant Executive Orders, guidelines, and regulations that may be found in *Labor Relations Reporter Expediter, Fair Employment Practice Manual, Individual Employment Rights Manual,* or *Wages and Hours Manual,* all published by The Bureau of National Affairs, Inc.

R. C. T.

Washington, D.C.
August 1987

CONTENTS

Part 5. Wage-Hour Laws

Part 6. Government Contracts Laws

Part 7. Occupational Safety Laws

Part 8. Alien Employment Laws

Part 9. Agricultural Worker Laws

Part 10. Appendix

Appendix

1

Constitutional Provisions

First Amendment (1791)

Congress shall make no law respecting an establishment of religion, or prohibiting the free exercise thereof; or abridging the freedom of speech, or of the press; or the right of the people peaceably to assemble, and to petition the Government for a redress of grievances.

Fifth Amendment (1791)

No person shall be held to answer for a capital, or otherwise infamous crime, unless on a presentment or indictment of a Grand Jury, except in cases arising in the land or naval forces, or in the Militia, when in actual service in time of War or public danger; nor shall any person be subject for the same offence to be twice put in jeopardy of life or limb; nor shall be compelled in any criminal case to be a witness against himself, nor be deprived of life, liberty, or property, without due process of law; nor shall private property be taken for public use, without just compensation.

Thirteenth Amendment (1865)

§ 1.

Neither slavery nor involuntary servitude, except as a punishment for crime whereof the party shall have been duly convicted, shall exist within the United States, or any place subject to their jurisdiction.

§ 2.

Congress shall have power to enforce this article by appropriate legislation.

Fourteenth Amendment (1868)

§ 1.

All persons born or naturalized in the United States, and subject to the jurisdiction thereof, are citizens of the United States and of the State wherein they reside. No State shall make or enforce any law which shall abridge the privileges or immunities of citizens of the United States; nor shall any State deprive any person of life, liberty, or property, without due process of law; nor deny to any person within its jurisdiction the equal protection of the laws.

* * *

§ 5.

The Congress shall have power to enforce, by appropriate legislation, the provisions of this article.

2

Antitrust Laws

Sherman Antitrust Act

(P.L. 190, approved July 2, 1890; as last amended by P.L. 97–290, approved October 8, 1982)

§ 1. Trusts, etc., in restraint of trade; penalty

[Sec. 1] Every contract, combination in the form of trust or otherwise, or conspiracy, in restraint of trade or commerce among the several States, or with foreign nations, is declared to be illegal. Every person who shall make any contract or engage in any combination or conspiracy hereby declared to be illegal shall be deemed guilty of a felony, and, on conviction thereof, shall be punished by fine not exceeding one million dollars if a corporation, or, if any other person, one hundred thousand dollars, or by imprisonment not exceeding three years, or by both said punishments, in the discretion of the court.

§ 2. Monopolizing trade a felony; penalty

[Seç. 2] Every person who shall monopolize, or attempt to monopolize, or combine or conspire with any other person or persons, to monopolize any part of the trade or commerce among the several States, or with foreign nations, shall be deemed guilty of a felony, and, on conviction thereof, shall be punished by fine not exceeding one million dollars if a corporation, or, if any other person, one hundred thousand dollars, or by imprisonment not exceeding three years, or by both said punishments, in the discretion of the court.

§ 3. Trusts in Territories or District of Columbia illegal; combination a felony

[Sec. 3] Every contract, combination in form of trust or otherwise, or conspiracy, in restraint of trade or commerce in any Territory of the United States or of the District of Columbia, or in restraint of trade or commerce between any such Territory and another, or between any such Territory or

Territories and any State or States or the District of Columbia, or with foreign nations, or between the District of Columbia and any State or States or foreign nations, is declared illegal. Every person who shall make any such contract or engage in any such combination or conspiracy, shall be deemed guilty of a felony, and, on conviction thereof, shall be punished by fine not exceeding one million dollars if a corporation, or, if any other person, one hundred thousand dollars, or by imprisonment not exceeding three years, or by both said punishments, in the discretion of the court.

§ 4. Jurisdiction of courts; duty of United States attorneys; procedure

[Sec. 4] The several district courts of the United States are invested with jurisdiction to prevent and restrain violations of sections 1 to 7 of this title; and it shall be the duty of the several United States attorneys, in their respective districts, under the direction of the Attorney General, to institute proceedings in equity to prevent and restrain such violations. Such proceedings may be by way of petition setting forth the case and praying that such violation shall be enjoined or otherwise prohibited. When the parties complained of shall have been duly notified of such petition the court shall proceed, as soon as may be, to the hearing and determination of the case; and pending such petition and before final decree, the court may at any time make such temporary restraining order or prohibition as shall be deemed just in the premises.

§ 5. Bringing in additional parties

[Sec. 5] Whenever it shall appear to the court before which any proceeding under section 4 of this title may be pending, that the ends of justice require that other parties should be brought before the court, the court may cause them to be summoned, whether they reside in the district in which the court is held or not; and subpoenas to that end may be served in any district by the marshal thereof.

§ 6. Forfeiture of property in transit

[Sec. 6] Any property owned under any contract or by any combination, or pursuant to any conspiracy (and being the subject thereof) mentioned in section 1 of this title, and being in the course of transportation from one State to another, or to a foreign country, shall be forfeited to the United States, and may be seized and condemned by like proceedings as those provided by law for the forfeiture, seizure, and condemnation of property imported into the United States contrary to law.

§ 6a.   Conduct involving trade or commerce with foreign nations

[Sec. 6a] Sections 1 to 7 of this title shall not apply to conduct involving trade or commerce (other than import trade or import commerce) with foreign nations unless—
  (1) such conduct has a direct, substantial, and reasonably foreseeable effect—
      (A) on trade or commerce which is not trade or commerce with foreign nations, or on import trade or import commerce with foreign nations; or
      (B) on export trade or export commerce with foreign nations, of a person engaged in such trade or commerce in the United States; and
  (2) such effect gives rise to a claim under the provisions of sections 1 to 7 of this title, other than this section.
If sections 1 to 7 of this title apply to such conduct only because of the operation of paragraph (1)(B), then sections 1 to 7 of this title shall apply to such conduct only for injury to export business in the United States.

§ 7.   "Person" defined

[Sec. 7] The word "person", or "persons", wherever used in sections 1 to 7 of this title shall be deemed to include corporations and associations existing under or authorized by the laws of either the United States, the laws of any of the Territories, the laws of any State, or the laws of any foreign country.

Clayton Antitrust Act

**(P.L. 212, approved October 15, 1914; as last amended by
P.L. 94–435, approved September 30, 1976)**

§ 17. Antitrust laws not applicable to labor organizations

[Sec. 6] The labor of a human being is not a commodity or article of commerce. Nothing contained in the antitrust laws shall be construed to forbid the existence and operation of labor, agricultural, or horticultural organizations, instituted for the purposes of mutual help, and not having capital stock or conducted for profit, or to forbid or restrain individual members of such organizations from lawfully carrying out the legitimate objects thereof; nor shall such organizations, or the members thereof, be held or construed to be illegal combinations or conspiracies in restraint of trade, under the antitrust laws.

* * *

§ 52. Statutory restriction of injunctive relief

[Sec. 20] No restraining order or injunction shall be granted by any court of the United States, or a judge or the judges thereof, in any case between an employer and employees, or between employers and employees, or between employees, or between persons employed and persons seeking employment, involving, or growing out of, a dispute concerning terms or conditions of employment, unless necessary to prevent irreparable injury to property, or to a property right, of the party making the application, for which injury there is no adequate remedy at law, and such property or property right must be described with particularity in the application, which must be in writing and sworn to by the applicant or by his agent or attorney.

And no such restraining order or injunction shall prohibit any person or persons, whether singly or in concert, from terminating any relation of employment, or from ceasing to perform any work or labor, or from

10

recommending, advising, or persuading others by peaceful means so to do; or from attending at any place where any such person or persons may lawfully be, for the purpose of peacefully obtaining or communicating information, or from peacefully persuading any person to work or to abstain from working; or from ceasing to patronize or to employ any party to such dispute, or from recommending, advising, or persuading others by peaceful and lawful means so to do; or from paying or giving to, or withholding from, any person engaged in such dispute, any strike benefits or other moneys or things of value; or from peaceably assembling in a lawful manner, and for lawful purposes; or from doing any act or thing which might lawfully be done in the absence of such dispute by any party thereto; nor shall any of the acts specified in this paragraph be considered or held to be violations of any law of the United States.

3

Labor-Management Relations Laws

Norris-LaGuardia Anti-Injunction Act

(P.L. 65, approved March 23, 1932, as last amended by P.L. 98–620, approved November 8, 1984)

§ 101. Issuance of restraining orders and injunctions; limitation; public policy

[Sec. 1] No court of the United States, as herein defined, shall have jurisdiction to issue any restraining order or temporary or permanent injunction in a case involving or growing out of a labor dispute, except in a strict conformity with the provisions of this Act; nor shall any such restraining order or temporary or permanent injunction be issued contrary to the public policy declared in this Act.

§ 102. Public policy in labor matters declared

[Sec. 2] In the interpretation of this Act and in determining the jurisdiction and authority of the court of the United States, as such jurisdiction and authority are herein defined and limited, the public policy of the United States is hereby declared as follows:

Whereas under prevailing economic conditions, developed with the aid of governmental authority for owners of property to organize in the corporate and other forms of ownership association, the individual unorganized worker is commonly helpless to exercise actual liberty of contract and to protect his freedom of labor, and thereby to obtain acceptable terms and conditions of employment, wherefore, though he should be free to decline to associate with his fellows, it is necessary that he have full freedom of association, self-organization, and designation of representatives of his own choosing, to negotiate the terms and conditions of his employment, and that he shall be free from the interference, restraint, or coercion of employers of labor, or their agents, in the designation of such representatives or in self-organization or in other concerted activities for the purpose of collective bargaining or

15

other mutual aid or protection; therefore, the following definitions of, and limitations upon, the jurisdiction and authority of the courts of the United States are hereby enacted.

§ 103. Nonenforceability of undertakings in conflict with public policy; "yellow dog" contracts

[Sec. 3] Any undertaking or promise, such as is described in this Section, or any other undertaking or promise in conflict with the public policy declared in Section 2 of this Act, is hereby declared to be contrary to the public policy of the United States, shall not be enforceable in any court of the United States and shall not afford any basis for the granting of legal or equitable relief by any such court, including specifically the following:

Every undertaking or promise hereafter made, whether written or oral, express or implied, constituting or contained in any contract or agreement of hiring or employment between any individual, firm, company, association, or corporation, and any employee or prospective employee of the same, whereby

(a) Either party to such contract or agreement undertakes or promises not to join, become, or remain a member of any labor organization or of any employer organization; or

(b) Either party to such contract or agreement undertakes or promises that he will withdraw from an employment relation in the event that he joins, becomes, or remains a member of any labor organization or of any employer organization.

§ 104. Enumeration of specific acts not subject to restraining orders or injunctions

[Sec. 4] No court of the United States shall have jurisdiction to issue any restraining order or temporary or permanent injunction in any case involving or growing out of any labor dispute to prohibit any person or persons participating or interested in such dispute (as these terms are herein defined) from doing, whether singly or in concert, any of the following acts:

(a) Ceasing or refusing to perform any work or to remain in any relation of employment;

(b) Becoming or remaining a member of any labor organization or of any employer organization, regardless of any such undertaking or promise as is described in Section 3 of this Act;

(c) Paying or giving to, or withholding from, any person participating or interested in such labor dispute, any strike or unemployment benefits or insurance, or other moneys or things of value;

(d) By all lawful means aiding any person participating or interested in any labor dispute who is being proceeded against in, or is prosecuting, any action or suit in any court of the United States or of any State;

(e) Giving publicity to the existence of, or the facts involved in, any labor dispute, whether by advertising, speaking, patrolling, or by any other method not involving fraud or violence;

(f) Assembling peaceably to act or organize to act in promotion of their interests in a labor dispute;

(g) Advising or notifying any person of an intention to do any of the acts heretofore specified;

(h) Agreeing with other persons to do or not to do any of the acts heretofore specified; and

(i) Advising, urging, or otherwise causing or inducing without fraud or violence the acts heretofore specified, regardless of any such undertaking or promise as is described in Section 3 of this Act.

§ 105. Doing in concert of certain acts as constituting unlawful combination or conspiracy subjecting person to injunctive remedies

[Sec. 5] No court of the United States shall have jurisdiction to issue a restraining order or temporary or permanent injunction upon the ground that any of the persons participating or interested in a labor dispute constitute or are engaged in an unlawful combination or conspiracy because of the doing in concert of the acts enumerated in Section 4 of this Act.

§ 106. Responsibility of officers and members of associations or their organizations for unlawful acts of individual officers, members, and agents

[Sec. 6] No officer or member of any association or organization, and no association or organization participating or interested in a labor dispute, shall be held responsible or liable in any court of the United States for the unlawful acts of individual officers, members, or agents, except upon clear proof of actual participation in, or actual authorization of, such acts, or of ratification of such acts after actual knowledge thereof.

§ 107. Issuance of injunctions in labor disputes; hearing; findings of court; notice to affected persons; temporary restraining order; undertakings

[Sec. 7] No court of the United States shall have jurisdiction to issue a temporary or permanent injunction in any case involving or growing out of a labor dispute, as herein defined, except after hearing the testimony of witnesses in open court (with opportunity for cross-examination) in support of the allegations of a complaint made under oath, and testimony in opposition thereto, if offered, and except after findings of fact by the court, to the effect—

(a) That unlawful acts have been threatened and will be committed unless restrained or have been committed and will be continued unless restrained, but no injunction or temporary restraining order shall be issued on account of any threat or unlawful act excepting against the person or persons, association, or organization making the threat or committing the unlawful act or actually authorizing or ratifying the same after actual knowledge thereof;

(b) That substantial and irreparable injury to complainant's property will follow;

(c) That as to each item of relief granted greater injury will be inflicted upon complainant by the denial of relief than will be inflicted upon defendants by the granting of relief;

(d) That complainant has no adequate remedy at law; and

(e) That the public officers charged with the duty to protect complainant's property are unable or unwilling to furnish adequate protection.

Such hearing shall be held after due and personal notice thereof has been given, in such manner as the court shall direct, to all known persons against whom relief is sought, and also to the chief of those public officials of the county and city within which the unlawful acts have been threatened or committed charged with the duty to protect complainant's property: *Provided, however,* That if a complainant shall also allege that, unless a temporary restraining order shall be issued without notice, a substantial and irreparable injury to complainant's property will be unavoidable, such a temporary restraining order may be issued upon testimony under oath, sufficient, if sustained, to justify the court in issuing a temporary injunction upon a hearing after notice. Such a temporary restraining order shall be effective for no longer than five days and shall become void at the expiration of said five days. No temporary restraining order or temporary injunction shall be issued except on condition that complainant shall first file an undertaking with adequate security in an amount to be fixed by the court sufficient to recompense those enjoined for any loss, expense, or damage caused by the improvident or erroneous issuance of such order or injunction, including all reasonable costs (together with a reasonable attorney's fee) and expense of defense against the order or against the granting of any injunctive relief sought in the same proceeding and subsequently denied by the court.

The undertaking herein mentioned shall be understood to signify an agreement entered into by the complainant and the surety upon which a decree may be rendered in the same suit or proceeding against said complainant and surety, upon a hearing to assess damages of which hearing complainant and surety shall have reasonable notice, the said complainant and surety submitting themselves to the jurisdiction of the court for that purpose. But nothing herein contained shall deprive any party having a claim or cause of action under or upon such undertaking from electing to pursue his ordinary remedy by suit at law or in equity.

§ 108. Noncompliance with obligations involved in labor disputes or failure to settle by negotiation or arbitration as preventing injunctive relief

[Sec. 8] No restraining order or injunctive relief shall be granted to any complainant who has failed to comply with any obligation imposed by law which is involved in the labor dispute in question, or who has failed to make every reasonable effort to settle such dispute either by negotiation or with the aid of any available governmental machinery of mediation or voluntary arbitration.

§ 109. Granting of restraining order or injunction as dependent on previous findings of fact; limitation on prohibitions included in restraining orders and injunctions

[Sec. 9] No restraining order or temporary or permanent injunction shall be granted in a case involving or growing out of a labor dispute, except on the basis of findings of fact made and filed by the court in the record of the case prior to the issuance of such restraining order or injunction; and every restraining order or injunction granted in a case involving or growing out of a labor dispute shall include only a prohibition of such specific act or acts as may be expressly complained of in the bill of complaint or petition filed in such case and as shall be expressly included in said findings of fact made and filed by the court as provided herein.

§ 110. Review by court of appeals of issuance or denial of temporary injunctions; records; precedence

[Sec. 10] Whenever any court of the United States shall issue or deny any temporary injunction in a case involving or growing out of a labor dispute, the court shall, upon the request of any party to the proceedings and on his filing the usual bond for costs, forthwith certify as in ordinary cases the record of the case to the court of appeals for its review. Upon the filing of such record in the court of appeals, the appeal shall be heard and the temporary injunctive order affirmed, modified, or set aside expeditiously.

§ 113. Definitions of terms and words used in chapter

[Sec. 13] When used in this Act, and for the purposes of this Act—
(a) A case shall be held to involve or to grow out of a labor dispute when the case involves persons who are engaged in the same industry, trade, craft, or occupation; or have direct or indirect interests therein; or who are

employees of the same employer; or who are members of the same or an affiliated organization of employers or employees; whether such dispute is (1) between one or more employers or associations of employers and one or more employees or associations of employees; (2) between one or more employers or associations of employers and one or more employers or associations of employers; or (3) between one or more employees or associations of employees and one or more employees or associations of employees; or when the case involves any conflicting or competing interests in a "labor dispute" (as hereinafter defined) of "persons participating or interested" therein (as hereinafter defined).

(b) A person or association shall be held to be a person participating or interested in a labor dispute if relief is sought against him or it, and if he or it is engaged in the same industry, trade, craft, or occupation in which such dispute occurs, or has a direct or indirect interest therein, or is a member, officer, or agent of any association composed in whole or in part of employers or employees engaged in such industry, trade, craft, or occupation.

(c) The term "labor dispute" includes any controversy concerning terms or conditions of employment, or concerning the association or representation of persons in negotiating, fixing, maintaining, changing, or seeking to arrange terms or conditions of employment, regardless of whether or not the disputants stand in the proximate relation of employer and employee.

(d) The term "court of the United States" means any court of the United States whose jurisdiction has been or may be conferred or defined or limited by Act of Congress, including the courts of the District of Columbia.

§ 114. Separability of provisions

[Sec. 14] If any provision of this Act or the application thereof to any person or circumstance is held unconstitutional or otherwise invalid, the remaining provisions of the Act and the application of such provisions to other persons or circumstances shall not be affected thereby.

§ 115. Repeal of conflicting acts

[Sec. 15] All Acts and parts of Acts in conflict with the provisions of this Act are hereby repealed.

National Labor Relations Act, as amended by the Labor Management Relations (Taft-Hartley) Act and the Labor-Management Reporting and Disclosure (Landrum-Griffin) Act

(P.L. 101, passed June 23, 1947; as last amended by P.L. 98–620, approved November 8, 1984)

Chapter 7. Labor-Management Relations

Subchapter I. General Provisions

§ 141. Short title; Congressional declaration of purpose and policy

[Sec. 1] (a) This Act may be cited as the "Labor Management Relations Act, 1947."

(b) Industrial strife which interferes with the normal flow of commerce and with the full production of articles and commodities for commerce, can be avoided or substantially minimized if employers, employees, and labor organizations each recognize under law one another's legitimate rights in their relations with each other, and above all recognize under law that neither party has any right in its relations with any other to engage in acts or practices which jeopardize the public health, safety, or interest.

It is the purpose and policy of this Act, in order to promote the full flow of commerce, to prescribe the legitimate rights of both employees and employers in their relations affecting commerce, to provide orderly and peaceful procedures for preventing the interference by either with the legitimate rights of the other, to protect the rights of individual employees in their relations with labor organizations whose activities affect commerce to define and proscribe practices on the part of labor and management which affect commerce and are inimical to the general welfare, and to protect the rights of the public in connection with labor disputes affecting commerce.

Title V [of Labor Management Relations Act].

§ 142. Definitions

[Sec. 501] When used in this Act—
(1) The term "industry affecting commerce" means any industry or activity in commerce or in which a labor dispute would burden or obstruct commerce or tend to burden or obstruct commerce or the free flow of commerce.
(2) The term "strike" includes any strike or other concerted stoppage of work by employees (including a stoppage by reason of the expiration of a collective-bargaining agreement) and any concerted slow down or other concerted interruption of operations by employees.
(3) The terms "commerce," "labor disputes," "employer," "employee," "labor organization," "representative," "person," and "supervisor" shall have the same meaning as when used in the National Labor Relations Act as amended by this Act.

§ 143. Saving provisions

[Sec. 502] Nothing in this Act shall be construed to require an individual employee to render labor or service without his consent, nor shall anything in this Act be construed to make the quitting of his labor by an individual employee an illegal act; nor shall any court issue any process to compel the performance by an individual employee of such labor or service, without his consent; nor shall the quitting of labor by an employee or employees in good faith because of abnormally dangerous conditions for work at the place of employment of such employee or employees be deemed a strike under this chapter.

§ 144. Separability of provisions

[Sec. 503] If any provision of this Act, or the application of such provision to any person or circumstance, shall be held invalid, the remainder of this Act, or the application of such provision to persons or circumstances other than those as to which it is held invalid, shall not be affected thereby.

Title I [of LMRA]. Amendment of National Labor Relations Act

Subchapter II. National Labor Relations

[Sec. 101] The National Labor Relations Act is hereby amended to read as follows:

§ 151. Findings and declaration of policy

"[Sec. 1] The denial by some employers of the right of employees to organize and the refusal by some employers to accept the procedure of collective bargaining lead to strikes and other forms of industrial strife or unrest, which have the intent or the necessary effect of burdening or obstructing commerce by (a) impairing the efficiency, safety, or operation of the instrumentalities of commerce; (b) occurring in the current of commerce; (c) materially affecting, restraining, or controlling the flow of raw materials or manufactured or processed goods from or into the channels of commerce, or the prices of such materials or goods in commerce; or (d) causing diminution of employment and wages in such volume as substantially to impair or disrupt the market for goods flowing from or into the channels of commerce.

"The inequality of bargaining power between employees who do not possess full freedom of association or actual liberty of contract, and employers who are organized in the corporate or other forms of ownership association substantially burdens and affects the flow of commerce, and tends to aggravate recurrent business depressions, by depressing wage rates and the purchasing power of wage earners in industry and by preventing the stabilization of competitive wage rates and working conditions within and between industries.

"Experience has proved that protection by law of the right of employees to organize and bargain collectively safeguards commerce from injury, impairment, or interruption, and promotes the flow of commerce by removing certain recognized sources of industrial strife and unrest, by encouraging practices fundamental to the friendly adjustment of industrial disputes arising out of differences as to wages, hours, or other working conditions, and by restoring equality of bargaining power between employers and employees.

"Experience has further demonstrated that certain practices by some labor organizations, their officers, and members have the intent or the necessary effect of burdening or obstructing commerce by preventing the free flow of goods in such commerce through strikes and other forms of industrial unrest or through concerted activities which impair the interest of the public in the free flow of such commerce. The elimination of such practices is a necessary condition to the assurance of the rights herein guaranteed.

"It is hereby declared to be the policy of the United States to eliminate the causes of certain substantial obstructions to the free flow of commerce and to mitigate and eliminate these obstructions when they have occurred by encouraging the practice and procedure of collective bargaining and by protecting the exercise by workers of full freedom of association, self-organization, and designation of representatives of their own choosing, for the purpose of negotiating the terms and conditions of their employment or other mutual aid or protection."

§ 152. Definitions

"**[Sec. 2]** When used in this Act—

"(1) The term 'person' includes one or more individuals, labor organizations, partnerships, associations, corporations, legal representatives, trustees, trustees in cases under Title 11 of the United States Code, or receivers.

"(2) The term 'employer' includes any person acting as an agent of an employer, directly or indirectly, but shall not include the United States or any wholly owned Government corporation, or any Federal Reserve Bank, or any State or political subdivision thereof, or any person subject to the Railway Labor Act [4 USC 151 et seq.], as amended from time to time, or any labor organization (other than when acting as an employer), or anyone acting in the capacity of officer or agent of such labor organization.

"(3) The term 'employee' shall include any employee, and shall not be limited to the employees of a particular employer, unless the Act explicitly states otherwise, and shall include any individual whose work has ceased as a consequence of, or in connection with, any current labor dispute or because of any unfair labor practice, and who has not obtained any other regular and substantially equivalent employment, but shall not include any individual employed as an agricultural laborer, or in the domestic service of any family or person at his home, or any individual employed by his parent or spouse, or any individual having the status of an independent contractor, or any individual employed as a supervisor, or any individual employed by an employer subject to the Railway Labor Act, as amended from time to time, or by any other person who is not an employer as herein defined.

"(4) The term 'representatives' includes any individual or labor organization.

"(5) The term 'labor organization' means any organization of any kind, or any agency or employee representation committee or plan, in which employees participated and which exists for the purpose, in whole or in part, of dealing with employers concerning grievances, labor disputes, wages, rates of pay, hours of employment, or conditions of work.

"(6) The term 'commerce' means trade, traffic, commerce, transportation, or communication among the several States, or between the District of Columbia or any Territory of the United States and any State or other Territory, or between any foreign country and any State, Territory, or the District of Columbia, or within the District of Columbia or any Territory, or between points in the same State but through any other State or any Territory or the District of Columbia or any foreign country.

"(7) The term 'affecting commerce' means in commerce, or burdening or obstructing commerce or the free flow of commerce, or having led or tending to lead to a labor dispute burdening or obstructing commerce or the free flow of commerce.

"(8) The term 'unfair labor practice' means any unfair labor practice listed in section 8.

"(9) The term 'labor dispute' includes any controversy concerning terms, tenure or conditions of employment, or concerning the association or representation of persons in negotiating, fixing, maintaining, changing, or seeking to arrange terms or conditions of employment, regardless of whether the disputants stand in the proximate relation of employer and employees.

"(10) The term 'National Labor Relations Board' means the National Labor Relations Board provided for in section 3 of this Act.

"(11) The term 'supervisor' means any individual having authority, in the interest of the employer, to hire, transfer, suspend, lay off, recall, promote, discharge, assign, reward, or discipline other employees, or responsibly to direct them or to adjust their grievances, or effectively to recommend such action, if in connection with the foregoing the exercise of such authority is not of a merely routine or clerical nature, but requires the use of independent judgment.

"(12) The term 'professional employee' means—

"(a) any employee engaged in work (i) predominantly intellectual and varied in character as opposed to routine mental, manual, mechanical, or physical work; (ii) involving the consistent exercise of discretion and judgment in its performance; (iii) of such a character that the output produced or the result accomplished cannot be standardized in relation to a given period of time; (iv) requiring knowledge of an advanced type in a field of science or learning customarily acquired by a prolonged course of specialized intellectual instruction and study in an institution of higher learning or a hospital, as distinguished from a general academic education or from an apprenticeship or from training in the performance of routine mental, manual, or physical processes; or

"(b) any employee, who (i) has completed the courses of specialized intellectual instruction and study described in clause (iv) of paragraph (a), and (ii) is performing related work under the supervision of a professional person to qualify himself to become a professional employee as defined in paragraph (a).

"(13) In determining whether any person is acting as an 'agent' of another person so as to make such other person responsible for his acts, the question of whether the specific acts performed were actually authorized or subsequently ratified shall not be controlling.

"(14) The term 'health care institution' shall include any hospital, convalescent hospital, health maintenance organization, health clinic, nursing home, extended care facility, or other institution devoted to the care of sick, infirm, or aged person."

§ 153. National Labor Relations Board

"[Sec. 3] (a) The National Labor Relations Board (hereinafter called the 'Board') created by this Act prior to its amendment by the Labor Management Relations Act, 1947, is hereby continued as an agency of the United States, except that the Board shall consist of five instead of three members, appointed by the President by and with the advice and consent of the Senate. Of the two additional members so provided for, one shall be appointed for a term of five years and the other for a term of two years. Their successors, and the successors of the other members, shall be appointed for terms of five years each, excepting that any individual chosen to fill a vacancy shall be appointed only for the unexpired term of the member whom he shall succeed. The President shall designate one member to serve as Chairman of the Board. Any member of the Board may be removed by the President, upon notice and hearing, for neglect of duty or malfeasance in office, but for no other cause.

"(b) The Board is authorized to delegate to any group of three or more members any or all of the powers which it may itself exercise. The Board is also authorized to delegate to its regional directors its powers under section 9 to determine the unit appropriate for the purpose of collective bargaining, to investigate and provide for hearings, and determine whether a question of representation exists, and to direct an election or take a secret ballot under subsection (c) or (e) of section 9 and certify the results thereof, except that upon the filing of a request therefor with the Board by any interested person, the Board may review any action of a regional director delegated to him under this paragraph, but such a review shall not, unless specifically ordered by the Board, operate as a stay of any action taken by the regional director. A vacancy in the Board shall not impair the right of the remaining members to exercise all of the powers of the Board, and three members of the Board shall, at all times constitute a quorum of the Board, except that two members shall constitute a quorum of any group designated pursuant to the first sentence hereof. The Board shall have an official seal which shall be judicially noticed.

"(c) The Board shall at the close of each fiscal year make a report in writing to Congress and to the President summarizing significant case activities and operations for that fiscal year.

"(d) There shall be a General Counsel of the Board who shall be appointed by the President by and with the advice and consent of the Senate, for a term of four years. The General Counsel of the Board shall exercise general supervision over all attorneys employed by the Board (other than administrative law judges and legal assistants to Board members) and over the officers and employees in the regional offices. He shall have final authority, on behalf of the Board, in respect of the investigation of charges and issuance of complaints under section 10, and in respect of the prosecution of such complaints before the Board, and shall have such other duties as the Board may prescribe or as may be provided by law. In case of a vacancy in the office of the General Counsel the President is authorized to designate the officer or employee who shall act as General Counsel during such vacancy, but no person or persons so designated shall so act (1) for more than forty days when the Congress is in session unless a nomination to fill such vacancy shall have been submitted to the Senate, or (2) after the adjournment sine die of the session of the Senate in which such nomination was submitted."

§ 154. Same; eligibility for reappointment; officers and employees; payment of expenses

"[Sec. 4] (a) Each member of the Board and the General Counsel of the Board shall be eligible for reappointment, and shall not engage in any other business, vocation, or employment. The Board shall appoint an executive secretary, and such attorneys, examiners, and regional directors, and such other employees as it may from time to time find necessary for the proper performance of its duties. The Board may not employ any attorneys for the purpose of reviewing transcripts of hearings or preparing drafts of opinions except that any attorney employed for assignment as a legal assistant to any Board member may for such Board member review such transcripts and prepare such drafts. No administrative law judge's report shall be reviewed, either before or after its publication, by any person other than a member of the Board or his legal assistant, and no administrative law judge shall advise or consult with the Board with respect to exceptions taken to his findings, rulings, or recommendations. The Board may establish or utilize such regional, local, or other agencies, and utilize such voluntary and uncompensated services, as may from time to time be needed. Attorneys appointed under this section may, at the direction of the Board, appear for and represent the Board in any case in court. Nothing in this subchapter shall be construed to authorize the Board to appoint individuals for the purpose of conciliation or mediation, or for economic analysis.

"(b) All of the expenses of the Board, including all necessary traveling and subsistence expenses outside the District of Columbia incurred by the members or employees of the Board under its orders, shall be allowed and paid on the presentation of itemized vouchers therefor approved by the Board or by any individual it designates for that purpose."

§ 155. Same; principal office; conducting inquiries throughout country; participation in decisions or inquiries conducted by member

"[Sec. 5] The principal office of the Board shall be in the District of Columbia, but it may meet and exercise any or all of its powers at any other place. The Board may, by one or more of its members or by such agents or agencies as it may designate, prosecute any inquiry necessary to its functions in any part of the United States. A member who participates in such an inquiry shall not be disqualified from subsequently participating in a decision of the Board in the same case."

§ 156. Same; rules and regulations

"[Sec. 6] The Board shall have authority from time to time to make, amend, and rescind, in the manner prescribed by the Administrative Procedure Act, such rules and regulations as may be necessary to carry out the provisions of this Act."

§ 157. Rights of employees as to organization, collective bargaining, etc.

"[Sec. 7] Employees shall have the right to self-organization, to form, join or assist labor organizations, to bargain collectively through representatives of their own choosing, and to engage in other concerted activities for the purpose of collective bargaining or other mutual aid or protection, and shall also have the right to refrain from any or all of such activities except to the extent that such right may be affected by an agreement requiring membership in a labor organization as a condition of employment as authorized in section 159(a)(3)."

§ 158. Unfair labor practices

"[Sec. 8] (a) It shall be an unfair labor practice for an employer—

"(1) to interfere with, restrain, or coerce employees in the exercise of the rights guaranteed in section 7;

"(2) to dominate or interfere with the formation or administration of any labor organization or contribute financial or other support to it: *Provided*, That subject to rules and regulations made and published by the Board pursuant to section 6, an employer shall not be prohibited from permitting employees to confer with him during working hours without loss of time or pay;

"(3) by discrimination in regard to hire or tenure of employment or any term or condition of employment to encourage or discourage membership in any labor organization; *Provided*, That nothing in this Act, or in any other statute of the United States, shall preclude an employer from making an agreement with a labor organization (not established, maintained, or assisted by any action defined in section 8(a) of this Act as an unfair labor practice) to require as a condition of employment membership therein on or after the thirtieth day following the beginning of such employment or the effective date of such agreement, whichever is the later, (i) if such labor organization is the representative of the employees as provided in section 9(a), in the appropriate collective-bargaining unit covered by such agreement when made; and (ii) unless following an election held as provided in section 9(e) within one year preceding the effective date of such agreement the Board shall have certified that at least a majority of the employees eligible to vote in such election have voted to rescind the authority of such labor organization to make such an agreement: *Provided further*, That no employer shall justify any discrimination against an employee for nonmembership in a labor organization (A) if he has reasonable grounds for believing that such membership was not available to the employee on the same terms and conditions generally applicable to other members or (B) if he has reasonable grounds for believing that membership was denied or terminated for reasons other than the failure of the employee to tender the periodic dues and the initiation fees uniformly required as a condition of acquiring or retaining membership;

"(4) to discharge or otherwise discriminate against an employee because he has filed charges or given testimony under this Act;

"(5) to refuse to bargain collectively with the representatives of his employees, subject to the provisions of section 9(a).

"(b) It shall be an unfair labor practice for a labor organization or its agents—

"(1) to restrain or coerce (A) employees in the exercise of the rights guaranteed in section 7: *Provided*, That this paragraph shall not impair the right of a labor organization to prescribe its own rules with respect to the acquisition or retention of membership therein; or (B) an employer in the selection of his representatives for the purposes of collective bargaining or the adjustment of grievances;

"(2) to cause or attempt to cause an employer to discriminate against an employee in violation of subsection (a)(3) or to discriminate against an employee with respect to whom membership in such organization has been denied or terminated on some ground other than his failure to tender the periodic dues and the initiation fees uniformly required as a condition of acquiring or retaining membership;

"(3) to refuse to bargain collectively with an employer, provided it is the representative of his employees subject to the provisions of section 9(a);

"(4)(i) to engage in, or to induce or encourage any individual employed by any person engaged in commerce or in an industry affecting commerce to engage in, a strike or a refusal in the course of his employment to use, manufacture, process, transport, or otherwise handle or work on any goods, articles, materials or commodities or to perform any services; or (ii) to threaten, coerce, or restrain any person engaged in commerce or in an industry affecting commerce, where in either case an object thereof is:

"(A) forcing or requiring any employer or self-employed person to join any labor or employer organization or to enter into any agreement which is prohibited by section 8(e);

"(B) forcing or requiring any person to cease using, selling, handling, transporting, or otherwise dealing in the products of any other producer, processor, or manufacturer, or to cease doing business with any other person, or forcing or requiring any other employer to recognize or bargain with a labor organization as the representative of his employees unless such labor organization has been certified as the representative of such employees under the provisions of section 9: *Provided*, That nothing contained in this clause (B) shall be construed to make unlawful, where not otherwise unlawful, any primary strike or primary picketing;

"(C) forcing or requiring any employer to recognize or bargain with a particular labor organization as the representative of his employees if another labor organization has been certified as the representative of such employees under the provisions of section 9;

"(D) forcing or requiring any employer to assign particular work to employees in a particular labor organization or in a particular trade, craft, or class rather than to employees in another labor organization or in another trade, craft, or class, unless such employer is failing to conform to an order or certification of the Board determining the bargaining representative for employees performing such work:

"*Provided*, That nothing contained in this subsection (b) shall be construed to make unlawful a refusal by any person to enter upon the premises of any employer (other than his own employer), if the employees of such employer are engaged in a strike ratified or approved by a representative of such employees whom such employer is required to recognize under this Act: *Provided further*, That for the purposes of this paragraph (4) only, nothing contained in such paragraph shall be construed to prohibit publicity, other than picketing, for the purpose of truthfully advising the public, including consumers and members of a labor organization, that a product or products are produced by an employer with whom the labor organization has a primary dispute and are distributed by another employer, as long as such publicity does not have an effect of inducing any individual employed by any person other than the primary employer in the course of his employment to refuse to pick up, deliver, or transport any goods, or not to perform any services, at the establishment of the employer engaged in such distribution;

"(5) to require of employees covered by an agreement authorized under subsection (a)(3) the payment, as a condition precedent to becoming a member of such organization, of a fee in an amount which the Board finds excessive or discriminatory under all the circumstances. In making such a finding, the Board shall consider, among other relevant factors, the practices and customs of labor organizations in the particular industry, and the wages currently paid to the employees affected;

"(6) to cause or attempt to cause an employer to pay or deliver or agree to pay or deliver any money or other thing of value, in the nature of an exaction, for services which are not performed or not to be performed; and

"(7) to picket or cause to be picketed, or threaten to picket or cause to be picketed, any employer where an object thereof is forcing or requiring an employer to recognize or bargain with a labor organization as the representative of his employees, or forcing or requiring the employees of an employer to accept or select such labor organization as their collective bargaining representative unless such labor organization is currently certified as the representative of such employees:

"(A) Where the employer has lawfully recognized in accordance with this Act any other labor organization and a question concerning representation may not appropriately be raised under section 9(c) of this Act,

"(B) where within the preceding twelve months a valid election under section 9(c) of this Act has been conducted, or

"(C) where such picketing has been conducted without a petition under section 9(c) being filed within a reasonable period of time not to exceed thirty days from the commencement of such picketing: *Provided*, That when such a petition has been filed the Board shall forthwith, without regard to the provisions of section 9(c)(1) or the absence of a showing of a substantial interest on the part of the labor organization, direct an election in such unit as the Board finds to be appropriate and shall certify the results thereof:

Provided further, That nothing in this subparagraph (C) shall be construed to prohibit any picketing or other publicity for the purpose of truthfully advising the public (including consumers) that an employer does not employ members of, or have a contract with, a labor organization, unless an effect of such picketing is to induce any individual employed by any other person in the course of his employment, not to pick up, deliver or transport any goods or not to perform any services.

"Nothing in this paragraph (7) shall be construed to permit any act which would otherwise be an unfair labor practice under this subsection.

"(c) The expressing of any views, argument, or opinion, or the dissemination thereof, whether in written, printed, graphic, or visual form, shall not constitute or be evidence of an unfair labor practice under any of the provisions of this Act, if such expression contains no threat of reprisal or force or promise of benefit.

"(d) For the purposes of this section, to bargain collectively is the performance of the mutual obligation of the employer and the representative of the employees to meet at reasonable times and confer in good faith with respect to wages, hours, and other terms and conditions of employment, or the negotiation of an agreement, or any question arising thereunder, and the execution of a written contract incorporating any agreement reached if requested by either party, but such obligation does not compel either party to agree to a proposal or require the making of a concession: *Provided*, That where there is in effect a collective-bargaining contract covering employees in an industry affecting commerce, the duty to bargain collectively shall also mean that no party to such contract shall terminate or modify such contract, unless the party desiring such termination or modification—

"(1) serves a written notice upon the other party to the contract of the proposed termination or modification sixty days prior to the expiration date thereof, or in the event such contract contains no expiration date, sixty days prior to the time it is proposed to make such termination or modification;

"(2) offers to meet and confer with the other party for the purpose of negotiating a new contract or a contract containing the proposed modifications;

"(3) notifies the Federal Mediation and Conciliation Service within thirty days after such notice of the existence of a dispute, and simultaneously therewith notifies any State or Territorial agency established to mediate and conciliate disputes within the State or Territory where the dispute occurred, provided no agreement has been reached by that time; and

"(4) continues in full force and effect, without resorting to strike or lock-out, all the terms and conditions of the existing contract for a period of sixty days after such notice is given or until the expiration date of such contract, whichever occurs later.

"The duties imposed upon employers, employees and labor organizations by paragraphs (2) to (4) of this subsection shall become inapplicable upon an intervening certification of the Board, under which the labor organization or individual, which is a party to the contract, has been superseded as or ceased to be the representative of the employees subject to the provisions of section 9(a), and the duties so imposed shall not be construed as requiring either party to discuss or agree to any modification of the terms and conditions contained in a contract for a fixed period, if such modification is to become effective before such terms and conditions can be reopened under the provisions of the contract. Any employee who engages in a strike within any notice period specified in this subsection, or who engages in any strike within the appropriate period specified in subsection (g) of this section, shall lose his status as an employee of the employer engaged in the particular labor dispute, for the purposes of sections 8, 9, and 10 of this Act, as amended, but such loss of status for such employee shall terminate if and when he is reemployed by such employer. Whenever the collective bargaining involves employees of a health care institution, the provisions of this section 8(d) shall be modified as follows:

"(A) The notice of section 8(d)(1) shall be ninety days; the notice of section 8(d)(3) shall be sixty days; and the contract period of section 8(d)(4) shall be ninety days.

"(B) Where the bargaining is for an initial agreement following certification or recognition, at least thirty days' notice of the existence of a dispute shall be given by the labor organization to the agencies set forth in section 8(d)(3).

"(C) After notice is given to the Federal Mediation and Conciliation Service under either clause (A) or (B) of this sentence, the Service shall promptly communicate with the parties and use its best efforts by mediation and conciliation to bring them to agreement. The parties shall participate fully and promptly in such meetings as may be undertaken by the Service for the purpose of aiding in a settlement of the dispute.

"(e) It shall be an unfair labor practice for any labor organization and any employer to enter into any contract or agreement, express or implied, whereby such employer ceases or refrains or agrees to cease or refrain from handling, using, selling, transporting or otherwise dealing in any of the products of any other employer, or to cease doing business with any other person, and any contract or agreement entered into heretofore or hereafter containing such an agreement shall be to such extent unenforcible and void: *Provided*, That nothing in this subsection (e) shall apply to an agreement between a labor organization and an employer in the construction industry relating to the contracting or subcontracting of work to be done at the site of the construction, alteration, painting, or repair of a building, structure, or other work: *Provided further*, That for the purposes of this subsection (e) and section 8(b)(4)(B) the terms 'any employer', 'any person engaged in commerce or any industry affecting commerce', and 'any person' when used in relation to the terms 'any other producer, processor, or manufacturer,' 'any other employer' or 'any other person' shall not include persons in the relation of a jobber, manufacturer, contractor, or subcontractor working on the goods or premises of the jobber or manufacturer or performing parts of an integrated process of production in the apparel and clothing industry: *Provided further*, That nothing in this Act shall prohibit the enforcement of any agreement which is within the foregoing exception.

"(f) It shall not be an unfair labor practice under subsections (a) and (b) of this section for an employer engaged primarily in the building and construction industry to make an agreement covering employees engaged (or who, upon their employment, will be engaged) in the building and construction industry with a labor organization of which building and construction employees are members (not established, maintained, or assisted by any action defined in section 8(a) of this Act as an unfair labor practice) because (1) the majority status of such labor organization has not been established under the provisions of section 9 of this Act prior to the making of such agreement, or (2) such agreement requires as a condition of employment, membership in such labor organization after the seventh day following the beginning of such employment or the effective date of the agreement, whichever is later, or (3) such agreement requires the employer to notify such labor organization of opportunities for employment with such employer, or gives such labor organization an opportunity to refer qualified applicants for such employment, or (4) such agreement specifies minimum training or experience qualifications for employment or provides for priority in opportunities for employment based upon length of service with such employer, in the industry or in the particular geographical area: *Provided*, That nothing in this subsection shall set aside the final proviso to section 8(a)(3) of this Act: *Provided further*, That any agreement which would be invalid but for clause (1) of this subsection, shall not be a bar to a petition filed pursuant to section 9(c) or 9(e).

"(g) A labor organization before engaging in any strike, picketing, or other concerted refusal to work at any health care institution shall, not less than ten days prior to such action, notify the institution in writing and the Federal Mediation and Conciliation Service of that intention, except that in the case of bargaining for an initial agreement following certification or recognition the notice required by this subsection shall not be given until the expiration of the period specified in clause (B) of the last sentence of section 8(d) of this Act. The notice shall state the date and time that such action will commence. The notice, once given, may be extended by the written agreement of both parties."

§ 158a. Providing facilities for operations of Federal Credit Unions

Provision by an employer of facilities for the operations of a Federal Credit Union on the premises of such employer shall not be deemed to be intimidation, coercion, interference, restraint or discrimination within the provisions of sections 157 and 158 of this title, or acts amendatory thereof.

§ 159. Representatives and elections

"[Sec. 9] (a) Representatives designated or selected for the purposes of collective bargaining by the majority of the employees in a unit appropriate for such purposes, shall be the exclusive representatives of all the employees in such unit for the purposes of collective bargaining in respect to rates of pay, wages, hours of employment, or other conditions of employment: *Provided,* That any individual employee or a group of employees shall have the right at any time to present grievances to their employer and to have such grievances adjusted, without the intervention of the bargaining representative, as long as the adjustment is not inconsistent with the terms of a collective-bargaining contract or agreement then in effect: *Provided further,* That the bargaining representative has been given opportunity to be present at such adjustment.

"(b) The Board shall decide in each case whether, in order to assure to employees the fullest freedom in exercising the rights guaranteed by this Act, the unit appropriate for the purposes of collective bargaining shall be the employer unit, craft unit, plant unit, or subdivision thereof: *Provided,* That the Board shall not (1) decide that any unit is appropriate for such purposes if such unit includes both professional employees and employees who are not professional employees unless a majority of such professional employees vote for inclusion in such unit; or (2) decide that any craft unit is inappropriate for such purposes on the ground that a different unit has been established by a prior Board determination, unless a majority of the employees in the proposed craft unit vote against separate representation or (3) decide that any unit is appropriate for such purposes if it includes, together with other employees, any individual employed as a guard to enforce against employees and other persons rules to protect property of the employer or to protect the safety of persons on the employer's premises; but no labor organization shall be certified as the representative of employees in a bargaining unit of guards if such organization admits to membership, or is affiliated directly or indirectly with an organization which admits to membership, employees other than guards.

"(c)(1) Whenever a petition shall have been filed, in accordance with such regulations as may be prescribed by the Board—

"(A) by an employee or group of employees or any individual or labor organization acting in their behalf alleging that a substantial number of employees (i) wish to be represented for collective bargaining and that their employer declines to recognize their representative as the representative defined in section 9(a), or (ii) assert that the individual or labor organization, which has been certified or is being currently recognized by their employer as the bargaining representative, is no longer a representative as defined in section 9(a); or

"(B) by an employer, alleging that one or more individuals or labor organizations have presented to him a claim to be recognized as the representative defined in section 9(a):

the Board shall investigate such petition and if it has reasonable cause to believe that a question of representation affecting commerce exists shall provide for an appropriate hearing upon due notice. Such hearing may be conducted by an officer or employee of the regional office, who shall not make any recommendations with respect thereto. If the Board finds upon the record of such hearing that such a question of representation exists, it shall direct an election by secret ballot and shall certify the results thereof.

"(2) In determining whether or not a question of representation affecting commerce exists, the same regulations and rules of decision shall apply irrespective of the identity of the persons filing the petition or the kind of relief sought and in no case shall the Board deny a labor organization a place on the ballot by reason of an order with respect to such labor organization or its predecessor not issued in conformity with section 10(c).

"(3) No election shall be directed in any bargaining unit or any subdivision within which, in the preceding twelve-month period, a valid election shall have been held. Employees engaged in an economic strike who are not entitled to reinstatement shall be eligible to vote under such regulations as the Board shall find are consistent with the purposes and provisions of this Act in any election conducted within twelve months after the commencement of the strike. In any election where none of the choices on the ballot receives a majority, a runoff shall be conducted, the ballot providing for a selection between the two choices receiving the largest and second largest number of valid votes cast in the election.

"(4) Nothing in this section shall be construed to prohibit the waiving of hearings by stipulation for the purpose of a consent election in conformity with regulations and rules of decision of the Board.

"(5) In determining whether a unit is appropriate for the purposes specified in subsection (b) the extent to which the employees have organized shall not be controlling.

"(d) Whenever an order of the Board made pursuant to section 10(c) is based in whole or in part upon facts certified following an investigation pursuant to subsection (c) of this section and there is a petition for the enforcement or review of such order, such certification and the record of such investigation shall be included in the transcript of the entire record required to be filed under section 10(e) or 10(f), and thereupon the decree of the court enforcing, modifying, or setting aside in whole or in part the order of the Board shall be made and entered upon the pleadings, testimony, and proceedings set forth in such transcript.

"(e)(1) Upon the filing with the Board, by 30 per centum or more of the employees in a bargaining unit covered by an agreement between their employer and a labor organization made pursuant to section 8(a)(3), of a petition alleging the desire that such authority be rescinded, the Board shall take a secret ballot of the employees in such unit and certify the results thereof to such labor organization and to the employer.

"(2) No election shall be conducted pursuant to this subsection in any bargaining unit or any subdivision within which, in the preceding twelve-month period, a valid election shall have been held."

§ 160. Prevention of unfair labor practices

"[Sec. 10] (a) The Board is empowered, as hereinafter provided, to prevent any person from engaging in any unfair labor practice (listed in section 8) affecting commerce. This power shall not be affected by any other means of adjustment or prevention that has been or may be established by agreement, law, or otherwise: *Provided,* That the Board is empowered by agreement with any agency of any State or Territory to cede to such agency jurisdiction over any cases in any industry (other than mining, manufacturing, communications, and transportation except where predominantly local in character) even though such cases may involve labor disputes affecting commerce, unless the provisions of the State or Territorial statute applicable to the determination of such cases by such agency is inconsistent with the corresponding provision of this Act or has received a construction inconsistent therewith.

"(b) Whenever it is charged that any person has engaged in or is engaging in any such unfair labor practice, the Board, or any agent or agency designated by the Board for such purposes, shall have power to issue and cause to be served upon such person a complaint stating the charges in that respect, and containing a notice of hearing before the Board or a member thereof, or before a designated agent or agency, at a place therein fixed, not less than five days after the serving of said complaint: *Provided,* That no complaint shall issue based upon any unfair labor practice occurring more than six months prior to the filing of the charge with the Board and the service of a copy thereof upon the person against whom such charge is made, unless the person aggrieved thereby was prevented from filing such charge by reason of service in the armed forces, in which event the six-month period shall be computed from the day of his discharge. Any such complaint may be amended by the member, agent, or agency conducting the hearing or the Board in its discretion at any time prior to the issuance of an order based thereon. The person so complained of shall have the right to file an answer to the original or amended complaint and to appear in person or otherwise and give testimony at the place and time fixed in the complaint. In the discretion of the member, agent, or agency conducting the hearing or the Board, any other person may be allowed to intervene in the said proceeding and to present testimony. Any such proceeding shall, so far as practicable, be conducted in accordance with the rules of evidence applicable in the district courts of the United States under the rules of civil procedure for the district courts of the United States, adopted by the Supreme Court of the United States pursuant to the Act of June 19, 1934 (U.S.C., title 28, secs. 723-B, 723-C).

"(c) The testimony taken by such member, agent, or agency or the Board shall be reduced to writing and filed with the Board. Thereafter, in its discretion, the Board upon notice may take further testimony or hear argument. If upon the preponderance of the testimony taken the Board shall be of the opinion that any person named in the complaint has engaged in or is engaging in any such unfair labor practice, then the Board shall state its findings of fact and shall issue and cause to be served on such person an order requiring such person to cease and desist from such unfair labor practice, and to take such affirmative action including reinstatement of employees with or without back pay, as will effectuate the policies of this Act: *Provided,* That where an order directs reinstatement of an employee, back pay may be required of the employer or labor organization, as the case may be, responsible for the discrimination suffered by him: *And provided further,* That in determining whether a complaint shall issue alleging a violation of section 8(a)(1) or section 8(a)(2), and in deciding such cases, the same regulations and rules of decision shall apply irrespective of whether or not the labor organization affected is affiliated with a labor organization national or international in scope. Such order may further require such person to make reports from time to time showing the extent to which it has complied with the order. If upon the preponderance of the testimony taken the Board shall not be of the opinion that the person named in the complaint has engaged in or is engaging in any such unfair labor practice, then the Board shall state its findings of fact and shall issue an order dismissing the said complaint. No order of the Board shall require the reinstatement of any individual as an employee who has been suspended or discharged, or the payment to him of any back pay, if such individual was suspended or discharged for cause. In case the evidence is presented before a member of the Board, or before an examiner or examiners thereof, such member, or such examiner or examiners, as the case may be, shall issue and cause to be served on the parties to the proceedings a proposed report, together with a recommended order, which shall be filed with the Board, and if no exceptions are filed within twenty days after service thereof upon such parties, or within such further period as the Board may authorize, such recommended order shall become the order of the Board and become effective as therein prescribed.

"(d) Until the record in a case shall have been filed in a court, as hereinafter provided, the Board may at any time upon reasonable notice and in such manner as it shall deem proper modify or set aside, in whole or in part, any finding or order made or issued by it.

"(e) The Board shall have power to petition any court of appeals of the United States, or if all the courts of appeals to which application may be made are in vacation, any district court of the United States, within any circuit or district, respectively, wherein the unfair labor practice in question occurred or wherein such person resides or transacts business, for the enforcement of such order and for appropriate temporary relief or restraining order, and shall file in the court the record in the proceedings, as provided in section 2112 of title 28, United States Code. Upon the filing of such petition, the court shall cause notice thereof to be served upon such person, and thereupon shall have jurisdiction of the proceeding and of the question determined therein, and shall have power to grant such temporary relief or restraining order as it deems just and proper, and to make and enter a decree enforcing, modifying, and enforcing as so modified, or setting aside in whole or in part the order of the Board. No objection that has not been urged before the Board, its member, agent, or agency, shall be considered by the court, unless the failure or neglect to urge such objection shall be excused because of extraordinary circumstances. The findings of the Board with respect to questions of fact if supported by substantial evidence on the record considered as a whole shall be conclusive. If either party shall apply to the court for leave to adduce additional evidence and shall show to the satisfaction of the court that such additional evidence is material and that there were reasonable grounds for the failure to adduce such evidence in the hearing before the Board, its member, agent, or agency, the court may order such additional evidence to be taken before the Board, its member, agent, or agency, and to be made a part of the record. The Board may modify its findings as to the facts, or make new findings, by reason of additional evidence so taken and filed, and it shall file such modified or new findings, which findings with respect to questions of fact if supported by substantial evidence on the record considered as a whole shall be conclusive, and shall file its recommendations, if any, for the modification or setting aside of its original order. Upon the filing of the record with it the jurisdiction of the court shall be exclusive and its judgment and decree shall be final, except that the same shall be subject to review by the appropriate United States court of appeals if application was made to the district court as hereinabove provided, and by the Supreme Court of the United States upon writ of certiorari or certification as provided in section 1254 of title 28.

"(f) Any person aggrieved by a final order of the Board granting or denying in whole or in part the relief sought may obtain a review of such order in any United States court of appeals in the circuit wherein the unfair labor practice in question was alleged to have been engaged in or wherein such person resides or transacts business, or in the United States Court of

Appeals for the District of Columbia, by filing in such court a written petition praying that the order of the Board be modified or set aside. A copy of such petition shall be forthwith transmitted by the clerk of the court to the Board, and thereupon the aggrieved party shall file in the court the record in the proceeding, certified by the Board, as provided in section 2112 of the title 28, United States Code. Upon the filing of such petition, the court shall proceed in the same manner as in the case of an application by the Board under subsection (e) of this section, and shall have the same jurisdiction to grant to the Board such temporary relief or restraining order as it deems just and proper, and in like manner to make and enter a decree enforcing, modifying, and enforcing as so modified, or setting aside in whole or in part the order of the Board; the findings of the Board with respect to questions of fact if supported by substantial evidence on the record considered as a whole shall in like manner be conclusive.

"(g) The commencement of proceedings under subsection (e) or (f) of this section shall not, unless specifically ordered by the court, operate as a stay of the Board's order.

"(h) When granting appropriate temporary relief or a restraining order, or making and entering a decree enforcing, modifying, or enforcing as so modified, or setting aside in whole or in part an order of the Board, as provided in this section, the jurisdiction of courts sitting in equity shall not be limited by the Act entitled 'An Act to amend the Judicial Code and to define and limit the jurisdiction of courts sitting in equity, and for other purposes', approved March 23, 1932 (U.S.C., Supp. VII, title 29, secs. 101–115).

"(i) [Repealed.]

"(j) The Board shall have power, upon issuance of a complaint as provided in subsection (b) charging that any person has engaged in or is engaging in an unfair labor practice, to petition any district court of the United States (including the District Court of the United States for the District of Columbia), within any district wherein the unfair labor practice in question is alleged to have occurred or wherein such person resides or transacts business, for appropriate temporary relief or restraining order. Upon the filing of any such petition the court shall cause notice thereof to be served upon such person, and thereupon shall have jurisdiction to grant to the Board such temporary relief or restraining order as it deems just and proper.

"(k) Whenever it is charged that any person has engaged in an unfair labor practice with the meaning of paragraph (4)(D) of section 8(b), the Board is empowered and directed to hear and determine the dispute out of which such unfair labor practice shall have arisen, unless, within ten days after notice that such charge has been filed, the parties to such dispute submit to the Board satisfactory evidence that they have adjusted, or agreed upon methods for the voluntary adjustment of, the dispute. Upon compliance by the parties to the dispute with the decision of the Board or upon such voluntary adjustment of the dispute, such charge shall be dismissed.

"(l) Whenever it is charged that any person has engaged in an unfair labor practice within the meaning of paragraph (4)(A), (B), or (C) of section 8(b) or section 8(e) or section 8(b)(7), the preliminary investigation of such charge shall be made forthwith and given priority over all other cases except cases of like character in the office where it is filed or to which it is referred. If, after such investigation, the officer or regional attorney to whom the matter may be referred has reasonable cause to believe such charge is true and that a complaint should issue, he shall, on behalf of the Board, petition any district court of the United States (including the District Court of the United States for the District of Columbia) within any district where the unfair labor practice in question has occurred, is alleged to have occurred, or wherein such person resides or transacts business, for appropriate injunctive relief pending the final adjudication of the Board with respect to such matter. Upon the filing of any such petition the district court shall have jurisdiction to grant such injunctive relief or temporary restraining order as it deems just and proper, notwithstanding any other provision of law: *Provided further*, that no temporary restraining order shall be issued without notice unless a petition alleges that substantial and irreparable injury to the charging party will be unavoidable and such temporary restraining order shall be effective for no longer than five days and will become void at the expiration of such period: *Provided further*, that such officer or regional attorney shall not apply for any restraining order under section 8(b)(7) if a charge against the employer under 8(a)(2) has been filed and after the preliminary investigation, he has reasonable cause to believe that such charge is true and that a complaint should issue. Upon filing of any such petition, the courts shall cause notice thereof to be served upon any person involved in the charge and such person, including the charging party, shall be given an opportunity to appear by counsel and present any relevant testimony: *Provided further*, that for the purposes of this subsection district courts shall be deemed to have jurisdiction of a labor organization (1) in the district in which such organization maintains its principal office, or (2) in any district in which its duly authorized officers or agents are engaged in promoting or protecting the interests of employee members. The service of legal process upon such officer or agent shall constitute service upon the labor organization and make such organization a party to the suit. In situations where such relief is appropriate the procedure specified herein shall apply to charges with respect to section 8(b)(4)(D).

"(m) Whenever it is charged that any person has engaged in an unfair labor practice within the meaning of subsection (a)(3) or (b)(2) of section 8, such charge shall be given priority over all other cases except cases of like character in the office where it is filed or to which it is referred and cases given priority under subsection (l)."

§ 161. Investigatory powers of Board

"[Sec. 11] For the purpose of all hearings and investigations, which, in the opinion of the Board, are necessary and proper for the exercise of the powers vested in it by section 9 and section 10—

"(1) The Board, or its duly authorized agents or agencies, shall at all reasonable times have access to, for the purpose of examination, and the right to copy any evidence of any person being investigated or proceeded against that relates to any matter under investigation or in question. The Board, or any member thereof, shall upon application of any party to such proceedings, forthwith issue to such party subpoenas requiring the attendance and testimony of witnesses or the production of any evidence in such proceeding or investigation requested in such application. Within five days after the service of a subpoena on any person requiring the production of any evidence in his possession or under his control, such person may petition the Board to revoke, and the Board shall revoke, such subpoena if in its opinion the evidence whose production is required does not relate to any matter under investigation, or any matter in question in such proceedings, or if in its opinion such subpoena does not describe with sufficient particularity the evidence whose production is required. Any member of the Board, or any agent or agency designated by the Board for such purposes, may administer oaths and affirmations, examine witnesses, and receive evidence. Such attendance of witnesses and the production of such evidence may be required from any place in the United States, or any Territory or possession thereof, at any designated place of hearing.

"(2) In case of contumacy or refusal to obey a subpoena issued to any person, any district court of the United States or the United States courts of any Territory or possession, or the District Court of the United States for the District of Columbia, within the jurisdiction of which the inquiry is carried on or within the jurisdiction of which said person guilty of contumacy or refusal to obey is found or resides or transacts business, upon application by the Board shall have jurisdiction to issue to such person an order requiring such person to appear before the Board, its member, agent, or agency, there to produce evidence if so ordered, or there to give testimony touching the matter under investigation or in question; and any failure to obey such order of the court may be punished by said court as a contempt thereof.

"(3) [Repealed.]

"(4) Complaints, orders and other process and papers of the Board, its member, agent, or agency, may be served either personally or by registered or certified mail or by telegraph or by leaving a copy thereof at the principal office or place of business of the person required to be served. The verified return by the individual so serving the same setting forth the manner of such service shall be proof of the same, and the return post office receipt or telegraph receipt thereof when registered or certified and mailed or when telegraphed as aforesaid shall be proof of service of the same. Witnesses summoned before the Board, its member, agent, or agency, shall be paid the same fees and mileage that are paid witnesses in the courts of the United States, and witnesses whose depositions are taken and the persons taking the same shall severally be entitled to the same fees as are paid for like services in the courts of the United States.

"(5) All process of any court to which application may be made under this Act may be served in the judicial district wherein the defendant or other person required to be served resides or may be found.

"(6) The several departments and agencies of the Government, when directed by the President, shall furnish the Board, upon its request, all records, papers, and information in their possession relating to any matter before the Board."

§ 162. Offenses and penalties

"[Sec. 12] Any person who shall willfully resist, prevent, impede, or interfere with any member of the Board or any of its agents or agencies in the performance of duties pursuant to this Act shall be punished by a fine of not more than $5,000 or by imprisonment for not more than one year, or both."

§ 163. Right to strike preserved

"[Sec. 13] Nothing in this Act, except as specifically provided for herein, shall be construed so as either to interfere with or impede or diminish in any way the right to strike, or to affect the limitations or qualifications on that right."

§ 164. Construction of provisions

"[Sec. 14] (a) Nothing herein shall prohibit any individual employed as a supervisor from becoming or remaining a member of a labor organization, but no employer subject to this Act shall be compelled to deem individuals defined herein as supervisors as employees for the purpose of any law, either national or local, relating to collective bargaining.

"(b) Nothing in this Act shall be construed as authorizing the execution or application of agreements requiring membership in a labor organization as a condition of employment in any State or Territory in which such execution or application is prohibited by State or Territorial law.

"(c)(1) The Board, in its discretion, may, by rule of decision or by published rules adopted pursuant to the Administrative Procedure Act, decline to assert jurisdiction over any labor dispute involving any class or category of employers, where, in the opinion of the Board, the effect of such labor dispute on commerce is not sufficiently substantial to warrant the exercise of its jurisdiction: *Provided*, That the Board shall not decline to assert jurisdiction over any labor dispute over which it would assert jurisdiction under the standards prevailing upon August 1, 1959.

"(2) Nothing in this Act shall be deemed to prevent or bar any agency or the courts of any State or Territory (including the Commonwealth of Puerto Rico, Guam, and the Virgin Islands), from assuming and asserting jurisdiction over labor disputes over which the Board declines, pursuant to paragraph (1) of this subsection, to assert jurisdiction."

§ 165. Conflict of laws

"[Sec. 15] Wherever the application of the provisions of section 272 of chapter 10 of the Act entitled 'An Act to establish a uniform system of bankruptcy throughout the United States', approved July 1, 1898, and Act amendatory thereof and supplementary thereto (U.S.C., title 11, sec. 672), conflicts with the application of the provisions of this Act, this Act shall prevail: *Provided*, That in any situation where the provisions of this Act cannot be validly enforced, the provisions of such other Acts shall remain in full force and effect."

§ 166. Separability of provisions

"[Sec. 16] If any provision of this Act, or the application of such provision to any person or circumstances, shall be held invalid, the remainder of this Act, or the application of such provision to persons or circumstances other than those as to which it is held invalid, shall not be affected thereby."

§ 167. Short title of [NLRA]

"[Sec. 17] This Act may be cited as the 'National Labor Relations Act'."

§ 168. Validation of certificates and other Board actions

"[Sec. 18] No petition entertained, no investigation made, no election held, and no certification issued by the National Labor Relations Board, under any of the provisions of section 9 of the National Labor Relations Act, as amended, shall be invalid by reason of the failure of the Congress of

Industrial Organizations to have complied with the requirements of section 9(f), (g), or (h) of the aforesaid Act prior to December 22, 1949, or by reason of the failure of the American Federation of Labor to have complied with the provisions of section 9(f), (g), or (h) of the aforesaid Act prior to November 7, 1947: *Provided,* That no liability shall be imposed under any provision of this Act upon any person for failure to honor any election or certificate referred to above, prior to the effective date of this amendment: *Provided, however,* That this proviso shall not have the effect of setting aside or in any way affecting judgments or decrees heretofore entered under section 10(e) or (f) and which have become final."

§ 169. Employees with religious convictions; payment of dues and fees

"[Sec. 19] Any employee who is a member of and adheres to established and traditional tenets or teachings of a bona fide religion, body, or sect which has historically held conscientious objections to joining or financially supporting labor organizations shall not be required to join or financially support any labor organization as a condition of employment; except that such employee may be required in a contract between such employees' employer and a labor organization in lieu of periodic dues and initiation fees, to pay sums equal to such dues and initiation fees to a nonreligious, nonlabor organization charitable fund exempt from taxation under section 501(c)(3) of title 26 of the Internal Revenue Code, chosen by such employee from a list of at least three such funds, designated in such contract or if the contract fails to designate such funds, then to any such fund chosen by the employee. If such employee who holds conscientious objections pursuant to this section requests the labor organization to pursue the grievance-arbitration procedure on the employee's behalf, the labor organization is authorized to charge the employee for the reasonable cost of using such procedure."

Title II [of LMRA]. Conciliation of Labor Disputes In Industries Affecting Commerce; National Emergencies

§ 171. Declaration of purpose and policy

[Sec. 201] It is the policy of the United States that—
(a) sound and stable industrial peace and the advancement of the general welfare, health, and safety of the Nation and of the best interests of employers and employees can most satisfactorily be secured by the settlement

of issues between employers and employees through the processes of conference and collective bargaining between employers and the representatives of
their employees;

(b) the settlement of issues between employers and employees through
collective bargaining may be advanced by making available full and adequate governmental facilities for conciliation, mediation, and voluntary
arbitration to aid and encourage employers and the representatives of their
employees to reach and maintain agreements concerning rates of pay, hours,
and working conditions, and to make all reasonable efforts to settle their
differences by mutual agreement reached through conferences and collective
bargaining or by such methods as may be provided for in any applicable
agreement for the settlement of disputes; and

(c) certain controversies which arise between parties to collective-
bargaining agreements may be avoided or minimized by making available
full and adequate governmental facilities for furnishing assistance to employers and the representatives of their employees in formulating for inclusion
within such agreements provision for adequate notice of any proposed
changes in the terms of such agreements, for the final adjustment of
grievances or questions regarding the application or interpretation of such
agreements, and other provisions designed to prevent the subsequent arising
of such controversies.

§ 172. Federal Mediation and Conciliation Service

[Sec. 202] (a) There is hereby created an independent agency to be known
as the Federal Mediation and Conciliation Service (herein referred to as the
"Service", except that for sixty days after the date of the enactment of this
Act such term shall refer to the Conciliation Service of the Department of
Labor). The Service shall be under the direction of a Federal Mediation and
Conciliation Director (hereinafter referred to as the "Director"), who shall
be appointed by the President by and with the advice and consent of the
Senate. The Director shall not engage in any other business, vocation, or
employment.

(b) The Director is authorized, subject to the civil-service laws, to appoint
such clerical and other personnel as may be necessary for the execution of the
functions of the Service, and shall fix their compensation in accordance with
the Classification Act of 1949, as amended, and may, without regard to the
provisions of the civil-service laws and the Classification Act of 1949 as
amended, appoint and fix the compensation of such conciliators and media-
tors as may be necessary to carry out the functions of the Service. The
Director is authorized to make such expenditures for supplies, facilities, and
services as he deems necessary. Such expenditures shall be allowed and paid

upon presentation of itemized vouchers therefor approved by the Director or by any employee designated by him for that purpose.

(c) The principal office of the Service shall be in the District of Columbia, but the Director may establish regional offices convenient to localities in which labor controversies are likely to arise. The Director may by order, subject to revocation at any time, delegate any authority and discretion conferred upon him by this Act to any regional director, or other officer or employee of the Service. The Director may establish suitable procedures for cooperation with State and local mediation agencies. The Director shall make an annual report in writing to Congress at the end of the fiscal year.

(d) All mediation and conciliation functions of the Secretary of Labor or the United States Conciliation Service under section 8 of the Act entitled "An Act to create a Department of Labor", approved March 4, 1913 (U.S.C., title 29, sec. 51), and all functions of the United States Conciliation Service under any other law are hereby transferred to the Federal Mediation and Conciliation Service, together with the personnel and records of the United States Conciliation Service. Such transfer shall take effect the sixtieth day after the date of enactment of this Act. Such transfer shall not affect any proceedings pending before the United States Conciliation Service or any certification, order, rule, or regulation theretofore made by it or by the Secretary of Labor. The Director and the Service shall not be subject in any way to the jurisdiction or authority of the Secretary of Labor or any official or division of the Department of Labor.

§ 173. Functions of Service

[Sec. 203] (a) It shall be the duty of the Service, in order to prevent or minimize interruptions of the free flow of commerce growing out of labor disputes, to assist parties to labor disputes in industries affecting commerce to settle such disputes through conciliation and mediation.

(b) The Service may proffer its services in any labor dispute in any industry affecting commerce, either upon its own motion or upon the request of one or more of the parties to the dispute, whenever in its judgment such dispute threatens to cause a substantial interruption of commerce. The Director and the Service are directed to avoid attempting to mediate disputes which would have only a minor effect on interstate commerce if State or other conciliation service are available to the parties. Whenever the Service does proffer its services in any disputes, it shall be the duty of the Service promptly to put itself in communication with the parties and to use its best efforts, by mediation and conciliation, to bring them to agreement.

(c) If the Director is not able to bring the parties to agreement by conciliation within a reasonable time, he shall seek to induce the parties voluntarily to seek other means of settling the dispute without resort to strike, lock-out, or other coercion, including submission to the employees in the bargaining unit of the employer's last offer of settlement for approval or rejection in a secret ballot. The failure or refusal of either party to agree to any procedure suggested by the Director shall not be deemed a violation of any duty or obligation imposed by this Act.

(d) Final adjustment by a method agreed upon by the parties is hereby declared to be the desirable method for settlement of grievance disputes arising over the application or interpretation of an existing collective-bargaining agreement. The Service is directed to make its conciliation and mediation services available in the settlement of such grievance disputes only as a last resort and in exceptional cases.

(e) The Service is authorized and directed to encourage and support the establishment and operation of joint labor management activities conducted by plant, area, and industrywide committees designed to improve labor management relationships, job security and organizational effectiveness, in accordance with the provisions of section 205A.

§ 174. Co-equal obligations of employees, their representatives, and management to minimize disputes

[Sec. 204] (a) In order to prevent or minimize interruptions of the free flow of commerce growing out of labor disputes, employers and employees and their representatives, in any industry affecting commerce, shall—

(1) exert every reasonable effort to make and maintain agreements concerning rates of pay, hours, and working conditions, including provision for adequate notice of any proposed change in the terms of such agreements;

(2) whenever a dispute arises over the terms or application of a collective-bargaining agreement and a conference is requested by a party or prospective party thereto, arrange promptly for such a conference to be held and endeavor in such conference to settle such dispute expeditiously; and

(3) in case such dispute is not settled by conference, participate fully and promptly in such meetings as may be undertaken by the Service under this Act for the purpose of aiding in a settlement of the dispute.

§ 175. National Labor-Management Panel; creation and composition; appointment, tenure, and compensation; duties

[Sec. 205] (a) There is hereby created a National Labor-Management Panel which shall be composed of twelve members appointed by the President, six of whom shall be selected from among persons outstanding in the field of management and six of whom shall be selected from among persons outstanding in the field of labor. Each member shall hold office for a term of three years, except that any member appointed to fill a vacancy occurring prior to the expiration of the term for which his predecessor was appointed shall be appointed for the remainder of such term, and the terms of office of the members first taking office shall expire, as designated by the President at the time of appointment, four at the end of the first year, four at the end of the second year, and four at the end of the third year after the date of appointment. Members of the panel, when serving on business of the panel, shall be paid compensation at the rate of $25 per day, and shall also be entitled to receive an allowance for actual and necessary travel and subsistence expenses while so serving away from their places of residence.

(b) It shall be the duty of the panel, at the request of the Director, to advise in the avoidance of industrial controversies and the manner in which mediation and voluntary adjustment shall be administered, particularly with reference to controversies affecting the general welfare of the country.

§ 175a. Assistance to plant, area, and industrywide labor management committees

[Sec. 205A] (a)(1) The Service is authorized and directed to provide assistance in the establishment and operation of plant, area and industrywide labor management committees which—

(A) have been organized jointly by employers and labor organizations representing employees in that plant, area, or industry; and

(B) are established for the purpose of improving labor management relationships, job security, organizational effectiveness, enhancing economic development or involving workers in decisions affecting their jobs including improving communication with respect to subjects of mutual interest and concern.

(2) The Service is authorized and directed to enter into contracts and to make grants, where necessary or appropriate, to fulfill its responsibilities under this section.

(b)(1) No grant may be made, no contract may be entered into and no other assistance may be provided under the provisions of this section to a plant labor management committee unless the employees in that plant are represented by a labor organization and there is in effect at that plant a collective bargaining agreement.

(2) No grant may be made, no contract may be entered into and no other assistance may be provided under the provisions of this section to an area or industrywide labor management committee unless its participants include any labor organizations certified or recognized as the representative of the employees of an employer participating in such committee. Nothing in this clause shall prohibit participation in an area or industrywide committee by an employer whose employees are not represented by a labor organization.

(3) No grant may be made under the provisions of this section to any labor management committee which the Service finds to have as one of its purposes the discouragement of the exercise of rights contained in section 7 of the National Labor Relations Act (29 U.S.C. 157), or the interference with collective bargaining in any plant, or industry.

(c) The Service shall carry out the provisions of this section through an office established for that purpose.

(d) There are authorized to be appropriated to carry out the provisions of this section $10,000,000 for the fiscal year 1979, and such sums as may be necessary thereafter.

§ 176. National emergencies; appointment of board of inquiry by President; report; contents; filing with Service

[Sec. 206] Whenever in the opinion of the President of the United States, a threatened or actual strike or lockout affecting an entire industry or a substantial part thereof engaged in trade, commerce, transportation, transmission, or communication among the several States or with foreign nations, or engaged in the production of goods for commerce, will, if permitted to occur or to continue, imperil the national health or safety, he may appoint a board of inquiry to inquire into the issues involved in the dispute and to make a written report to him within such time as he shall prescribe. Such report shall include a statement of the facts with respect to the dispute, including each party's statement of its position but shall not contain any recommendations. The President shall file a copy of such report with the Service and shall make its contents available to the public.

§ 177. Board of inquiry

[Sec. 207] (a) A board of inquiry shall be composed of a chairman and such other members as the President shall determine, and shall have power to sit and act in any place within the United States and to conduct such hearings either in public or in private, as it may deem necessary or proper, to ascertain the facts with respect to the causes and circumstances of the dispute.

(b) Members of a board of inquiry shall receive compensation at the rate of $50 for each day actually spent by them in the work of the board, together with necessary travel and subsistence expenses.

(c) For the purpose of any hearing or inquiry conducted by any board appointed under this title, the provisions of sections 9 and 10 (relating to the attendance of witnesses and the production of books, papers, and documents) of the Federal Trade Commission Act of September 16, 1914, as amended

(U.S.C., title 15, secs. 49 and 50, as amended), are hereby made applicable to the powers and duties of such board.

§ 178. Injunctions during national emergency

[Sec. 208] (a) Upon receiving a report from a board of inquiry the President may direct the Attorney General to petition any district court of the United States having jurisdiction of the parties to enjoin such strike or lock-out or the continuing thereof, and if the court finds that such threatened or actual strike or lock-out—

> (i) affects an entire industry or a substantial part thereof engaged in trade, commerce, transportation, transmission, or communication among the several States or with foreign nations, or engaged in the production of goods for commerce; and
>
> (ii) if permitted to occur or to continue, will imperil the national health or safety, it shall have jurisdiction to enjoin any such strike or lock-out, or the continuing thereof, and to make such other orders as may be appropriate.

(b) In any case, the provisions of the Act of March 23, 1932, entitled "An Act to amend the Judicial Code and to define and limit the jurisdiction of courts sitting in equity, and for other purposes", shall not be applicable.

(c) The order or orders of the court shall be subject to review by the appropriate circuit court of appeals and by the Supreme Court upon writ of certiorari or certification as provided in section 1254 of title 28.

§ 179. Injunctions during national emergency; adjustment efforts by parties during injunction period

[Sec. 209] (a) Whenever a district court has issued an order under section 208 enjoining acts or practices which imperil or threaten to imperil the national health or safety, it shall be the duty of the parties to the labor dispute giving rise to such order to make every effort to adjust and settle their differences, with the assistance of the Service created by this Act. Neither party shall be under any duty to accept, in whole or in part, any proposal of settlement made by the Service.

(b) Upon the issuance of such order, the President shall reconvene the board of inquiry which has previously reported with respect to the dispute. At the end of a sixty-day period (unless the dispute has been settled by that time), the board of inquiry shall report to the President the current position of the parties and the efforts which have been made for settlement, and shall include a statement by each party of its position and a statement of the employer's last offer of settlement. The President shall make such report available to the public. The National Labor Relations Board, within the succeeding fifteen days, shall take a secret ballot of the employees of each employer involved in the dispute on the question of whether they wish to accept the final offer of settlement made by their employer as stated by him and shall certify the results thereof to the Attorney General within five days thereafter.

§ 180. Discharge of injunction upon certification of results of election or settlement; report to Congress

[Sec. 210] Upon the certification of the results of such ballot or upon a settlement being reached, whichever happens sooner, the Attorney General shall move the court to discharge the injunction, which motion shall then be granted and the injunction discharged. When such motion is granted, the President shall submit to the Congress a full and comprehensive report of the proceedings, including the findings of the board of inquiry and the ballot taken by the National Labor Relations Board, together with such recommendations as he may see fit to make for consideration and appropriate action.

§ 181. Compilation of collective bargaining agreements, etc.; use of data

[Sec. 211] (a) For the guidance and information of interested representatives of employers, employees, and the general public, the Bureau of Labor Statistics of the Department of Labor shall maintain a file of copies of all available collective bargaining agreements and other available agreements and actions thereunder settling or adjusting labor disputes. Such file shall be open to inspection under appropriate conditions prescribed by the Secretary of Labor, except that no specific information submitted in confidence shall be disclosed.

(b) The Bureau of Labor Statistics in the Department of Labor is authorized to furnish upon request of the Service, or employers, employees, or their representatives, all available data and factual information which may aid in the settlement of any labor dispute, except that no specific information submitted in confidence shall be disclosed.

§ 182. Exemption of Railway Labor Act

[Sec. 212] The provisions of this title shall not be applicable with respect to any matter which is subject to the provisions of the Railway Labor Act, as amended from time to time.

§ 183. Conciliation of labor disputes in the health care industry

[Sec. 213] (a) If, in the opinion of the Director of the Federal Mediation and Conciliation Service a threatened or actual strike or lockout affecting a health care institution will, if permitted to occur or to continue, substantially interrupt the delivery of health care in the locality concerned, the Director may further assist in the resolution of the impasse by establishing within 30 days after the notice to the Federal Mediation and Conciliation Service under clause (A) of the last sentence of section 8(d) (which is required by clause (3) of such section 8(d)), or within 10 days after the notice under clause (B), an impartial Board of Inquiry to investigate the issues involved in the dispute and to make a written report thereon to the parties within fifteen (15) days after the establishment of such a Board. The written report shall contain the findings of fact together with the Board's recommendations for settling the dispute, with the objective of achieving a prompt, peaceful and just settlement of the dispute. Each such Board shall be composed of such number of individuals as the Director may deem desirable. No member appointed under this section shall have any interest or involvement in the health care institutions or the employee organizations involved in the dispute.

(b)(1) Members of any board established under this section who are otherwise employed by the Federal Government shall serve without compensation but shall be reimbursed for travel, subsistence, and other necessary expenses incurred by them in carrying out its duties under this section.

(2) Members of any board established under this section who are not subject to paragraph (1) shall receive compensation at a rate prescribed by the Director but not to exceed the daily rate prescribed for GS-18 of the General Schedule under section 5332 of title 5, United States Code, including travel for each day they are engaged in the performance of their duties under this section and shall be entitled to reimbursement for travel, subsistence, and other necessary expenses incurred by them in carrying out their duties under this section.

(c) After the establishment of a board under subsection (a) of this section and for 15 days after any such board has issued its report, no change in the status quo in effect prior to the expiration of the contract in the case of negotiations for a contract renewal, or in effect prior to the time of the impasse in the case of an initial bargaining negotiation, except by agreement, shall be made by the parties to the controversy.

(d) There are authorized to be appropriated such sums as may be necessary to carry out the provisions of this section.

Title III [of LMRA]. Liabilities of and Restrictions on Labor and Management

§ 185. Suits by and against labor organizations

[Sec. 301] (a) Suits for violation of contracts between an employer and a labor organization representing employees in an industry affecting commerce as defined in this Act, or between any such labor organizations, may be brought in any district court of the United States having jurisdiction of the parties, without respect to the amount in controversy or without regard to the citizenship of the parties.

(b) Any labor organization which represents employees in an industry affecting commerce as defined in this Act and any employer whose activities affect commerce as defined in this Act shall be bound by the acts of its agents. Any such labor organization may sue or be sued as an entity and in behalf of the employees whom it represents in the courts of the United States. Any money judgment against a labor organization in a district court of the United States shall be enforceable only against the organization as an entity and against its assets, and shall not be enforceable against any individual member or his assets.

(c) For the purposes of actions and proceedings by or against labor organizations in the district courts of the United States, district courts shall be deemed to have jurisdiction of a labor organization (1) in the district in which such organization maintains its principal office, or (2) in any district in which its duly authorized officers or agents are engaged in representing or acting for employee members.

(d) The service of summons, subpoena, or other legal process of any court of the United States upon an officer or agent of a labor organization, in his capacity as such, shall constitute service upon the labor organization.

(e) For the purposes of this section, in determining whether any person is acting as an "agent" of another person so as to make such other person responsible for his acts, the question of whether the specific acts performed were actually authorized or subsequently ratified shall not be controlling.

§ 186. Restrictions on financial transactions

[Sec. 302] (a) It shall be unlawful for any employer or association of employers or any person who acts as a labor relations expert, adviser, or consultant to an employer or who acts in the interest of an employer to pay, lend, or deliver, or agree to pay, lend, or deliver, any money or other thing of value—

(1) to any representative of any of his employees who are employed in an industry affecting commerce; or

(2) to any labor organization or any officer or employee thereof, which represents, seeks to represent, or would admit to membership, any of the employees of such employer who are employed in an industry affecting commerce; or

(3) to any employee or group or committee of employees of such employer employed in an industry affecting commerce in excess of their normal compensation for the purpose of causing such employee or group or committee directly or indirectly to influence any other employees in the exercise of the right to organize and bargain collectively through representatives of their own choosing; or

(4) to any officer or employee of a labor organization engaged in an industry affecting commerce with intent to influence him in respect to any of his actions, decisions, or duties as a representative of employees or as such officer or employee of such labor organization.

(b)(1) It shall be unlawful for any person to request, demand, receive, or accept, or agree to receive or accept, any payment, loan, or delivery of any money or other thing of value prohibited by subsection (a).

(2) It shall be unlawful for any labor organization, or for any person acting as an officer, agent, representative, or employee of such labor organization, to demand or accept from the operator of any motor vehicle (as defined in part II of the Interstate Commerce Act) employed in the transportation of property in commerce, or the employer of any such operator, any money or other thing of value payable to such organization or to an officer, agent, representative or employee thereof as a fee or charge for the unloading, or in connection with the unloading, of the cargo of such vehicle: *Provided*, That nothing in this paragraph shall be construed to make unlawful any payment by an employer to any of his employees as compensation for their services as employees.

(c) The provisions of this section shall not be applicable (1) in respect to any money or other thing of value payable by an employer to any of his employees whose established duties include acting openly for such employer in matters of labor relations or personnel administration or to any representative of his employees, or to any officer or employee of a labor organization, who is also an employee or former employee of such employer, as compensation for, or by reason of, his service as an employee of such employer; (2) with respect to the payment or delivery of any money or other thing of value in satisfaction of a judgment of any court or a decision or award of an arbitrator or impartial chairman or in compromise, adjustment, settlement, or release of any claim, complaint, grievance, or dispute in the absence of fraud or duress; (3) with respect to the sale or purchase of an article or commodity at the prevailing market price in the regular course of business; (4) with respect to money deducted from the wages of employees in payment of membership dues in a labor organization: *Provided*, That the employer has received from each employee, on whose account such deductions are made, a written assignment which shall not be irrevocable for a period of more than one year, or beyond the termination date of the applicable collective agreement, whichever occurs sooner; (5) with respect to money or other thing of value paid to a trust fund established by such representative, for the sole and exclusive benefit of the employees of such employer, and their families and dependents (or of such employees, families, and dependents jointly with the employees of other employers making similar payments, and their families and dependents): *Provided*, That (A) such payments are held in trust for the purpose of paying, either from principal or income or both, for the benefit of employees, their families and dependents, for medical or hospital care, pensions on retirement or death of employees, compensation for injuries or illness resulting from occupational activity or insurance to provide any of the foregoing, or unemployment benefits or life insurance, disability and sickness insurance, or accident insurance; (B) the detailed basis on which such payments are to be made is specified in a written agreement with the employer, and employees and employers are equally represented in the administration of such fund, together with such neutral persons as the representatives of the employers and the representatives of employees may agree upon, and in the event the employer and employee groups deadlock on the administration of such fund and there are no neutral persons empowered to break such deadlock, such agreement provides that the two groups shall agree on an impartial umpire to decide such dispute, or in event of failure to agree within a reasonable length of time, an impartial umpire to decide such dispute shall, on petition of either group, be appointed by the district court of the United States for the district where the trust fund has its principal office, and shall also contain provisions for an annual audit of the trust fund, a statement of the results of which shall be available for inspection by interested persons at the principal office of the trust fund and at such other places as may be designated in such written agreement; and (C) such payments as are intended to be used for the purpose of providing pensions or annuities for employees are made to a separate trust which provides that the funds held therein cannot be used for any purpose other than paying such pensions or annuities; (6) with respect to money or other thing of value paid by any employer to a trust fund established by such representative for the purpose of pooled vacation, holiday, severance or similar benefits, or defraying costs of apprenticeship or other training programs: *Provided*, That the requirements of clause (B) of the proviso to clause (5) of this subsection shall apply to such trust funds; (7) with respect to money or other thing of value paid by any employer to a pooled or individual trust fund established by such representative for the purpose of (A) scholarships for the benefit of employees, their families, and dependents for study at educational institutions, or (B) child care centers for preschool and school age dependents of employees: *Provided*, That no labor organization or employer shall be required to bargain on the establishment of any such trust fund, and refusal to do so shall not constitute an unfair labor practice: *Provided further,* That the requirements of clause (B) of the proviso to clause (5) of this subsection shall apply to such trust funds; (8) with respect to money or any other thing of value paid by any employer to a trust fund established by such representative for the purpose of defraying the costs of legal services for employees, their families, and dependents for counsel or plan of their choice: *Provided*, That the requirements of clause (B) of the proviso to clause (5) of this subsection shall apply to such trust funds: *Provided further,* That no such legal services shall be furnished: (A) to initiate any proceeding directed (i) against any such employer or its officers or agents except in workman's compensation cases, or (ii) against such labor organization, or its parent or subordinate bodies, or their officers or agents, or (iii) against any other employer or labor organization, or their officers or agents, in any matter arising under the National Labor Relations Act, as amended, or this Act; and (B) in any proceeding where a labor organization would be prohibited from defraying the costs of legal services by the provisions of the Labor-Management Reporting and Disclosure Act of 1959 [29 USC 401 et seq.]; or (9) with respect to money or other things of value paid by an employer to a plant, area or industrywide labor management committee established for one or more of the purposes set forth in section 5(b) of the Labor Management Cooperation Act of 1978.

(d)(1) Any person who participates in a transaction involving a payment, loan, or delivery of money or other thing of value to a labor organization in payment of membership dues or to a joint labor-management trust fund as defined by clause (B) of the proviso to clause (5) of subsection (c) of this section or to a plant, area, or industry-wide labor-management committee that is received and used by such labor organization, trust fund, or committee, which transaction does not satisfy all the applicable requirements of subsections (c)(4) through (c)(9) of this section, and willfully and with intent to benefit himself or to benefit other persons he knows are not permitted to receive a payment, loan, money, or other thing of value under subsections (c)(4) through (c)(9) violates this subsection, shall, upon conviction thereof, be guilty of a felony and be subject to a fine of not more than $15,000, or imprisoned for not more than five years, or both; but if the value of the amount of money or thing of value involved in any violation of the provisions of this section does not exceed $1,000, such person shall be guilty of a misdemeanor and be subject to a fine of not more than $10,000, or imprisoned for not more than one year, or both.

(2) Except for violations involving transactions covered by subsection (d)(1) of this section, any person who willfully violates this section shall, upon conviction thereof, be guilty of a felony and be subject to a fine of not more than $15,000, or imprisoned for not more than five years, or both; but if the value of the amount of money or thing of value involved in any violation of the provisions of this section does not exceed $1,000, such person shall be guilty of a misdemeanor and be subject to a fine of not more than $10,000, or imprisoned for not more than one year, or both.

(e) The district courts of the United States and the United States courts of the Territories and possessions shall have jurisdiction, for cause shown, and subject to the provisions of section 17 (relating to notice to opposite party) of the Act entitled "An Act to supplement existing laws against unlawful restraints and monopolies, and for other purposes", approved October 15, 1914, as amended (U.S.C., title 28, sec. 381), to restrain violations of this section, without regard to the provisions of sections 6 and 20 of such Act of October 15, 1914, as amended (U.S.C., title 15, sec. 17, and title 29, sec. 52), and the provisions of the Act entitled "An Act to amend the Judicial Code and to define and limit the jurisdiction of courts sitting in equity, and for other purposes", approved March 23, 1932 (U.S.C., title 29, secs. 101–115).

(f) This section shall not apply to any contract in force on the date of enactment of this Act, until the expiration of such contract, or until July 1, 1948, whichever first occurs.

(g) Compliance with the restrictions contained in subsection (c)(5)(B) upon contributions to trust funds, otherwise lawful, shall not be applicable to contributions to such trust funds established by collective agreement prior to January 1, 1946, nor shall subsection (c)(5)(A) be construed as prohibiting contributions to such trust funds if prior to January 1, 1947, such funds contained provisions for pooled vacation benefits.

§ 187. Unlawful activities or conduct; right to sue; jurisdiction; limitations; damages

[Sec. 303] (a) It shall be unlawful, for the purpose of this section only, in an industry or activity affecting commerce, for any labor organization to engage in any activity or conduct defined as an unfair labor practice in section 8(b)(4) of the National Labor Relations Act, as amended.

(b) Whoever shall be injured in his business or property by reason of any violation of subsection (a) may sue therefor in any district court of the United States subject to the limitations and provisions of section 301 hereof without respect to the amount in controversy, or in any other court having jurisdiction of the parties, and shall recover the damages by him sustained and the cost of the suit.

Landrum-Griffin Labor Management Reporting and Disclosure Act

(P.L. 86–257, approved September 14, 1959; as last amended by P.L. 98–473, approved October 12, 1984)

§ 401. Congressional declaration of findings, purposes, and policy

[Sec. 2] (a) The Congress finds that, in the public interest, it continues to be the responsibility of the Federal Government to protect employees' rights to organize, choose their own representatives, bargain collectively, and otherwise engage in concerted activities for their mutual aid or protection; that the relations between employers and labor organizations and the millions of workers they represent have a substantial impact on the commerce of the Nation; and that in order to accomplish the objective of a free flow of commerce it is essential that labor organizations, employers, and their officials adhere to the highest standards of responsibility and ethical conduct in administering the affairs of their organizations, particularly as they affect labor-management relations.

(b) The Congress further finds, from recent investigations in the labor and management fields, that there have been a number of instances of breach of trust, corruption, disregard of the rights of individual employees, and other failures to observe high standards of responsibility and ethical conduct which require further and supplementary legislation that will afford necessary protection of the rights and interests of employees and the public generally as they relate to the activities of labor organizations, employers, labor relations consultants, and their officers and representatives.

(c) The Congress, therefore, further finds and declares that the enactment of this Act is necessary to eliminate or prevent improper practices on the part of labor organizations, employers, labor relations consultants, and their officers and representatives which distort and defeat the policies of the Labor Management Relations Act, 1947, as amended, and the Railway Labor Act, as amended, and have the tendency or necessary effect of burdening or obstructing commerce by (1) impairing the efficiency, safety, or operation of

59

the instrumentalities of commerce; (2) occurring in the current of commerce; (3) materially affecting, restraining, or controlling the flow of raw materials or manufactured or processed goods into or from the channels of commerce, or the prices of such materials or goods in commerce; or (4) causing diminution of employment and wages in such volume as substantially to impair or disrupt the market for goods flowing into or from the channels of commerce.

§ 402. Definitions

[Sec. 3] For the purposes of titles I, II, III, IV, V (except section 505), and VI of this Act—

(a) "Commerce" means trade, traffic, commerce, transportation, transmission, or communication among the several States or between any State and any place outside thereof.

(b) "State" includes any State of the United States, the District of Columbia, Puerto Rico, the Virgin Islands, American Samoa, Guam, Wake Island, the Canal Zone, and Outer Continental Shelf lands defined in the Outer Continental Shelf Lands Act (43 U.S.C. 1331–1343).

(c) "Industry affecting commerce" means any activity, business, or industry in commerce or in which a labor dispute would hinder or obstruct commerce or the free flow of commerce and includes any activity or industry "affecting commerce" within the meaning of the Labor Management Relations Act, 1947, as amended, or the Railway Labor Act, as amended.

(d) "Person" includes one or more individuals, labor organizations, partnerships, associations, corporations, legal representatives, mutual companies, joint-stock companies, trusts, unincorporated organizations, trustees, trustees in cases under title 11, or receivers.

(e) "Employer" means any employer or any group or association of employers engaged in an industry affecting commerce (1) which is, with respect to employees engaged in an industry affecting commerce, an employer within the meaning of any law of the United States relating to the employment of any employees or (2) which may deal with any labor organization concerning grievances, labor disputes, wages, rates of pay, hours of employment, or conditions of work, and includes any person acting directly or indirectly as an employer or as an agent of an employer in relation to an employee but does not include the United States or any corporation wholly owned by the Government of the United States or any State or political subdivision thereof.

(f) "Employee" means any individual employed by an employer, and includes any individual whose work has ceased as a consequence of, or in connection with, any current labor dispute or because of any unfair labor practice or because of exclusion or expulsion from a labor organization in any manner or for any reason inconsistent with the requirements of this Act.

(g) "Labor dispute" includes any controversy concerning terms, tenure, or conditions of employment, or concerning the association or representation of persons in negotiating, fixing, maintaining, changing, or seeking to arrange terms or conditions of employment, regardless of whether the disputants stand in the proximate relation of employer and employee.

(h) "Trusteeship" means any receivership, trusteeship, or other method of supervision or control whereby a labor organization suspends the autonomy otherwise available to a subordinate body under its constitution or bylaws.

(i) "Labor organization" means a labor organization engaged in an industry affecting commerce and includes any organization of any kind, any agency, or employee representation committee, group, association, or plan so engaged in which employees participate and which exists for the purpose, in whole or in part, of dealing with employers concerning grievances, labor disputes, wages, rates of pay, hours, or other terms or conditions of employment, and any conference, general committee, joint or system board, or joint council so engaged which is subordinate to a national or international labor organization, other than a State or local central body.

(j) A labor organization shall be deemed to be engaged in an industry affecting commerce if it—

(1) is the certified representative of employees under the provisions of the National Labor Relations Act, as amended, or the Railway Labor Act, as amended; or

(2) although not certified, is a national or international labor organization or a local labor organization recognized or acting as the representative of employees of an employer or employers engaged in an industry affecting commerce; or

(3) has chartered a local labor organization or subsidiary body which is representing or actively seeking to represent employees of employers within the meaning of paragraph (1) or (2); or

(4) has been chartered by a labor organization representing or actively seeking to represent employees within the meaning of paragraph (1) or (2) as the local or subordinate body through which such employees may enjoy membership or become affiliated with such labor oganization; or

(5) is a conference, general committee, joint or system board, or joint council, subordinate to a national or international labor organization, which includes a labor organization engaged in an industry affecting commerce within the meaning of any of the preceding paragraphs of this subsection, other than a State or local central body.

(k) "Secret ballot" means the expression by ballot, voting machine, or otherwise, but in no event by proxy, of a choice with respect to any election or vote taken upon any matter, which is cast in such a manner that the person expressing such choice cannot be identified with the choice expressed.

(l) "Trust in which a labor organization is interested" means a trust or other fund or organization (1) which was created or established by a labor organization, or one or more of the trustees or one or more members of the governing body of which is selected or appointed by a labor organization, and (2) a primary purpose of which is to provide benefits for the members of such labor organization or their beneficiaries.

(m) "Labor relations consultant" means any person who, for compensation, advises or represents an employer, employer organization, or labor organization concerning employee organizing, concerted activities, or collective bargaining activities.

(n) "Officer" means any constitutional officer, any person authorized to perform the functions of president, vice president, secretary treasurer, or other executive functions of a labor organization, and any member of its executive board or similar governing body.

(o) "Member" or "member in good standing", when used in reference to a labor organization, includes any person who has fulfilled the requirements for membership in such organization, and who neither has voluntarily withdrawn from membership nor has been expelled or suspended from membership after appropriate proceedings consistent with lawful provisions of the constitution and bylaws of such organization.

(p) "Secretary" means the Secretary of Labor.

(q) "Officer, agent, shop steward, or other representative", when used with respect to a labor organization, includes elected officials and key administrative personnel, whether elected or appointed (such as business agents, heads of departments or major units, and organizers who exercise substantial independent authority), but does not include salaried nonsupervisory professional staff, stenographic, and service personnel.

(r) "District court of the United States" means a United States district court and a United States court of any place subject to the jurisdiction of the United States.

Title I [of LMRDA]. Bill of Rights of Members of Labor Organizations

§ 411. Bill of rights; constitution and bylaws of labor organizations

[Sec. 101] (a)(1) Every member of a labor organization shall have equal rights and privileges within such organization to nominate candidates, to vote in elections or referendums of the labor organization, to attend membership meetings, and to participate in the deliberations and voting upon the business of such meetings, subject to reasonable rules and regulations in such organization's constitution and bylaws.

(2) Every member of any labor organization shall have the right to meet and assemble freely with other members; and to express any views,

arguments, or opinions, and to express at meetings of the labor organization his views, upon candidates in an election of the labor organization or upon any business properly before the meeting, subject to the organization's established and reasonable rules pertaining to the conduct of meetings: *Provided,* That nothing herein shall be construed to impair the right of a labor organization to adopt and enforce reasonable rules as to the responsibility of every member toward the organization as an institution and to his refraining from conduct that would interfere with its performance of its legal or contractual obligations.

(3) Except in the case of a federation of national or international labor organizations, the rates of dues and initiation fees payable by members of any labor organization in effect on the date of enactment of this Act shall not be increased, and no general or special assessment shall be levied upon such members, except—

(A) in the case of a local labor organization, (i) by majority vote by secret ballot of the members in good standing voting at a general or special membership meeting, after reasonable notice of the intention to vote upon such question, or (ii) by majority vote of the members in good standing voting in a membership referendum conducted by secret ballot; or

(B) in the case of a labor organization, other than a local labor organization or a federation of national or international labor organizations, (i) by majority vote of the delegates voting at a regular convention, or at a special convention of such labor organization held upon not less than thirty days' written notice to the principal office of each local or constituent labor organization entitled to such notice, or (ii) by majority vote of the members in good standing of such labor organization voting in a membership referendum conducted by secret ballot, or (iii) by majority vote of the members of the executive board or similar governing body of such labor organization, pursuant to express authority contained in the constitution and bylaws of such labor organization: *Provided,* That such action on the part of the executive board or similar governing body shall be effective only until the next regular convention of such labor organization.

(4) No labor organization shall limit the right of any member thereof to institute an action in any court, or in a proceeding before any administrative agency, irrespective of whether or not the labor organization or its officers are named as defendants or respondents in such action or proceeding, or the right of any member of a labor organization to appear as a witness in any judicial, administrative, or legislative proceeding, or to petition any legislature or to communicate with any legislator: *Provided,* That any such member may be required to exhaust reasonable hearing procedures (but not to exceed a four-

month lapse of time) within such organization, before instituting legal or administrative proceedings against such organizations or any officer thereof: *And provided further,* That no interested employer or employer association shall directly or indirectly finance, encourage, or participate in, except as a party, any such action, proceeding, appearance, or petition.

(5) No member of any labor organization may be fined, suspended, expelled, or otherwise disciplined except for nonpayment of dues by such organization or by any officer thereof unless such member has been (A) served with written specific charges; (B) given a reasonable time to prepare his defense; (C) afforded a full and fair hearing.

(b) Any provision of the constitution and bylaws of any labor organization which is inconsistent with the provisions of this section shall be of no force or effect.

§ 412. Civil action for infringement of rights; jurisdiction

[Sec. 102] Any person whose rights secured by the provisions of this title have been infringed by any violation of this title may bring a civil action in a district court of the United States for such relief (including injunctions) as may be appropriate. Any such action against a labor organization shall be brought in the district court of the United States for the district where the alleged violation occurred, or where the principal office of such labor organization is located.

§ 413. Retention of existing rights of members

[Sec. 103] Nothing contained in this title shall limit the rights and remedies of any member of a labor organization under any State or Federal law or before any court or other tribunal, or under the constitution and bylaws of any labor organization.

§ 414. Right to copies of collective bargaining agreements

[Sec. 104] It shall be the duty of the secretary or corresponding principal officer of each labor organization, in the case of a local labor organization, to forward a copy of each collective bargaining agreement made by such labor organization with any employer to any employee who requests such a copy and whose rights as such employee are directly affected by such agreement, and in the case of a labor organization other than a local labor organization, to forward a copy of any such agreement to each constituent unit which has members directly affected by such agreement; and such officer shall maintain at the principal office of the labor organization of which he is an officer copies of any such agreement made or received by such labor organization, which copies shall be available for inspection by any member or by any employee whose rights are affected by such agreement. The provisions of section 210 shall be applicable in the enforcement of this section.

§ 415.   Information to members of provisions of Act

[Sec. 105] Every labor organization shall inform its members concerning the provisions of this Act.

Title II [of LMRDA]. Reporting by Labor Organizations, Officers and Employees of Labor Organizations, and Employers

§ 431.   Report of labor organizations

[Sec. 201] (a) Every labor organization shall adopt a constitution and bylaws and shall file a copy thereof with the Secretary, together with a report, signed by its president and secretary or corresponding principal officers, containing the following information—

(1) the name of the labor organization, its mailing address, and any other address at which it maintains its principal office or at which it keeps the records referred to in this title;

(2) the name and title of each of its officers;

(3) the initiation fee or fees required from a new or transferred member and fees for work permits required by the reporting labor organization;

(4) the regular dues or fees or other periodic payments required to remain a member of the reporting labor organization; and

(5) detailed statements, or references to specific provisions of documents filed under this subsection which contain such statements, showing the provision made and procedures followed with respect to each of the following: (A) qualifications for or restrictions on membership, (B) levying of assessments, (C) participation in insurance or other benefit plans, (D) authorization for disbursement of funds of the labor organization, (E) audit of financial transactions of the labor organiza-tion, (F) the calling of regular and special meetings, (G) the selection of officers and stewards and of any representatives to other bodies

composed of labor organizations' representatives, with a specific statement of the manner in which each officer was elected, appointed, or otherwise selected, (H) discipline or removal of officers or agents for breaches of their trust, (I) imposition of fines, suspensions, and expulsions of members, including the grounds for such action and any provision made for notice, hearing, judgment on the evidence, and appeal procedures, (J) authorization for bargaining demands, (K) ratification of contract terms, (L) authorization for strikes, and (M) issuance of work permits. Any change in the information required by this subsection shall be reported to the Secretary at the time the reporting labor organization files with the Secretary the annual financial report required by subsection (b).

(b) Every labor organization shall file annually with the Secretary a financial report signed by its president and treasurer or corresponding principal officers containing the following information in such detail as may be necessary accurately to disclose its financial condition and operations for its preceding fiscal year—

(1) assets and liabilities at the beginning and end of the fiscal year;

(2) receipts of any kind and the sources thereof;

(3) salary, allowances, and other direct or indirect disbursements (including reimbursed expenses) to each officer and also to each employee who, during such fiscal year, received more than $10,000 in the aggregate from such labor organization and any other labor organization affiliated with it or with which it is affiliated, or which is affiliated with the same national or international labor organization;

(4) direct and indirect loans made to any officer, employee, or member, which aggregated more than $250 during the fiscal year, together with a statement of the purpose, security, if any, and arrangements for repayment;

(5) direct and indirect loans to any business enterprise, together with a statement of the purpose, security, if any, and arrangements for repayment; and

(6) other disbursements made by it including the purposes thereof; all in such categories as the Secretary may prescribe.

(c) Every labor organization required to submit a report under this title shall make available the information required to be contained in such report to all of its members, and every such labor organization and its officers shall be under a duty enforceable at the suit of any member of such organization in any State court of competent jurisdiction or in the district court of the United States for the district in which such labor organization maintains its principal office, to permit such member for just cause to examine any books, records, and accounts necessary to verify such report. The court in such action may, in its discretion, in addition to any judgment awarded to the plaintiff or plaintiffs, allow a reasonable attorney's fee to be paid by the defendant, and costs of the action.

(d) Subsections (f), (g), and (h) of section 9 of the National Labor Relations Act, as amended, are hereby repealed.

(e) Clause (1) of section 8(a)(3) of the National Labor Relations Act, as amended, is amended by striking out the following: "and has at the time the agreement was made or within the preceding twelve months received from the Board a notice of compliance with sections 9(f), (g), (h)".

§ 432. Report of officers and employees of labor organizations

[Sec. 202] (a) Every officer of a labor organization and every employee of a labor organization (other than an employee performing exclusively clerical or custodial services) shall file with the Secretary a signed report listing and describing for his preceding fiscal year—

(1) any stock, bond, security, or other interest, legal or equitable, which he or his spouse or minor child directly or indirectly held in, and any income or any other benefit with monetary value (including reimbursed expenses) which he or his spouse or minor child derived directly or indirectly from, an employer whose employees such labor organization represents or is actively seeking to represent, except payments and other benefits received as a bona fide employee of such employer;

(2) any transaction in which he or his spouse or minor child engaged, directly or indirectly, involving any stock, bond, security, or loan to or from, or other legal or equitable interest in the business of an employer whose employees such labor organization represents or is actively seeking to represent;

(3) any stock, bond, security, or other interest, legal or equitable, which he or his spouse or minor child directly or indirectly held in, and any income or any other benefit with monetary value (including reimbursed expenses) which he or his spouse or minor child directly or indirectly derived from, any business a substantial part of which consists of buying from, selling or leasing to, or otherwise dealing with, the business of an employer whose employees such labor organization represents or is actively seeking to represent;

(4) any stock, bond, security, or other interest, legal or equitable, which he or his spouse or minor child directly or indirectly held in, and any income or any other benefit with monetary value (including reimbursed expenses) which he or his spouse or minor child directly or indirectly derived from, a business any part of which consists of buying from, or selling or leasing directly or indirectly to, or otherwise dealing with such labor organization;

(5) any direct or indirect business transaction or arrangement between him or his spouse or minor child and any employer whose employees his organization represents or is actively seeking to represent, except

work performed and payments and benefits received as a bona fide employee of such employer and except purchases and sales of goods or services in the regular course of business at prices generally available to any employee of such employer; and

(6) any payment of money or other thing of value (including reimbursed expenses) which he or his spouse or minor child received directly or indirectly from any employer or any person who acts as a labor relations consultant to an employer, except payments of the kinds referred to in section 302(c) of the Labor Management Relations Act, 1947, as amended.

(b) The provisions of paragraphs (1), (2), (3), (4), and (5) of subsection (a) shall not be construed to require any such officer or employee to report his bona fide investments in securities traded on a securities exchange registered as a national securities exchange under the Securities Exchange Act of 1934, in shares in an investment company registered under the Investment Company Act of 1940, or in securities of a public utility holding company registered under the Public Utility Holding Company Act of 1935, or to report any income derived therefrom.

(c) Nothing contained in this section shall be construed to require any officer or employee of a labor organization to file a report under subsection (a) unless he or his spouse or minor child holds or has held an interest, has received income or any other benefit with monetary value or a loan, or has engaged in a transaction described therein.

§ 433. Report of employers

[Sec. 203] (a) Every employer who in any fiscal year made—

(1) any payment or loan, direct or indirect, of money or other thing of value (including reimbursed expenses), or any promise or agreement therefor, to any labor organization or officer, agent, shop steward, or other representative of a labor organization, or employee of any labor organization, except (A) payments or loans made by any national or State bank, credit union, insurance company, savings and loan association or other credit institution and (B) payments of the kind referred to in section 302(c) of the Labor Management Relations Act, 1947, as amended;

(2) any payment (including reimbursed expenses) to any of his employees, or any group or committee of such employees, for the purpose of causing such employee or group or committee of employees to persuade other employees to exercise or not to exercise, or as the manner of exercising, the right to organize and bargain collectively through representatives of their own choosing unless such payments were contemporaneously or previously disclosed to such other employees;

(3) any expenditure, during the fiscal year, where an object thereof, directly or indirectly, is to interfere with, restrain, or coerce employees in the exercise of the right to organize and bargain collectively through representatives of their own choosing, or is to obtain information concerning the activities of employees or a labor organization in connection with a labor dispute involving such employer, except for use solely in conjunction with an administrative or arbitral proceeding or a criminal or civil judicial proceeding;

(4) any agreement or arrangement with a labor relations consultant or other independent contractor or organization pursuant to which such person undertakes activities where an object thereof, directly or indirectly, is to persuade employees to exercise or not to exercise, or persuade employees as to the manner of exercising, the right to organize and bargain collectively through representatives of their own choosing, or undertakes to supply such employer with information concerning the activities of employees or a labor organization in connection with a labor dispute involving such employer, except information for use solely in conjunction with an administrative or arbitral proceeding or a criminal or civil judicial proceeding; or

(5) any payment (including reimbursed expenses) pursuant to an agreement or arrangement described in subdivision (4);

shall file with the Secretary a report, in a form prescribed by him, signed by its president and treasurer or corresponding principal officers showing in detail the date and amount of each such payment, loan, promise, agreement, or arrangement and the name, address, and position, if any, in any firm or labor organization of the person to whom it was made and a full explanation of the circumstances of all such payments, including the terms of any agreement or understanding pursuant to which they were made.

(b) Every person who pursuant to any agreement or arrangement with an employer undertakes activities where an object thereof is, directly or indirectly—

(1) to persuade employees to exercise or not to exercise, or persuade employees as to the manner of exercising, the right to organize and bargain collectively through representatives of their own choosing; or

(2) to supply an employer with information concerning the activities of employees or a labor organization in connection with a labor dispute involving such employer, except information for use solely in conjunction with an administrative or arbitral proceeding or a criminal or civil judicial proceeding;

shall file within 30 days after entering into such agreement or arrangement a report with the Secretary, signed by its president and treasurer or corresponding principal officers, containing the name under which such person is engaged in doing business and the address of its principal office, and a detailed statement of the terms and conditions of such agreement or arrangement. Every such person shall file annually, with respect to each fiscal year during which payments were made as a result of such an agreement or arrangement, a report with the Secretary, signed by its president and treasurer or corresponding principal officers, containing a statement (A) of its receipts of any kind from employers on account of labor relations advice or services, designating the sources thereof, and (B) of its disbursements of any kind, in connection with such services and the purposes thereof. In each such case such information shall be set forth in such categories as the Secretary may prescribe.

(c) Nothing in this section shall be construed to require any employer or other person to file a report covering the services of such person by reason of his giving or agreeing to give advice to such employer or representing or agreeing to represent such employer before any court, administrative agency, or tribunal of arbitration or engaging or agreeing to engage in collective bargaining on behalf of such employer with respect to wages, hours, or other terms or conditions of employment or the negotiation of an agreement or any question arising thereunder.

(d) Nothing contained in this section shall be construed to require an employer to file a report under subsection (a) unless he has made an expenditure, payment, loan, agreement, or arrangement of the kind described therein. Nothing contained in this section shall be construed to require any other person to file a report under subsection (b) unless he was a party to an agreement or arrangement of the kind described therein.

(e) Nothing contained in this section shall be construed to require any regular officer, supervisor, or employee of an employer to file a report in connection with services rendered to such employer nor shall any employer be required to file a report covering expenditures made to any regular officer, supervisor, or employee of an employer as compensation for service as a regular officer, supervisor, or employee of such employer.

(f) Nothing contained in this section shall be construed as an amendment to, or modification of the rights protected by, section 8(c) of the National Labor Relations Act, as amended.

(g) The term "interfere with, restrain, or coerce" as used in this section means interference, restraint, and coercion which, if done with respect to the exercise of rights guaranteed in section 7 of the National Labor Relations Act, as amended, would, under section 8(a) of such Act, constitute an unfair labor practice.

§ 434. Exemption of attorney-client communications

[Sec. 204] Nothing contained in this Act shall be construed to require an attorney who is a member in good standing of the bar of any State, to include in any report required to be filed pursuant to the provisions of this Act any information which was lawfully communicated to such attorney by any of his clients in the course of a legitimate attorney-client relationship.

§ 435. Reports and documents as public information

[Sec. 205] (a) The contents of the reports and documents filed with the Secretary pursuant to sections 201, 202, 203, and 211, of this title shall be public information, and the Secretary may publish any information and data which he obtains pursuant to the provisions of this subchapter. The Secretary may use the information and data for statistical and research purposes, and compile and publish such studies, analyses, reports, and surveys based thereon as he may deem appropriate.

(b) The Secretary shall by regulation make reasonable provision for the inspection and examination, on the request of any person, of the information and data contained in any report or other document filed with him pursuant to section 201, 202, 203, or 211.

(c) The Secretary shall by regulation provide for the furnishing by the Department of Labor of copies of reports or other documents filed with the Secretary pursuant to this title, upon payment of a charge based upon the cost of the service. The Secretary shall make available without payment of a charge, or require any person to furnish, to such State agency as is designated by law or by the Governor of the State in which such person has his principal place of business or headquarters, upon request of the Governor of such State, copies of any reports and documents filed by such person with the Secretary pursuant to section 201, 202, 203, or 211, or of information and data contained therein. No person shall be required by reason of any law of any State to furnish to any officer or agency of such State any information included in a report filed by such person with the Secretary pursuant to the provisions of this title, if a copy of such report, or of the portion thereof containing such information, is furnished to such officer or agency. All moneys received in payment of such charges fixed by the Secretary pursuant to this subsection shall be deposited in the general fund of the Treasury.

§ 436. Retention of records

[Sec. 206] Every person required to file any report under this title shall maintain records on the matters required to be reported which will provide in sufficient detail the necessary basic information and data from which the documents filed with the Secretary may be verified, explained or clarified, and checked for accuracy and completeness, and shall include vouchers, worksheets, receipts, and applicable resolutions, and shall keep such records available for examination for a period of not less than five years after the filing of the documents based on the information which they contain.

§ 437. Time for making reports

[Sec. 207] (a) Each labor organization shall file the initial report required under section 201(a) within ninety days after the date on which it first becomes subject to this Act.

(b) Each person required to file a report under section 201(b), 202, 203 (a), the second sentence of 203(b), or 211 shall file such report within ninety days after the end of each of its fiscal years; except that where such person is subject to section 201(b), 202, 203(a), the second sentence of 203(b), or 211, as the case may be, for only a portion of such a fiscal year (because the date of enactment of this Act occurs during such person's fiscal year or such person becomes subject to this Act during its fiscal year) such person may consider that portion as the entire fiscal year in making such report.

§ 438. Rules and regulations; simplified reports

[Sec. 208] The Secretary shall have authority to issue, amend, and rescind rules and regulations prescribing the form and publication of reports required to be filed under this title and such other reasonable rules and regulations (including rules prescribing reports concerning trusts in which a labor organization is interested) as he may find necessary to prevent the circumvention or evasion of such reporting requirements. In exercising his power under this section the Secretary shall prescribe by general rule simplified reports for labor organizations or employers for whom he finds that by virtue of their size a detailed report would be unduly burdensome, but the Secretary may revoke such provision for simplified forms of any labor organization or employer if he determines, after such investigation as he deems proper and due notice and opportunity for a hearing, that the purposes of this section would be served thereby.

§ 439. Violations and penalties

[Sec. 209] (a) Any person who willfully violates this title shall be fined not more than $10,000 or imprisoned for not more than one year, or both.

(b) Any person who makes a false statement or representation of a material fact, knowing it to be false, or who knowingly fails to disclose a material fact, in any document, report, or other information required under the provisions of this title shall be fined not more than $10,000 or imprisoned for not more than one year, or both.

(c) Any person who willfully makes a false entry in or willfully conceals, withholds, or destroys any books, records, reports, or statements required to be kept by any provision of this title shall be fined not more than $10,000 or imprisoned for not more than one year, or both.

(d) Each individual required to sign reports under sections 201 and 203 shall be personally responsible for the filing of such reports and for any statement contained therein which he knows to be false.

§ 440. Civil action for enforcement by Secretary; jurisdiction

[Sec. 210] Whenever it shall appear that any person has violated or is about to violate any of the provisions of this title, the Secretary may bring a civil action for such relief (including injunctions) as may be appropriate. Any such action may be brought in the district court of the United States where the violation occurred or, at the option of the parties, in the United States District Court for the District of Columbia.

§ 441. Surety company reports; contents; waiver or modification of requirements respecting contents of reports

[Sec. 211] Each surety company which issues any bond required by this Act or the Employee Retirement Income Security Act of 1974 [29 U.S.C. 1001 et seq.] shall file annually with the Secretary, with respect to each fiscal year during which any such bond was in force, a report, in such form and detail as he may prescribe by regulation, filed by the president and treasurer or corresponding principal officers of the surety company, describing its bond experience under each such Act, including information as to the premiums received, total claims paid, amounts recovered by way of subrogation, administrative and legal expense, and such related data and information as the Secretary shall determine to be necessary in the public interest and to carry out the policy of the Act. Notwithstanding the foregoing, if the Secretary finds that any such specific information cannot be practicably ascertained or would be uninformative, the Secretary may modify or waive the requirement for such information.

Title III [of LMRDA]. Trusteeships

§ 461. Reports

[Sec. 301] (a) Every labor organization which has or assumes trusteeship over any subordinate labor organization shall file with the Secretary within thirty days after the date of the enactment of this Act or the imposition of any such trusteeship, and semiannually thereafter, a report, signed by its president and treasurer or corresponding principal officers, as well as by the trustees of such subordinate labor organization, containing the following information: (1) the name and address of the subordinate organization; (2) the date of establishing the trusteeship; (3) a detailed statement of the reason or reasons for establishing or continuing the trusteeship; and (4) the nature and extent of participation by the membership of the subordinate organization in the selection of delegates to represent such organization in regular or special conventions or other policy-determining bodies and in the election of officers of the labor organization which has assumed trusteeship over such subordinate organizations. The initial report shall also include a full and complete account of the financial condition of such subordinate organization as of the time trusteeship was assumed over it. During the continuance of a trusteeship the labor organization which has assumed trusteeship over a subordinate labor organization shall file on behalf of the subordinate labor organization the annual financial report required by section 201(b) signed by the president and treasurer or corresponding principal officers of the labor organization which has assumed such trusteeship and the trustees of the subordinate labor organization.

(b) The provisions of sections 201(c), 205, 206, 208, and 210 shall be applicable to reports filed under this title.

(c) Any person who willfully violates this section shall be fined not more than $10,000 or imprisoned for not more than one year, or both.

(d) Any person who makes a false statement or representation of a material fact, knowing it to be false, or who knowingly fails to disclose a material fact, in any report required under the provisions of this section or willfully makes any false entry in or willfully withholds, conceals, or destroys any documents, books, records, reports, or statements upon which such report is based, shall be fined not more than $10,000 or imprisoned for not more than one year, or both.

(e) Each individual required to sign a report under this section shall be personally responsible for the filing of such report and for any statement contained therein which he knows to be false.

§ 462. Purposes for establishment of trusteeship

[Sec. 302] Trusteeships shall be established and administered by a labor organization over a subordinate body only in accordance with the constitution and bylaws of the organization which has assumed trusteeship over the subordinate body and for the purpose of correcting corruption or financial malpractice, assuring the performance of collective bargaining agreements or other duties of a bargaining representative, restoring democratic procedures, or otherwise carrying out the legitimate objects of such labor organization.

§ 463. Unlawful acts relating to labor organization under trusteeship

[Sec. 303] (a) During any period when a subordinate body of a labor organization is in trusteeship, it shall be unlawful (1) to count the vote of delegates from such body in any convention or election of officers of the labor organization unless the delegates have been chosen by secret ballot in an election in which all the members in good standing of such subordinate body were eligible to participate, or (2) to transfer to such organization any current receipts or other funds of the subordinate body except the normal per capita tax and assessments payable by subordinate bodies not in trusteeship: *Provided,* That nothing herein contained shall prevent the distribution of the assets of a labor organization in accordance with its constitution and bylaws upon the bona fide dissolution thereof.

(b) Any person who willfully violates this section shall be fined not more than $10,000 or imprisoned for not more than one year, or both.

§ 464. Civil action for enforcement

[Sec. 304] (a) Upon the written complaint of any member or subordinate body of a labor organization alleging that such organization has violated the provisions of this title (except section 301) the Secretary shall investigate the complaint and if the Secretary finds probable cause to believe that such violation has occurred and has not been remedied he shall, without disclosing the identity of the complainant, bring a civil action in any district court of the United States having jurisdiction of the labor organization for such relief (including injunctions) as may be appropriate. Any member or subordinate body of a labor organization affected by any violation of this title (except section 301) may bring a civil action in any district court of the United States having jurisdiction of the labor organization for such relief (including injunctions) as may be appropriate.

(b) For the purpose of actions under this section, district courts of the United States shall be deemed to have jurisdiction of a labor organization (1) in the district in which the principal office of such labor organization is located, or (2) in any district in which its duly authorized officers or agents are engaged in conducting the affairs of the trusteeship.

(c) In any proceeding pursuant to this section a trusteeship established by a labor organization in conformity with the procedural requirements of its constitution and bylaws and authorized or ratified after a fair hearing either before the executive board or before such other body as may be provided in accordance with its constitution or bylaws shall be presumed valid for a period of eighteen months from the date of its establishment and shall not be subject to attack during such period except upon clear and convincing proof that the trusteeship was not established or maintained in good faith for a purpose allowable under section 302. After the expiration of eighteen months the trusteeship shall be presumed invalid in any such proceeding and its discontinuance shall be decreed unless the labor organization shall show by clear and convincing proof that the continuation of the trusteeship is necessary for a purpose allowable under section 302. In the latter event the court may dismiss the complaint or retain jurisdiction of the cause on such conditions and for such period as it deems appropriate.

§ 465. Report to Congress

[Sec. 305] The Secretary shall submit to the Congress at the expiration of three years from the date of enactment of this Act a report upon the operation of this title.

§ 466. Additional rights and remedies; exclusive jurisdiction of district court; res judicata

[Sec. 306] The rights and remedies provided by this title shall be in addition to any and all other rights and remedies at law or in equity: *Provided*, That upon the filing of a complaint by the Secretary the jurisdiction of the district court over such trusteeship shall be exclusive and the final judgment shall be res judicata.

Title IV [of LMRDA]. Elections

§ 481. Terms of office and election procedures

[Sec. 401] (a) Every national or international labor organization, except a federation of national or international labor organizations, shall elect its officers not less often than once every five years either by secret ballot among the members in good standing or at a convention of delegates chosen by secret ballot.

(b) Every local labor organization shall elect its officers not less often than once every three years by secret ballot among the members in good standing.

(c) Every national or international labor organization, except a federation of national or international labor organizations, and every local labor organization, and its officers, shall be under a duty, enforceable at the suit of any bona fide candidate for office in such labor organization in the district court of the United States in which such labor organization maintains its principal office, to comply with all reasonable requests of any candidate to distribute by mail or otherwise at the candidate's expense campaign literature in aid of such person's candidacy to all members in good standing of such labor organization and to refrain from discrimination in favor of or against any candidate with respect to the use of lists of members, and whenever such labor organizations or its officers authorize the distribution by mail or otherwise to members of campaign literature on behalf of any candidate or of the labor organization itself with reference to such election, similar distribution at the request of any other bona fide candidate shall be made by such labor organization and its officers, with equal treatment as to the expense of such distribution. Every bona fide candidate shall have the right, once within 30 days prior to an election of a labor organization in which he is a candidate, to inspect a list containing the names and last known addresses of all members of the labor organization who are subject to a collective bargaining agreement requiring membership therein as a condition of employment, which list shall be maintained and kept at the principal office of such labor organization by a designated official thereof. Adequate safeguards to insure a fair election shall be provided, including the right of any candidate to have an observer at the polls and at the counting of the ballots.

(d) Officers of intermediate bodies, such as general committees, system boards, joint boards, or joint councils, shall be elected not less often than once every four years by secret ballot among the members in good standing or by labor organization officers representative of such members who have been elected by secret ballot.

(e) In any election required by this section which is to be held by secret ballot a reasonable opportunity shall be given for the nomination of candidates and every member in good standing shall be eligible to be a candidate and to hold office (subject to section 504 and to reasonable qualifications uniformly imposed) and shall have the right to vote for or otherwise support the candidate or candidates of his choice, without being subject to penalty, discipline, or improper interference or reprisal of any kind by such organization or any member thereof. Not less than fifteen days prior to the election notice thereof shall be mailed to each member at his last known home address. Each member in good standing shall be entitled to one vote. No member whose dues have been withheld by his employer for payment to such organization pursuant to his voluntary authorization provided for in a collective bargaining agreement shall be declared ineligible to vote or be a candidate for office in such organization by reason of alleged delay or default in the payment of dues. The votes cast by members of each local labor organization shall be counted, and the results published, separately. The election officials designated in the constitution and bylaws or the secretary, if no other official is designated shall preserve for one year the ballots and all other records pertaining to the election. The election shall be conducted in accordance with the constitution and bylaws of such organization insofar as they are not inconsistent with the provisions of this title.

(f) When officers are chosen by a convention of delegates elected by secret ballot, the convention shall be conducted in accordance with the constitution and bylaws of the labor organization insofar as they are not inconsistent with the provisions of this title. The officials designated in the constitution and bylaws or the secretary, if no other is designated, shall preserve for one year the credentials of the delegates and all minutes and other records of the convention pertaining to the election of officers.

(g) No moneys received by any labor organization by way of dues, assessments, or similar levy, and no moneys of an employer shall be contributed or applied to promote the candidacy of any person in an election subject to the provisions of this title. Such moneys of a labor organization may be utilized for notices, factual statements of issues not involving candidates, and other expenses necessary for the holding of an election.

(h) If the Secretary, upon application of any member of a local labor organization, finds after hearing in accordance with the Administrative Procedure Act that the constitution and bylaws of such labor organization do not provide an adequate procedure for the removal of an elected officer guilty of serious misconduct, such officer may be removed, for cause shown and after notice and hearing, by the members in good standing voting in a secret ballot conducted by the officers of such labor organization in accordance with its constitution and bylaws insofar as they are not inconsistent with the provisions of this title.

(i) The Secretary shall promulgate rules and regulations prescribing minimum standards and procedures for determining the adequacy of the removal procedures to which reference is made in subsection (h).

§ 482. Enforcement

[Sec. 402] (a) A member of a labor organization—
(1) who has exhausted the remedies available under the constitution and bylaws of such organization and of any parent body, or
(2) who has invoked such available remedies without obtaining a final decision within three calendar months after their invocation, may file a complaint with the Secretary within one calendar month thereafter alleging the violation of any provision of section 401 (including violation of the constitution and bylaws of the labor organization pertaining to the election and removal of officers). The challenged election shall be presumed valid pending a final decision thereon (as hereinafter provided) and in the interim the affairs of the organization

shall be conducted by the officers elected or in such other manner as its constitution and bylaws may provide.

(b) The Secretary shall investigate such complaint and, if he finds probable cause to believe that a violation of this title has occurred and has not been remedied, he shall, within sixty days after the filing of such complaint, bring a civil action against the labor organization as an entity in the district court of the United States in which such labor organization maintains its principal office to set aside the invalid election, if any, and to direct the conduct of an election or hearing and vote upon the removal of officers under the supervision of the Secretary and in accordance with the provisions of this title and such rules and regulations as the Secretary may prescribe. The court shall have power to take such action as it deems proper to preserve the assets of the labor organization.

(c) If, upon a preponderance of the evidence after a trial upon the merits, the court finds—

(1) that an election has not been held within the time prescribed by section 401, or

(2) that the violation of section 401 may have affected the outcome of an election,

the court shall declare the election, if any, to be void and direct the conduct of a new election under supervision of the Secretary and, so far as lawful and practicable, in conformity with the constitution and bylaws of the labor organization. The Secretary shall promptly certify to the court the names of the persons elected, and the court shall thereupon enter a decree declaring such persons to be the officers of the labor organization. If the proceeding is for the removal of officers pursuant to subsection (h) of section 401, the Secretary shall certify the results of the vote and the court shall enter a decree declaring whether such persons have been removed as officers of the labor organization.

(d) An order directing an election, dismissing a complaint, or designating elected officers of a labor organization shall be appealable in the same manner as the final judgment in a civil action, but an order directing an election shall not be stayed pending appeal.

§ 483. Application of other laws; existing rights and remedies; exclusiveness of remedy for challenging election

[Sec. 403] No labor organization shall be required by law to conduct elections of officers with greater frequency or in a different form or manner than is required by its own constitution or bylaws, except as otherwise provided by this title. Existing rights and remedies to enforce the constitution and bylaws of a labor organization with respect to elections prior to the conduct thereof shall not be affected by the provisions of this title. The remedy provided by this title for challenging an election already conducted shall be exclusive.

Title V [of LMRDA]. Safeguards for Labor Organizations

§ 501. Fiduciary responsibility of officers of labor organizations

[Sec. 501] (a) The officers, agents, shop stewards, and other representatives of a labor organization occupy positions of trust in relation to such organization and its members as a group. It is, therefore, the duty of each such person, taking into account the special problems and functions of a labor organization, to hold its money and property solely for the benefit of the organization and its members and to manage, invest, and expend the same in accordance with its constitution and bylaws and any resolutions of the governing bodies adopted thereunder, to refrain from dealing with such organization as an adverse party or in behalf of an adverse party in any matter connected with his duties and from holding or acquiring any pecuniary or personal interest which conflicts with the interests of such organization, and to account to the organization for any profit received by him in whatever capacity in connection with transactions conducted by him or under his direction on behalf of the organization. A general exculpatory provision in the constitution and bylaws of such a labor organization or a general exculpatory resolution of a governing body purporting to relieve any such person of liability for breach of the duties declared by this section shall be void as against public policy.

(b) When any officer, agent, shop steward, or representative of any labor organization is alleged to have violated the duties declared in subsection (a) and the labor organization or its governing board or officers refuse or fail to sue or recover damages or secure an accounting or other appropriate relief within a reasonable time after being requested to do so by any member of the labor organization, such member may sue such officer, agent, shop steward, or representative in any district court of the United States or in any State court of competent jurisdiction to recover damages or secure an accounting or other appropriate relief for the benefit of the labor organization. No such proceeding shall be brought except upon leave of the court obtained upon verified application and for good cause shown, which application may be made ex parte. The trial judge may allot a reasonable part of the recovery in any action under this subsection to pay the fees of counsel prosecuting the suit at the instance of the member of the labor organization and to compensate such member for any expenses necessarily paid or incurred by him in connection with the litigation.

(c) Any person who embezzles, steals, or unlawfully and wilfully abstracts or converts to his own use, or the use of another, any of the moneys, funds, securities, property, or other assets of a labor organization of which he is an officer, or by which he is employed, directly or indirectly, shall be fined not more than $10,000 or imprisoned for not more than five years, or both.

§ 502. Bonding of officers and employees of labor organizations; amount, form, and placement of bonds; penalty for violation

[Sec. 502] (a) Every officer, agent, shop steward, or other representative or employee of any labor organization (other than a labor organization whose property and annual financial receipts do not exceed $5,000 in value), or of a trust in which a labor organization is interested, who handles funds or other property thereof shall be bonded to provide protection against loss by reason of acts of fraud or dishonesty on his part directly or through connivance with others. The bond of each such person shall be fixed at the beginning of the organization's fiscal year and shall be in an amount not less than 10 per centum of the funds handled by him and his predecessor or predecessors, if any, during the preceding fiscal year, but in no case more than $500,000. If the labor organization or the trust in which a labor organization is interested does not have a preceding fiscal year, the amount of the bond shall be, in the case of a local labor organization, not less than $1,000, and in the case of any other labor organization or of a trust in which a labor organization is interested, not less than $10,000. Such bonds shall be individual or schedule in form, and shall have a corporate surety company as surety thereon. Any person who is not covered by such bonds shall not be permitted to receive, handle, disburse, or otherwise exercise custody or control of the funds or other property of a labor organization or of a trust in which a labor organization is interested. No such bond shall be placed through an agent or broker or with a surety company, in which any labor organization or any officer, agent, shop steward, or other representative of a labor organization has any direct or indirect interest. Such surety company shall be a corporate surety which holds a grant of authority from the Secretaty of the Treasury under the Act of July 30, 1947 (6 U.S.C. 6–13), as an acceptable surety on Federal bonds: *Provided,* That when in the opinion of the Secretary a labor organization has made other bonding arrangements which would provide the protection required by this section at comparable cost or less, he may exempt such labor organization from placing a bond through a surety company holding such grant of authority.

(b) Any person who wilfully violates this section shall be fined not more than $10,000 or imprisoned for not more than one year, or both.

§ 503. Financial transactions between labor organizations and officers and employees

[Sec. 503] (a) No labor organization shall make directly or indirectly any loan or loans to any officer or employee of such organization which results in a total indebtedness on the part of such officer or employee to the labor organization in excess of $2,000.

(b) No labor organization or employer shall directly or indirectly pay the fine of any officer or employee convicted of any willful violation of this Act.

(c) Any person who willfully violates this section shall be fined not more than $5,000 or imprisoned for not more than one year, or both.

§ 504. Prohibition against certain persons holding office

[Sec. 504] (a) No person who is or has been a member of the Communist Party or who has been convicted of, or served any part of a prison term resulting from his conviction of, robbery, bribery, extortion, embezzlement, grand larceny, burglary, arson, violation of narcotics laws, murder, rape, assault with intent to kill, assault which inflicts grievous bodily injury, or a violation of title II or III of this Act, any felony involving abuse or misuse of such person's position or employment in a labor organization or employee benefit plan to seek or obtain an illegal gain at the expense of the members of the labor organization or the beneficiaries of the employee benefit plan, or conspiracy to commit any such crimes or attempt to commit any such crimes, or a crime in which any of the foregoing crimes is an element, shall serve or be permitted to serve—

(1) as a consultant or adviser to any labor organization,

(2) as an officer, director, trustee, member of any executive board or similar governing body, business agent, manager, organizer, employee, or representative in any capacity of any labor organization,

(3) as a labor relations consultant or adviser to a person engaged in an industry or activity affecting commerce, or an officer, director, agent, or employee of any group or association of employers dealing with any labor organization, or in a position having specific collective bargaining authority or direct responsibility in the area of labor-management relations in any corporation or association engaged in an industry or activity affecting commerce, or

(4) in a position which entitles its occupant to a share of the proceeds of, or as an officer or executive or administrative employee of, any entity whose activities are in whole or substantial part devoted to providing goods or services to any labor organization, or

(5) in any capacity, other than in his capacity as a member of such labor organization, that involves decisionmaking authority concerning, or decisionmaking authority over, or custody of, or control of the moneys, funds, assets, or property of any labor organization,

during or for the period of thirteen years after such conviction or after the end of such imprisonment, whichever is later, unless the sentencing court on the motion of the person convicted sets a lesser period of at least three years after such conviction or after the end of such imprisonment, whichever is later, or unless prior to the end of such period, in the case of a person so convicted or imprisoned, (A) his citizenship rights, having been revoked as a result of such conviction, have been fully restored, or (B) the United States Parole Commission determines that such person's service in any capacity referred to in clauses (1) through (5) would not be contrary to the purposes of this chapter. Prior to making any such determination the Commission shall hold an administrative hearing and shall give notice of such proceeding by certified mail to the Secretary of Labor and to State, county, and Federal prosecuting officials in the jurisdiction or jurisdictions in which such person was convicted. The Commission's determination in any such proceeding shall be final. No person shall knowingly hire, retain, employ, or otherwise place any other person to serve in any capacity in violation of this subsection.

(b) Any person who willfully violates this section shall be fined not more than $10,000 or imprisoned for not more than five years, or both.

(c) For the purpose of this section—

(1) A person shall be deemed to have been "convicted" and under the disability of "conviction" from the date of the judgment of the trial court, regardless of whether that judgment remains under appeal.

(2) A period of parole shall not be considered as part of a period of imprisonment.

(d) Whenever any person—

(1) by operation of this section, has been barred from office or other position in a labor organization as a result of a conviction, and

(2) has filed an appeal of that conviction,

any salary which would be otherwise due such person by virtue of such office or position, shall be placed in escrow by the individual employer or organization responsible for payment of such salary. Payment of such salary into escrow shall continue for the duration of the appeal or for the period of time during which such salary would be otherwise due, whichever period is shorter. Upon the final reversal of such person's conviction on appeal, the amounts in escrow shall be paid to such person. Upon the final sustaining of such person's conviction on appeal, the amounts in escrow shall be returned to the individual employer or organization responsible for payment of those amounts. Upon final reversal of such person's conviction, such person shall no longer be barred by this statute from assuming any position from which such person was previously barred.

Title VI [of LMRDA]. Miscellaneous Provisions

§ 521. Investigations by Secretary; applicability of other laws

[Sec. 601] (a) The Secretary shall have power when he believes it necessary in order to determine whether any person has violated or is about to violate any provision of this Act (except title I or amendments made by this Act to other statutes) to make an investigation and in connection therewith he may enter such places and inspect such records and accounts and question such persons as he may deem necessary to enable him to determine the facts relative thereto. The Secretary may report to interested persons or officials concerning the facts required to be shown in any report required by this Act and concerning the reasons for failure or refusal to file such a report or any other matter which he deems to be appropriate as a result of such an investigation.

(b) For the purpose of any investigation provided for in this Act, the provisions of sections 9 and 10 (relating to the attendance of witnesses and the production of books, papers, and documents) of the Federal Trade Commission Act of September 16, 1914, as amended (15 U.S.C. 49, 50), are hereby made applicable to the jurisdiction, powers, and duties of the Secretary or any officers designated by him.

§ 522. Extortionate picketing; penalty for violation

[Sec. 602] (a) It shall be unlawful to carry on picketing on or about the premises of any employer for the purpose of, or as part of any conspiracy or in furtherance of any plan or purpose for, the personal profit or enrichment of any individual (except a bona fide increase in wages or other employee benefits) by taking or obtaining any money or other thing of value from such employer against his will or with his consent.

(b) Any person who willfully violates this section shall be fined not more than $10,000 or imprisoned not more than twenty years, or both.

§ 523. Retention of rights under other Federal and State laws

[Sec. 603] (a) Except as explicitly provided to the contrary, nothing in this Act shall reduce or limit the responsibilities of any labor organization or any officer, agent, shop steward, or other representative of a labor organization, or of any trust in which a labor organization is interested, under any other Federal law or under the laws of any State, and, except as explicitly provided to the contrary, nothing in this Act shall take away any right or bar any remedy to which members of a labor organization are entitled under such other Federal law or law of any State.

(b) Nothing contained in titles I, II, III, IV, V, or VI of this Act shall be construed to supersede or impair or otherwise affect the provisions of the

Railway Labor Act, as amended, or any of the obligations, rights, benefits, privileges, or immunities of any carrier, employee, organization, representative, or person subject thereto; nor shall anything contained in said titles (except section 505) of this Act be construed to confer any rights, privileges, immunities, or defenses upon employers, or to impair or otherwise affect the rights of any person under the National Labor Relations Act, as amended.

§ 524. Effect on State laws

[Sec. 604] Nothing in this Act shall be construed to impair or diminish the authority of any State to enact and enforce general criminal laws with respect to robbery, bribery, extortion, embezzlement, grand larceny, burglary, arson, violation of narcotics laws, murder, rape, assault with intent to kill, or assault which inflicts grievous bodily injury, or conspiracy to commit any of such crimes.

§ 524a. Elimination of racketeering activities threat; State legislation governing collective bargaining representative

Notwithstanding this or any other Act regulating labor-management relations, each State shall have the authority to enact and enforce, as part of a comprehensive statutory system to eliminate the threat of pervasive racketeering activity in an industry that is, or over time has been, affected by such activity, a provision of law that applies equally to employers, employees, and collective bargaining representatives, which provision of law governs service in any position in a local labor organization which acts or seeks to act in that State as a collective bargaining representative pursuant to the National Labor Relations Act [29 U.S.C.A. § 151 et seq.], in the industry that is subject to that program.

§ 525. Service of process

[Sec. 605] For the purposes of this Act, service of summons, subpena, or other legal process of a court of the United States upon an officer or agent of a labor organization in his capacity as such shall constitute service upon the labor organization.

§ 526. Applicability of administrative procedure provisions

[Sec. 606] The provisions of the Administrative Procedure Act shall be applicable to the issuance, amendment, or rescission of any rules or regulations, or any adjudication, authorized or required pursuant to the provisions of this Act.

§ 527. Cooperation with other agencies and departments

[Sec. 607] In order to avoid unnecessary expense and duplication of functions among Government agencies, the Secretary may make such arrangements or agreements for cooperation or mutual assistance in the performance of his functions under this Act and the functions of any such agency as he may find to be practicable and consistent with law. The Secretary may utilize the facilities or services of any department, agency, or establishment of the United States or of any State or political subdivision of a State, including the services of any of its employees, with the lawful consent of such department, agency, or establishment; and each department, agency, or establishment of the United States is authorized and directed to cooperate with the Secretary and, to the extent permitted by law, to provide such information and facilities as he may request for his assistance in the performance of his functions under this Act. The Attorney General or his representative shall receive from the Secretary for appropriate action such evidence developed in the performance of his functions under this Act as may be found to warrant consideration for criminal prosecution under the provisions of this Act or other Federal law.

§ 528. Criminal contempt

[Sec. 608] No person shall be punished for any criminal contempt allegedly committed outside the immediate presence of the court in connection with any civil action prosecuted by the Secretary or any other person in any court of the United States under the provisions of this Act unless the facts constituting such criminal contempt are established by the verdict of the jury in a proceeding in the district court of the United States, which jury shall be chosen and empaneled in the manner prescribed by the law governing trial juries in criminal prosecutions in the district courts of the United States.

§ 529. Prohibition on certain discipline by labor organization

[Sec. 609] It shall be unlawful for any labor organization, or any officer, agent, shop steward, or other representative of a labor organization, or any employee thereof to fine, suspend, expel, or otherwise discipline any of its members for exercising any right to which he is entitled under the provisions of this Act. The provisions of section 102 shall be applicable in the enforcement of this section.

§ 530. Deprivation of rights by violence; penalty

[Sec. 610] It shall be unlawful for any person through the use of force or violence, or threat of the use of force or violence, to restrain, coerce, or intimidate, or attempt to restrain, coerce, or intimidate any member of a labor organization for the purpose of interfering with or preventing the exercise of any right to which he is entitled under the provisions of this Act. Any person who wilfully violates this section shall be fined not more than $1,000 or imprisoned for not more than one year, or both.

§ 531. Separability of provisions

[Sec. 611] If any provision of this Act, or the application of such provision to any person or circumstances, shall be held invalid, the remainder of this Act or the application of such provision to persons or circumstances other than those as to which it is held invalid, shall not be affected thereby.

Labor Management Cooperation Act

(P.L. 95–524, approved October 27, 1978; incorporated into text of 29 U.S.C. 173, 175a, and 186)

[Sec. 6] (a) This section may be cited as the "Labor Management Cooperation Act of 1978".

(b) It is the purpose of this section—

(1) to improve communication between representatives of labor and management;

(2) to provide workers and employers with opportunities to study and explore new and innovative joint approaches to achieving organizational effectiveness;

(3) to assist workers and employers in solving problems of mutual concern not susceptible to resolution within the collective bargaining process;

(4) to study and explore ways of eliminating potential problems which reduce the competitiveness and inhibit the economic development of the plant, area or industry;

(5) to enhance the involvement of workers in making decisions that affect their working lives;

(6) to expand and improve working relationships between workers and managers; and

(7) to encourage free collective bargaining by establishing continuing mechanisms for communication between employers and their employees through Federal assistance to the formation and operation of labor management committees.

(c)(1) Section 203 of the Labor-Management Relations Act, 1947, is amended by adding at the end thereof the following new subsection:

"(e) The Service is authorized and directed to encourage and support the establishment and operation of joint labor management activities conducted by plant, area, and industrywide committees designed to improve labor management relationships, job security and organizational effectiveness, in accordance with the provisions of section 205A."

(2) Title II of the Labor-Management Relations Act, 1947, is amended by adding after section 205 the following new section:

"Sec. 205A. (a)(1) The Service is authorized and directed to provide assistance in the establishment and operation of plant, area and industrywide labor management committees which—

"(A) have been organized jointly by employers and labor organizations representing employees in that plant, area, or industry; and

"(B) are established for the purpose of improving labor management relationships, job security, organizational effectiveness, enhancing economic development or involving workers in decisions affecting their jobs including improving communication with respect to subjects of mutual interest and concern.

"(2) The Service is authorized and directed to enter into contracts and to make grants, where necessary or appropriate, to fulfill its responsibilities under this section.

"(b)(1) No grant may be made, no contract may be entered into and no other assistance may be provided under the provisions of this section to a plant labor management committee unless the employees in that plant are represented by a labor organization and there is in effect at that plant a collective bargaining agreement.

"(2) No grant may be made, no contract may be entered into and no other assistance may be provided under the provisions of this section to an area or industrywide labor management committee unless its participants include any labor organizations certified or recognized as the representative of the employees of an employer participating in such committee. Nothing in this clause shall prohibit participation in an area or industrywide committee by an employer whose employees are not represented by a labor organization.

"(3) No grant may be made under the provisions of this section to any labor management committee which the Service finds to have as one of its purposes the discouragement of the exercise of rights contained in section 7 of the National Labor Relations Act (29 U.S.C. 157), or the interference with collective bargaining in any plant, or industry.

"(c) The Service shall carry out the provisions of this section through an office established for that purpose.

"(d) There are authorized to be appropriated to carry out the provisions of this section $10,000,000 for the fiscal year 1979, and such sums as may be necessary thereafter.".

(d) Section 302(c) of the Labor Management Relations Act, 1947, is amended by striking the word "or" after the semicolon at the end of subparagraph (8) thereof and by inserting the following before the period at the end thereof: "; or (9) with respect to money or other things of value paid by an employer to a plant, area or industrywide labor management committee established for one or more of the purposes set forth in section 5(b) of the Labor Management Cooperation Act of 1978".

(e) Nothing in this section or the amendments made by this section shall affect the terms and conditions of any collective bargaining agreement whether in effect prior to or entered into after the date of enactment of this section.

Civil Service Reform Act

(Title VII of P.L. 95–454, effective January 1, 1979, as last amended by P.L. 98–224, approved March 2, 1984)

Title VII. Federal Service Labor-Management Relations

Chapter 71 [of Title 5, U.S. Code]. Labor-Management Relations

Subchapter I.   General Provisions

§ 7101.   Findings and purpose

[Sec. 701] (a) The Congress finds that—
(1) experience in both private and public employment indicates that the statutory protection of the right of employees to organize, bargain collectively, and participate through labor organizations of their own choosing in decisions which affect them—
   (A) safeguards the public interest,
   (B) contributes to the effective conduct of public business, and
   (C) facilitates and encourages the amicable settlements of disputes between employees and their employers involving conditions of employment; and
(2) the public interest demands the highest standards of employee performance and the continued development and implementation of modern and progressive work practices to facilitate and improve employee performance and the efficient accomplishment of the operations of the Government.
Therefore, labor organizations and collective bargaining in the civil service are in the public interest.
   (b) It is the purpose of this chapter to prescribe certain rights and obligations of the employees of the Federal Government and to establish procedures which are designed to meet the special requirements and needs of the Government. The provisions of this chapter should be interpreted in a

90

manner consistent with the requirement of an effective and efficient Government.

§ 7102. Employees' rights

Each employee shall have the right to form, join, or assist any labor organization, or to refrain from any such activity, freely and without fear of penalty or reprisal, and each employee shall be protected in the exercise of such right. Except as otherwise provided under this chapter, such right includes the right—

(1) to act for a labor organization in the capacity of a representative and the right, in that capacity, to present the views of the labor organization to heads of agencies and other officials of the executive branch of the Government, the Congress, or other appropriate authorities, and

(2) to engage in collective bargaining with respect to conditions of employment through representatives chosen by employees under this chapter.

§ 7103. Definitions; application

(a) For the purpose of this chapter—

(1) "person" means an individual, labor organization, or agency;

(2) "employee" means an individual—

(A) employed in an agency; or

(B) whose employment in an agency has ceased because of any unfair labor practice under section 7116 of this title and who has not obtained any other regular and substantially equivalent employment, as determined under regulations prescribed by the Federal Labor Relations Authority;

but does not include—

(i) an alien or noncitizen of the United States who occupies a position outside the United States;

(ii) a member of the uniformed services;

(iii) a supervisor or a management official;

(iv) an officer or employee in the Foreign Service of the United States employed in the Department of State, the International Communication Agency, the United States International Development Cooperation Agency, the Department of Agriculture, or the Department of Commerce; or

(v) any person who participates in a strike in violation of section 7311 of this title;

(3) "agency" means an Executive agency (including a nonappropriated fund instrumentality described in section 2105(c) of this title and the

Veterans' Canteen Service, Veterans' Administration), the Library of Congress, and the Government Printing Office, but does not include—
- (A) the General Accounting Office;
- (B) the Federal Bureau of Investigation;
- (C) the Central Intelligence Agency;
- (D) the National Security Agency;
- (E) the Tennessee Valley Authority;
- (F) the Federal Labor Relations Authority; or
- (G) the Federal Service Impasses Panel;

(4) "labor organization" means an organization composed in whole or in part of employees, in which employees participate and pay dues, and which has as a purpose the dealing with an agency concerning grievances and conditions of employment, but does not include—
- (A) an organization which, by its constitution, bylaws, tacit agreement among its members, or otherwise, denies membership because of race, color, creed, national origin, sex, age, preferential or nonpreferential civil service status, political affiliation, marital status, or handicapping condition;
- (B) an organization which advocates the overthrow of the constitutional form of government of the United States;
- (C) an organization sponsored by an agency; or
- (D) an organization which participates in the conduct of a strike against the Government or any agency thereof or imposes a duty or obligation to conduct, assist, or participate in such a strike;

(5) "dues" means dues, fees, and assessments;

(6) "Authority" means the Federal Labor Relations Authority described in section 7104(a) of this title;

(7) "Panel" means the Federal Service Impasses Panel described in section 7119(c) of this title;

(8) "collective bargaining agreement" means an agreement entered into as a result of collective bargaining pursuant to the provisions of this chapter;

(9) "grievance" means any complaint—
- (A) by any employee concerning any matter relating to the employment of the employee;
- (B) by any labor organization concerning any matter relating to the employment of any employee; or
- (C) by any employee, labor organization, or agency concerning—
  - (i) the effect or interpretation, or a claim of breach, of a collective bargaining agreement; or
  - (ii) any claimed violation, misinterpretation, or misapplication of any law, rule, or regulation affecting conditions of employment;

(10) "supervisor" means an individual employed by an agency having authority in the interest of the agency to hire, direct, assign, promote,

reward, transfer, furlough, layoff, recall, suspend, discipline, or remove employees, to adjust their grievances, or to effectively recommend such action, if the exercise of the authority is not merely routine or clerical in nature but requires the consistent exercise of independent judgment, except that, with respect to any unit which includes firefighters or nurses, the term "supervisor" includes only those individuals who devote a preponderance of their employment time to exercising such authority;

(11) "management official" means an individual employed by an agency in a position the duties and responsibilities of which require or authorize the individual to formulate, determine, or influence the policies of the agency;

(12) "collective bargaining" means the performance of the mutual obligation of the representative of an agency and the exclusive representative of employees in an appropriate unit in the agency to meet at reasonable times and to consult and bargain in a good-faith effort to reach agreement with respect to the conditions of employment affecting such employees and to execute, if requested by either party, a written document incorporating any collective bargaining agreement reached, but the obligation referred to in this paragraph does not compel either party to agree to a proposal or to make a concession;

(13) "confidential employee" means an employee who acts in a confidential capacity with respect to an individual who formulates or effectuates management policies in the field of labor-management relations;

(14) "conditions of employment" means personnel policies, practices, and matters, whether established by rule, regulation, or otherwise, affecting working conditions, except that such term does not include policies, practices, and matters—

(A) relating to political activities prohibited under subchapter III of chapter 73 of this title;

(B) relating to the classification of any position; or

(C) to the extent such matters are specifically provided for by Federal statute;

(15) "professional employee" means—

(A) an employee engaged in the performance of work—

(i) requiring knowledge of an advanced type in a field of science or learning customarily acquired by a prolonged course of specialized intellectual instruction and study in an institution of higher learning or a hospital (as distinguished from knowledge acquired by a general academic education, or from an apprenticeship, or from training in the performance of routine mental, manual, mechanical, or physical activities);

(ii) requiring the consistent exercise of discretion and judgment in its performance;

(iii) which is predominantly intellectual and varied in character (as distinguished from routine mental, manual, mechanical, or physical work); and

(iv) which is of such character that the output produced or the result accomplished by such work cannot be standardized in relation to a given period of time; or

(B) an employee who has completed the courses of specialized intellectual instruction and study described in subparagraph (A)(i) of this paragraph and is performing related work under appropriate direction or guidance to qualify the employee as a professional employee described in subparagraph (A) of this paragraph;

(16) "exclusive representative" means any labor organization which—

(A) is certified as the exclusive representative of employees in an appropriate unit pursuant to section 7111 of this title; or

(B) was recognized by an agency immediately before the effective date of this chapter as the exclusive representative of employees in an appropriate unit—

(i) on the basis of an election, or

(ii) on any basis other than an election, and continues to be so recognized in accordance with the provisions of this chapter;

(17) "firefighter" means any employee engaged in the performance of work directly connected with the control and extinguishment of fires or the maintenance and use of firefighting apparatus and equipment; and

(18) "United States" means the 50 States, the District of Columbia, the Commonwealth of Puerto Rico, Guam, the Virgin Islands, the Trust Territory of the Pacific Islands, and any territory or possession of the United States.

(b)(1) The President may issue an order excluding any agency or subdivision thereof from coverage under this chapter if the President determines that—

(A) the agency or subdivision has as a primary function intelligence, counterintelligence, investigative, or national security work, and

(B) the provisions of this chapter cannot be applied to that agency or subdivision in a manner consistent with national security requirements and considerations.

(2) The President may issue an order suspending any provision of this chapter with respect to any agency, installation, or activity located outside the 50 States and the District of Columbia, if the President determines that the suspension is necessary in the interest of national security.

§ 7104. Federal Labor Relations Authority

(a) The Federal Labor Relations Authority is composed of three members, not more than 2 of whom may be adherents of the same political party. No member shall engage in any other business or employment or hold another office or position in the Government of the United States except as otherwise provided by law.

(b) Members of the Authority shall be appointed by the President by and with the advice and consent of the Senate, and may be removed by the President only upon notice and hearing and only for inefficiency, neglect of duty, or malfeasance in office. The President shall designate one member to serve as Chairman of the Authority. The Chairman is the chief executive and administrative officer of the Authority.

(c) A member of the Authority shall be appointed for a term of 5 years. An individual chosen to fill a vacancy shall be appointed for the unexpired term of the member replaced. The term of any member shall not expire before the earlier of—

(1) the date on which the member's successor takes office, or

(2) the last day of the Congress beginning after the date on which the member's term of office would (but for this paragraph) expire.

(d) A vacancy in the Authority shall not impair the right of the remaining members to exercise all of the powers of the Authority.

(e) The Authority shall make an annual report to the President for transmittal to the Congress which shall include information as to the cases it has heard and the decisions it has rendered.

(f)(1) The General Counsel of the Authority shall be appointed by the President, by and with the advice and consent of the Senate, for a term of 5 years. The General Counsel may be removed at any time by the President. The General Counsel shall hold no other office or position in the Government of the United States except as provided by law.

(2) The General Counsel may—

(A) investigate alleged unfair labor practices under this chapter,

(B) file and prosecute complaints under this chapter, and

(C) exercise such other powers of the Authority as the Authority may prescribe.

(3) The General Counsel shall have direct authority over, and responsibility for, all employees in the office of General Counsel, including employees of the General Counsel in the regional offices of the Authority.

§ 7105. Powers and duties of the Authority

(a)(1) The Authority shall provide leadership in establishing policies and guidance relating to matters under this chapter, and, except as otherwise provided, shall be responsible for carrying out the purpose of this chapter.

(2) The Authority shall, to the extent provided in this chapter and in accordance with regulations prescribed by the Authority—

(A) determine the appropriateness of units for labor organization representation under section 7112 of this title;

    (B) supervise or conduct elections to determine whether a labor organization has been selected as an exclusive representative by a majority of the employees in an appropriate unit and otherwise administer the provisions of section 7111 of this title relating to the according of exclusive recognition to labor organizations;

    (C) prescribe criteria and resolve issues relating to the granting of national consultation rights under section 7113 of this title;

    (D) prescribe criteria and resolve issues relating to determining compelling need for agency rules or regulations under section 7117(b) of this title;

    (E) resolves issues relating to the duty to bargain in good faith under section 7117(c) of this title;

    (F) prescribe criteria relating to the granting of consultation rights with respect to conditions of employment under section 7117(d) of this title;

    (G) conduct hearings and resolve complaints of unfair labor practices under section 7118 of this title;

    (H) resolve exceptions to arbitrator's awards under section 7122 of this title; and

    (I) take such other actions as are necessary and appropriate to effectively administer the provisions of this chapter.

(b) The Authority shall adopt an official seal which shall be judicially noticed.

(c) The principal office of the Authority shall be in or about the District of Columbia, but the Authority may meet and exercise any or all of its powers at any time or place. Except as otherwise expressly provided by law, the Authority may, by one or more of its members or by such agents as it may designate, make any appropriate inquiry necessary to carry out its duties wherever persons subject to this chapter are located. Any member who participates in the inquiry shall not be disqualified from later participating in a decision of the Authority in any case relating to the inquiry.

(d) The Authority shall appoint an Executive Director and such regional directors, administrative law judges under section 3105 of this title, and other individuals as it may from time to time find necessary for the proper performance of its functions. The Authority may delegate to officers and employees appointed under this subsection authority to perform such duties and make such expenditures as may be necessary.

(e)(1) The Authority may delegate to any regional director its authority under this chapter—

    (A) to determine whether a group of employees is an appropriate unit;

    (B) to conduct investigations and to provide for hearings;

    (C) to determine whether a question of representation exists and to direct an election; and

    (D) to supervise or conduct secret ballot elections and certify the results thereof.

(2) The Authority may delegate to any administrative law judge appointed under subsection (d) of this section its authority under section 7118 of this title to determine whether any person has engaged in or is engaging in an unfair labor practice.

(f) If the Authority delegates any authority to any regional director or administrative law judge to take any action pursuant to subsection (e) of this section, the Authority may, upon application by any interested person filed within 60 days after the date of the action, review such action, but the review ·shall not, unless specifically ordered by the Authority, operate as a stay of action. The Authority may affirm, modify, or reverse any action reviewed under this subsection. If the Authority does not undertake to grant review of the action under this subsection within 60 days after the later of—

(1) the date of the action; or

(2) the date of the filing of any application under this subsection for review of the action;

the action shall become the action of the Authority at the end of such 60-day period.

(g) In order to carry out its functions under this chapter, the Authority may—

(1) hold hearings;

(2) administer oaths, take the testimony or deposition of any person under oath, and issue subpenas as provided in section 7132 of this title; and

(3) may require an agency or a labor organization to cease and desist from violations of this chapter and require it to take any remedial action it considers appropriate to carry out the policies of this chapter.

(h) Except as provided in section 518 of title 28, relating to litigation before the Supreme Court, attorneys designated by the Authority may appear for the Authority and represent the Authority in any civil action brought in connection with any function carried out by the Authority pursuant to this title or as otherwise authorized by law.

(i) In the exercise of the functions of the Authority under this title, the Authority may request from the Director of the Office of Personnel Management an advisory opinion concerning the proper interpretation of rules, regulations, or policy directives issued by the Office of Personnel Management in connection with any matter before the Authority.

§ 7106. Management rights

(a) Subject to subsection (b) of this section, nothing in this chapter shall affect the authority of any management official of any agency—

(1) to determine the mission, budget, organization, number of employees, and internal security practices of the agency; and

(2) in accordance with applicable laws—
  (A) to hire, assign, direct, layoff, and retain employees in the agency, or to suspend, remove, reduce in grade or pay, or take other disciplinary action against such employees;
  (B) to assign work, to make determinations with respect to contracting out, and to determine the personnel by which agency operations shall be conducted;
  (C) with respect to filling positions, to make selections for appointments from—
    (i) among properly ranked and certified candidates for promotion; or
    (ii) any other appropriate source; and
  (D) to take whatever actions may be necessary to carry out the agency mission during emergencies.

(b) Nothing in this section shall preclude any agency and any labor organization from negotiating—
  (1) at the election of the agency, on the numbers, types, and grades of employees or positions assigned to any organizational subdivision, work project, or tour of duty, or on the technology, methods, and means of performing work;
  (2) procedures which management officials of the agency will observe in exercising any authority under this section; or
  (3) appropriate arrangements for employees adversely affected by the exercise of any authority under this section by such management officials.

Subchapter II [of 5 U.S.C.]. Rights and Duties of Agencies and Labor Organizations

§ 7111. Exclusive recognition of labor organizations

(a) An agency shall accord exclusive recognition to a labor organization if the organization has been selected as the representative, in a secret ballot election, by a majority of the employees in an appropriate unit who cast valid ballots in the election.

(b) If a petition is filed with the Authority—
(1) by any person alleging—
  (A) in the case of an appropriate unit for which there is no exclusive representative, that 30 percent of the employees in the appropriate unit wish to be represented for the purpose of collective bargaining by an exclusive representative, or
  (B) in the case of an appropriate unit for which there is an exclusive representative, that 30 percent of the employees in the unit allege

that the exclusive representative is no longer the representative of the majority of the employees in the unit; or

(2) by any person seeking clarification of, or an amendment to, a certification then in effect or a matter relating to representation;

the Authority shall investigate the petition, and if it has reasonable cause to believe that a question of representation exists, it shall provide an opportunity for a hearing (for which a transcript shall be kept) after reasonable notice. If the Authority finds on the record of the hearing that a question of representation exists, the Authority shall supervise or conduct an election on the question by secret ballot and shall certify the results thereof. An election under this subsection shall not be conducted in any appropriate unit or in any subdivision thereof within which, in the preceding 12 calendar months, a valid election under this subsection has been held.

(c) A labor organization which—

(1) has been designated by at least 10 percent of the employees in the unit specified in any petition filed pursuant to subsection (b) of this section;

(2) has submitted a valid copy of a current or recently expired collective bargaining agreement for the unit; or

(3) has submitted other evidence that it is the exclusive representative of the employees involved;

may intervene with respect to a petition filed pursuant to subsection (b) of this section and shall be placed on the ballot of any election under such subsection (b) with respect to the petition.

(d) The Authority shall determine who is eligible to vote in any election under this section and shall establish rules governing any such election, which shall include rules allowing employees eligible to vote the opportunity to choose—

(1) from labor organizations on the ballot, that labor organization which the employees wish to have represent them; or

(2) not to be represented by a labor organization.

In any election in which no choice on the ballot receives a majority of the votes cast, a runoff election shall be conducted between the two choices receiving the highest number of votes. A labor organization which receives the majority of the votes cast in an election shall be certified by the Authority as the exclusive representative.

(e) A labor organization seeking exclusive recognition shall submit to the Authority and the agency involved a roster of its officers and representatives, a copy of its constitution and bylaws, and a statement of its objectives.

(f) Exclusive recognition shall not be accorded to a labor organization—

(1) if the Authority determines that the labor organization is subject to corrupt influences or influences opposed to democratic principles;

(2) in the case of a petition filed pursuant to subsection (b)(1)(A) of this section, if there is not credible evidence that at least 30 percent of the employees in the unit specified in the petition wish to be represented for the purpose of collective bargaining by the labor organization

seeking exclusive recognition;

(3) if there is then in effect a lawful written collective bargaining agreement between the agency involved and an exclusive representative (other than the labor organization seeking exclusive recognition) covering any employees included in the unit specified in the petition, unless—

    (A) the collective bargaining agreement has been in effect for more than 3 years, or

    (B) the petition for exclusive recognition is filed not more than 105 days and not less than 60 days before the expiration date of the collective bargaining agreement; or

(4) if the Authority has, within the previous 12 calendar months, conducted a secret ballot election for the unit described in any petition under this section and in such election a majority of the employees voting chose a labor organization for certification as the unit's exclusive representative.

(g) Nothing in this section shall be construed to prohibit the waiving of hearings by stipulation for the purpose of a consent election in conformity with regulations and rules or decisions of the Authority.

§ 7112. Determination of appropriate units for labor organization representation

(a)(1) The Authority shall determine the appropriateness of any unit. The Authority shall determine in each case whether, in order to ensure employees the fullest freedom in exercising the rights guaranteed under this chapter, the appropriate unit should be established on an agency, plant, installation, functional, or other basis and shall determine any unit to be an appropriate unit only if the determination will ensure a clear and identifiable community of interest among the employees in the unit and will promote effective dealings with, and efficiency of the operations of, the agency involved.

(b) A unit shall not be determined to be appropriate under this section solely on the basis of the extent to which employees in the proposed unit have organized, nor shall a unit be determined to be appropriate if it includes—

(1) except as provided under section 7135(a)(2) of this title, any management official or supervisor;

(2) a confidential employee;

(3) an employee engaged in personnel work in other than a purely clerical capacity;

(4) an employee engaged in administering the provisions of this chapter;

(5) both professional employees and other employees, unless a majority of the professional employees vote for inclusion in the unit;

(6) any employee engaged in intelligence, counterintelligence, investigative, or security work which directly affects national security; or

(7) any employee primarily engaged in investigation or audit functions relating to the work of individuals employed by an agency whose duties directly affect the internal security of the agency, but only if the functions are undertaken to ensure that the duties are discharged honestly and with integrity.

(c) Any employee who is engaged in administering any provision of law relating to labor-management relations may not be represented by a labor organization—

(1) which represents other individuals to whom such provision applies; or

(2) which is affiliated directly or indirectly with an organization which represents other individuals to whom such provision applies.

(d) Two or more units which are in an agency and for which a labor organization is the exclusive representative may, upon petition by the agency or labor organization, be consolidated with or without an election into a single larger unit if the Authority considers the larger unit to be appropriate. The Authority shall certify the labor organization as the exclusive representative of the new larger unit.

§ 7113. National consultation rights

(a)(1) If, in connection with any agency, no labor organization has been accorded exclusive recognition on an agency basis, a labor organization which is the exclusive representative of a substantial number of the employees of the agency, as determined in accordance with criteria prescribed by the Authority, shall be granted national consultation rights by the agency. National consultation rights shall terminate when the labor organization no longer meets the criteria prescribed by the Authority. Any issue relating to any labor organization's eligibility for, or continuation of, national consultation rights shall be subject to determination by the Authority.

(b)(1) Any labor organization having national consultation rights in connection with any agency under subsection (a) of this section shall—

(A) be informed of any substantive change in conditions of employment proposed by the agency, and

(B) be permitted reasonable time to present its views and recommendations regarding the changes.

(2) If any views or recommendations are presented under paragraph (1) of this subsection to an agency by any labor organization—

(A) the agency shall consider the views or recommendations before taking final action on any matter with respect to which the views or recommendations are presented; and

(B) the agency shall provide the labor organization a written statement of the reasons for taking the final action.

(c) Nothing in this section shall be construed to limit the right of any agency or exclusive representative to engage in collective bargaining.

§ 7114. Representation rights and duties

(a)(1) A labor organization which has been accorded exclusive recognition is the exclusive representative of the employees in the unit it represents and is entitled to act for, and negotiate collective bargaining agreements covering, all employees in the unit. An exclusive representative is responsible for representing the interests of all employees in the unit it represents without discrimination and without regard to labor organization membership.

(2) An exclusive representative of an appropriate unit in an agency shall be given the opportunity to be represented at—

(A) any formal discussion between one or more representatives of the agency and one or more employees in the unit or their representatives concerning any grievance or any personnel policy or practices or other general condition of employment; or

(B) any examination of an employee in the unit by a representative of the agency in connection with an investigation if—

(i) the employee reasonably believes that the examination may result in disciplinary action against the employee; and

(ii) the employee requests representation.

(3) Each agency shall annually inform its employees of their rights under paragraph (2)(B) of this subsection.

(4) Any agency and any exclusive representative in any appropriate unit in the agency, through appropriate representatives, shall meet and negotiate in good faith for the purposes of arriving at a collective bargaining agreement. In addition, the agency and the exclusive representative may determine appropriate techniques, consistent with the provisions of section 7119 of this title, to assist in any negotiation.

(5) The rights of an exclusive representative under the provisions of this subsection shall not be construed to preclude an employee from—

(A) being represented by an attorney or other representative, other than the exclusive representative, of the employee's own choosing in any grievance or appeal action; or

(B) exercising grievance or appellate rights established by law, rule, or regulation; except in the case of grievance or appeal procedures negotiated under this chapter.

(b) The duty of an agency and an exclusive representative to negotiate in good faith under subsection (a) of this section shall include the obligation—

(1) to approach the negotiations with a sincere resolve to reach a collective bargaining agreement;

(2) to be represented at the negotiations by duly authorized representatives prepared to discuss and negotiate on any condition of employment;

(3) to meet at reasonable times and convenient places as frequently as may be necessary, and to avoid unnecessary delays;

(4) in the case of an agency, to furnish to the exclusive representative

involved, or its authorized representative, upon request and, to the extent not prohibited by law, data—

(A) which is normally maintained by the agency in the regular course of business;

(B) which is reasonably available and necessary for full and proper discussion, understanding, and negotiation of subjects within the scope of collective bargaining; and

(C) which does not constitute guidance, counsel, or training provided for management officials or supervisors, relating to collective bargaining; and

(5) if agreement is reached, to execute on the request of any party to the negotiation a written document embodying the agreed terms, and to take such steps as are necessary to implement such agreement.

(c)(1) An agreement between any agency and an exclusive representative shall be subject to approval by the head of the agency.

(2) The head of the agency shall approve the agreement within 30 days from the date the agreement is executed if the agreement is in accordance with the provisions of this chapter and any other applicable law, rule, or regulation (unless the agency has granted an exception to the provision).

(3) If the head of the agency does not approve or disapprove the agreement within the 30-day period, the agreement shall take effect and shall be binding on the agency and the exclusive representative subject to the provisions of this chapter and any other applicable law, rule, or regulation.

(4) A local agreement subject to a national or other controlling agreement at a higher level shall be approved under the procedures of the controlling agreement or, if none, under regulations prescribed by the agency.

§ 7115. Allotments to representatives

(a) If an agency has received from an employee in an appropriate unit a written assignment which authorizes the agency to deduct from the pay of the employee amounts for the payment of regular and periodic dues of the exclusive representative of the unit, the agency shall honor the assignment and make an appropriate allotment pursuant to the assignment. Any such allotment shall be made at no cost to the exclusive representative or the employee. Except as provided under subsection (b) of this section, any such assignment may not be revoked for a period of 1 year.

(b) An allotment under subsection (a) of this section for the deduction of dues with respect to any employee shall terminate when—

(1) the agreement between the agency and the exclusive representative involved ceases to be applicable to the employee; or

(2) the employee is suspended or expelled from membership in the exclusive representative.

(c)(1) Subject to paragraph (2) of this subsection, if a petition has been filed with the Authority by a labor organization alleging that 10 percent of the employees in an appropriate unit in an agency have membership in the labor organization, the Authority shall investigate the petition to determine its validity. Upon certification by the Authority of the validity of the petition, the agency shall have a duty to negotiate with the labor organization solely concerning the deduction of dues of the labor organization from the pay of the members of the labor organization who are employees in the unit and who make a voluntary allotment for such purpose.

(2)(A) The provisions of paragraph (1) of this subsection shall not apply in the case of any appropriate unit for which there is an exclusive representative.

(B) Any agreement under paragraph (1) of this subsection between a labor organization and an agency with respect to an appropriate unit shall be null and void upon the certification of an exclusive representative of the unit.

§ 7116. Unfair labor practices

(a) For the purpose of this chapter, it shall be an unfair labor practice for an agency—

(1) to interfere with, restrain, or coerce any employee in the exercise by the employee of any right under this chapter;

(2) to encourage or discourage membership in any labor organization by discrimination in connection with hiring, tenure, promotion, or other conditions of employment;

(3) to sponsor, control, or otherwise assist any labor organization, other than to furnish, upon request, customary and routine services and facilities if the services and facilities are also furnished on an impartial basis to other labor organizations having equivalent status;

(4) to discipline or otherwise discriminate against an employee because the employee has filed a complaint, affidavit, or petition, or has given any information or testimony under this chapter;

(5) to refuse to consult or negotiate in good faith with a labor organization as required by this chapter;

(6) to fail or refuse to cooperate in impasse procedures and impasse decisions as required by this chapter;

(7) to enforce any rule or regulation (other than a rule or regulation implementing section 2302 of this title) which is in conflict with any applicable collective bargaining agreement if the agreement was in effect before the date the rule or regulation was prescribed; or

(8) to otherwise fail or refuse to comply with any provision of this chapter.

(b) For the purpose of this chapter, it shall be an unfair labor practice for a labor organization—

(1) to interfere with, restrain, or coerce any employee in the exercise by the employee of any right under this chapter;

(2) to cause or attempt to cause an agency to discriminate against any employee in the exercise by the employee of any right under this chapter;

(3) to coerce, discipline, fine, or attempt to coerce a member of the labor organization as punishment, reprisal, or for the purpose of hindering or impeding the member's work performance or productivity as an employee or the discharge of the member's duties as an employee;

(4) to discriminate against an employee with regard to the terms or conditions of membership in the labor organization on the basis of race, color, creed, national origin, sex, age, preferential or nonpreferential civil service status, political affiliation, marital status, or handicapping condition;

(5) to refuse to consult or negotiate in good faith with an agency as required by this chapter;

(6) to fail or refuse to cooperate in impasse procedures and impasse decisions as required by this chapter;

(7)(A) to call, or participate in, a strike, work stoppage, or slowdown, or picketing of an agency in a labor-management dispute if such picketing interferes with an agency's operations, or

(B) to condone any activity described in subparagraph (A) of this paragraph by failing to take action to prevent or stop such activity; or

(8) to otherwise fail or refuse to comply with any provision of this chapter.

Nothing in paragraph (7) of this subsection shall result in any informational picketing which does not interfere with an agency's operations being considered as an unfair labor practice.

(c) For the purpose of this chapter it shall be an unfair labor practice for an exclusive representative to deny membership to any employee in the appropriate unit represented by such exclusive representative except for failure—

(1) to meet reasonable occupational standards uniformly required for admission, or

(2) to tender dues uniformly required as a condition of acquiring and retaining membership.

This subsection does not preclude any labor organization from enforcing discipline in accordance with procedures under its constitution or bylaws to the extent consistent with the provisions of this chapter.

(d) Issues which can properly be raised under an appeals procedure may not be raised as unfair labor practices prohibited under this section. Except for matters wherein, under section 7121(e) and (f) of this title, an employee has an option of using the negotiated grievance procedure or an appeals procedure, issues which can be raised under a grievance procedure may, in the discretion of the aggrieved party, be raised under the grievance procedure or as an unfair labor practice under this section, but not under both procedures.

(e) The expression of any personal view, argument, opinion or the making of any statement which—

(1) publicizes the fact of a representational election and encourages employees to exercise their right to vote in such election,

(2) corrects the record with respect to any false or misleading statement made by any person, or

(3) informs employees of the Government's policy relating to labor-management relations and representation,

shall not, if the expression contains no threat of reprisal or force or promise of benefit or was not made under coercive conditions, (A) constitute an unfair labor practice under any provision of this chapter, or (B) constitute grounds for the setting aside of any election conducted under any provisions of this chapter.

§ 7117. Duty to bargain in good faith; compelling need; duty to consult

(a)(1) Subject to paragraph (2) of this subsection, the duty to bargain in good faith shall, to the extent not inconsistent with any Federal law or any Government-wide rule or regulation, extend to matters which are the subject of any rule or regulation only if the rule or regulation is not a Government-wide rule or regulation.

(2) The duty to bargain in good faith shall, to the extent not inconsistent with Federal law or any Government-wide rule or regulation, extend to matters which are the subject of any agency rule or regulation referred to in paragraph (3) of this subsection only if the Authority has determined under subsection (b) of this section that no compelling need (as determined under regulations prescribed by the Authority) exists for rule or regulation.

(3) Paragraph (2) of the subsection applies to any rule or regulation issued by any agency or issued by any primary national subdivision of such agency, unless an exclusive representative represents an appropriate unit including not less than a majority of the employees in the issuing agency or primary national subdivision, as the case may be, to whom the rule or regulation is applicable.

(b)(1) In any case of collective bargaining in which an exclusive representative alleges that no compelling need exists for any rule or regulation referred to in subsection (a)(3) of this section which is then in effect and which governs any matter at issue in such collective bargaining, the Authority shall determine under paragraph (2) of this subsection, in accordance with regulations prescribed by the Authority, whether such a compelling need exists.

(2) For the purpose of this section, a compelling need shall be determined not to exist for any rule or regulation only if—

(A) the agency, or primary national subdivision, as the case may be, which issued the rule or regulation informs the Authority in writing that a compelling need for the rule or regulation does not exist; or

(B) the Authority determines that a compelling need for a rule or regulation does not exist.

(3) A hearing may be held, in the discretion of the Authority, before a determination is made under this subsection. If a hearing is held, it shall be expedited to the extent practicable and shall not include the General Counsel as a party.

(4) The agency, or primary national subdivision, as the case may be, which issued the rule or regulation shall be a necessary party at any hearing under this subsection.

(c)(1) Except in any case to which subsection (b) of this section applies, if an agency involved in collective bargaining with an exclusive representative alleges that the duty to bargain in good faith does not extend to any matter, the exclusive representative may appeal the allegation to the Authority in accordance with the provisions of this subsection.

(2) The exclusive representative may, on or before the 15th day after the date on which the agency first makes the allegation referred to in paragraph (1) of this subsection, institute an appeal under this subsection by—

(A) filing a petition with the Authority; and

(B) furnishing a copy of the petition to the head of the agency.

(3) On or before the 30th day after the date of the receipt by the head of the agency of the copy of the petition under paragraph (2)(B) of this subsection, the agency shall—

(A) file with the Authority a statement—

(i) withdrawing the allegation; or

(ii) setting forth in full its reasons supporting the allegation; and

(B) furnish a copy of such statement to the exclusive representative.

(4) On or before the 15th day after the date of the receipt by the exclusive representative of a copy of a statement under paragraph (3)(B) of this subsection, the exclusive representative shall file with the Authority its response to the statement.

(5) A hearing may be held, in the discretion of the Authority, before a determination is made under this subsection. If a hearing is held, it shall not include the General Counsel as a party.

(6) The Authority shall expedite proceedings under this subsection to the extent practicable and shall issue to the exclusive representative and to

the agency a written decision on the allegation and specific reasons therefor at the earliest practicable date.

(d)(1) A labor organization which is the exclusive representative of a substantial number of employees, determined in accordance with criteria prescribed by the Authority, shall be granted consultation rights by any agency with respect to any Government-wide rule or regulation issued by the agency effecting any substantive change in any condition of employment. Such consultation rights shall terminate when the labor organization no longer meets the criteria prescribed by the Authority. Any issue relating to a labor organization's eligibility for, or continuation of, such consultation rights shall be subject to determination by the Authority.

(2) A labor organization having consultation rights under paragraph (1) of this subsection shall—

(A) be informed of any substantive change in conditions of employment proposed by the agency, and

(B) shall be permitted reasonable time to present its views and recommendations regarding the changes.

(3) If any views or recommendations are presented under paragraph (2) of this subsection to an agency by any labor organization—

(A) the agency shall consider the views or recommendations before taking final action on any matter with respect to which the views or recommendations are presented; and

(B) the agency shall provide the labor organization a written statement of the reasons for taking the final action.

§ 7118. Prevention of unfair labor practices

(a)(1) If any agency or labor organization is charged by any person with having engaged in or engaging in an unfair labor practice, the General Counsel shall investigate the charge and may issue and cause to be served upon the agency or labor organization a complaint. In any case in which the General Counsel does not issue a complaint because the charge fails to state an unfair labor practice, the General Counsel shall provide the person making the charge a written statement of the reasons for not issuing a complaint.

(2) Any complaint under paragraph (1) of this subsection shall contain a notice—

(A) of the charge;

(B) that a hearing will be held before the Authority (or any member thereof or before an individual employed by the authority and designated for such purpose); and

(C) of the time and place fixed for the hearing.

(3) The labor organization or agency involved shall have the right to file an answer to the original and any amended complaint and to appear

in person or otherwise and give testimony at the time and place fixed in the complaint for the hearing.

(4)(A) Except as provided in subparagraph (B) of this paragraph, no complaint shall be issued based on any alleged unfair labor practice which occurred more than 6 months before the filing of the charge with the Authority.

    (B) If the General Counsel determines that the person filing any charge was prevented from filing the charge during the 6-month period referred to in subparagraph (A) of this paragraph by reason of—

        (i) any failure of the agency or labor organization against which the charge is made to perform a duty owed to the person, or

        (ii) any concealment which prevented discovery of the alleged unfair labor practice during the 6-month period,

the General Counsel may issue a complaint based on the charge if the charge was filed during the 6-month period beginning on the day of the discovery by the person of the alleged unfair labor practice.

(5) The General Counsel may prescribe regulations providing for informal methods by which the alleged unfair labor practice may be resolved prior to the issuance of a complaint.

(6) The Authority (or any member thereof or any individual employed by the Authority and designated for such purpose) shall conduct a hearing on the complaint not earlier than 5 days after the date on which the complaint is served. In the discretion of the individual or individuals conducting the hearing, any person involved may be allowed to intervene in the hearing and to present testimony. Any such hearing shall, to the extent practicable, be conducted in accordance with the provisions of subchapter II of chapter 5 of this title, except that the parties shall not be bound by rules of evidence, whether statutory, common law, or adopted by a court. A transcript shall be kept of the hearing. After such a hearing the Authority, in its discretion, may upon notice receive further evidence or hear argument.

(7) If the Authority (or any member thereof or any individual employed by the Authority and designated for such purpose) determines after any hearing on a complaint under paragraph (5) of this subsection that the preponderance of the evidence received demonstrates that the agency or labor organization named in the complaint has engaged in or is engaging in an unfair labor practice, then the individual or individuals conducting the hearing shall state in writing their findings of fact and shall issue and cause to be served on the agency or labor organization an order—

    (A) to cease and desist from any such unfair labor practice in which the agency or labor organization is engaged;

    (B) requiring the parties to renegotiate a collective bargaining agreement in accordance with the order of the Authority and requiring that the agreement, as amended, be given retroactive effect;

(C) requiring reinstatement of an employee with backpay in accordance with section 5596 of this title; or

(D) including any combination of the actions described in subparagraphs (A) through (C) of this paragraph or such other action as will carry out the purpose of this chapter.

If any such order requires reinstatement of an employee with backpay, backpay may be required of the agency (as provided in section 5596 of this title) or of the labor organization, as the case may be, which is found to have engaged in the unfair labor practice involved.

(8) If the individual or individuals conducting the hearing determine that the preponderance of the evidence received fails to demonstrate that the agency or labor organization named in the complaint has engaged in or is engaging in an unfair labor practice, the individual or individuals shall state in writing their findings of fact and shall issue an order dismissing the complaint.

(b) In connection with any matter before the Authority in any proceeding under this section, the Authority may request, in accordance with the provisions of section 7105(i) of this title, from the Director of the Office of Personnel Management an advisory opinion concerning the proper interpretation of rules, regulations, or other policy directives issued by the Office of Personnel Management.

§ 7119. Negotiation impasses; Federal Service Impasses Panel

(a) The Federal Mediation and Conciliation Service shall provide services and assistance to agencies and exclusive representatives in the resolution of negotiation impasses. The Service shall determine under what circumstances and in what manner it shall provide services and assistance.

(b) If voluntary arrangements, including the services of the Federal Mediation and Conciliation Service or any other third-party mediation, fail to resolve a negotiation impasse—

(1) either party may request the Federal Service Impasses Panel to consider the matter, or

(2) the parties may agree to adopt a procedure for binding arbitration of the negotiation impasse, but only if the procedure is approved by the Panel.

(c)(1) The Federal Service Impasses Panel is an entity within the Authority, the function of which is to provide assistance in resolving negotiation impasses between agencies and exclusive representatives.

(2) The Panel shall be composed of a Chairman and at least six other members, who shall be appointed by the President, solely on the basis of fitness to perform the duties and functions involved, from among individuals who are familiar with Government operations and knowledgeable in labor-management relations.

(3) Of the original members of the Panel, 2 members shall be appointed for a term of 1 year, 2 members shall be appointed for a term of 3 years, and the Chairman and the remaining members shall be appointed for a term of 5 years. Thereafter each member shall be appointed for a term of 5 years, except that an individual chosen to fill a vacancy shall be appointed for the unexpired term of the member replaced. Any member of the Panel may be removed by the President.

(4) The Panel may appoint an Executive Director and any other individuals it may from time to time find necessary for the proper performance of its duties. Each member of the Panel who is not an employee (as defined in section 2105 of this title) is entitled to pay at a rate equal to the daily equivalent of the maximum annual rate of basic pay then currently paid under the General Schedule for each day he is engaged in the performance of official business of the Panel, including travel time, and is entitled to travel expenses as provided under section 5703 of this title.

(5)(A) The Panel or its designee shall promptly investigate any impasse presented to it under subsection (b) of this section. The Panel shall consider the impasse and shall either—

  (i) recommend to the parties procedures for the resolution of the impasse; or

  (ii) assist the parties in resolving the impasse through whatever methods and procedures, including factfinding and recommendations, it may consider appropriate to accomplish the purpose of this section.

(B) If the parties do not arrive at a settlement after assistance by the Panel under subparagraph (A) of this paragraph, the Panel may—

  (i) hold hearings;

  (ii) administer oaths, take the testimony or deposition of any person under oath, and issue subpenas as provided in section 7132 of this title; and

  (iii) take whatever action is necessary and not inconsistent with this chapter to resolve the impasse.

(C) Notice of any final action of the Panel under this section shall be promptly served upon the parties, and the action shall be binding on such parties during the term of the agreement, unless the parties agree otherwise.

§ 7120. Standards of conduct for labor organizations

(a) An agency shall only accord recognition to a labor organization that is free from corrupt influences and influences opposed to basic democratic principles. Except as provided in subsection (b) of this section, an organization is not required to prove that it is free from such influences if it is subject to governing requirements adopted by the organization or by a national or international labor organization or federation of labor organizations with which it is affiliated, or in which it participates, containing explicit and detailed provisions to which it subscribes calling for—

(1) the maintenance of democratic procedures and practices including provisions for periodic elections to be conducted subject to recognized safeguards and provisions defining and securing the right of individual members to participate in the affairs of the organization, to receive fair and equal treatment under the governing rules of the organization, and to receive fair process in disciplinary proceedings;

(2) the exclusion from office in the organization of persons affiliated with communist or other totalitarian movements and persons identified with corrupt influences;

(3) the prohibition of business or financial interests on the part of organization officers and agents which conflict with their duty to the organization and its members; and

(4) the maintenance of fiscal integrity in the conduct of the affairs of the organization, including provisions for accounting and financial controls and regular financial reports or summaries to be made available to members.

(b) Notwithstanding the fact that a labor organization has adopted or subscribed to standards of conduct as provided in subsection (a) of this section, the organization is required to furnish evidence of its freedom from corrupt influences or influences opposed to basic democratic principles if there is reasonable cause to believe that—

(1) the organization has been suspended or expelled from, or is subject to other sanction, by a parent labor organization, or federation of organizations with which it had been affiliated, because it had demonstrated an unwillingness or inability to comply with governing requirements comparable in purpose to those required by subsection (a) of this section; or

(2) the organization is in fact subject to influences that would preclude recognition under this chapter.

(c) A labor organization which has or seeks recognition as a representative of employees under this chapter shall file financial and other reports with the Assistant Secretary of Labor for Labor Management Relations, provide for bonding of officials and employees of the organization, and comply with trusteeship and election standards.

(d) The Assistant Secretary shall prescribe such regulations as are necessary to carry out the purposes of this section. Such regulations shall conform generally to the principles applied to labor organizations in the private sector. Complaints of violations of this section shall be filed with the Assistant Secretary. In any matter arising under this section, the Assistant Secretary may require a labor organization to cease and desist from violations of this section and require it to take such actions as he considers appropriate to carry out the policies of this section.

(e) This chapter does not authorize participation in the management of a labor organization or acting as a representative of a labor organization by a management official, a supervisor, or a confidential employee, except as specifically provided in this chapter, or by an employee if the participation or activity would result in a conflict or apparent conflict of interest or would otherwise be incompatible with law or with the official duties of the employee.

(f) In the case of any labor organization which by omission or commission has willfully and intentionally, with regard to any strike, work stoppage, or slowdown, violated section 7116(b)(7) of this title, the Authority shall, upon an appropriate finding by the Authority of such violation—

(1) revoke the exclusive recognition status of the labor organization, which shall then immediately cease to be legally entitled and obligated to represent employees in the unit; or

(2) take any other appropriate disciplinary action.

Subchapter III [of 5 U.S.C.].   Grievances, Appeals, and Review

§ 7121.   Grievance procedures

(a)(1) Except as provided in paragraph (2) of this subsection, any collective bargaining agreement shall provide procedures for the settlement of grievances, including questions of arbitrability. Except as provided in subsections (d) and (e) of this section, the procedures shall be the exclusive procedures for resolving grievances which fall within its coverage.

(2) Any collective bargaining agreement may exclude any matter from the application of the grievance procedures which are provided for in the agreement.

(b) Any negotiated grievance procedure referred to in subsection (a) of this section shall—

(1) be fair and simple,

(2) provide for expeditious processing, and

(3) include procedures that—

(A) assure an exclusive representative the right, in its own behalf or on behalf of any employee in the unit represented by the exclusive representative, to present and process grievances;

(B) assure such an employee the right to present a grievance on the employee's own behalf, and assure the exclusive representative the right to be present during the grievance proceeding; and

(C) provide that any grievance not satisfactorily settled under the negotiated grievance procedure shall be subject to binding arbitration which may be invoked by either the exclusive representative or the agency.

(c) The preceding subsections of this section shall not apply with respect to any grievance concerning—

(1) any claimed violation of subchapter III of chapter 73 of this title (relating to prohibited political activities);

(2) retirement, life insurance, or health insurance;

(3) a suspension or removal under section 7532 of this title;

(4) any examination, certification, or appointment; or

(5) the classification of any position which does not result in the reduction in grade or pay of an employee.

(d) An aggrieved employee affected by a prohibited personnel practice under section 2302(b)(1) of this title which also falls under the coverage of the negotiated grievance procedure may raise the matter under a statutory procedure or the negotiated procedure, but not both. An employee shall be deemed to have exercised his option under this subsection to raise the matter under either a statutory procedure or the negotiated procedure at such time as the employee timely initiates an action under the applicable statutory procedure or timely files a grievance in writing, in accordance with the provisions of the parties' negotiated procedure, whichever event occurs first. Selection of the negotiated procedure in no manner prejudices the right of an aggrieved employee to request the Merit Systems Protection Board to review the final decision pursuant to section 7702 of this title in the case of any personnel action that could have been appealed to the Board, or, where applicable, to request the Equal Employment Opportunity Commission to review a final decision in any other matter involving a complaint of discrimination of the type prohibited by any law administered by the Equal Employment Opportunity Commission.

(e)(1) Matters covered under sections 4303 and 7512 of this title which also fall within the coverage of the negotiated grievances procedure may, in the discretion of the aggrieved employee, be raised either under the appellate procedures of section 7701 of this title or under the negotiated grievance procedure, but not both. Similar matters which arise under other personnel systems applicable to employees covered by this chapter may, in the discretion of the aggrieved employee, be raised either under the appellate procedures, if any, applicable to those matters, or under the negotiated grievance procedure, but not both. An employee shall be deemed to have exercised his option under this subsection to raise a matter either under the applicable appellate procedures or under negotiated grievance procedure at such time as the employee timely files a notice of appeal under the applicable appellate procedures or timely files a grievance in writing in accordance with the provisions of the parties' negotiated grievance procedure, whichever event occurs first.

(2) In matters covered under sections 4303 and 7512 of this title which have been raised under the negotiated grievance procedure in accordance with this section, an arbitrator shall be governed by section 7701(c)(1) of this title, as applicable.

(f) In matters covered under sections 4303 and 7512 of this title which have been raised under the negotiated grievance procedure in accordance with this section, section 7703 of this title pertaining to judicial review shall apply to the award of an arbitrator in the same manner and under the same conditions as if the matter had been decided by the Board. In matters similar to those covered under sections 4303 and 7512 of this title which arise under other personnel systems and which an aggrieved employee has raised under the negotiated grievance procedure, judicial review of an arbitrator's award may be obtained in the same manner and on the same basis as could be obtained of a final decision in such matters raised under applicable appellate procedures.

§ 7122. Exceptions to arbitral awards

(a) Either party to arbitration under this chapter may file with the Authority an exception to any arbitrator's award pursuant to the arbitration (other than an award relating to a matter described in section 7121(f) of this title). If upon review the Authority finds that the award is deficient—
  (1) because it is contrary to any law, rule, or regulation; or
  (2) on other grounds similar to those applied by Federal courts in private
      sector labor-management relations;
the Authority may take such action and make such recommendations concerning the award as it considers necessary, consistent with applicable laws, rules, or regulations.

(b) If no exception to an arbitrator's award is filed under subsection (a) of this section during the 30-day period beginning on the date the award is served on the party, the award shall be final and binding. An agency shall take the actions required by an arbitrator's final award. The award may include the payment of backpay (as provided in section 5596 of this title).

§ 7123. Judicial review; enforcement

(a) Any person aggrieved by any final order of the Authority other than an order under—
  (1) section 7122 of this title (involving an award by an arbitrator), unless
      the order involves an unfair labor practice under section 7118 of this
      title, or
  (2) section 7112 of this title (involving an appropriate unit
      determination),
may, during the 60-day period beginning on the date on which the order was issued, institute an action for judicial review of the Authority's order in the United States court of appeals in the circuit in which the person resides or transacts business or in the United States Court of Appeals for the District of Columbia.

(b) The Authority may petition any appropriate United States court of appeals for the enforcement of any order of the Authority and for appropriate temporary relief or restraining order.

(c) Upon the filing of a petition under subsection (a) of this section for judicial review or under subsection (b) of this section for enforcement, the Authority shall file in the court the record in the proceedings, as provided in section 2112 of title 28. Upon the filing of the petition, the court shall cause notice thereof to be served to the parties involved, and thereupon shall have jurisdiction of the proceeding and of the question determined therein and may grant any temporary relief (including a temporary restraining order) it considers just and proper, and may make and enter a decree affirming and enforcing, modifying and enforcing as so modified, or setting aside in whole or in part the order of the Authority. The filing of a petition under subsection (a) or (b) of this section shall not operate as a stay of the Authority's order unless the court specifically orders the stay. Review of the Authority's order shall be on the record in accordance with section 706 of this title. No objection that has not been urged before the Authority, or its designee, shall be considered by the court, unless the failure or neglect to urge the objection is excused because of extraordinary circumstances. The findings of the Authority with respect to questions of fact, if supported by substantial evidence on the record considered as a whole, shall be conclusive. If any person applies to the court for leave to adduce additional evidence and shows to the satisfaction of the court that the additional evidence is material and that there were reasonable grounds for the failure to adduce the evidence in the hearing before the Authority, or its designee, the court may order the additional evidence to be taken before the Authority, or its designee, and to be made a part of the record. The Authority may modify its findings as to the facts, or make new findings by reason of additional evidence so taken and filed. The Authority shall file its modified or new findings, which, with respect to questions of facts, if supported by substantial evidence on the record considered as a whole, shall be conclusive. The Authority shall file its recommendations, if any, for the modification or setting aside of its original order. Upon the filing of the record with the court, the jurisdiction of the court shall be exclusive and its judgment and decree shall be final, except that the judgment and decree shall be subject to review by the Supreme Court of the United States upon writ of certiorari or certification as provided in section 1254 of title 28.

(d) The Authority may, upon issuance of a complaint as provided in section 7118 of this title charging that any person has engaged in or is engaging in an unfair labor practice, petition any United States district court within any district in which the unfair labor practice in question is alleged to have occurred or in which such person resides or transacts business for appropriate temporary relief (including a restraining order). Upon the filing of the petition, the court shall cause notice thereof to be served upon the person, and thereupon shall have jurisdiction to grant any temporary relief (including a temporary restraining order) it considers just and proper. A court shall not grant any temporary relief under this section if it would interfere with the ability of the agency to carry out its essential functions or if the Authority fails to establish probable cause that an unfair labor practice is being committed.

Subchapter IV [of 5 U.S.C.]. Administrative and Other Provisions

§ 7131. Official time

(a) Any employee representing an exclusive representative in the negotiation of a collective bargaining agreement under this chapter shall be authorized official time for such purposes, including attendance at impasse proceeding, during the time the employee otherwise would be in a duty status. The number of employees for whom official time is authorized under this subsection shall not exceed the number of individuals designated as representing the agency for such purposes.

(b) Any activities performed by any employee relating to the internal business of a labor organization (including the solicitation of membership, elections of labor organization officials, and collection of dues) shall be performed during the time the employee is in a nonduty status.

(c) Except as provided in subsection (a) of this section, the Authority shall determine whether any employee participating for, or on behalf of, a labor organization in any phase of proceedings before the Authority shall be authorized official time for such purpose during the time the employee otherwise would be in a duty status.

(d) Except as provided in the preceding subsections of this section—

(1) any employee representing an exclusive representative, or

(2) in connection with any other matter covered by this chapter, any employee in an appropriate unit represented by an exclusive representative,

shall be granted official time in any amount the agency and the exclusive representative involved agree to be reasonable, necessary, and in the public interest.

§ 7132. Subpenas

(a) Any member of the Authority, the General Counsel, or the Panel, any administrative law judge appointed by the authority under section 3105 of this title, and any employee of the Authority designated by the Authority may—

(1) issue subpenas requiring the attendance and testimony of witnesses and the production of documentary or other evidence from any place in the United States; and

(2) administer oaths, take or order the taking of depositions, order responses to written interrogatories, examine witnesses, and receive evidence.

No subpena shall be issued under this section which requires the disclosure of intramanagement guidance, advice, counsel, or training within an agency or between an agency and the Office of Personnel Management.

(b) In the case of contumacy or failure to obey a subpena issued under subsection (a)(1) of this section, the United States district court for the judicial district in which the person to whom the subpena is addressed resides or is served may issue an order requiring such person to appear at any designated place to testify or to produce documentary or other evidence. Any failure to obey the order of the court may be punished by the court as a contempt thereof.

(c) Witnesses (whether appearing voluntarily or under subpena) shall be paid the same fee and mileage allowances which are paid subpenaed witnesses in the courts of the United States.

§ 7133. Compilation and publication of data

(a) The Authority shall maintain a file of its proceedings and copies of all available agreements and arbitration decisions, and shall publish the texts of its decisions and the actions taken by the Panel under section 7119 of this title.

(b) All files maintained under subsection (a) of this section shall be open to inspection and reproduction in accordance with the provisions of sections 552 and 552a of this title.

§ 7134. Regulations

The Authority, the General Counsel, the Federal Mediation and Conciliation Service, the Assistant Secretary of Labor for Labor Management Relations, and the Panel shall each prescribe rules and regulations to carry out the provisions of this chapter applicable to each of them, respectively. Provisions of subchapter II of chapter 5 of this title shall be applicable to the issuance, revision, or repeal of any such rule or regulation.

§ 7135. Continuation of existing laws, recognitions, agreements, and procedures

(a) Nothing contained in this chapter shall preclude—

(1) the renewal or continuation of an exclusive recognition, certification of an exclusive representative, or a lawful agreement between an agency

and an exclusive representative of its employees, which is entered into before the effective date of this chapter; or
(2) the renewal, continuation, or initial according of recognition for units of management officials or supervisors represented by labor organizations which historically or traditionally represent management officials or supervisors in private industry and which hold exclusive recognition for units of such officials or supervisors in any agency on the effective date of this chapter.

(b) Policies, regulations, and procedures established under and decisions issued under Executive Orders 11491, 11616, 11636, 11787, and 11838, or under any other Executive order, as in effect on the effective date of this chapter, shall remain in full force and effect until revised or revoked by the President, or unless superseded by specific provisions of this chapter or by regulations or decisions issued pursuant to this chapter.

* * *

§ 5596(b). Backpay due to unjustified personnel action

[Sec. 702] (b)(1) An employee of an agency who, on the basis of a timely appeal or an administrative determination (including a decision relating to an unfair labor practice or a grievance) is found by appropriate authority under applicable law, rule, regulation, or collective bargaining agreement, to have been affected by an unjustified or unwarranted personnel action which has resulted in the withdrawal or reduction of all or part of the pay, allowances, or differentials of the employee—
(A) is entitled, on correction of the personnel action, to receive for the period for which the personnel action was in effect—
(i) an amount equal to all or any part of the pay, allowances, or differentials, as applicable which the employee normally would have earned or received during the period if the personnel action had not occurred, less any amounts earned by the employee through other employment during that period; and
(ii) reasonable attorney fees related to the personnel action which, with respect to any decision relating to an unfair labor practice or a grievance processed under a procedure negotiated in accordance with chapter 71 of this title, shall be awarded in accordance with standards established under section 7701(g) of this title; and
(B) for all purposes, is deemed to have performed service for the agency during that period, except that—
(i) annual leave restored under this paragraph which is in excess of the maximum leave accumulation permitted by law shall be

credited to a separate leave account for the employee and shall be available for use by the employee within the time limits prescribed by regulations of the Office of Personnel Management, and

(ii) annual leave credited under clause (i) of this subparagraph but unused and still available to the employee under regulations prescribed by the Office shall be included in the lump-sum payment under section 5551 or 5552(1) of this title but may not be retained to the credit of the employee under section 5552(2) of this title.

(2) This subsection does not apply to any reclassification action nor authorize the setting aside of an otherwise proper promotion by a selecting official from a group of properly ranked and certified candidates.

(3) For the purpose of this subsection, "grievance" and "collective bargaining agreement" have the meanings set forth in section 7103 of this title, "unfair labor practice" means an unfair labor practice described in section 7116 of this title, and "personnel action" includes the omission or failure to take an action or confer a benefit.

* * *

Chapter 72 [of 5 U.S.C.]. Antidiscrimination; Right to Petition Congress

Subchapter II. Employees' Right to Petition Congress

§ 7211. Employees' right to petition Congress

[Sec. 703] The right of employees, individually or collectively, to petition Congress or a Member of Congress, or to furnish information to either House of Congress, or to a committee or Member thereof, may not be interfered with or denied.

4

Fair Employment Practices Laws

Civil Rights Act (1866)

(Act of April 9, 1866)

§ 1982. Property rights of citizens

All citizens of the United States shall have the same right, in every State and Territory, as is enjoyed by white citizens thereof to inherit, purchase, lease, sell, hold, and convey real and personal property.

Civil Rights Act (1870)

(Act of May 31, 1870)

§ 1981. Equal rights under the law

All persons within the jurisdiction of the United States shall have the same right in every State and Territory to make and enforce contracts, to sue, be parties, give evidence, and to the full and equal benefit of all laws and proceedings for the security of persons and property as is enjoyed by white citizens, and shall be subject to like punishment, pains, penalties, taxes, licenses, and exactions of every kind, and to no other.

Civil Rights Act (1871)

(Act of April 20, 1871; as last amended by P.L. 96–170, effective December 29, 1979)

§ 1983. Civil action for deprivation of rights

Every person who, under color of any statute, ordinance, regulation, custom or usage, of any State or Territory, subjects, or causes to be subjected, any citizen of the United States or other person within the jurisdiction thereof to the deprivation of any rights, privileges, or immunities secured by the Constitution and laws, shall be liable to the party injured in an action at law, suit in equity, or other proper proceeding for redress. For the purposes of this section, any Act of Congress applicable exclusively to the District of Columbia shall be considered to be a statute of the District of Columbia.

Civil Rights Act (1964)

(P.L. 88–352, approved July 2, 1964, as last amended by P.L. 96–191, effective October 1, 1980)

Title VI. Nondiscrimination in Federally Assisted Programs

§ 2000d. Prohibition against exclusion from participation in, denial of benefits of, and discrimination under Federally assisted programs on ground of race, color, or national origin

[Sec. 601] No person in the United States shall, on the ground of race, color, or national origin, be excluded from participation in, be denied the benefits of, or be subjected to discrimination under any program or activity receiving Federal financial assistance.

§ 2000d–1. Federal authority and financial assistance to programs or activities by way of grant, loan, or contract other than contract of insurance or guaranty; rules and regulations; approval by President; compliance with requirements; reports to Congressional committees; effective date of administrative action

[Sec. 602] Each Federal department and agency which is empowered to extend Federal financial assistance to any program or activity, by way of grant, loan, or contract other than a contract of insurance or guaranty, is authorized and directed to effectuate the provisions of section 601 with respect to such program or activity by issuing rules, regulations, or orders of general applicability which shall be consistent with achievement of the objectives of the statute authorizing the financial assistance in connection with which the action is taken. No such rule, regulation, or order shall become effective unless and until approved by the President. Compliance

125

with any requirement adopted pursuant to this section may be effected (1) by the termination of or refusal to grant or to continue assistance under such program or activity to any recipient as to whom there has been an express finding on the record, after opportunity for hearing, of a failure to comply with such requirement, but such termination or refusal shall be limited to the particular political entity, or part thereof, or other recipient as to whom such a finding has been made and, shall be limited in its effect to the particular program, or part thereof, in which such noncompliance has been so found, or (2) by any other means authorized by law: *Provided, however,* That no such action shall be taken until the department or agency concerned has advised the appropriate person or persons of the failure to comply with the requirement and has determined that compliance cannot be secured by voluntary means. In the case of any action terminating, or refusing to grant or continue, assistance because of failure to comply with a requirement imposed pursuant to this section, the head of the Federal department or agency shall file with the committees of the House and Senate having legislative jurisdiction over the program or activity involved a full written report of the circumstances and the grounds for such action. No such action shall become effective until thirty days have elapsed after the filing of such report.

§ 2000d–2. Judicial review; administrative procedure provisions

[Sec. 603] Any department or agency action taken pursuant to section 602 shall be subject to such judicial review as may otherwise be provided by law for similar action taken by such department or agency on other grounds. In the case of action, not otherwise subject to judicial review, terminating or refusing to grant or to continue financial assistance upon a finding of failure to comply with a requirement imposed pursuant to section 602, any person aggrieved (including any State or political subdivision thereof and any agency of either) may obtain judicial review of such action in accordance with section 10 of the Administrative Procedure Act, and such action shall not be deemed committed to unreviewable agency discretion within the meaning of that section.

§ 2000d–3. Construction of provisions not to authorize administrative action with respect to employment practices except where primary objective of Federal financial assistance is to provide employment

[Sec. 604] Nothing contained in this title shall be construed to authorize action under this title by any department or agency with respect to any employment practice of any employer, employment agency, or labor organization except where a primary objective of the Federal financial assistance is to provide employment.

§ 2000d–4. Federal authority and financial assistance to programs or activities by way of contract of insurance or guaranty

[Sec. 605] Nothing in this title shall add to or detract from any existing authority with respect to any program or activity under which Federal financial assistance is extended by way of a contract of insurance or guaranty.

* * *

Title VII. Equal Employment Opportunities

§ 2000e. Definitions

[Sec. 701] For the purposes of this title—

(a) The term "person" includes one or more individuals, governments, governmental agencies, political subdivisions, labor unions, partnerships, associations, corporations, legal representatives, mutual companies, joint-stock companies, trusts, unincorporated organizations, trustees, trustees in bankruptcy, or receivers.

(b) The term "employer" means a person engaged in an industry affecting commerce who has fifteen or more employees for each working day in each of twenty or more calendar weeks in the current or preceding calendar year, and any agent of such a person, but such term does not include (1) the United States, a corporation wholly owned by the Government of the United States, an Indian tribe, or any department or agency of the District of Columbia subject by statute to procedures of the competitive service (as defined in section 2102 of title 5 of the United States Code), or (2) a bona fide private membership club (other than a labor organization) which is exempt from taxation under section 501(c) of the Internal Revenue Code of 1954, except that during the first year after the date of enactment of the Equal Employment Opportunity Act of 1972, persons having fewer than twenty-five employees (and their agents) shall not be considered employers.

(c) The term "employment agency" means any person regularly under-taking with or without compensation to procure employees for an employer or to procure for employees opportunities to work for an employer and includes an agent of such a person.

(d) The term "labor organization" means a labor organization engaged in an industry affecting commerce, and any agent of such an organization, and includes any organization of any kind, any agency, or employee representation committee, group, association, or plan so engaged in which employees participate and which exists for the purpose, in whole or in part, of dealing with employers concerning grievances, labor disputes, wages, rates of pay, hours, or other terms or conditions of employment, and any conference, general committee, joint or system board, or joint council so engaged which is subordinate to a national or international labor organization.

(e) A labor organization shall be deemed to be engaged in an industry affecting commerce if (1) it maintains or operates a hiring hall or hiring office which procures employees for an employer or procures for employees opportunities to work for an employer, or (2) the number of its members (or, where it is a labor organization composed of other labor organizations or their representatives, if the aggregate number of the members of such other labor organization) is (A) twenty-five or more during the first year after the date of enactment of the Equal Employment Opportunity Act of 1972, or (B) fifteen or more thereafter, and such labor organization—

(1) is the certified representative of employees under the provisions of the National Labor Relations Act, as amended, or the Railway Labor Act, as amended;

(2) although not certified, is a national or international labor organization or a local labor organization recognized or acting as the representative of employees of an employer or employers engaged in an industry affecting commerce; or

(3) has chartered a local labor organization or subsidiary body which is representing or actively seeking to represent employees of employers within the meaning of paragraph (1) or (2); or

(4) has been chartered by a labor organization representing or actively seeking to represent employees within the meaning of paragraph (1) or (2) as the local or subordinate body through which such employees may enjoy membership or become affiliated with such labor organization; or

(5) is a conference, general committee, joint or system board, or joint council subordinate to a national or international labor organization, which includes a labor organization engaged in an industry affecting commerce within the meaning of any of the preceding paragraphs of this subsection.

(f) The term "employee" means an individual employed by an employer, except that the term "employee" shall not include any person elected to public office in any State or political subdivision of any State by the qualified voters thereof, or any person chosen by such officer to be on such officer's personal staff, or an appointee on the policy making level or an immediate adviser with respect to the exercise of the constitutional or legal powers of the office. The exemption set forth in the preceding sentence shall not include employees subject to the civil service laws of a State government, governmental agency or political subdivision.

(g) The term "commerce" means trade, traffic, commerce, transportation, transmission, or communication among the several States; or between a State and any place outside thereof; or within the District of Columbia, or a possession of the United States, or between points in the same State but through a point outside thereof.

(h) The term "industry affecting commerce" means any activity, business, or industry in commerce or in which a labor dispute would hinder or obstruct commerce or the free flow of commerce and includes any activity or industry "affecting commerce" within the meaning of the Labor-Management Reporting and Disclosure Act of 1959, and further includes any governmental industry, business, or activity.

(i) The term "State" includes a State of the United States, the District of Columbia, Puerto Rico, the Virgin Islands, American Samoa, Guam, Wake Island, the Canal Zone, and Outer Continental Shelf Lands defined in the Outer Continental Shelf Lands Act.

(j) The term "religion" includes all aspects of religious observance and practice, as well as belief, unless an employer demonstrates that he is unable to reasonably accommodate to an employee's or prospective employee's religious observance or practice without undue hardship on the conduct of the employer's business.

(k) The terms "because of sex" or "on the basis of sex" include, but are not limited to, because of or on the basis of pregnancy, childbirth or related medical conditions; and women affected by pregnancy, childbirth, or related medical conditions shall be treated the same for all employment-related purposes, including receipt of benefits under fringe benefit programs, as other persons not so affected but similar in their ability or inability to work, and nothing in Section 703(h) of this title shall be interpreted to permit otherwise. This subsection shall not require an employer to pay for health insurance benefits for abortion, except where the life of the mother would be endangered if the fetus were carried to term, or except where medical complications have arisen from an abortion: *Provided,* That nothing herein shall preclude an employer from providing abortion benefits or otherwise affect bargaining agreements in regard to abortion.

§ 2000e-1. Title not applicable to employment of aliens outside State and individuals for performance of activities of religious corporations, associations, educational institutions, or societies

[Sec. 702] This title shall not apply to an employer with respect to the employment of aliens outside any State, or to a religious corporation, association, educational institution, or society with respect to the employment of individuals of a particular religion to perform work connected with the carrying on by such corporation, association, educational institution, or society of its activities.

§ 2000e-2. Unlawful employment practices

[Sec. 703] (a) It shall be an unlawful employment practice for an employer—

(1) to fail or refuse to hire or to discharge any individual, or otherwise to discriminate against any individual with respect to his compensation, terms, conditions, or privileges of employment, because of such individual's race, color, religion, sex, or national origin; or

(2) to limit, segregate, or classify his employees or applicants for employment in any way which would deprive or tend to deprive any individual of employment opportunities or otherwise adversely affect his status as an employee, because of such individual's race, color, religion, sex, or national origin.

(b) It shall be an unlawful employment practice for an employment agency to fail or refuse to refer for employment, or otherwise to discriminate against, any individual because of his race, color, religion, sex, or national origin, or to classify or refer for employment any individual on the basis of his race, color, religion, sex, or national origin.

(c) It shall be an unlawful employment practice for a labor organization—

(1) to exclude or to expel from its membership, or otherwise to discriminate against, any individual because of his race, color, religion, sex, or national origin;

(2) to limit, segregate, or classify its membership or applicants for membership or to classify or fail or refuse to refer for employment any individual, in any way which would deprive or tend to deprive any individual of employment opportunities, or would limit such employment opportunities or otherwise adversely affect his status as an employee or as an applicant for employment, because of such individual's race, color, religion, sex, or national origin; or

(3) to cause or attempt to cause an employer to discriminate against an individual in violation of this section.

(d) It shall be an unlawful employment practice for any employer, labor organization, or joint labor-management committee controlling apprenticeship or other training or retraining, including on-the-job training programs, to discriminate against any individual because of his race, color, religion, sex, or national origin in admission to, or employment in, any program established to provide apprenticeship or other training.

(e) Notwithstanding any other provision of this title, (1) it shall not be an unlawful employment practice for an employer to hire and employ employees, for an employment agency to classify, or refer for employment any individual, for a labor organization to classify its membership or to classify or refer for employment any individual, or for an employer, labor organization, or joint labor-management committee controlling apprenticeship or other training or retraining programs to admit or employ any individual in any such program, on the basis of his religion, sex, or national origin in those certain instances where religion, sex, or national origin is a bona fide occupational qualification reasonably necessary to the normal operation of that particular business or enterprise, and (2) it shall not be an unlawful employment practice for a school, college, university, or other educational institution or institution of learning to hire and employ employees of a particular religion if such school, college, university, or other educational institution or institution of learning is, in whole or in substantial part, owned, supported, controlled, or managed by a particular religion or by a particular religious corporation, association, or society, or if the curriculum of such school, college, university, or other educational institution or institution of learning is directed toward the propagation of a particular religion.

(f) As used in this title, the phrase "unlawful employment practice" shall not be deemed to include any action or measure taken by an employer, labor organization, joint labor-management committee, or employment agency with respect to an individual who is a member of the Communist Party of the United States or of any other organization required to register as a Communist-action or Communist-front organization by final order of the Subversive Activities Control Board pursuant to the Subversive Activities Control Act of 1950.

(g) Notwithstanding any other provision of this title, it shall not be an unlawful employment practice for an employer to fail or refuse to hire and employ any individual for any position, for an employer to discharge an individual from any position, or for an employment agency to fail or refuse to refer any individual for employment in any position, or for a labor organization to fail or refuse to refer any individual for employment in any position, if—

(1) the occupancy of such position, or access to the premises in or upon which any part of the duties of such position is performed or is to be performed, is subject to any requirement imposed in the interest of the national security of the United States under any security program in effect pursuant to or administered under any statute of the United States or any Executive order of the President; and

(2) such individual has not fulfilled or has ceased to fulfill that requirement.

(h) Notwithstanding any other provision of this title, it shall not be an unlawful employment practice for an employer to apply different standards of compensation, or different terms, conditions, or privileges of employment pursuant to a bona fide seniority or merit system, or a system which measures earnings by quantity or quality of production or to employees who work in different locations, provided that such differences are not the result of an intention to discriminate because of race, color, religion, sex, or national origin; nor shall it be an unlawful employment practice for an employer to give and to act upon the results of any professionally developed ability test provided that such test, its administration or action upon the results is not designed, intended, or used to discriminate because of race, color, religion, sex, or national origin. It shall not be an unlawful employment practice under this title for any employer to differentiate upon the basis of sex in determining the amount of the wages or compensation paid or to be paid to employees of such employer if such differentiation is authorized by the provisions of Section 6(d) of the Fair Labor Standards Act of 1938 as amended (29 U.S.C. 206(d)).

(i) Nothing contained in this title shall apply to any business or enterprise on or near an Indian reservation with respect to any publicly announced employment practice of such business or enterprise under which a preferential treatment is given to any individual because he is an Indian living on or near a reservation.

(j) Nothing contained in this title shall be interpreted to require any employer, employment agency, labor organization, or joint labor-management committee subject to this title to grant preferential treatment to any individual or to any group because of the race, color, religion, sex, or national origin of such individual or group on account of an imbalance which may exist with respect to the total number or percentage of persons of any race, color, religion, sex, or national origin employed by any employer, referred or classified for employment by any employment agency or labor organization, admitted to membership or classified by any labor organization, or admitted to, or employed in, any apprenticeship or other training program, in comparison with the total number or percentage of persons of such race, color, religion, sex, or national origin in any community, State, section, or other area, or in the available work force in any community, State, section, or other area.

§ 2000e–3. Other unlawful employment practices

[Sec. 704] (a) It shall be an unlawful employment practice for an employer to discriminate against any of his employees or applicants for employment, for an employment agency, or joint labor-management committee controlling apprenticeship or other training or retraining, including on-the-job training programs, to discriminate against any individual, or for a labor organization to discriminate against any member thereof or applicant for membership, because he has opposed any practice made an unlawful employment practice by this title, or because he has made a charge, testified, assisted, or participated in any manner in an investigation, proceeding, or hearing under this title.

(b) It shall be an unlawful employment practice for an employer, labor organization, employment agency, or joint labor-management committee controlling apprenticeship or other training or retraining, including on-the-job training programs, to print or cause to be printed or published any notice or advertisement relating to employment by such an employer or membership in or any classification or referral for employment by such a labor organization, or relating to any classification or referral for employment by such an employment agency, or relating to admission to, or employment in, any program established to provide apprenticeship or other training by such a joint labor-management committee, indicating any preference, limitation, specification, or discrimination, based on race, color, religion, sex or national origin, except that such a notice or advertisement may indicate a preference, limitation, specification, or discrimination based on religion, sex or national origin when religion, sex, or national origin is a bona fide occupational qualification for employment.

§ 2000e–4. Equal Employment Opportunity Commission

[Sec. 705] (a) There is hereby created a Commission to be known as the Equal Employment Opportunity Commission, which shall be composed of five members, not more than three of whom shall be members of the same political party. Members of the Commission shall be appointed by the President by and with the advice and consent of the Senate for a term of five years. Any individual chosen to fill a vacancy shall be appointed only for the unexpired term of the member whom he shall succeed, and all members of the Commission shall continue to serve until their successors are appointed and qualified, except that no such member of the Commission shall continue to serve (1) for more than sixty days when the Congress is in session unless a nomination to fill such vacancy shall have been submitted to the Senate, or (2) after the adjournment sine die of the session of the Senate in which such nomination was submitted. The President shall designate one member to serve as Chairman of the Commission, and one member to serve as Vice Chairman. The Chairman shall be responsible on behalf of the Commission for the administrative operations of the Commission, and, except as provided in subsection (b), shall appoint, in accordance with the provisions of title 5, United States Code, governing appointments in the competitive service, such officers, agents, attorneys, administrative law judges, and employees as he deems necessary to assist it in the performance of its functions and to fix their compensation in accordance with the provisions of chapter 51 and subchapter III of chapter 53 of title 5, United States Code, relating to classification and General Schedule pay rates: *Provided*, That assignment, removal, and compensation of administrative law judges shall be in accordance with sections 3105, 3344, 5362, and 7521 of title 5, United States Code.

(b)(1) There shall be a General Counsel of the Commission appointed by the President, by and with the advice and consent of the Senate, for a term of four years. The General Counsel shall have responsibility for the conduct of litigation as provided in sections 706 and 707 of this title. The General Counsel shall have such other duties as the Commission may prescribe or as may be provided by law and shall concur with the Chairman of the Commission on the appointment and supervision of regional attorneys. The General Counsel of the Commission on the effective date of this Act shall continue in such position and perform the functions specified in this subsection until a successor is appointed and qualified.

(2) Attorneys appointed under this section may, at the direction of the Commission, appear for and represent the Commission in any case in court, provided that the Attorney General shall conduct all litigation to which the Commission is a party in the Supreme Court pursuant to this title.

(c) A vacancy in the Commission shall not impair the right of the remaining members to exercise all the powers of the Commission and three members thereof shall constitute a quorum.

(d) The Commission shall have an official seal which shall be judicially noticed.

(e) The Commission shall at the close of each fiscal year report to the Congress and to the President concerning the action it has taken, and the moneys it has disbursed. It shall make such further reports on the cause of and means of eliminating discrimination and such recommendations for further legislation as may appear desirable.

(f) The principal office of the Commission shall be in or near the District of Columbia, but it may meet or exercise any or all its powers at any other place. The Commission may establish such regional or State offices as it deems necessary to accomplish the purpose of this title.

(g) The Commission shall have power—

(1) to cooperate with and, with their consent, utilize regional, State, local, and other agencies, both public and private, and individuals;

(2) to pay to witnesses whose depositions are taken or who are summoned before the Commission or any of its agents the same witness and mileage fees as are paid to witnesses in the courts of the United States;

(3) to furnish to persons subject to this title such technical assistance as they may request to further their compliance with this title or an order issued thereunder;

(4) upon the request of (i) any employer, whose employees or some of them, or (ii) any labor organization, whose members or some of them, refuse or threaten to refuse to cooperate in effectuating the provisions of this title, to assist in such effectuation by conciliation or such other remedial action as is provided by this title;

(5) to make such technical studies as are appropriate to effectuate the purposes and policies of this title and to make the results of such studies available to the public;

(6) to intervene in a civil action brought under section 706 by an aggrieved party against a respondent other than a government, governmental agency or political subdivision.

(h) The Commission shall, in any of its educational or promotional activities, cooperate with other departments and agencies in the performance of such educational and promotional activities.

(i) All officers, agents, attorneys and employees of the Commission, including the members of the Commission, shall be subject to the provisions of section 9 of the Act of August 2, 1939, as amended (the Hatch Act), notwithstanding any exemption contained in such section.

§ 2000e–5. Enforcement provisions

[Sec. 706] (a) The Commission is empowered, as hereinafter provided, to prevent any person from engaging in any unlawful employment practice as set forth in section 703 or 704 of this title.

(b) Whenever a charge is filed by or on behalf of a person claiming to be aggrieved, or by a member of the Commission, alleging that an employer, employment agency, labor organization, or joint labor-management committee controlling apprenticeship or other training or retraining, including on-the-job training programs, has engaged in an unlawful employment practice, the Commission shall serve a notice of the charge (including the date, place and circumstances of the alleged unlawful employment practice) on such employer, employment agency, labor organization, or joint labor-manage-ment committee (hereinafter referred to as the 'respondent') within ten days and shall make an investigation thereof. Charges shall be in writing under oath or affirmation and shall contain such information and be in such form as the Commission requires. Charges shall not be made public by the Commission. If the Commission determines after such investigation that there is not reasonable cause to believe that the charge is true, it shall dismiss the charge and promptly notify the person claiming to be aggrieved and the respondent of its action. In determining whether reasonable cause exists, the Commission shall accord substantial weight to final findings and orders made by State or local authorities in proceedings commenced under State or local law pursuant to the requirements of subsections (c) and (d). If the Commission determines after such investigation that there is reasonable cause to believe that the charge is true, the Commission shall endeavor to eliminate any such alleged unlawful employment practice by informal methods of conference, conciliation, and persuasion. Nothing said or done during and as a part of such informal endeavors may be made public by the Commission, its officers or employees, or used as evidence in a subsequent proceeding without the written consent of the persons concerned. Any person who makes public information in violation of this subsection shall be fined not more than $1,000 or imprisoned for not more than one year, or both. The Commission shall make its determination on reasonable cause as promptly as possible and, so far as practicable, not later than one hundred and twenty days from the filing of the charge or, where applicable under subsection (c) or (d) from the date upon which the Commission is authorized to take action with respect to the charge.

(c) In the case of an alleged unlawful employment practice occurring in a State, or political subdivision of a State, which has a State or local law prohibiting the unlawful employment practice alleged and establishing or authorizing a State or local authority to grant or seek relief from such practice or to institute criminal proceedings with respect thereto upon receiving notice thereof, no charge may be filed under subsection (a) by the person aggrieved before the expiration of sixty days after proceedings have been commenced under the State or local law, unless such proceedings have been earlier terminated, provided that such sixty-day period shall be extended to one hundred and twenty days during the first year after the effective date of such State or local law. If any requirement for the commencment of such proceedings is imposed by a State or local authority other than a requirement of the filing of a written and signed statement of the facts upon which the proceeding is based, the proceeding shall be deemed to have been commenced for the purposes of this subsection at the time such statement is sent by registered mail to the appropriate State or local authority.

(d) In the case of any charge filed by a member of the Commission alleging an unlawful employment practice occurring in a State or political subdivision of a State which has a State or local law prohibiting the practice alleged and establishing or authorizing a State or local authority to grant or seek relief from such practice or to institute criminal proceedings with respect thereto upon receiving notice thereof, the Commission shall, before taking any action with respect to such charge, notify the appropriate State or local officials and, upon request, afford them a reasonable time, but not less than sixty days (provided that such sixty-day period shall be extended to one hundred and twenty days during the first year after the effective day of such State or local law), unless a shorter period is requested, to act under such State or local law to remedy the practice alleged.

(e) A charge under this section shall be filed within one hundred and eighty days after the alleged unlawful employment practice occurred and notice of the charge (including the date, place and circumstances of the alleged unlawful employment practice) shall be served upon the person against whom such charge is made within ten days thereafter, except that in a case of an unlawful employment practice with respect to which the person aggrieved has initially instituted proceedings with a State or local agency with authority to grant or seek relief from such practice or to institute criminal proceedings with respect thereto upon receiving notice thereof, such charge shall be filed by or on behalf of the person aggrieved within three hundred days after the alleged unlawful employment practice occurred, or within thirty days after receiving notice that the State or local agency has terminated the proceedings under the State or local law, whichever is earlier, and a copy of such charge shall be filed by the Commission with the State or local agency.

(f)(1) If within thirty days after a charge is filed with the Commission or within thirty days after expiration of any period of reference under subsection (c) or (d), the Commission has been unable to secure from the respondent a conciliation agreement acceptable to the Commission, the Commission may bring a civil action against any respondent not a government, governmental agency, or political subdivision named in the charge. In the case of a respondent which is a government, governmental agency, or political subdivision, if the Commission has been unable to secure from the respondent a conciliation agreement acceptable to the Commission, the Commission shall take no further action and shall refer the case to the Attorney General who may bring a civil action against such respondent in the appropriate United States district court. The person or persons aggrieved shall have the right to intervene in a civil action brought by the Commission or the Attorney General in a case involving a government, governmental agency, or political subdivision. If a charge filed with the Commission pursuant to subsection (b) is dismissed by the Commission, or if within one hundred and eighty days from the filing of such charge or the expiration of any period of reference under subsection (c) or (d), whichever is later, the Commission has not filed a civil action under this section or the Attorney General has not filed a civil action in a case involving a government, governmental agency, or political subdivision, or the Commission has not entered into a conciliation agreement to which the person aggrieved is a party, the Commission, or the Attorney General in a case involving a government, governmental agency, or political subdivision, shall so notify the person aggrieved and within ninety days after the giving of such notice a civil action may be brought against the respondent named in the charge (A) by the person claiming to be aggrieved or (B) if such charge was filed by a member of the Commission, by any person whom the charge alleges was aggrieved by the alleged unlawful employment practice. Upon application by the complainant and in such circumstances as the court may deem just, the court may appoint an attorney for such complainant and may authorize the commencement of the action without the payment of fees, costs, or security. Upon timely application, the court may, in its discretion, permit the Commission, or the Attorney General in a case involving a government, governmental agency, or political subdivision, to intervene in such civil action upon certification that the case is of general public importance. Upon request, the court may, in its discretion, stay further proceedings for not more than sixty days pending the termination of State or local proceedings described in subsections (c) or (d) of this section or further efforts of the Commission to obtain voluntary compliance.

(2) Whenever a charge is filed with the Commission and the Commission concludes on the basis of a preliminary investigation that prompt judicial action is necessary to carry out the purposes of this Act, the Commission, or the Attorney General in a case involving a government, governmental agency, or political subdivision, may bring an action for appropriate temporary or preliminary relief pending final

disposition of such charge. Any temporary restraining order or other order granting preliminary or temporary relief shall be issued in accordance with rule 65 of the Federal Rules of Civil Procedure. It shall be the duty of a court having jurisdiction over proceedings under this section to assign cases for hearing at the earliest practicable date and to cause such cases to be in every way expedited.

(3) Each United States district court and each United States court of a place subject to the jurisdiction of the United States shall have jurisdiction of actions brought under this title. Such an action may be brought in any judicial district in the State in which the unlawful employment practice is alleged to have been committed, in the judicial district in which the employment records relevant to such practice are maintained and administered, or in the judicial district in which the aggrieved person would have worked but for the alleged unlawful employment practice, but if the respondent is not found within any such district, such an action may be brought within the judicial district in which the respondent has his principal office. For purposes of sections 1404 and 1406 of title 28 of the United States Code, the judicial district in which the respondent has his principal office shall in all cases be considered a district in which the action might have been brought.

(4) It shall be the duty of the chief judge of the district (or in his absence, the acting chief judge) in which the case is pending immediately to designate a judge in such district to hear and determine the case. In the event that no judge in the district is available to hear and determine the case, the chief judge of the district, or the acting chief judge, as the case may be, shall certify this fact to the chief judge of the circuit (or in his absence, the acting chief judge) who shall then designate a district or circuit judge of the circuit to hear and determine the case.

(5) It shall be the duty of the judge designated pursuant to this subsection to assign the case for hearing at the earliest practicable date and to cause the case to be in every way expedited. If such judge has not scheduled the case for trial within one hundred and twenty days after issue has been joined that judge may appoint a master pursuant to rule 53 of the Federal Rules of Civil Procedure.

(g) If the court finds that the respondent has intentionally engaged in or is intentionally engaging in an unlawful employment practice charged in the complaint, the court may enjoin the respondent from engaging in such unlawful employment practice, and order such affirmative action as may be appropriate, which may include, but is not limited to, reinstatement or hiring of employees, with or without back pay (payable by the employer, employment agency, or labor organization, as the case may be, responsible for the unlawful employment practice), or any other equitable relief as the court deems appropriate. Back pay liability shall not accrue from a date more than two years prior to the filing of a charge with the Commission. Interim earnings or amounts earnable with reasonable diligence by the person or persons discriminated against shall operate to reduce the back pay otherwise allowable. No order of the court shall require the admission or reinstatement of an individual as a member of a union, or the hiring, reinstatement, or promotion of an individual as an employee, or the payment to him of any back pay, if such individual was refused admission, suspended, or expelled, or was refused employment or advancement or was suspended or discharged for any reason other than discrimination on account of race, color, religion, sex, or national origin or in violation of section 704(a).

(h) The provisions of the Act entitled "An Act to amend the Judicial Code and to define and limit the jurisdiction of courts sitting in equity, and for other purposes," approved March 23, 1932 (29 U.S.C. 101–115), shall not apply with respect to civil actions brought under this section.

(i) In any case in which an employer, employment agency, or labor organization fails to comply with an order of a court issued in a civil action brought under this section the Commission may commence proceedings to compel compliance with such order.

(j) Any civil action brought under this section and any proceedings brought under subsection (j) shall be subject to appeal as provided in sections 1291 and 1292, title 28, United States Code.

(k) In any action or proceeding under this title the court, in its discretion, may allow the prevailing party, other than the Commission or the United States, a reasonable attorney's fee as part of the costs, and the Commission and the United States shall be liable for costs the same as a private person.

§ 2000e-6. Civil actions by the Attorney General

[Sec. 707] (a) Whenever the Attorney General has reasonable cause to believe that any person or group of persons is engaged in a pattern or practice of resistance to the full enjoyment of any of the rights secured by this title, and that the pattern or practice is of such a nature and is intended to deny the full exercise of the rights herein described, the Attorney General may bring a civil action in the appropriate district court of the United States by filing with it a complaint (1) signed by him (or in his absence the Acting Attorney General), (2) setting forth facts pertaining to such pattern or practice, and (3) requesting such relief, including an application for a permanent or temporary injunction, restraining order or other order against the person or persons responsible for such pattern or practice, as he deems necessary to insure the full enjoyment of the rights herein described.

(b) The district courts of the United States shall have and shall exercise jurisdiction of proceedings instituted pursuant to this section, and in any such proceeding the Attorney General may file with the clerk of such court a request that a court of three judges be convened to hear and determine the case. Such request by the Attorney General shall be accompanied by a certificate that, in his opinion, the case is of general public importance. A copy of the certificate and request for a three-judge court shall be immediately furnished by such clerk to the chief judge of the circuit (or in his absence, the presiding circuit judge of the circuit) in which the case is pending. Upon receipt of such request it shall be the duty of the chief judge of the circuit or the presiding circuit judge, as the case may be, to designate immediately three judges in such circuit, of whom at least one shall be a circuit judge and another of whom shall be a district judge of the court in which the proceeding was instituted, to hear and determine such case, and it shall be the duty of the judges so designated to assign the case for hearing at the earliest practicable date, to participate in the hearing and determination thereof, and to cause the case to be in every way expedited. An appeal from the final judgment of such court will lie to the Supreme Court.

In the event the Attorney General fails to file such a request in any such proceeding, it shall be the duty of the chief judge of the district (or in his absence, the acting chief judge) in which the case is pending immediately to designate a judge in such district to hear and determine the case. In the event that no judge in the district is available to hear and determine the case, the chief judge of the district, or the acting chief judge, as the case may be, shall certify this fact to the chief judge of the circuit (or in his absence, the acting chief judge) who shall then designate a district or circuit judge of the circuit to hear and determine the case.

It shall be the duty of the judge designated pursuant to this section to assign the case for hearing at the earliest practicable date and to cause the case to be in every way expedited.

(c) Effective two years after the date of enactment of the Equal Employment Opportunity Act of 1972, the functions of the Attorney General under this section shall be transferred to the Commission, together with such personnel, property, records, and unexpended balances of appropriations, allocations, and other funds employed, used, held, available, or to be made available in connection with such functions unless the President submits, and neither House of Congress vetoes, a reorganization plan pursuant to chapter 9 of title 5, United States Code, inconsistent with the provisions of this subsection. The Commission shall carry out such functions in accordance with subsections (d) and (e) of this section.

(d) Upon the transfer of functions provided for in subsection (c) of this section, in all suits commenced pursuant to this section prior to the date of such transfer, proceedings shall continue without abatement, all court orders and decrees shall remain in effect, and the Commission shall be substituted as a party for the United States of America, the Attorney General, or the Acting Attorney General, as appropriate.

(e) Subsequent to the date of enactment of the Equal Employment Opportunity Act of 1972, the Commission shall have authority to investigate and act on a charge of a pattern or practice of discrimination, whether filed by or on behalf of a person claiming to be aggrieved or by a member of the Commission. All such actions shall be conducted in accordance with the procedures set forth in section 706 of this Act.

§ 2000e–7. Effect on State laws

[Sec. 708] Nothing in this title shall be deemed to exempt or relieve any person from any liability, duty, penalty, or punishment provided by any present or future law of any State or political subdivision of a State, other than any such law which purports to require or permit the doing of any act which would be an unlawful employment practice under this title.

§ 2000e–8. Investigations

[Sec. 709] (a) In connection with any investigation of a charge filed under section 706, the Commission or its designated representative shall at all reasonable times have access to, for the purposes of examination, and the right to copy any evidence of any person being investigated or proceeded against that relates to unlawful employment practices covered by this title and is relevant to the charge under investigation.

(b) The Commission may cooperate with State and local agencies charged with the administration of State fair employment practices laws and, with the consent of such agencies, may, for the purpose of carrying out its functions and duties under this title and within the limitation of funds appropriated specifically for such purpose, engage in and contribute to the cost of research and other projects of mutual interest undertaken by such agencies, and utilize the services of such agencies and their employees, and, notwithstanding any other provision of law, pay by advance or reimbursement such agencies and their employees for services rendered to assist the Commission in carrying out this title. In furtherance of such cooperative efforts, the Commission may enter into written agreements with such State or local agencies and such agreements may include provisions under which the Commission shall refrain from processing a charge in any cases or class of cases specified in such agreements or under which the Commission shall relieve any person or class of persons in such State or locality from requirements imposed under this section. The Commission shall rescind any such agreement whenever it determines that the agreement no longer serves the interest of effective enforcement of this title.

(c) Every employer, employment agency, and labor organization subject to this title shall (1) make and keep such records relevant to the determinations of whether unlawful employment practices have been or are being committed, (2) preserve such records for such periods, and (3) make such reports therefrom as the Commission shall prescribe by regulation or order, after public hearing, as reasonable, necessary, or appropriate for the enforcement of this title or the regulations or orders thereunder. The Commission shall, by regulation, require each employer, labor organization, and joint labor-management committee subject to this title which controls an apprenticeship or other training program to maintain such records as are reasonably necessary to carry out the purposes of this title, including, but not limited to, a list of applicants who wish to participate in such program, including the chronological order in which applications were received, and to furnish to the Commission upon request, a detailed description of the manner in which persons are selected to participate in the apprenticeship or other training program. Any employer, employment agency, labor organization, or joint labor-management committee which believes that the application to it of any regulation or order issued under this section would result in undue hardship may apply to the Commission for an exemption from the application of such regulation or order, and, if such application for an exemption is denied, bring a civil action in the United States district court for the district where such records are kept. If the Commission or the court, as the case may be, finds that the application of the regulation or order to the employer, employment agency, or labor organization in question would impose an undue hardship, the Commission or the court, as the case may be, may grant appropriate relief. If any person required to comply with the provisions of this subsection fails or refuses to do so, the United States district court for the district in which such person is found, resides, or transacts business, shall, upon application of the Commission, or the Attorney General in a case involving a government, governmental agency or political subdivision, have jurisdiction to issue to such person an order requiring him to comply.

(d) In prescribing requirements pursuant to subsection (c) of this section, the Commission shall consult with other interested State and Federal agencies and shall endeavor to coordinate its requirements with those adopted by such agencies. The Commission shall furnish upon request and without cost to any State or local agency charged with the administration of a fair employment practice law information obtained pursuant to subsection (c) of this section from any employer, employment agency, labor organization, or joint labor-management committee subject to the jurisdiction of such agency. Such information shall be furnished on condition that it not be made public by the recipient agency prior to the institution of a proceeding under State or local law involving such information. If this condition is violated by a recipient agency, the Commission may decline to honor subsequent requests pursuant to this subsection.

(e) It shall be unlawful for any officer or employee of the Commission to make public in any manner whatever any information obtained by the Commission pursuant to its authority under this section prior to the institution of any proceeding under this title involving such information. Any officer or employee of the Commission who shall make public in any manner whatever any information in violation of this subsection shall be guilty of a misdemeanor and upon conviction thereof, shall be fined not more than $1,000, or imprisoned not more than one year.

§ 2000e–9. Conduct of hearings and investigations pursuant to section 161 of title 29

[Sec. 710] For the purpose of all hearings and investigations conducted by the Commission or its duly authorized agents or agencies, section 11 of the National Labor Relations Act (49 Stat. 455; 29 U.S.C. 161) shall apply.

§ 2000e–10. Posting of notices; penalties

[Sec. 711] (a) Every employer, employment agency and labor organization, as the case may be, shall post and keep posted in conspicuous places upon its premises where notices to employees, applicants for employment, and members are customarily posted a notice to be prepared or approved by the Commission setting forth excerpts from, or summaries of, the pertinent provisions of this title and information pertinent to the filing of a complaint.

(b) A willful violation of this section shall be punishable by a fine of not more than $100 for each separate offense.

§ 2000e–11. Veterans' special rights or preference

[Sec. 712] Nothing contained in this title shall be construed to repeal or modify any Federal, State, territorial, or local law creating special rights or preference for veterans.

§ 2000e–12. Regulations; conformity of regulations with administrative procedure provisions; reliance on interpretations and instructions of Commission

[Sec. 713] (a) The Commission shall have authority from time to time to issue, amend, or rescind suitable procedural regulations to carry out the provisions of this title. Regulations issued under this section shall be in conformity with the standards and limitations of the Administrative Procedure Act.

(b) In any action or proceeding based on any alleged unlawful employment practice, no person shall be subject to any liability or punishment for or on account of (1) the commission by such person of an unlawful employment practice if he pleads and proves that the act or omission complained of was in good faith, in conformity with, and in reliance on any written interpretation or opinion of the Commission, or (2) the failure of such person to publish and file any information required by any provision of this title if he pleads and proves that he failed to publish and file such information in good faith, in conformity with the instructions of the Commission issued under this title regarding the filing of such information. Such a defense, if established, shall be a bar to the action or proceeding, notwithstanding that (A) after such act or omission, such interpretation or opinion is modified or rescinded or is determined by judicial authority to be invalid or of no legal effect, or (B) after publishing or filing the description and annual reports, such publication or filing is determined by judicial authority not to be in conformity with the requirements of this title.

§ 2000e–13. Application of personnel to Commission of sections 111 and 1114 of title 18; punishment for violation of section 1114 of title 18

[Sec. 714] The provisions of sections 111 and 1114, title 18, United States Code, shall apply to officers, agents, and employees of the Commission in the performance of their official duties. Notwithstanding the provisions of sections 111 and 1114 of title 18, United States Code, whoever in violation of the provisions of section 1114 of such title kills a person while engaged in or on account of the performance of his official functions under this Act shall be punished by imprisonment for any term of years or for life.

§ 2000e–14. Coordination of efforts and elimination of competition among Federal departments, agencies, etc. in implementation and enforcement of equal employment opportunity legislation, orders, and policies; report to President and Congress

[Sec. 715] The Equal Employment Opportunity Commission shall have the responsibility for developing and implementing agreements, policies and practices designed to maximize effort, promote efficiency, and eliminate conflict, competition, duplication and inconsistency among the operations, functions and jurisdictions of the various departments, agencies and branches of the Federal Government responsible for the implementation and enforcement of equal employment opportunity legislation, orders, and policies. On or before October 1 of each year, the Equal Employment Opportunity Commission shall transmit to the President and to the Congress a report of its activities, together with such recommendations for legislative or administrative changes as it concludes are desirable to further promote the purposes of this section.

§ 2000e–15.   Presidential conferences; acquaintance of leadership with provisions for employment rights and obligations; plans for fair administration; membership

[Sec. 716(c)] The President shall, as soon as feasible after the enactment of this title, convene one or more conferences for the purpose of enabling the leaders of groups whose members will be affected by this title to become familiar with the rights afforded and obligations imposed by its provisions, and for the purpose of making plans which will result in the fair and effective administration of this title when all of its provisions become effective. The President shall invite the participation in such conference or conferences of (1) the members of the President's Committee on Equal Employment Opportunity, (2) the members of the Commission on Civil Rights, (3) representatives of State and local agencies engaged in furthering equal employment opportunity, (4) representatives of private agencies engaged in furthering equal employment opportunity, and (5) representatives of employers, labor organizations, and employment agencies who will be subject to this title.

§ 2000e–16.   Employment by Federal Government

[Sec. 717] (a) All personnel actions affecting employees or applicants for employment (except with regard to aliens employed outside the limits of the United States) in military departments as defined in section 102 of title 5, United States Code in executive agencies as defined in section 105 of title 5, United States Code (including employees and applicants for employment who are paid from nonappropriated funds), in the United States Postal Service and the Postal Rate Commission, in those units of the Government of the District of Columbia having positions in the competitive service, and in those units of the legislative and judicial branches of the Federal Government having positions in the competitive service, and in the Library of Congress shall be made free from any discrimination based on race, color, religion, sex, or national origin.

(b) Except as otherwise provided in this subsection, the Equal Employment Opportunity Commission shall have authority to enforce the provisions of subsection (a) through appropriate remedies, including reinstatement or hiring of employees with or without back pay, as will effectuate the policies of this section, and shall issue such rules, regulations, orders and instructions as it deems necessary and appropriate to carry out its responsibilities under this section. The Equal Employment Opportunity Commission shall—

(1) be responsible for the annual review and approval of a national and regional equal employment opportunity plan which each department and agency and each appropriate unit referred to in subsection (a) of this section shall submit in order to maintain an affirmative program

of equal employment opportunity for all such employees and applicants for employment;

(2) be responsible for the review and evaluation of the operation of all agency equal employment opportunity programs, periodically obtaining and publishing (on at least a semi-annual basis) progress reports from each such department, agency, or unit; and

(3) consult with and solicit the recommendations of interested individuals, groups, and organizations relating to equal employment opportunity.

The head of each such department, agency, or unit shall comply with such rules, regulations, orders, and instructions which shall include a provision that an employee or applicant for employment shall be notified of any final action taken on any complaint of discrimination filed by him thereunder. The plan submitted by each department, agency, and unit shall include, but not be limited to—

(1) provision for the establishment of training and education programs designed to provide a maximum opportunity for employees to advance so as to perform at their largest potential; and

(2) a description of the qualifications in terms of training and experience relating to equal employment opportunity for the principal and operating officials of each such department, agency, or unit responsible for carrying out the equal employment opportunity program and of the allocation of personnel and resources proposed by such department, agency, or unit to carry out its equal employment opportunity program.

With respect to employment in the Library of Congress, authorities granted in this subsection to the Equal Employment Opportunity Commission shall be exercised by the Librarian of Congress.

(c) Within thirty days of receipt of notice of final action taken by a department, agency, or unit referred to in subsection 717(a), or by the Equal Employment Opportunity Commission upon an appeal from a decision or order such department, agency, or unit on a complaint of discrimination based on race, color, religion, sex or national origin, brought pursuant to subsection (a) of this section, Executive Order 11478 or any succeeding Executive orders, or after one hundred and eighty days from the filing of the initial charge with the department, agency, or unit or with the Equal Employment Opportunity Commission on appeal from a decision or order of such department, agency or unit until such time as final action may be taken by a department, agency, or unit, an employee or applicant for employment, if aggrieved by the final disposition of his complaint, or by the failure to take final action on his complaint, may file a civil action as provided in section 706, in which civil action the head of department, agency, or unit, as appropriate, shall be the defendant.

(d) The provisions of section 706(f) through (k), as applicable, shall govern civil actions brought hereunder.

(e) Nothing contained in this Act shall relieve any Government agency or official of its or his primary responsibility to assure nondiscrimination in employment as required by the Constitution and statutes or of its or his responsibilities under Executive Order 11478 relating to equal employment opportunity in the Federal Government.

§ 2000e-17 Procedure for denial, withholding, termination, or suspension of Government contract subsequent to acceptance by Government of affirmative action plan of employer; time of acceptance of plan

[Sec. 718] No Government contract, or portion thereof, with any employer, shall be denied, withheld, terminated, or suspended, by any agency or officer of the United States under any equal employment opportunity law or order, where such employer has an affirmative action plan which has previously been accepted by the Government for the same facility within the past twelve months without first according such employer full hearing and adjudication under the provisions of title 5, United States Code, section 554, and the following pertinent section: *Provided,* That if such employer has deviated substantially from such previously agreed to affirmative action plan, this section shall not apply. *Provided further,* That for the purposes of this section an affirmative action plan shall be deemed to have been accepted by the Government at the time the appropriate compliance agency has accepted such plan unless within forty-five days thereafter the Office of Federal Contract Compliance has disapproved such plan.

* * *

Title IX. Intervention and Procedure After Removal in Civil Rights Cases

§ 2000h-2. Intervention by Attorney General; denial of equal protection on account of race, color, religion, sex or national origin

[Sec. 902] Whenever an action has been commenced in any court of the United States seeking relief from the denial of equal protection of the laws under the fourteenth amendment to the Constitution on account of race, color, religion, sex or national origin, the Attorney General for or in the name of the United States may intervene in such action upon timely application if the Attorney General certifies that the case is of general public importance. In such action the United States shall be entitled to the same relief as if it had instituted the action.

* * *

Title XI. Miscellaneous

§ 2000h. Criminal contempt proceedings; trial by jury, criminal practice, penalties, exceptions, intent; civil contempt proceedings

[Sec. 1101] In any proceeding for criminal contempt arising under titles * * * VI, or VII of this Act, the accused, upon demand therefor, shall be entitled to a trial by jury, which shall conform as near as may be to the practice in criminal cases. Upon conviction, the accused shall not be fined more than $1,000 or imprisoned for more than six months.

This section shall not apply to contempts committed in the presence of the court, or so near thereto as to obstruct the administration of justice, nor to the misbehavior, misconduct, or disobedience of any officer of the court in respect to writs, orders, or process of the court. No person shall be convicted of criminal contempt hereunder unless the act or omission constituting such contempt shall have been intentional, as required in other cases of criminal contempt.

Nor shall anything herein be construed to deprive courts of their power, by civil contempt proceedings, without a jury, to secure compliance with or to prevent obstructions of, as distinguished from punishment for violations of, any lawful writ, process, order, rule, decree, or command of the court in accordance with the prevailing usages of law and equity, including the power of detention.

§ 2000h-1. Double jeopardy; specific crimes and criminal contempts

[Sec. 1102] No person should be put twice in jeopardy under the laws of the United States for the same act or omission. For this reason, an acquittal or conviction in a prosecution for a specific crime under the laws of the United States shall bar a proceeding for criminal contempt, which is based upon the same act or omission and which arises under the provisions of this Act; and an acquittal or conviction in a proceeding for criminal contempt, which arises under the provisions of this Act, shall bar a prosecution for a specific crime under the laws of the United States based upon the same act or omission.

§ 2000h–3. Construction of provisions not to affect authority of Attorney General, etc., to institute or intervene in actions or proceedings

[Sec. 1103] Nothing in this Act shall be construed to deny, impair, or otherwise affect any right or authority of the Attorney General or of the United States or any agency or officer thereof under existing law to institute or intervene in any action or proceeding.

§ 2000h–4. Construction of provisions not to exclude operation of State laws and not to invalidate consistent State laws

[Sec. 1104] Nothing contained in any title of this Act shall be construed as indicating an intent on the part of Congress to occupy the field in which any such title operates to the exclusion of State laws on the same subject matter, nor shall any provision of this Act be construed as invalidating any provision of State law unless such provision is inconsistent with any of the purposes of this Act, or any provision thereof.

§ 2000h–5. Authorization of appropriations

[Sec. 1105] There are hereby authorized to be appropriated such sums as are necessary to carry out the provisions of this Act.

§ 2000h–6. Separability of provisions

[Sec. 1106] If any provision of this Act or the application thereof to any person or circumstances is held invalid, the remainder of the Act and the application of the provision to other persons not similarly situated or to other circumstances shall not be affected thereby.

Civil Rights Act (1968)

(P.L. 90–284, effective April 11, 1968)

Title I. Interference With Federally Protected Activities

§ 245. Federally protected activities

[Sec. 101(a)] (a)(1) Nothing in this section shall be construed as indicating an intent on the part of Congress to prevent any State, any possession or Commonwealth of the United States, or the District of Columbia, from exercising jurisdiction over any offense over which it would have jurisdiction in the absence of this section, nor shall anything in this section be construed as depriving State and local law enforcement authorities of responsibility for prosecuting acts that may be violations of this section and that are violations of State and local law. No prosecution of any offense described in this section shall be undertaken by the United States except upon the certification in writing of the Attorney General or the Deputy Attorney General that in his judgment a prosecution by the United States is in the public interest and necessary to secure substantial justice, which function of certification may not be delegated.

(2) Nothing in this subsection shall be construed to limit the authority of Federal officers, or a Federal grand jury, to investigate possible violations of this section.

(b) Whoever, whether or not acting under color of law, by force or threat of force willfully injures, intimidates or interferes with, or attempts to injure, intimidate or interfere with—

(1) any person because he is or has been, or in order to intimidate such person or any other person or any class of persons from—

(A) voting or qualifying to vote, qualifying or campaigning as a candidate for elective office, or qualifying or acting as a poll watcher, or any legally authorized election official, in any primary, special, or general election;

150

(B) participating in or enjoying any benefit, service, privilege, program, facility, or activity provided or administered by the United States;

(C) applying for or enjoying employment, or any perquisite thereof, by any agency of the United States;

(D) serving, or attending upon any court in connection with possible service, as a grand or petit juror in any court of the United States;

(E) participating in or enjoying the benefits of any program or activity receiving Federal financial assistance; or

(2) any person because of his race, color, religion or national origin and because he is or has been—

(A) enrolling in or attending any public school or public college;

(B) participating in or enjoying any benefit service, privilege, program, facility or activity provided or administered by any State or subdivision thereof;

(C) applying for or enjoying employment, or any perquisite thereof, by any private employer or any agency of any State or subdivision thereof, or joining or using the services or advantages of any labor organization, hiring hall, or employment agency;

(D) serving, or attending upon any court of any State in connection with possible service, as a grand or petit juror;

(E) traveling in or using any facility of interstate commerce, or using any vehicle, terminal, or facility of any common carrier by motor, rail, water, or air;

(F) enjoying the goods, services, facilities, privileges, advantages, or accommodations of any inn, hotel, motel, or other establishment which provides lodging to transient guests, or of any restaurant, cafeteria, lunchroom, lunch counter, soda fountain, or other facility which serves the public and which is principally engaged in selling food or beverages for consumption on the premises, or of any gasoline station, or of any motion picture house, theater, concert hall, sports arena, stadium, or any other place of exhibition or entertainment which serves the public, or of any other establishment which serves the public and (i) which is located within the premises of any of the aforesaid establishments or within the premises of which is physically located any of the aforesaid establishments, and (ii) which holds itself out as serving patrons of such establishments; or

(3) during or incident to a riot or civil disorder, any person engaged in a business in commerce or affecting commerce, including, but not limited to, any person engaged in a business which sells or offers for sale to interstate travelers a substantial portion of the articles, commodities, or services which it sells or where a substantial portion of the articles or commodities which it sells or offers for sale have moved in commerce; or

(4) any person because he is or has been, or in order to intimidate such person or any other person or any class of persons from—
  (A) participating, without discrimination on account of race, color, religion or national origin, in any of the benefits or activities described in subparagraphs (1)(A) through (1)(E) or subparagraphs (2)(A) through (2)(F); or
  (B) affording another person or class of persons opportunity or protection to so participate; or
(5) any citizen because he is or has been, or in order to intimidate such citizen or any other citizen from lawfully aiding or encouraging other persons to participate, without discrimination on account of race, color, religion or national origin, in any of the benefits or activities described in subparagraphs (1)(A) through (1)(E) or subparagraphs (2)(A) through (2)(F), or participating lawfully in speech or peaceful assembly opposing any denial of the opportunity to so participate—

shall be fined not more than $1,000, or imprisoned not more than one year, or both; and if bodily injury results shall be fined not more than $10,000, or imprisoned not more than ten years, or both; and if death results shall be subject to imprisonment for any term of years or for life. As used in this section, the term "participating lawfully in speech or peaceful assembly" shall not mean the aiding, abetting, or inciting of other persons to riot or to commit any act of physical violence upon any individual or against any real or personal property in furtherance of a riot. Nothing in subparagraph (2)(F) or (4)(A) of this subsection shall apply to the proprietor of any establishment which provides lodging to transient guests, or to any employee acting on behalf of such propietor, with respect to the enjoyment of the goods, services, facilities, privileges, advantages, or accommodations of such establishment if such establishment is located within a building which contains not more than five rooms for rent or hire and which is actually occupied by the proprietor as his residence.

(c) Nothing in this section shall be construed so as to deter any law enforcement officer from lawfully carrying out the duties of his office; and no law enforcement officer shall be considered to be in violation of this section for lawfully carrying out the duties of his office or lawfully enforcing ordinances and laws of the United States, the District of Columbia, any of the several States, or any political subdivision of a State. For purposes of the preceding sentence, the term "law enforcement officer" means any officer of the United States, the District of Columbia, a State, or political subdivision of a State, who is empowered by law to conduct investigations of, or make arrests because of, offenses against the United States, the District of Columbia, a State, or a political subdivision of a State.

Age Discrimination In Employment Act

(P.L. 90–202, effective June 12, 1968; as last amended by
P.L. 99–509, effective January 1, 1988)

§ 621. Congressional statement of findings and purpose

[Sec. 2] (a) The Congress hereby finds and declares that—
(1) in the face of rising productivity and affluence, older workers find themselves disadvantaged in their efforts to retain employment, and especially to regain employment when displaced from jobs;
(2) the setting of arbitrary age limits regardless of potential for job performance has become a common practice, and certain otherwise desirable practices may work to the disadvantage of older persons;
(3) the incidence of unemployment, especially long-term unemployment with resultant deterioration of skill, morale, and employer acceptability is, relative to the younger ages, high among older workers; their numbers are great and growing; and their employment problems grave;
(4) the existence in industries affecting commerce of arbitrary discrimination in employment because of age burdens commerce and the free flow of goods in commerce.

(b) It is therefore the purpose of this Act to promote employment of older persons based on their ability rather than age; to prohibit arbitrary age discrimination in employment; to help employers and workers find ways of meeting problems arising from the impact of age on employment.

§ 622. Education and research program; recommendation to Congress

[Sec. 3] (a) The Secretary of Labor shall undertake studies and provide information to labor unions, management, and the general public concerning the needs and abilities of older workers, and their potentials for continued employment and contribution to the economy. In order to achieve the purposes of this Act, the Secretary of Labor shall carry on a continuing program of education and information, under which he may, among other measures:

(1) undertake research, and promote research, with a view to reducing barriers to the employment of older persons, and the promotion of measures for utilizing their skills;

(2) publish and otherwise make available to employers, professional societies, the various media of communication and other interested persons the findings of studies and other materials for the promotion of employment;

(3) foster, through the public employment service system and through cooperative effort, the development of facilities of public and private agencies for expanding the opportunities and potentials of older persons;

(4) sponsor and assist State and community informational and educational programs.

(b) Not later than six months after the effective date of this Act, the Secretary shall recommend to the Congress any measures he may deem desirable to change the lower or upper age limits set forth in section 12.

§ 623. Prohibition of age discrimination

[Sec. 4] (a) It shall be unlawful for an employer—

(1) to fail or refuse to hire or to discharge any individual or otherwise discriminate against any individual with respect to his compensation, terms, conditions, or privileges of employment, because of such individual's age;

(2) to limit, segregate, or classify his employees in any way which would deprive or tend to deprive any individual of employment opportunities or otherwise adversely affect his status as an employee, because of such individual's age; or

(3) to reduce the wage rate of any employee in order to comply with this Act.

(b) It shall be unlawful for an employment agency to fail or refuse to refer for employment, or otherwise to discriminate against, any individual because of such individual's age, or to classify or refer for employment any individual on the basis of such individual's age.

(c) It shall be unlawful for a labor organization—

(1) to exclude or to expel from its membership or otherwise to discriminate against, any individual because of his age;

(2) to limit, segregate, or classify its membership, or to classify or fail or refuse to refer for employment any individual, in any way which would deprive or tend to deprive any individual of employment opportunities, or would limit such employment opportunities or otherwise adversely affect his status as an employee or as an applicant for employment, because of such individual's age;

(3) to cause or attempt to cause an employer to discriminate against an individual in violation of this section.

(d) It shall be unlawful for any employer to discriminate against any of his employees or applicants for employment, for an employment agency to discriminate against any individual, or for a labor organization to discriminate against any member thereof or applicant for membership, because such individual member, or applicant for membership, has opposed any practice made unlawful by this section, or because such individual, member, or applicant for membership has made a charge, testified, assisted, or participated in any manner in an investigation, proceeding, or litigation under this Act.

(e) It shall be unlawful for an employer, labor organization, or employment agency to print or publish, or cause to be printed or published, any notice or advertisement relating to employment by such an employer or membership in or any classification or referral for employment by such a labor organization, or relating to any classification or referral for employment by such an employment agency, indicating any preference, limitation, specification, or discrimination, based on age.

(f) It shall not be unlawful for an employer, employment agency, or labor organization—

(1) to take any action otherwise prohibited under subsection (a), (b), (c), or (e) of this section where age is a bona fide occupational qualification reasonably necessary to the normal operation of the particular business, or where the differentiation is based on reasonable factors other than age, or where such practices involve an employee in a workplace in a foreign country, and compliance with such subsections would cause such employer, or a corporation controlled by such employer, to violate the laws of the country in which such workplace is located;

(2) to observe the terms of a bona fide seniority system or any bona fide employee benefit plan such as retirement, pension, or insurance plan, which is not a subterfuge to evade the purpose of this Act, except that no such employee benefit plan shall excuse the failure to hire any individual, and no such seniority system or employee benefit plan shall require or permit the involuntary retirement of any individual specified by section 12(a) of this Act because of the age of such individual; or

(3) to discharge or otherwise discipline an individual for good cause.

(g)(1) For purposes of this section, any employer must provide that any employee aged 65 or older, and any employee's spouse aged 65 or older, shall be entitled to coverage under any group health plan offered to such employees under the same conditions as any employee, and the spouse of such employee, under age 65.

(2) For purposes of paragraph (1), the term "group health plan" has the meaning given to such term in section 162(i)(2) of title 26.

(h)(1) If an employer controls a corporation whose place of incorporation is in a foreign country, any practice by such corporation prohibited under this section shall be presumed to be such practice by such employer.

(2) The prohibitions of this section shall not apply where the employer is a foreign person not controlled by an American employer.

(3) For the purpose of this subsection, the determination of whether an employer controls a corporation shall be based upon the—

(A) interrelation of operations,

(B) common management,

(C) centralized control of labor relations, and

(D) common ownership or financial control,

of the employer and the corporation.

(i) [As added and designated by Sec. 9201 of P.L. 99–509] (1) Except as otherwise provided in this subsection, it shall be unlawful for an employer, an employment agency, a labor organization, or any combination thereof to establish or maintain an employee pension benefit plan which requires or permits—

(A) in the case of defined benefit plan, the cessation of an employee's benefit accrual, or the reduction of the rate of an employee's benefit accrrual, because of age, or

(B) in the case of a defined contribution plan, the cessation of allocations to an employee's account, or the reduction of the rate at which amounts are allocated to an employee's account, because of age.

(2) Nothing in this section shall be construed to prohibit an employer, employment agency, or labor organization from observing any provision of an employee pension benefit plan to the extent that such provision imposes (without regard to age) a limitation on the amount of benefits that the plan provides or a limitation on the number of years of service or years of participation which are taken into account for purposes of determining benefit accrual under the plan.

(3) In the case of any employee who, as of the end of any plan year under a defined benefit plan, has attained normal retirement age under such plan—

(A) if distribution of benefits under such plan with respect to such employee has commenced as of the end of such plan year, then any requirement of this subsection for continued accrual of benefits under such plan with respect to such employee during such plan year shall be treated as satisfied to the extent of the actuarial equivalent of in-service distribution of benefits, and

(B) if distribution of benefits under such plan with respect to such employee has not commenced as of the end of such year in accordance with section 1056(a)(3) of this title [the Employee Retirement Income Social Security Act of 1974] and section 401(a)(14)(C) of title 26, and the payment of benefits under such plan with respect to such employee is not suspended during such plan year pursuant to section 1053(a)(3)(B) of this title or section 411(a)(3)(B) of title 26, then any requirement of this subsection for continued accrual of benefits under such plan with respect to such employee during such plan year shall be treated as satisfied to the extent of any adjustment in the benefit payable under the plan during such plan year attributable to the delay in the distribution of benefits after the attainment of normal retirement age.

The provisions of this paragraph shall apply in accordance with regulations of the Secretary of the Treasury. Such regulations shall provide for the application of the preceding provisions of this paragraph to all employee pension benefit plans subject to this subsection and may provide for the application of such provisions, in the case of any such employee, with respect to any period of time within a plan year.

(4) Compliance with the requirements of this subsection with respect to an employee pension benefit plan shall constitute compliance with the requirements of this section relating to benefit accrual under such plan.

(5) Paragraph (1) shall not apply with respect to any employee who is a highly compensated employee (within the meaning of section 414(q) of title 26), to the extent provided in regulations prescribed by the Secretary of the Treasury for purposes of precluding discrimination in favor of highly compensated employees within the meaning of subchapter D of chapter 1 of title 26.

(6) A plan shall not be treated as failing to meet the requirements of paragraph (1) solely because the subsidized portion of any early retirement benefit is disregarded in determining benefit accruals.

(7) Any regulations prescribed by the Secretary of the Treasury pursuant to clause (v) of section 411(b)(1)(H) of title 26 and subparagraphs (C) and (D) of section 411(b)(2) of title 26 shall apply with respect to the requirements of this subsection in the same manner and to the same extent as such regulations apply with respect to the requirements of such sections 411(b)(1)(H) and 411(b)(2) of title 26.

(8) A plan shall not be treated as failing to meet the requirements of this section solely because such plan provides a normal retirement age described in section 1002(24)(B) of this title and section 411(a)(8)(B) of title 26.

(9) For purposes of this subsection—

  (A) The terms "employee pension benefit plan", "defined benefit plan", "defined contribution plan", and "normal retirement age" have the meanings provided such terms in section 1002 of this title.

  (B) The term "compensation" has the meaning provided by section 414(s) of title 26.

(i) [As added and designated by Sec. 3 of P.L. 99–592] It shall not be unlawful for an employer which is a State, a political subdivision of a State, an agency or instrumentality of a State or a political subdivision of a State, or an interstate agency to fail refuse to hire or to discharge any individual because of such individual's age if such action is taken—

(1) with respect to the employment of an individual as a firefighter or as a law enforcement officer and the individual has attained the age of hiring or retirement in effect under applicable State or local law on March 3, 1983, and

(2) pursuant to a bona fide hiring or retirement plan that is not a subterfuge to evade the purposes of this chapter.

§ 624. Study by Secretary of Labor; reports to President and Congress; scope of study; implementation of study; transmittal date of reports

[Sec. 5] (a)(1) The Secretary of Labor is directed to undertake an appropriate study of institutional and other arrangements giving rise to involuntary retirement, and report his findings and any appropriate legislative recommendations to the President and to the Congress. Such study shall include—

(A) an examination of the effect of the amendment made by section 3(a) of the Age Discrimination in Employment Act Amendments of 1978 in raising the upper age limitation established by section 12(a) of this act to 70 years of age;

(B) a determination of the feasibility of eliminating such limitation;

(C) a determination of the feasibility of raising such limitation above 70 years of age; and

(D) an examination of the effect of the exemption contained in section 12(c), relating to certain executive employees, and the exemption contained in section 12(d), relating to tenured teaching personnel.

(2) The Secretary may undertake the study required by paragraph (1) of this subsection directly or by contract or other arrangement.

(b) The report required by subsection (a) of this section, shall be transmitted to the President and to the Congress as an interim report not later than January 1, 1981, and in final form not later than January 1, 1982.

§ 625. Administration

[Sec. 6] The Secretary shall have the power—

(a) to make delegations, to appoint such agents and employees, and to pay for technical assistance on a fee-for-service basis, as he deems necessary to assist him in the performance of his functions under this Act;

(b) to cooperate with regional, State, local, and other agencies, and to cooperate with and furnish technical assistance to employers, labor organizations, and employment agencies to aid in effectuating the purposes of this Act.

§ 626. Recordkeeping, investigation, and enforcement

[Sec. 7] (a) The Equal Employment Opportunity Commission shall have the power to make investigations and require the keeping of records necessary or appropriate for the administration of this Act in accordance with the powers and procedures provided in sections 9 and 11 of the Fair Labor Standards Act of 1938, as amended (29 U.S.C. 209 and 211).

(b) The provisions of this Act shall be enforced in accordance with the powers, remedies, and procedures provided in sections 11(b), 16 (except for subsection (a) thereof), and 17 of the Fair Labor Standards Act of 1938, as amended (29 U.S.C. 211(b), 216, 217) and subsection (c) of this section. Any act prohibited under section 4 of this Act shall be deemed to be a prohibited act under section 15 of the Fair Labor Standards Act of 1938, as amended (29 U.S.C. 215). Amounts owing to an individual as a result of a violation of this Act shall be deemed to be unpaid minimum wages or unpaid overtime compensation for purposes of sections 16 and 17 of the Fair Labor Standards Act of 1938, as amended (29 U.S.C. 216, 217): *Provided*, That liquidated damages shall be payable only in cases of willful violations of this Act. In any action brought to enforce this Act the court shall have jurisdiction to grant such legal or equitable relief as may be appropriate to effectuate the purposes of this Act, including without limitation judgments compelling employment, reinstatement or promotion, or enforcing the liability for amounts deemed to be unpaid minimum wages or unpaid overtime compensation under this section. Before instituting any action under this section, the Equal Employment Opportunity Commission shall attempt to eliminate the discriminatory practice or practices alleged, and to effect voluntary compliance with the requirements of this Act through informal methods of conciliation, conference, and persuasion.

(c)(1) Any aggrieved individual may bring a civil action in any court of competent jurisdiction for such legal or equitable relief as will effectuate the purposes of this Act: *Provided*, That the right of any individual to bring such action shall terminate upon the commencement of an action by the Equal Employment Opportunity Commission to enforce the right of such individual under this Act.

(2) In an action brought under paragraph (1), a person shall be entitled to a trial by jury of any issue of fact in any such action for recovery of amounts owing as a result of a violation of this Act, regardless of whether equitable relief is sought by any party in such action.

(d) No civil action may be commenced by an individual under this section until 60 days after a charge alleging unlawful discrimination has been filed with the Equal Employment Opportunity Commission. Such a charge shall be filed—

(1) within 180 days after the alleged unlawful practice occurred; or

(2) in a case to which section 14(b) applies, within 300 days after the alleged unlawful practice occurred, or within 30 days after receipt by the individual of notice of termination of proceedings under State law, whichever is earlier.

Upon receiving such a charge, the Commission shall promptly notify all persons named in such charge as prospective defendants in the action and shall promptly seek to eliminate any alleged unlawful practice by informal methods of conciliation, conference, and persuasion.

(e)(1) Sections 6 and 10 of the Portal-to-Portal Act of 1947 shall apply to actions under this Act.

(2) For the period during which the Equal Employment Opportunity Commission is attempting to effect voluntary compliance with requirements of this Act through informal methods of conciliation, conference, and persuasion pursuant to subsection (b), the statute of limitations as provided in section 6 of the Portal-to-Portal Act of 1947 shall be tolled, but in no event for a period in excess of one year.

§ 627. Notices to be posted

[Sec. 8] Every employer, employment agency, and labor organization shall post and keep posted in conspicuous places upon its premises a notice to be prepared or approved by the Equal Employment Opportunity Commission setting forth information as the Commission deems appropriate to effectuate the purposes of this Act.

§ 628. Rules and regulations; exemptions

[Sec. 9] In accordance with the provisions of subchapter II of chapter 5 of title 5, United States Code, the Equal Employment Opportunity Commission may issue such rules and regulations as it may consider necessary or appropriate for carrying out this Act, and may establish such reasonable exemptions to and from any or all provisions of this Act as it may find necessary and proper in the public interest.

§ 629. Criminal penalties

[Sec. 10] Whoever shall forcibly resist, oppose, impede, intimidate, or interfere with a duly authorized representative of the Equal Employment Opportunity Commission while it is engaged in the performance of duties under this Act shall be punished by a fine of not more than $500 or by imprisonment for not more than one year, or by both: *Provided, however,* That no person shall be imprisoned under this section except when there has been a prior conviction hereunder.

§ 630. Definitions

[Sec. 11] For the purposes of this Act—

(a) The term "person" means one or more individuals, partnerships, associations, labor organizations, corporations, business trusts, legal representatives, or any organized groups of persons.

(b) The term "employer" means a person engaged in an industry affecting commerce who has twenty or more employees for each working day in each of twenty or more calendar weeks in the current or preceding calendar year: *Provided,* That prior to June 30, 1968, employers having fewer than fifty employees shall not be considered employers. The term also means (1) any agent of such a person, and (2) a State or political subdivision of a State and any agency or instrumentality of a State or a political subdivision of a State, and any interstate agency but such term does not include the United States, or a corporation wholly owned by the Government of the United States.

(c) The term "employment agency" means any person regularly undertaking with or without compensation to procure employees for an employer and includes an agent of such a person; but shall not include an agency of the United States.

(d) The term "labor organization" means a labor organization engaged in an industry affecting commerce, and any agent of such an organization, and includes any organization of any kind, any agency, or employee representation committee, group, association, or plan so engaged in which employees participate and which exists for the purpose, in whole or in part, of dealing with employers concerning grievances, labor disputes, wages, rates of pay, hours, or other terms or conditions of employment, and any conference, general committee, joint or system board, or joint council so engaged which is subordinate to a national or international labor organization.

(e) A labor organization shall be deemed to be engaged in an industry affecting commerce if (1) it maintains or operates a hiring hall or hiring office which procures employees for an employer or procures for employees opportunities to work for an employer, or (2) the number of its members (or, where it is a labor organization composed of other labor organizations or their representatives, if the aggregate number of the members of such other labor organization) is fifty or more prior to July 1, 1968, or twenty-five or more on or after July 1, 1968, and such labor organization—

(1) is the certified representative of employees under the provisions of the National Labor Relation Act, as amended, or the Railway Labor Act, as amended; or

(2) although not certified, is a national or international labor organization or a local labor organization recognized or acting as the representative

of employees of an employer or employers engaged in an industry affecting commerce; or

(3) has chartered a local labor organization or subsidiary body which is representing or actively seeking to represent employees of employers within the meaning of paragraph (1) or (2); or

(4) has been chartered by a labor organization representing or actively seeking to represent employees within the meaning of paragraph (1) or (2) as the local or subordinate body through which such employees may enjoy membership or become affiliated with such labor organization; or

(5) is a conference, general committee, joint or system board or joint council subordinate to a national or international labor organization, which includes a labor organization engaged in an industry affecting commerce within the meaning of any of the preceding paragraphs of this subsection.

(f) The term "employee" means an individual employed by an employer except that the term "employee" shall not include any person elected to public office in any State or political subdivision of any State by the qualified voters thereof, or any person chosen by such officer to be on such officer's personal staff, or an appointee on the policy-making level or an immediate adviser with respect to the exercise of the constitutional or legal powers of the office. The exemption set forth in the preceding sentence shall not include employees subject to the civil service laws of a State government, governmental agency, or political subdivision. The term "employee" includes any individual who is a citizen of the United States employed by an employer in a workplace in a foreign country.

(g) The term "commerce" means trade, traffic, commerce, transportation, transmission, or communication among the several States, or between a State and any place outside thereof; or within the District of Columbia, or a possession of the United States, or between points in the same State but through a point outside thereof.

(h) The term "industry affecting commerce" means any activity, business, or industry in commerce or in which a labor dispute would hinder or obstruct commerce or the free flow of commerce and includes any activity or industry "affecting commerce" within the meaning of the Labor-Management Reporting and Disclosure Act of 1959.

(i) The term "State" includes a State of the United States, the District of Columbia, Puerto Rico, the Virgin Islands, American Samoa, Guam, Wake Island, the Canal Zone, and Outer Continental Shelf Lands defined in the Outer Continental Shelf Lands Act.

(j) The term "firefighter" means an employee, the duties of whose position are primarily to perform work directly connected with the control and extinguishment of fires or the maintenance and use of firefighting apparatus and equipment, including an employee engaged in this activity who is transferred to a supervisory or administrative position.

(k) The term "law enforcement officer" means an employee, the duties of whose position are primarily the investigation, apprehension, or detention of individuals suspected or convicted of offenses against the criminal laws of a State, including an employee engaged in this activity who is transferred to a supervisory or administration position. For the purpose of this subsection, "detention" includes the duties of employees assigned to guard individuals incarcerated in any penal institution.

§ 631. Age limits

[Sec. 12] (a) The prohibitions in this Act (except the provisions of section 4(g)) shall be limited to individuals who are at least 40 years of age.

(b) In the case of any personnel action affecting employees or applicants for employment which is subject to the provisions of section 15 of this Act, the prohibitions established in section 15 of this Act shall be limited to individuals who are at least 40 years of age.

(c)(1) Nothing in this Act shall be construed to prohibit compulsory retirement of any employee who has attained 65 years of age, and who, for the two-year period immediately before retirement, is employed in a bona fide executive or a high policymaking position, if such employee is entitled to an immediate nonforfeitable annual retirement benefit from a pension, profitsharing, savings, or deferred compensation plan, or any combination of such plans, which equals, in aggregate, at least $44,000.

(2) In applying the retirement benefit test of pargraph (1) of this subsection, if any such retirement benefit is in a form other than a straight life annuity (with no ancillary benefits), or if employees contribute to any such plan or make rollover contributions, such benefit shall be adjusted in accordance with regulations prescribed by the Equal Employment Opportunity Commission, after consultation with the Secretary of the Treasury, so that the benefit is the equivalent of a straight life annuity (with no ancillary benefits) under a plan to which employees do not contribute and under which no rollover contributions are made.

(d) Nothing in this Act shall be construed to prohibit compulsory retirement of any employee who has attained 70 years of age, and who is serving under a contract of unlimited tenure (or similar arrangement providing for unlimited tenure) at an institution of higher education (as defined by section 1201(a) of the Higher Education Act of 1985).

§ 632. Annual report to Congress

[Sec. 13] The Equal Employment Opportunity Commission shall submit annually in January a report to the Congress covering its activities for the preceding year and including such information, data, and recommendations for further legislation in connection with the matters covered by this Act as it may find advisable. Such report shall contain an evaluation and appraisal by the Commission of the effect of the minimum and maximum ages established by this Act, together with its recommendation to the Congress. In making such evaluation and appraisal, the Commission shall take into consideration any changes which may have occurred in the general age level of the population, the effect of the Act upon workers not covered by its provisions, and such other factors as it may deem pertinent.

§ 633. Federal-state relationship

[Sec. 14] (a) Nothing in this Act shall affect the jurisdiction of any agency of any State performing like functions with regard to discriminatory employment practices on account of age except that upon commencement of an action under this Act such action shall supersede any State action.

(b) In the case of an alleged unlawful practice occurring in a State which has a law prohibiting discrimination in employment because of age and establishing or authorizing a State authority to grant or seek relief from such discriminatory practice, no suit may be brought under section 7 of this Act before the expiration of sixty days after proceedings have been commenced under the State law, unless such proceedings have been earlier terminated: *Provided*, That such sixty-day period shall be extended to one hundred and twenty days during the first year after the effective day of such State law. If any requirement for the commencement of such proceedings is imposed by a State authority other than a requirement of the filing of a written and signed statement of the facts upon which the proceeding is based, the proceeding shall be deemed to have been commenced for the purposes of this subsection at the time such statement is sent by registered mail to the appropriate State authority.

§ 633a. Nondiscrimination on account of age in Federal Government employment

[Sec. 15] (a) All personnel actions affecting employees or applicants for employment who are at least 40 years of age (except personnel actions with regard to aliens employed outside the limits of the United States) in military departments as defined in section 102 of title 5, in executive agencies as defined in section 105 of title 5 (including employees and applicants for employment who are paid from nonappropriated funds), in the United States Postal Service and the Postal Rate Commission, in those units in the government of the District of Columbia having positions in the competitive service, and in those units of the legislative and judicial branches of the Federal Government having positions in the competitive service, and in the Library of Congress shall be made free from any discrimination based on age.

(b) Except as otherwise provided in this subsection, the Equal Employment Opportunity Commission is authorized to enforce the provisions of subsection (a) of this section through appropriate remedies, including reinstatement or hiring of employees with or without backpay, as will effectuate the policies of this section. The Equal Employment Opportunity Commission shall issue such rules, regulations, orders, and instructions as it deems necessary and appropriate to carry out its responsibilities under this section. The Equal Employment Opportunity Commission shall—

(1) be responsible for the review and evaluation of the operation of all agency programs designed to carry out the policy of this section, periodically obtaining and publishing (on at least a semiannual basis) progress reports from each department, agency, or unit referred to in subsection (a) of this section;

(2) consult with and solicit the recommendations of interested individuals, groups, and organizations relating to nondiscrimination in employment on account of age; and

(3) provide for the acceptance and processing of complaints of discrimination in Federal employment on account of age.

The head of each such department, agency, or unit shall comply with such rules, regulations, orders, and instructions of the Equal Employment Opportunity Commission which shall include a provision that an employee or applicant for employment shall be notified of any final action taken on any complaint of discrimination filed by him thereunder. Reasonable exemptions to the provisions of this section may be established by the Commission but only when the Commission has established a maximum age requirement on the basis of a determination that age is a bona fide occupational qualification necessary to the performance of the duties of the position. With respect to employment in the Library of Congress, authorities granted in this subsection to the Equal Employment Opportunity Commission shall be exercised by the Librarian of Congress.

(c) Any person aggrieved may bring a civil action in any Federal district court of competent jurisdiction for such legal or equitable relief as will effectuate the purposes of this Act.

(d) When the individual has not filed a complaint concerning age discrimination with the Commission, no civil action may be commenced by any individual under this section until the individual has given the Commission not less than thirty days' notice of an intent to file such action. Such notice shall be filed within one hundred and eighty days after the alleged unlawful practice occurred. Upon receiving a notice of intent to sue, the Commission shall promptly notify all persons named therein as prospective defendants in the action and take any appropriate action to ensure the elimination of any unlawful practice.

(e) Nothing contained in this section shall relieve any Government agency or official of the responsibility to assure nondiscrimination on account of age in employment as required under any provision of Federal law.

(f) Any personnel action of any department, agency, or other entity referred to in subsection (a) of this section shall not be subject to, or affected by, any provision of this Act, other than the provisions of section 631(b) of this Act and the provisions of this section.

(g)(1) The Equal Employment Opportunity Commission shall undertake a study relating to the effects of the amendments made to this section by the Age Discrimination in Employment Act Amendments of 1978, and the effects of section 631(b) of this Act, as added by the Age Discrimination in Employment Act Amendments of 1978.

(2) The Equal Employment Opportunity Commission shall transmit a report to the President and to the Congress containing the findings of the Commission resulting from the study of the Commission under paragraph (1) of this subsection. Such report shall be transmitted no later than January 1, 1980.

[Sec. 16] [Deleted.]

§ 634. Authorization of appropriations

[Sec. 17] There are hereby authorized to be appropriated such sums as may be necessary to carry out this chapter.

Age Discrimination in Employment Amendments of 1986

(P.L. 99–592, approved October 31, 1986)

§ 3.   Employment as firefighter or law enforcement officer

(a) Section 4 of the Age Discrimination in Employment Act of 1967 (29 U.S.C. 623) is amended by adding at the end thereof the following new subsection:

"(i) It shall not be unlawful for an employer which is a State, a political subdivision of a State, an agency or instrumentality of a State or a political subdivision of a State, or an interstate agency to fail or refuse to hire or to discharge any individual because of such individual's age if such action is taken—

"(1) with respect to the employment of an individual as a firefighter or as a law enforcement officer and the individual has attained the age of hiring or retirement in effect under applicable State or local law on March 3, 1983, and

"(2) pursuant to a bona fide hiring or retirement plan that is not a subterfuge to evade the purposes of this Act."

(b) The amendment made by subsection (a) of this section is repealed December 31, 1993.

§ 4.   Definitions

Section 11 of the Age Discrimination in Employment Act of 1967 (29 U.S.C. 630) is amended by adding at the end thereof the following new subsections:

"(j) The term 'firefighter' means an employee, the duties of whose position are primarily to perform work directly connected with the control and extinguishment of fires or the maintenance and use of firefighting apparatus and equipment, including an employee engaged in this activity who is transferred to a supervisory or administrative position.

"(k) The term 'law enforcement officer' means an employee, the duties of whose position are primarily the investigation, apprehension, or detention of individuals suspected or convicted of offenses against the criminal laws of a State, including an employee engaged in this activity who is transferred to a supervisory or administrative position. For the purpose of this subsection, 'detention' includes the duties of employees assigned to guard individuals incarcerated in any penal institution."

§ 5. Study and proposed guidelines relating to police officers and firefighters

(a) Not later than 4 years after the date of enactment of this Act, the Secretary of Labor and the Equal Employment Opportunity Commission, jointly, shall—

(1) conduct a study—
  (A) to determine whether physical and mental fitness tests are valid measurements of the ability and competency of police officers and firefighters to perform the requirements of their jobs,
  (B) if such tests are found to be valid measurements of such ability and competency, to determine which particular types of tests most effectively measure such ability and competency, and
  (C) to develop recommendations with respect to specific standards that such tests, and the administration of such tests should satisfy, and
(2) submit a report to the Speaker of the House of Representatives and the President pro tempore of the Senate that includes—
  (A) a description of the results of such study, and
  (B) a statement of the recommendations developed under paragraph (1)(C).

(b) The Secretary of Labor and the Equal Employment Opportunity Commission shall, during the conduct of the study required under subsection (a) and prior to the development of recommendations under paragraph (1)(C), consult with the United States Fire Administration, the Federal Emergency Management Agency, organizations representing law enforcement officers, firefighters, and their employers, and organizations representing older Americans.

(c) Not later than 5 years after the date of the enactment of this Act, the Equal Employment Opportunity Commission shall propose, in accordance with subchapter II of chapter 5 of title 5 of the United States Code, guidelines for the administration and use of physical and mental fitness tests to measure the ability and competency of police officers and firefighters to perform the requirements of their jobs.

§ 6. Special rule for tenured faculty

(a) Section 12 of the Age Discrimination in Employment Act of 1967 (29

U.S.C. 631) is amended by adding at the end thereof the following new subsection:

"(d) Nothing in this Act shall be construed to prohibit compulsory retirement of any employee who has attained 70 years of age, and who is serving under a contract of unlimited tenure (or similar arrangement providing for unlimited tenure) at an institution of higher education (as defined by section 1201(a) of the Higher Education Act of 1965).".

(b) The amendment made by subsection (a) of this section is repealed December 31, 1993.

(c)(1) The Equal Employment Opportunity Commission shall, not later than 12 months after the date of enactment of this Act, enter into an agreement with the National Academy of Sciences for the conduct of a study to analyze the potential consequences of the elimination of mandatory retirement on institutions of higher education.

(2) The study required by paragraph (1) of this subsection shall be conducted under the general supervision of the National Academy of Sciences by a study panel composed of 9 members. The study panels shall consist of—

(A) 4 members who shall be administrators at institutions of higher education selected by the National Academy of Sciences after consultation with the American Council of Education, the Association of American Universities, and the National Association of State Universities and Land Grant Colleges;

(B) 4 members who shall be teachers or retired teachers at institutions of higher education (who do not serve in an administrative capacity at such institutions), selected by the National Academy of Sciences after consultation with the American Federation of Teachers, the National Education Association, the American Association of University Professors, and the American Association of Retired Persons; and

(C) one member selected by the National Academy of Sciences.

(3) The results of the study shall be reported, with recommendations, to the President and to the Congress not later than 5 years after the date of enactment of this Act.

(4) The expenses of the Study required by this subsection shall be paid from funds available to the Equal Employment Opportunity Commission.

§ 7.   Effective date; application of amendments

(a) Except as provided in subsection (b), this Act and the amendments made by this Act shall take effect on January 1, 1987, except that with respect to any employee who is subject to a collective-bargaining agreement—

(1) which is in effect on June 30, 1986,

(2) which terminates after January 1, 1987,

(3) any provision of which was entered into by a labor organization (as defined by section 6(d)(4) of the Fair Labor Standards Act of 1938 (29 U.S.C. 206(d)(4)), and

(4) which contains any provision that would be superseded by such amendments, but for the operation of this section,

such amendments shall not apply until the termination of such collective bargaining agreement or January 1, 1990, whichever occurs first.

(b) The amendments made by sections 3 and 4 of this Act shall not apply with respect to any cause of action arising under the Age Discrimination in Employment Act of 1967 as in effect before January 1, 1987.

Omnibus Budget Reconciliation Act of 1986

(P.L. 99–509, approved October 21, 1986, amending 29 U.S.C. 623)

Title IX. Income Security, Medicare, Medicaid, and Maternal and Child Health Programs

* * *

Subtitle C. Older Americans Pension Benefits

* * *

§ 9204. Effective date; regulations

(a)(1) The amendments made by [section] 9201 * * * shall apply only with respect to plan years beginning on or after January 1, 1988, and only to employees who have 1 hour of service in any plan year to which such amendments apply.

   (2) In the case of a plan maintained pursuant to 1 or more collective bargaining agreements between employee representatives and 1 or more employers ratified before March 1, 1986, paragraph (1) shall be applied to benefits pursuant to, and individuals covered by, any such agreement by substituting for "January 1, 1988" the date of the commencement of the first plan year beginning on or after the earlier of—

   (A) the later of—

      (i) January 1, 1988, or

      (ii) the date on which the last of such collective bargaining agreements terminate (determined without regard to any extension thereof after February 28, 1986), or

   (B) January 1, 1990.

* * *

171

(c) If any amendment made by this subtitle requires an amendment to any plan, such plan amendment shall not be required to be made before the first plan year beginning on or after January 1, 1989, if—

(1) during the period after such amendment takes effect and before such first plan year, the plan is operated in accordance with the requirements of such amendment, and

(2) such plan amendment applied retroactively to the period after such amendment takes effect and such first plan year.

A pension plan shall not be treated as failing to provide definitely determinable benefits or contributions, or to be operated in accordance with the provisions of the plan, merely because it operates in accordance with this subsection.

(d) The regulations and rulings issued by the Secretary of Labor, the regulations and rulings issued by the Secretary of the Treasury, and the regulations and rulings issued by the Equal Employment Opportunity Commission pursuant to the amendments made by this subtitle shall each be consistent with the others. The Secretary of Labor, the Secretary of the Treasury, and the Equal Employment Opportunity Commission shall each consult with the others to the extent necessary to meet the requirements of the preceding sentence.

(e) The Secretary of Labor, the Secretary of the Treasury, and the Equal Employment Opportunity Commission shall each issue before February 1, 1988, such final regulations as may be necessary to carry out the amendments made by this subtitle.

Age Discrimination Act of 1975

(P.L. 94–135, approved November 28, 1975; as last amended by P.L. 99–272, effective October 18, 1986)

§ 6101. Statement of purpose

[Sec. 302] It is the purpose of this title to prohibit discrimination on the basis of age in programs or activities receiving Federal financial assistance.

§ 6102. Prohibition of discrimination

[Sec. 303] Pursuant to regulations prescribed under section 304, and except as provided by section 304(b) and section 304(c), no person in the United States shall, on the basis of age, be excluded from participation in, be denied the benefits of, or be subjected to discrimination under any program or activity receiving Federal financial assistance.

§ 6103. Regulations

[Sec. 304] (a)(1) Not later than one year after the transmission of the report required by section 307(b), or two and one-half years after the date of the enactment of this Act, whichever occurs first, the Secretary of Health and Human Services shall publish in the Federal Register proposed general regulations to carry out the provisions of section 303.

(2)(A) The Secretary shall not publish such proposed general regulations until the expiration of a period comprised of:

    (i) the forty-five day period specified in section 307(e); and

    (ii) an additional forty-five day period immediately following the period described in clause (i), during which any committee of the Congress having jurisdiction over the subject matter involved may conduct hearings with respect to the report which the Commission is required to transmit under section 307(d), and with respect to the comments and recommendations submitted by Federal departments and agencies under section 307(e).

(B) The forty-five day period specified in subparagraph (A)(ii) shall include only days during which both Houses of the Congress are in session.

(3) Not later than ninety days after the Secretary publishes proposed regulations under paragraph (1), the Secretary shall publish in the Federal Register final general regulations to carry out the provisions of section 303, after taking into consideration any comments received by the Secretary with respect to the regulations proposed under paragraph (1).

(4) Not later than ninety days after the Secretary publishes final general regulations under paragraph (a)(3), the head of each Federal department or agency which extends Federal financial assistance to any program or activity by way of grant, entitlement, loan, or contract other than a contract of insurance or guaranty, shall transmit to the Secretary and publish in the Federal Register proposed regulations to carry out the provisions of section 303 and to provide appropriate investigative, conciliation, and enforcement procedures. Such regulations shall be consistent with the final general regulations issued by the Secretary and shall not become effective until approved by the Secretary.

(5) Notwithstanding any other provision of this section, no regulations issued pursuant to this section shall be effective before July 1, 1979.

(b)(1) It shall not be a violation of any provision of this title, or of any regulation issued under this title, for any person to take any action otherwise prohibited by the provisions of section 303 if, in the program or activity involved:

(A) such action reasonably takes into account age as a factor necessary to the normal operation or the achievement of any statutory objective of such program or activity; or

(B) the differentiation made by such action is based upon reasonable factors other than age.

(2) The provisions of this title shall not apply to any program or activity established under authority of any law which:

(A) provides any benefits or assistance to persons based upon the age of such persons; or

(B) establishes criteria for participation in age related terms or describes intended beneficiaries or target groups in such terms.

(c)(1) Except with respect to any program or activity receiving Federal financial assistance for public service employment under the Job Training Partnership Act, as amended, nothing in this title shall be construed to authorize action under this title by any Federal department or agency with respect to any employment practice of any employer, employment agency, or labor organization, or with respect to any labor-management joint apprenticeship training program.

(2) Nothing in this title shall be construed to amend or modify the Age Discrimination in Employment Act of 1967 as amended, or to affect the rights or responsibilities of any person or party pursuant to such Act.

§ 6104. Enforcement

[Sec. 305] (a) The head of any Federal department or agency who prescribes regulations under section 304 may seek to achieve compliance with any such regulation:

(1) by terminating or refusing to grant or to continue assistance under the program or activity involved to any recipient with respect to whom there has been an express finding on the record, after reasonable notice and opportunity for hearing, of a failure to comply with any such regulation: or

(2) by any other means authorized by law.

(b) Any termination of, or refusal to grant or to continue, assistance under subsection (a)(1) shall be limited to the particular political entity or other recipient with respect to which a finding has been made under subsection (a)(1). Any such termination or refusal shall be limited in its effect to the particular program or activity, or part of such program or activity, with respect to which such finding has been made. No such termination or refusal shall be based in whole or in part on any finding with respect to any program or activity which does not receive Federal financial assistance.

(c) No action may be taken under subsection (a) until the head of the Federal department or agency involved has advised the appropriate person of the failure to comply with the regulation involved and has determined that compliance cannot be secured by voluntary means.

(d) In the case of any action taken under subsection (a), the head of the Federal department or agency involved shall transmit a written report of the circumstances and grounds of such action to the committees of the House of Representatives and the Senate having legislative jurisdiction over the program or activity involved. No such action shall take effect until thirty days after the transmission of any such report.

(e)(1) When any interested person brings an action in any United States district court for the district in which the defendant is found or transacts business to enjoin a violation of this Act by any program or activity receiving Federal financial assistance, such interested person shall give notice by registered mail not less than 30 days prior to the commencement of that action to the Secretary of Health and Human Services, the Attorney General of the United States, and the person against whom the action is directed. Such interested person may elect, by a demand for such relief in his complaint, to recover reasonable attorney's fees, in which case the court shall award the costs of suit, including a reasonable attorney's fee, to the prevailing plaintiff.

(2) The notice referred to in paragraph (1) shall state the nature of the alleged violation, the relief to be requested, the court in which the action will be brought, and whether or not attorney's fees are being demanded in the event that the plaintiff prevails. No action described in paragraph (1) shall be brought (A) if at the time the action is brought the same alleged violation by the same defendant is the subject of a pending action in any court of the United States; or (B) if administrative remedies have not been exhausted.

(f) With respect to actions brought for relief based on an alleged violation of the provisions of this title, administrative remedies shall be deemed exhausted upon the expiration of 180 days from the filing of an administrative complaint during which time the Federal department or agency makes no finding with regard to the complaint, or upon the day that the Federal department or agency issues a finding in favor of the recipient of financial assistance, whichever occurs first.

§ 6105. Judicial review

[Sec. 306] (a) Any action by any Federal department or agency under section 305 shall be subject to such judicial review as may otherwise be provided by law for similar action taken by any such department or agency on other grounds.

(b) In the case of any action by any Federal department or agency under section 305 which is not otherwise subject to judicial review, any person aggrieved (including any State or political subdivision thereof and any agency of either) may obtain judicial review of such action in accordance with the provisions of chapter 7 of title 5. United States Code. For purposes of this subsection, any such action shall not be considered committed to unreviewable agency discretion within the meaning of section 701(a)(2) of such title.

§ 6106. Study of discrimination based on age

[Sec. 307] (a) The Commission on Civil Rights shall (1) undertake a study of unreasonable discrimination based on age in programs and activities receiving Federal financial assistance; and (2) identify with particularity any such federally assisted program or activity in which there is found evidence of persons who are otherwise qualified being, on the basis of age, excluded from participation in, denied the benefits of, or subjected to discrimination under such program or activity.

(b) As part of the study required by this section, the Commission shall conduct public hearings to elicit the views of interested parties, including Federal departments and agencies, on issues relating to age discrimination in programs and activities receiving Federal financial assistance, and particularly with respect to the reasonableness of distinguishing, on the basis of age, among potential participants in, or beneficiaries of, specific federally assisted programs.

(c) The Commission is authorized to obtain, through grant or contract, analyses, research and studies by independent experts of issues relating to age discrimination and to publish the results thereof. For purposes of the study required by this section, the Commission may accept and utilize the services of voluntary or uncompensated personnel, without regard to the provisions of section 105(b) of the Civil Rights Act of 1957 (42 U.S.C. 1975d(b)).

(d) Not later than two years after November 28, 1975, the Commission shall transmit a report of its findings and its recommendations for statutory changes (if any) and administrative action, including suggested general regulations, to the Congress and to the President and shall provide a copy of its report to the head of each Federal department and agency with respect to which the Commission makes findings or recommendations.

(e) Not later than forty-five working days after receiving a copy of the report required by subsection (d), each Federal department or agency with respect to which the Commission makes findings or recommendations shall submit its comments and recommendations regarding such report to the President and to the Committee on Labor of the House of Representatives.

(f) The head of each Federal department or agency shall cooperate in all respects with the Commission with respect to the study required by subsection (a), and shall provide to the Commission such data, reports, and documents in connection with the subject matter of such study as the Commission may request.

(g) There are authorized to be appropriated such sums as may be necessary to carry out the provisions of this section.

§ 6106a.   Reports to the Secretary and Congress

[Sec. 307a] (a) Not later than December 31 of each year (beginning in 1979), the head of each Federal department or agency shall submit to the Secretary of Health and Human Services a report (1) describing in detail the steps taken during the preceding fiscal year by such department or agency to carry out the provisions of section 303; and (2) containing specific data about program participants or beneficiaries, by age, sufficient to permit analysis of how well the department or agency is carrying out the provisions of Section 303.

(b) Not later than March 31 of each year (beginning in 1980), the Secretary of Health and Human Services shall compile the reports made pursuant to subsection (a) and shall submit them to the Congress, together with an evaluation of the performance of each department or agency with respect to carrying out the provisions of Section 303.

§ 6107. Definitions

[Sec. 308] For purposes of this title—

(1) the term "Commission" means the Commission on Civil Rights;

(2) the term "Secretary" means the Secretary of Health and Human Services; and

(3) the term "Federal department or agency" means any agency as defined in section 551 of title 5, United States Code, and includes the United States Postal Service and the Postal Rate Commission.

Rehabilitation Act of 1973

(P.L. 93–112, approved September 26, 1973; as last amended by P.L. 99–506, effective October 21, 1986)

General Provisions

* * *

§ 706. Definitions

[Sec. 7] For purposes of this Act:

* * *

(6) The term "employability," with respect to an individual, means a determination that, with the provision of vocational rehabilitation services, the individual is likely to enter or retain, as a primary objective, full-time employment, and when appropriate, part-time employment, consistent with the capacities or abilities of the individual in the competitive labor market or any other vocational outcome the Secretary may determine consistent with this Act.

* * *

(8)(A) Except as otherwise provided in subparagraph (B), the term "handicapped individual" means any individual who (i) has a physical or mental disability which for such individual constitutes or results in a substantial handicap to employment and (ii) can reasonably be expected to benefit in terms of employability from vocational rehabilitation services provided pursuant to subchapters I and III of this chapter.

(B) Subject to the second sentence of this subparagraph, the term "handicapped individual" means, for purposes of titles IV and V of this Act, any person who (i) has a physical or mental impairment which substantially limits one or more of such person's major life activities, (ii) has a record of such an impairment, or (iii) is regarded as having such an impairment. For purposes of sections 503 and 504 as such sections relate to employment, such term does not include any individual who is an alcoholic or drug abuser whose current use of alcohol or drugs prevents such individual from performing the duties of the job in question or whose employment, by reason of such current alcohol or drug abuse, would constitute a direct threat to property or the safety of others.

* * *

Subchapter V. Miscellaneous Provisions

* * *

§ 791. Employment of handicapped individuals

[Sec. 501] (a) There is established within the Federal Government an Interagency Committee on Handicapped Employees (hereinafter in this section referred to as the "Committee"), comprised of such members as the President may select, including the following (or their designees whose positions are Executive Level IV or higher); the Chairman of the Equal Employment Opportunity Commission, the Administrator of Veterans' Affairs, and the Secretaries of Labor and Education and Health and Human Services. The Secretary of Education and the Chairman of the Equal Employment Opportunity Commission shall serve as cochairmen of the Committee. The resources of the President's Committees on Employment of the Handicapped and on Mental Retardation shall be made fully available to the Committee. It shall be the purpose and function of the Committee (1) to provide a focus for Federal and other employment of handicapped individuals, and to review, on a periodic basis, in cooperation with the Equal Employment Opportunity Commission, the adequacy of hiring, placement, and advancement practices with respect to handicapped individuals, by each department, agency, and instrumentality in the executive branch of Government, and to insure that the special needs of such individuals are being met; and (2) to consult with the Equal Employment Opportunity Commission to assist the Commission to carry out its responsibilities under subsections (b), (c), and (d) of this section. On the basis of such review and consultation, the Committee shall periodically make to the Equal Employment Opportunity Commission such recommendations for legislative and administrative changes, as it deems necessary or desirable. The Equal Employment Opportunity Commission shall timely transmit to the appropriate committees of Congress any such recommendations.

(b) Each department, agency, and instrumentality (including the United States Postal Service and the Postal Rate Commission) in the executive branch shall, within one hundred and eighty days after the date of enactment of this Act, submit to the Equal Employment Opportunity Commission and to the Committee an affirmative action program plan for the hiring, placement, and advancement of handicapped individuals in such department, agency or instrumentality. Such plan shall include a description of the extent to which and methods whereby the special need of handicapped employees are being met. Such plan shall be updated annually, and shall be reviewed annually, and approved by the Commission, if the Commission determines, after consultation with the Committee, that such plan provides sufficient assurances, procedures and commitments to provide adequate hiring, placement, and advancement opportunities for handicapped individuals.

(c) The Equal Employment Opportunity Commission, after consultation with the Committee, shall develop and recommend to the Secretary for referral to the appropriate State agencies, policies and procedures which will facilitate the hiring, placement, and advancement in employment of individuals who have received rehabilitation services under State vocational rehabilitation programs, veterans' programs, or any other program for handicapped individuals, including the promotion of job opportunities for such individuals. The Secretary shall encourage such State agencies to adopt and implement such policies and procedures.

(d) The Equal Employment Opportunity Commission, after consultation with the Committee, shall on June 30, 1974, and at the end of each subsequent fiscal year, make a complete report to the appropriate committees of the Congress with respect to the practices of and achievements in hiring, placement, and advancement of handicapped individuals by each department, agency, and instrumentality and the effectiveness of the affirmative action programs required by subsection (b) of this section, together with recommendations as to legislation which have been submitted to the Equal Employment Opportunity Commission under subsection (a) of this section, or other appropriate action to insure the adequacy of such practices. Such report shall also include an evaluation by the Committee of the effectiveness of the activities of the Equal Employment Opportunity Commission under subsections (b) and (c) of this section.

(e) An individual who, as a part of an individualized written rehabilitation program under a State plan approved under this Act, participates in a program of unpaid work experience in a Federal agency, shall not, by reason thereof, be considered to be a Federal employee or to be subject to the provisions of law relating to Federal employment, including those relating to hours of work, rates of compensation, leave, unemployment compensation, and Federal employee benefits.

(f)(1) The Secretary of Labor and the Secretary of Education are authorized and directed to cooperate with the President's Committee on Employment of the Handicapped in carrying out its functions.

(2) In selecting personnel to fill all positions on the President's Committee

on Employment of the Handicapped, special consideration shall be given to qualified handicapped individuals.

* * *

§ 793. Employment under Federal contracts

[Sec. 503] (a) Any contract in excess of $2,500 entered into by any Federal department or agency for the procurement of personal property and nonpersonal services (including construction) for the United States shall contain a provision requiring that, in employing persons to carry out such contract the party contracting with the United States shall take affirmative action to employ and advance in employment qualified handicapped individuals as defined in section 706(7) of this title. The provisions of this section shall apply to any subcontract in excess of $2,500 entered into by a prime contractor in carrying out any contract for the procurement of personal property and nonpersonal services (including construction) for the United States. The President shall implement the provisions of this section by promulgating regulations within ninety days after September 26, 1973.

(b) If any handicapped individual believes any contractor has failed or refused to comply with the provisions of a contract with the United States, relating to employment of handicapped individuals, such individual may file a complaint with the Department of Labor. The Department shall promptly investigate such complaint and shall take such action thereon as the facts and circumstances warrant, consistent with the terms of such contract and the laws and regulations applicable thereto.

(c) The requirements of this section may be waived, in whole or in part, by the President with respect to a particular contract or subcontract in accordance with guidelines set forth in regulations which the President shall prescribe, when the President determines that special circumstances in the national interest so require and states in writing the reasons for such determination.

§ 794. Nondiscrimination under Federal grants and programs; promulgation of rules and regulations

[Sec. 504] No otherwise qualified handicapped individual in the United States, as defined in section 7(8), shall, solely by reason of his handicap, be excluded from the participation in, be denied the benefits of, or be subjected to discrimination under any program or activity receiving Federal financial assistance or under any program or activity conducted by any Executive agency or by the United States Postal Service. The head of each such agency shall promulgate such regulations as may be necessary to carry out the amendments to this section made by the Rehabilitation, Comprehensive

Services, and Developmental Disabilities Act of 1978. Copies of any proposed regulation shall be submitted to appropriate authorizing committees of the Congress, and such regulation may take effect no earlier than the thirtieth day after the date on which such regulation is so submitted to such committees.

§ 794a. Remedies and attorney fees

[Sec. 505] (a)(1) The remedies, procedures, and rights set forth in section 717 of the Civil Rights Act of 1964 (42 U.S.C. 2000e-16), including the application of sections 706(f) through 706(k) (42 U.S.C. 2000e-5(f) through (k), shall be available, with respect to any complaint under section 501 of this Act, to any employee or applicant for employment aggrieved by the final disposition of such complaint, or by the failure to take final action on such complaint. In fashioning an equitable or affirmative action remedy under such section, a court may take into account the reasonableness of the cost of any necessary work place accommodation, and the availability of alternatives therefor or other appropriate relief in order to achieve an equitable and appropriate remedy.

(2) The remedies, procedures, and rights set forth in title VI of the Civil Rights Act of 1964 shall be available to any person aggrieved by any act or failure to act by any recipient of Federal assistance or Federal provider of such assistance under section 504 of this Act.

(b) In any action or proceeding to enforce or charge a violation of a provision of this title, the court, in its discretion, may allow the prevailing party, other than the United States, a reasonable attorney's fee as part of the costs.

* * *

Subchapter VI. Employment Opportunities for Handicapped Individuals

Part A. Community Service Employment Pilot Programs for Handicapped Individuals

§ 795. Pilot programs

[Sec. 611] (a) In order to promote useful opportunities in community service activities for handicapped individuals who have poor employment prospects, the Secretary of Labor (hereinafter in this part referred to as the "Secretary") is authorized to establish a community service employment pilot program for handicapped individuals. For purposes of this part, the term "eligible individuals" means persons who are handicapped individuals (as defined in section 7(8) of this Act) and who are referred to programs under this part by designated State units.

(b)(1) The Secretary may enter into agreements with public or private nonprofit agencies or organizations, including national organizations, agencies of a State government or a political subdivision of a State (having elected or duly appointed governing officials), or a combination of such political subdivisions, or tribal organizations in order to carry out the pilot program referred to in subsection (a). Such agreements may include provisions consistent with subsection (c) for the payment of the costs of projects developed by such organizations and agencies in cooperation with the Secretary. No payment shall be made by the Secretary toward the cost of any such project unless the Secretary determines that:

(A) Such project will provide employment only for eligible individuals, except that if eligible individuals are not available to serve as technical, administrative, or supervisory personnel for a project then such personnel may be recruited from among other individuals.

(B) Such project will provide employment for eligible individuals in the community in which such individuals reside, or in nearby communities.

(C) Such project will employ eligible individuals in services related to publicly owned and operated facilities and projects, or projects sponsored by organizations, other than political parties, exempt from taxation under section 501(c)(3) of the Internal Revenue Code of 1954, except for projects involving the construction, operation, or maintenance of any facility used or to be used as a place for sectarian religious instruction or worship.

(D) Such project will contribute to the general welfare of the community in which eligible individuals are employed under such project.

(E) Such project (i) will result in an increase in employment opportunities over those opportunities which would otherwise be available, (ii) will not result in any displacement of currently employed workers (including partial displacement, such as a reduction in the hours of nonovertime work or wages or employment benefits), and (iii) will not impair existing contracts or result in the substitution of Federal funds for other funds in connection with work that would otherwise be performed.

(F) Such project will not employ any eligible individual to perform work which is the same or substantially the same as that performed by any other person who is on layoff from employment with the agency or organization sponsoring such project.

(G) Such project will utilize methods of recruitment and selection (including the listing of job vacancies with the State agency units designated under section 721(a)(2)(A) of this title to administer vocational rehabilitation services under this chapter) which will assure that the maximum number of eligible individuals will have an opportunity to participate in the project.

(H) Such project will provide for (i) such training as may be necessary to make the most effective use of the skills and talents of individuals who are participating in the project, and (ii) during the period of such training, a reasonable subsistence allowance for such individuals and the payment of any other reasonable expenses related to such training.

(I) Such project will provide safe and healthy working conditions for any eligible individual employed under such project and will pay any such individual at a rate of pay not lower than the rate of pay described in paragraph (2).

(J) Such project will be established or administered with the advice of (i) persons competent in the field of service in which employment is being provided, and (ii) persons who are knowledgeable with regard to the needs of handicapped individuals.

(K) Such project will pay any reasonable costs for work-related expenses, transportation, and attendant care incurred by eligible individuals employed under such project in accordance with regulations prescribed by the Secretary.

(L) Such project will provide appropriate placement services for employees under the project to assist them in locating unsubsidized employment when the Federal assistance for the project terminates.

(2) The rate of pay referred to in subparagraph (I) of paragraph (1) is the highest of the following:

(A) the prevailing rate of pay for persons employed in similar occupations by the same employer.

(B) The minimum wage which would be applicable to the employee under the Fair Labor Standards Act of 1938 if such employee were not exempt from such Act under section 13 thereof.

(C) The State or local minimum wage for the most nearly comparable covered employment.

The Department of Labor shall not issue any certificate of exemption under section 14(c) of the Fair Labor Standards Act of 1938 with respect to any person employed in a project under this section.

(c)(1) The Secretary may pay not to exceed 90 percent of the cost of any project which is the subject of an agreement entered into under subsection (b). Notwithstanding the preceding sentence, the Secretary may pay all of the costs of any such project which is (A) an emergency or disaster project, or (B) a project located in an economically depressed area, as determined by the Secretary in consultation with the Secretary of Commerce and the Director of the Community Services Administration.

(2) The non-Federal share of any project under this part may be in cash or in kind. In determining the amount of the non-Federal share, the Secretary may attribute fair market value to services and facilities contributed from non-Federal sources.

(d) Payments under this part may be made in advance or by way of reimbursement, and in such installments as the Secretary may determine. (29 U.S.C. § 795).

§ 795a. Administration

[Sec. 612] (a) In order to effectively carry out the provisions of this part, the Secretary shall, through the Commissioner of the Rehabilitation Services Administration, consult with any designated State unit with regard to—

(1) the localities in which community service projects of the type authorized by this part are most needed;

(2) the employment situations and types of skills possessed by eligible individuals in such localities; and

(3) potential projects suitable for funding in such localities.

(b) The Secretary shall coordinate the pilot program established under this part with programs authorized under the Emergency Jobs and Unemployment Assistance Act of 1974, the Job Training Partnership Act, the Community Services Act of 1974, and the Emergency Employment Act of 1971. Appropriations under this part may not be used to carry out any program under the Acts referred to in the preceding sentence.

(c) In carrying out this part, the Secretary may, with the consent of any other Federal, State, or local agency, use the services, equipment, personnel, and facilities of such agency with or without providing such agency with reimbursement and may use the services, equipment, and facilities of any other public or private entity on a similar basis.

(d) Within one hundred and eighty days after the effective date of this part, the Secretary shall issue and publish in the Federal Register such regulations as may be necessary to carry out this part.

(e) The Secretary shall not delegate any function of the Secretary under this part to any other department or agency of the Federal Government.

§ 795b. Employment

[Sec. 613] (a) Eligible individuals who are employed in any project funded under this part shall not be considered to be Federal employees as a result of such employment and shall not be subject to the provisions of part III of title 5.

(b) No contract shall be entered into under this part with a contractor who is, or whose employees are, under State law, exempted from operation of any

State workmen's compensation law generally applicable to employees, unless the contractor shall undertake to provide for persons to be employed under such contract, through insurance by a recognized carrier or by self-insurance authorized by State law, workmen's compensation coverage equal to that provided by law for covered employment.

(c) No part of the wages, allowances, or reimbursement for transportation and attendant care costs made available to an eligible individual employed in any project funded under this part shall be treated as income or benefits for the purpose of any other program or provision of State or Federal law, unless the Secretary makes a case by case determination that disallowance of such income or benefit is inequitable or does not carry out the purposes of this title.

§ 795c. Interagency cooperation

[Sec. 614] (a) The Secretary shall consult with, and obtain the written views of, the Commissioner of the Rehabilitation Services Administration before establishing rules or general policy in the administration of this part.

(b) The Secretary shall consult and cooperate with the Director of the Community Services Administration, the Secretary of Education, and the heads of other Federal agencies carrying out related programs, in order to achieve maximum coordination between such programs and the program established under this part. Each Federal agency shall cooperate with the Secretary in disseminating information relating to the availability of assistance under this part and in identifying individuals eligible for employment in projects assisted under this part.

§ 795d. Award of grants or contracts

[Sec. 615] (a)(1) Preference in awarding grants or contracts under this part shall be given to organizations of proven ability in providing employment services to handicapped individuals under this program and similar programs. The Secretary, in awarding grants and contracts under this section, shall, to the extent feasible, assure an equitable distribution of activities under such grants and contracts among the States, taking into account the needs of underserved States and the needs of Indian tribes.

(2) The Secretary shall allot for projects within each State the sums appropriated for any fiscal year under section 795f of this title so that each State will receive an amount which bears the same ratio to such sums as the population of the State bears to the population of all the States.

(b) The amount allotted for projects within any fiscal year which the Secretary determines will not be required for such year shall be reallotted, from time to time and on such dates during such year as the Secretary may fix, to projects within other States in proportion to the original allotments to projects within such States under subsection (a) for such year, but with such proportionate amount for any of such other States being reduced to the extent it exceeds the sum the Secretary estimates that projects within such State need and will be able to use for such year. The total of such reductions shall be similarly reallotted among the States whose proportionate amounts were not so reduced. Any amount reallotted to a State under this subsection during a year shall be deemed part of its allotment under subsection (a) for such year.

(c) The amount apportioned for projects within each State under subsection (a) shall be apportioned among areas within each such State in an equitable manner, taking into consideration (1) the proportion which eligible individuals in each such area bears to the total number of such individuals, respectively, in that State, and (2) the relative distribution of such individuals residing in rural and urban areas within the State (including individuals residing on Indian reservations).

§ 795e. Definitions

[Sec. 616] For purposes of this part—
(1) the term "community service" means social, health, welfare, and educational services, legal and other counseling services and assistance, including tax counseling and assistance and financial counseling, and library, recreational, and other similar services; conservation, maintenance, or restoration of natural resources; community betterment or beautification; antipollution and environmental quality efforts; economic development; and such other services essential and necessary to the community as the Secretary, by regulation, may prescribe;
(2) the term "pilot program" means the community service employment program for handicapped individuals established under this part; and
(3) the term "attendant care" means interpreter services for the deaf, reader services for the blind, and services provided to assist mentally retarded individuals to perform duties of employment.

§ 795f. Authorization of appropriations

[Sec. 617] There are authorized to be appropriated to carry out the provisions of this part such sums as may be necessary for each of the fiscal years 1987, 1988, 1989, 1990, and 1991.

Part B. Projects With Industry and Business Opportunities for Handicapped Individuals

§ 795g. Projects with industry

[Sec. 621] (a)(1) The purpose of this title is to promote opportunities for competitive employment of individuals with handicaps, to provide appropriate placement resources, to engage the talent and leadership of private industry as partners in the rehabilitation process, to create practical settings for job readiness and training programs, and to secure the participation of private industry in identifying and providing job opportunities and the necessary skills and training to qualify people with handicaps for competetive employment.

(2) The Commissioner, in consultation with the Secretaries of Labor and Commerce and with designated State units, may enter into agreements with individual employers, designated State units and other entities to establish jointly financed projects which—

   (A) shall create and expand job opportunities for individuals with handicaps by providing for the establishment of appropriate job placement services;

   (B) shall provide individuals with handicaps with training in a realistic work setting in order to prepare them for employment in the competitive market;

   (C) shall provide handicapped individuals with such supportive services as may be required to permit them to continue to engage in the employment for which they have received training under this section;

   (D) shall, to the extent appropriate, expand job opportunities for handicapped individuals by providing for (i) the development and modification of jobs to accommodate the special needs of such individuals, (ii) the distribution of special aids, appliances, or adapted equipment to such individuals, and (iii) the modification of any facilities or equipment of the employer which are to be used primarily by handicapped individuals; and

   (E) shall provide for business advisory councils comprised of representatives of private industry, business concerns, and organized labor who will identify job availability within the community and the skills necessary to fill jobs identified, and prescribe training and programs tailored to their need.

(3) Any agreement under this subsection shall be jointly developed by the Commissioner, the prospective employer, and, to the extent practicable, the appropriate designated State unit and the handicapped individuals involved. Such agreements shall specify the terms of training and employment under the project, provide for the payment by the Commissioner of part of the costs of the project (in accordance with subsection (e)), and contain the items required under subsection (b) and such other provisions as the parties to the agreement consider to be appropriate.

(4) Any agreement developed under this subsection shall include a description of an evaluation plan which at the end of each project year reflects at a minimum the following—

    (A) the numbers and types of handicapped individuals assisted;

    (B) the types of assistance provided;

    (C) the sources of funding;

    (D) the percentage of resources committed to each type of assistance provided;

    (E) the extent to which the employment status and earning power of handicapped individuals changed following assistance;

    (F) the extent of capacity building activities, including collaboration with other organizations, agencies, and institutions; and

    (G) a comparison, when appropriate, of activities in prior years with activities in the most recent year.

(b) No payment shall be made by the Commissioner under any agreement with an employer entered into under subsection (a) unless such agreement—

    (1) provides assurances that handicapped individuals placed with such employer shall receive at least the applicable minimum wage;

    (2) specifies that the Commissioner, together with the designated State unit, has the right to review any termination of employment, and that, in the event such termination occurs less than three years after the date of the commencement of employment of the handicapped individual involved, the Commissioner shall be entitled to require the repayment of a portion of the funds made available to the employer if such termination is without reasonable cause, as determined by the Commissioner in consultation with such designated State unit;

    (3) provides assurances that any handicapped individual placed with such employer shall be afforded terms and benefits of employment equal to those which are afforded to other employees of such employer, and that such handicapped individuals shall not be unreasonably segregated from other employees; and

    (4) provides assurances that an evaluation report containing data specified under subsection (a)(4) shall be submitted to the Commissioner.

    (4) [enacted with same number as above] provides assurances that an evaluation report containing data specified under subsection (a)(4) of this section shall be submitted as determined by the Commissioner.

(c) Payments under this section with respect to any project may not exceed 80 per centum of the costs of the project.

(d)(1) The Commissioner shall, not later than February 1, 1985, develop and publish standards for evaluation consistent with the provisions in section (a)(3) to assist each recipient under the Projects With Industry Program receiving assistance under this title to review and evaluate the operation of its projects. Such standards shall be revised as necessary, subject to paragraph (4) of this subsection.

    (2) The Commissioner shall, pursuant to section 14 of this Act conduct a comprehensive evaluation of the Projects With Industry Program and submit a report on February 1, 1986, to Congress on the evaluation, including recommendations for the improvement and continuation of

each recipient and for the support of new Projects With Industry recipients. In conducting the comprehensive evaluation, the Commissioner shall apply standards for evaluation criteria which are consistent with those required in section (a)(3).

(3) In developing standards for evaluation to be used by the Projects With Industry recipients, and in developing the standards for evaluation to be used in the comprehensive evaluation, the Commissioner shall obtain and consider recommendations for such standards from State Vocational Rehabilitation Agencies, current Projects With Industry recipients, professional organizations representing industry, organizations representing handicapped individuals, individuals assisted by Projects With Industry recipients, and labor organizations.

(4) No standards may be established under this subsection unless the standards are approved by the National Council on the Handicapped. The Council shall approve the standards within 90 days after receiving the standards. If the Secretary of Education has not received notification of approval or disapproval from the Council within 90 days, the standards shall be deemed approved. A Council decision on such standards shall occur at a regularly scheduled meeting of the Council, and shall be the result of a simple majority of those present at the meeting.

(e)(1) Subject to the availability of appropriations, an agreement for financial assistance under this section may be effective for a period not to exceed five years. Any subsequent agreement for financial assistance under this section may be effective for not more than five years. In making a determination concerning any subsequent agreement, the Commissioner shall consider performance under the previous agreement and evaluation reports submitted under subsection (b)(4).

(2) The Commissioner shall annually review each evaluation report submitted under subsection (b)(4) and make a determination concerning the termination, modification, or renewal of each agreement for financial assistance under this section.

(f)(1) By July 1, 1988, the Commissioner shall publish in the Federal Register in final form indicators of what constitutes minimum compliance consistent with the evaluation standards under subsection (d)(1).

(2) Each grantee shall report to the Commissioner at the end of each project year the extent to which the grantee is in compliance with the evaluation standards, beginning with fiscal year 1989.

(3) By the end of fiscal year 1991, the Commissioner shall have conducted on-site compliance reviews of at least one-third of the grantees receiving funding under this part in fiscal year 1987. The Commissioner shall conduct on-site compliance reviews of at least 15 percent of grantees annually in subsequent years. Selection of grantees for compliance reviews shall be on a random basis. The Commissioner shall use the indicators of the evaluation standards in determining

compliance. At least one member of an on-site compliance review shall be a non-Federal employee with experience or expertise in conducting Projects With Industry.

(4) Beginning with the annual report to Congress for fiscal year 1990 and in subsequent years, the Commissioner shall include an analysis of the extent to which grantees have complied with the evaluation standards. The Commissioner may identify individual grantees in the analysis. In addition, the Commissioner shall report the results of on-site compliance reviews, identifying individual grantees.

(g) The Commissioner may provide, directly or by way of grant or contract, technical assistance to (1) entities conducting Projects With Industry for the purpose of assisting such entities in the improvement of or in the development of relationships with private industry or labor, and (2) entities planning the development of new Projects With Industry.

(h)(1)(A) From sums appropriated for the purposes of this section for fiscal year 1990, an amount which is 80 percent of the amount appropriated for fiscal year 1989 shall be available only for grantees receiving assistance in fiscal year 1989.

(B) The Secretary shall ensure that grants are made under subparagraph (A) only to Projects With Industry recipients that meet the evaluation standards and shall make a determination concerning the termination, modification, or renewal of each grant on the basis of such evaluation.

(2) To the extent funds are available under paragraph (1), the Secretary shall award grants to new Projects With Industry recipients located in unserved geographic areas. Grants to new recipients shall be awarded on a competitive basis.

(3) For fiscal year 1991 and for any subsequent fiscal year, new grant awards shall be made on a competitive basis and shall include consideration of past performance, where appropriate.

(4)(A) Each grant recipient receiving assistance under this section in fiscal year 1986 shall continue to receive assistance through September 30, 1987, unless the Commissioner determines that the grant recipient is not in compliance with the provisions of the approved application of the grant recipient.

(B) Grant recipients continuing to receive assistance on the basis of the review described in subparagraph (A) of this paragraph shall be evaluated by the Commissioner using standards described in subsection (d) and (f) of this section. Each such grant recipient shall continue to receive assistance for 3 years unless the Commissioner determines that the grantee is not substantially in compliance with such standards and with the provisions of the approved application of the grant recipient.

(i) In approving applications under this section, the Commissioner shall give priority to the geographic areas among the States which are currently not served or underserved by Projects With Industry.

§ 795h. Business opportunities for handicapped; promulgation of regulations

[Sec. 622] The Commissioner, in consultation with the Secretaries of Labor and Commerce, may make grants to, or enter into contracts with, handicapped individuals to enable them to establish or operate commercial or other enterprises to develop or market their products or services. Within ninety days after the effective date of this section, the Commissioner shall promulgate regulations to carry out this section, including regulations specifying (1) the maximum amount of money which may be provided under this section to any participant, and (2) procedures for certification, by designated State units, of individuals eligible to participate in any program under this section.

§ 795i. Authorization of appropriations

[Sec. 623] There are authorized to be appropriated to carry out the provisions of section 621, $16,070,000 for fiscal year 1987, $17,010,000 for fiscal year 1988, $18,030,000 for fiscal year 1989, $19,149,000 for fiscal year 1990, and $19,925,000 for fiscal year 1991 and for section 622 such sums may be as necessary for each of the fiscal years 1987, 1988, 1989, 1990 and 1991.

Part C. Supported Employment Services for Individuals With Severe Handicaps

§ 795j. Purpose

[Sec. 631] It is the purpose of this part to authorize grants (supplementary to grants for vocational rehabilitation services under title I) to assist States in developing collaborative programs with appropriate public agencies and private nonprofit organizations for training and traditionally time-limited post-employment services leading to supported employment for individuals with severe handicaps.

§ 795k. Eligibility

[Sec. 632] Services may be provided under this part to any individual with severe handicaps whose ability or potential to engage in a training program and whose ability to engage in a supported employment setting has been determined by an evaluation of rehabilitation potential as defined in section 7 of this Act.

§ 7951. Allotments

[Sec. 633] (a)(1) The Secretary shall allot the sums appropriated for each fiscal year under this section among the States on the basis of relative population of each State, except that no State shall receive less than $250,000 or one-third of 1 percent of the sums made available for the fiscal year for which the allotment is made, whichever is greater.

    (2)(A) For the purposes of this subsection, the term "States" does not include Guam, American Samoa, the Virgin Islands, the Trust Territory of the Pacific Islands, and the Commonwealth of the Northern Mariana Islands.

    (B) The jurisdictions described in subparagraph (A) shall be allotted not less than one-eighth of 1 percent of the amounts made available for purposes of this subpart for each such clause for the fiscal year for which the allotment is made.

    (b) Whenever the Commissioner determines that any amount of an allotment to a State for any fiscal year will not be expended by such State to carry out the provisions of this part, the Commissioner shall make such amount available for carrying out the provisions of this part to one or more of the States which the Commissioner determines will be able to use additional amounts during such year for carrying out such provisions. Any amount made available to a State for any fiscal year pursuant to the preceding sentence shall, for the purposes of this section, be regarded as an increase in the State's allotment for such year.

    (c)(1) In the first fiscal year in which appropriations are made pursuant to section 638 a State may, in lieu of receiving its allotment under this part, make an application for a planning grant for that fiscal year. The Secretary is authorized to approve the appropriation of States which meet the requirements of this subsection.

    (2)(A) The grant made under this subsection shall be used for planning activities designed to facilitate the State using its allotment under this part.

    (B) No grant under this subsection may exceed a period of 18 months.

    (3) No planning grant made under this subsection may exceed $250,000.

§ 795m. State plan

[Sec. 634] (a) In order to be eligible for grants under this part, a State shall submit to the Commissioner as part of the State plan under title I of this Act a State plan supplement for a three-year period for providing training and traditionally time-limited post-employment services leading to supported employment for individuals with severe handicaps. Each State shall make such annual revisions in the plan supplement as may be necessary.

(b) Each such plan supplement shall—

(1) designate each agency of such State designated under section 101(a)(2)(B) of this Act as the agency to administer the program assisted under this part;

(2)(A) specify results of the needs assessment conducted as required by title I of this Act of individuals with severe handicaps as such assessment identifies the need for supported employment services, including the coordination and use of the information within the State relating to section 618(b)(3) of the Education of the Handicapped Act; and

   (B) describe the quality, scope, and extent of supported employment services to be provided to individuals with severe handicaps under this part, and specify the State's goals and plans with respect to the distribution of funds received under section 635 of this part;

(3) provide assurances that—

   (A) an evaluation for each individual describes training and tradition-ally time-limited post-employment services leading to supported employment;

   (B) an individualized written rehabilitation program as required by section 102 will be developed outlining the services to be provided;

   (C) such services will be provided in accordance with such program or a program specified under subsection (b)(3)(D) of this part;

   (D) such services will be coordinated with the evaluation results, the individual written rehabilitation plan or education plan as re-quired under section 102 of this Act, section 123 of the Develop-mental Disabilities Act of 1984, and sections 612(4) and 614(5) of the Education of the Handicapped Act, respectively;

   (E) the State will conduct periodic reviews of the progress of individ-uals assisted under this part to determine whether services pro-vided to such individuals should be continued, modified, or discontinued; and

   (F) the State will make maximum use of services from public agen-cies, private nonprofit organizations, and other appropriate re-sources in the community to carry out this part;

(4) demonstrate evidence of collaboration by and funding from relevant State agencies and private nonprofit organizations to assist in the provision of supported employment services;

(5) provide assurance that all designated State agencies will expend not more than 5 percent of the State's allotment under this part for administrative costs for carrying out this part; and

(6) contain such other information and be submitted in such form and in accordance with such procedures as the Commissioner may require.

§ 795n. Services, availability and comparability

[Sec. 635] (a)(1) Services available under this part may include but are not limited to an evaluation of rehabilitation potential, provision of skilled job trainers who accompany the worker for intensive on-the-job training, systematic training, job development, follow-up services (including regular contact with the employer, trainee, and the parent or guardian), and consistent with subsection (b) regular observation or supervision of the individual with severe handicaps at the training site and other services needed to support the individual in employment.

(2) The evaluation of rehabilitation potential authorized by paragraph (1) of this subsection shall be supplementary to the evaluation of rehabilitation potential provided under title I of this Act.

(b) Services authorized under this part are limited to training and traditionally time-limited post-employment services leading to supported employment. Extended supported employment services shall be provided by the relevant State agencies and private organizations as specified under section 634(b)(4) of this part or any other available source.

(c) Services provided under this part shall be complementary to services provided under title I of this Act.

§ 795o. Restriction

[Sec. 636] Each designated State agency shall collect the client information required by section 13 of this Act separately for supported employment clients under this part and for supported employment clients under title I.

§ 795p. Saving provision

[Sec. 637] Nothing in this Act shall be construed to prohibit a State from conducting or from carrying out training and traditionally time-limited post-employment services leading to supported employment in accordance with the State plan submitted under section 101 from its State allotment under section 110.

§ 795q. Authorization of appropriations

[Sec. 638] There are authorized to be appropriated to carry out this part $25,000,000 for the fiscal year 1987, $26,470,000 for the fiscal year 1988, $28,060,000 for the fiscal year 1989, $29,730,000 for the fiscal year 1990, $30,949,000 for the fiscal year 1991.

Rehabilitation Act Amendments of 1986 — (Unincorporated)
(P.L. 99–506, approved October 21, 1986)

Title VII. Employment Opportunities for Individuals With Handicaps

* * *

[Sec. 703.] Projects with industry

(a) * * *
(4) The amendment made by paragraph (2), adding clause (E) to section 621(a)(2) of the Act, shall take effect one year after the date of enactment of this Act.

* * *

Title X. Technical and Miscellaneous Provisions

[Sec. 1003.] Civil rights remedies equalization

(a)(1) A State shall not be immune under the Eleventh Amendment of the Constitution of the United States from suit in Federal court for a violation of section 504 of the Rehabilitation Act of 1973, title IX of the Education Amendments of 1972, the Age Discrimination Act of 1975, title VI of the Civil Rights Act of 1964, or the provisions of any other Federal statute prohibiting discrimination by recipients of Federal financial assistance.

(2) In a suit against a State for a violation of a statute referred to in paragraph (1), remedies (including remedies both at law and in equity) are available for such a violation to the same extent as such remedies are available for such a violation in the suit against any public or private entity other than a State.

(b) The provisions of subsection (a) shall take effect with respect to violations that occur in whole or in part after the date of enactment of the Rehabilitation Act Amendments of 1986.

Vietnam Era Veterans' Readjustment Assistance Act of 1974

(P.L. 93–508, approved December 3, 1974; as last amended by P.L. 98–543, effective October 24, 1984)

Chapter 42. Employment and Training of Disabled and Vietnam Era Veterans

§ 2011. Definitions

[Sec. 2011] As used in this chapter—
(1) The term "special disabled veteran" means—
   (A) a veteran who is entitled to compensation (or who but for the receipt of military retired pay would be entitled to compensation) under laws administered by the Veterans' Administration for a disability (i) rated at 30 percent or more, or (ii) rated at 10 or 20 percent in the case of a veteran who has been determined under section 1506 of this title to have a serious employment handicap; or
   (B) a person who was discharged or released from active duty because of a service-connected disability.
(2)(A) Subject to subparagraph (B) of this paragraph, the term "veteran of the Vietnam era" means an eligible veteran any part of whose active military, naval, or air service was during the Vietnam era.
   (B) No veteran may be considered to be a veteran of the Vietnam era under this paragraph after December 31, 1991.
(3) The term "disabled veteran" means (A) a veteran who is entitled to compensation (or who but for the receipt of military retired pay would be entitled to compensation) under laws administered by the Veterans' Administration, or (B) a person who was discharged or released from active duty because of a service-connected disability.
(4) The term "eligible veteran" means a person who (A) served on active duty for a period of more than 180 days and was discharged or

released therefrom with other than a dishonorable discharge, or (B) was discharged or released from active duty because of a service-connected disability.

(5) The term "department or agency" means any agency of the Federal Government or the District of Columbia, including any Executive agency as defined in section 105 of title 5 and the United States Postal Service and the Postal Rate Commission, and the term "department, agency, or instrumentality in the executive branch" includes the United States Postal Service and the Postal Rate Commission.

§ 2012. Veterans' employment emphasis under Federal contracts

[Sec. 2012] (a) Any contract in the amount of $10,000 or more entered into by any department or agency for the procurement of personal property and non-personal services (including construction) for the United States, shall contain a provision requiring that the party contracting with the United States shall take affirmative action to employ and advance in employment qualified special disabled veterans and veterans of the Vietnam era. The provisions of this section shall apply to any subcontract entered into by a prime contractor in carrying out any contract for the procurement of personal property and nonpersonal services (including construction) for the United States. In addition to requiring affirmative action to employ such veterans under such contracts and subcontracts and in order to promote the implementation of such requirement, the President shall implement the provisions of this section by promulgating regulations which shall require that (1) each such contractor undertake in such contract to list immediately with the appropriate local employment service office all of its suitable employment openings, and (2) each such local office shall give such veterans priority in referral to such employment openings.

(b) If any special disabled veteran or veteran of the Vietnam era believes any contractor of the United States has failed to comply or refuses to comply with the provisions of the contractor's contract relating to the employment of veterans, the veteran may file a complaint with the Secretary of Labor, who shall promptly investigate such complaint and take appropriate action in accordance with the terms of the contract and applicable laws and regulations.

(c) The Secretary shall include as part of the annual report required by section 2007(c) of this title the number of complaints filed pursuant to subsection (b) of this section, the actions taken thereon and the resolutions thereof. Such report shall also include the number of contractors listing suitable employment openings, the nature, types, and number of positions listed and the number of veterans receiving priority pursuant to subsection (a)(2) of this section.

(d)(1) Each contractor to whom subsection (a) of this section applies shall, in accordance with regulations which the Secretary shall prescribe, report at least annually to the Secretary on

  (A) the number of employees in the work force of such contractor, by job category and hiring location, who are veterans of the Vietnam era or special disabled veterans; and

  (B) the total number of new employees hired by the contractor during the period covered by the report and the number of such employees who are veterans of the Vietnam era or special disabled veterans.

(2) The Secretary shall ensure that the administration of the reporting requirement under paragraph (1) of this subsection is coordinated with respect to any requirement for the contractor to make any other report to the Secretary.

§ 2013. Eligibility requirements for veterans under Federal employment and training programs

[Sec. 2013] Any (1) amounts received as pay or allowances by any person while serving on active duty, (2) period of time during which such person served on such active duty, and (3) amounts received under chapters 11, 13, 31, 34, 35, and 36 of this title by an eligible veteran, and any amounts received by an eligible person under chapter 13 and 35 of such title, shall be disregarded in determining the needs or qualifications of participants in any public service employment program, any emergency employment program, any job training program assisted under the Economic Opportunity Act of 1964, any employment or training program assisted under the Comprehensive Employment and Training Act, or any other employment or training (or related) program financed in whole or in part with Federal funds.

§ 2014. Employment within the Federal Government

[Sec. 2014] (a)(1) It is the policy of the United States and the purpose of this section to promote the maximum of employment and job advancement opportunities within the Federal Government for qualified disabled veterans and veterans of the Vietnam era.

(2) For the purposes of this section, the term "agency" means a department, agency, or instrumentality in the executive branch.

(b)(1) To further the policy stated in subsection (a) of this section, veterans of the Vietnam era shall be eligible, in accordance with regulations which the Office of Personnel Management shall prescribe, for veterans readjustment appointments, and for subsequent career-conditional appointments, under the terms and conditions specified in Executive Order Numbered 11521 (March 26, 1970), except that—

(A) such an appointment may be made up to and including the level GS-9 or its equivalent;

(B) a veteran of the Vietnam era shall be eligible for such an appointment without any time limitation with respect to eligibility for such an appointment; and

(C) a veteran of the Vietnam era who is entitled to disability compensation under the laws administered by the Veterans' Administration or whose discharge or release from active duty was for a disability incurred or aggravated in line of duty shall be eligible for such an appointment without regard to the number of years of education completed by such veteran; and

(D) a veteran given an appointment under the authority of this subsection whose employment under the appointment is terminated within one year after the date of such appointment shall have the same right to appeal that termination to the Merit Systems Protection Board as a career or career-conditional employee has during the first year of employment.

(2) No veterans readjustment appointment may be made under authority of this subsection after December 31, 1989.

(c) Each agency shall include in its affirmative action plan for the hiring, placement, and advancement of handicapped individuals in such agency as required by section 501(b) of the Rehabilitation Act of 1973 (29 U.S.C. 791(b)), a separate specification of plans (in accordance with regulations which the Office of Personnel Management shall prescribe in consultation with the Administrator, the Secretary of Labor, and the Secretary of Health and Human Services, consistent with the purposes, provisions, and priorities of such Act) to promote and carry out such affirmative action with respect to disabled veterans in order to achieve the purpose of this section.

(d) The Office of Personnel Management shall be responsible for the review and evaluation of the implementation of this section and the activities of each agency to carry out the purpose and provisions of this section. The Office shall periodically obtain (on at least an annual basis) information on the implementation of this section by each agency and on the activities of each agency to carry out the purpose and provisions of this section. The information obtained shall include specification of the use and extent of appointments made by each agency under subsection (b) of this section and the results of the plans required under subsection (c) of this section.

(e)(1) The Office of Personnel Management shall submit to the Congress annually a report on activities carried out under this section. Each such report shall include the following information with respect to each agency:

(A) The number of appointments made under subsection (b) of this section since the last such report and the grade levels in which such appointments were made.

(B) The number of individuals receiving appointments under such subsection whose appointments were converted to career conditional appointments, or whose employment under such an appointment has terminated, since the last such report, together with a complete listing of categories of causes of appointment terminations and the number of such individuals whose employment has terminated falling into each such category.

(C) The number of such terminations since the last such report that were initiated by the agency involved and the number of such terminations since the last such report that were initiated by the individual involved.

(D) A description of the education and training programs in which individuals appointed under such subsection are participating at the time of such report.

(2) Information shown for an agency under clauses (A) through (D) of paragraph (1) of this subsection—

(A) shall be shown for all veterans; and

(B) shall be shown separately (i) for veterans of the Vietnam era who are entitled to disability compensation under the laws administered by the Veterans' Administration or whose discharge or release from active duty was for a disability incurred or aggravated in line of duty, and (ii) for other veterans.

(f) Notwithstanding section 2011 of this title, the terms "veteran" and "disabled veteran" as used in subsection (a) of this section shall have the meaning provided for under generally applicable civil service law and regulations.

(g) To further the policy stated in subsection (a) of this section, the Administrator may give preference to qualified special disabled veterans and qualified veterans of the Vietnam era for employment in the Veterans' Administration as veterans' benefits counselors and veterans' claims examiners and in positions to provide the outreach services required under section 241 of this title, to serve as veterans' representatives at certain educational institutions as provided in section 243 of this title, or to provide readjustment counseling under section 612A of this title to veterans of the Vietnam era.

5

Wage-Hour Laws

Fair Labor Standards Act of 1938

(P.L. 75–718, effective October 24, 1938; as last amended
by P.L. 99–486, approved October 16, 1986)

§ 201. Short title

[Sec. 1] This Act may be cited as the "Fair Labor Standards Act of 1938."

§ 202. Congressional finding and declaration of policy

[Sec. 2] (a) The Congress hereby finds that the existence, in industries engaged in commerce or in the production of goods for commerce, of labor conditions detrimental to the maintenance of the minimum standard of living necessary for health, efficiency, and general well-being of workers (1) causes commerce and the channels and instrumentalities of commerce to be used to spread and perpetuate such labor conditions among the workers of the several States; (2) burdens commerce and the free flow of goods in commerce; (3) constitutes an unfair method of competition in commerce; (4) leads to labor disputes burdening and obstructing commerce and the free flow of goods in commerce; and (5) interferes with the orderly and fair marketing of goods in commerce. That Congress further finds that the employment of persons in domestic service in households affects commerce.

(b) It is hereby declared to be the policy of this Act, through the exercise by Congress of its power to regulate commerce among the several States and with foreign nations, to correct and as rapidly as practicable to eliminate the conditions above referred to in such industries without substantially curtailing employment or earning power.

§ 203. Definitions

[Sec. 3] As used in this Act—

(a) "Person" means an individual, partnership, association, corporation, business trust, legal representative, or any organized group of persons.

(b) "Commerce" means trade, commerce, transportation, transmission, or communication among the several States or between any State and any place outside thereof.

(c) "State" means any State of the United States or the District of Columbia or any Territory or possession of the United States.

(d) "Employer" includes any person acting directly or indirectly in the interest of an employer in relation to an employee and includes a public agency, but does not include any labor organization (other than when acting as an employer) or anyone acting in the capacity of officer or agent of such labor organization.

(e)(1) Except as provided in paragraphs (2), (3), and (4), the term "employee" means any individual employed by an employer.

(2) In the case of an individual employed by a public agency such term means—

    (A) any individual employed by the Government of the United States—

        (i) as a civilian in the military departments (as defined in section 102 of title 5, United States Code),

        (ii) in any executive agency (as defined in section 105 of such title),

        (iii) in any unit of the legislative or judicial branch of the Government which has positions in the competitive service,

        (iv) in a nonappropriated fund instrumentality under the jurisdiction of the Armed Forces, or

        (v) in the Library of Congress;

    (B) any individual employed by the United States Postal Service or the Postal Rate Commission; and

    (C) any individual employed by a State, political subdivision of a State, or an interstate governmental agency, other than such an individual—

        (i) who is not subject to the civil service laws of the State, political subdivision, or agency which employs him; and

        (ii) who—

            (I) holds a public elective office of that State, political subdivision, or agency,

            (II) is selected by the holder of such an office to be a member of his personal staff,

            (III) is appointed by such an officeholder to serve on a policy-making level,

            (IV) is an immediate adviser to such an officeholder with respect to the constitutional or legal powers of his office, or

            (V) is an employee in the legislative branch or legislative body of that State, political subdivision, or agency and is not employed by the legislative library of such State, political subdivision, or agency.

(3) For purposes of subsection (u), such term does not include any individual employed by an employer engaged in agriculture if such individual is the parent, spouse, child, or other member of the

employer's immediate family.

(4)(A) The term "employee" does not include any individual who volunteers to perform services for a public agency which is a State, a political subdivision of a State, or an interstate governmental agency, if—

    (i) the individual receives no compensation or is paid expenses, reasonable benefits, or a nominal fee to perform the services for which the individual volunteered; and

    (ii) such services are not the same type of services which the individual is employed to perform for such public agency.

(B) An employee of a public agency which is a State, political subdivision of a State, or an interstate governmental agency may volunteer to perform services for any other State, political subdivision, or interstate governmental agency, including a State, political subdivision or agency with which the employing State, political subdivision, or agency has a mutual aid agreement.

(f) "Agriculture" includes farming in all its branches and among other things includes the cultivation and tillage of the soil, dairying, the production, cultivation, growing, and harvesting of any agricultural or horticultural commodities (including commodities defined as agricultural commodities in section 15(g) of the Agricultural Marketing Act, as amended), the raising of livestock, and any practices (including any forestry, or lumbering operations) bees, fur-bearing animals, or poultry, performed by a farmer or on a farm as an incident to or in conjunction with such farming operations, including preparation for market, delivery to storage or to market or to carriers for transportation to market.

(g) "Employ" includes to suffer or permit to work.

(h) "Industry" means a trade, business, industry, or other activity, or branch or group thereof, in which individuals are gainfully employed.

(i) "Goods" means goods (including ships and marine equipment), wares, products, commodities, merchandise, or articles or subjects of commerce of any character, or any part or ingredient thereof, but does not include goods after their delivery into the actual physical possession of the ultimate consumer thereof other than a producer, manufacturer, or processor thereof.

(j) "Produced" means produced, manufactured, mined, handled, or in any other manner worked on in any State; and for the purposes of this Act an employee shall be deemed to have been engaged in the production of goods if such employee was employed in producing, manufacturing, mining, handling, transporting, or in any other manner working on such goods, or in any closely related process or occupation directly essential to the production thereof, in any State.

(k) "Sale" or "sell" includes any sale, exchange, contract to sell, consignment for sale, shipment for sale, or other disposition.

(l) "Oppressive child labor" means a condition of employment under which (1) any employee under the age of sixteen years is employed by an employer (other than a parent or a person standing in place of a parent employing his own child or a child in his custody under the age of sixteen years in an occupation other than manufacturing or mining or an occupation found by the Secretary of Labor to be particularly hazardous for the employment of children between the ages of sixteen and eighteen years or detrimental to their health or well-being) in any occupation, or (2) any employee between the ages of sixteen and eighteen years is employed by an employer in any occupation which the Secretary of Labor shall find and by order declare to be particularly hazardous for the employment of children between such ages or detrimental to their health or well-being; but oppressive child labor shall not be deemed to exist by virtue of the employment in any occupation of any person with respect to whom the employer shall have on file an unexpired certificate issued and held pursuant to regulations of the Secretary of Labor certifying that such person is above the oppressive child-labor age. The Secretary of Labor shall provide by regulation or by order that the employment of employees between the ages of fourteen and sixteen years in occupations other than manufacturing and mining shall not be deemed to constitute oppressive child labor if and to the extent that the Secretary of Labor determines that such employment is confined to periods which will not interfere with their schooling and to conditions which will not interfere with their health and well-being.

(m) "Wage" paid to any employee includes the reasonable cost, as determined by the Administrator, to the employer of furnishing such employee with board, lodging, or other facilities, if such board, lodging, or other facilities are customarily furnished by such employer to his employee: *Provided*, That the cost of board, lodging, or other facilities shall not be included as a part of the wage paid to any employee to the extent it is excluded therefrom under the terms of a bona fide collective-bargaining agreement applicable to the particular employee: *Provided further*, That the Secretary is authorized to determine the fair value of such board, lodging, or other facilities for defined classes of employees and in defined areas, based on average cost to the employer or to groups of employers similarly situated, or average value to groups of employees, or other appropriate measures of fair value. Such evaluations, where applicable and pertinent, shall be used in lieu of actual measure of cost in determining the wage paid to any employee. In determining the wage of a tipped employee, the amount paid such employee by his employer shall be deemed to be increased on account of tips by an amount determined by the employer, but not by an amount in excess of 40 per centum of the applicable minimum wage rate, except that the amount of the increase on account of tips determined by the employer may not exceed the value of the tips actually received by the employee. The previous sentence shall not apply with respect to any tipped employee unless (1) such employee has been informed by the employer of the provisions of this subsection, and (2) all tips received by such employee have been retained by the employee, except that this subsection shall not be construed to prohibit the pooling of tips among employees who customarily and regularly receive tips.

(n) "Resale" shall not include the sale of goods to be used in residential or farm building construction, repair, or maintenance: *Provided*, That the sale is recognized as a bona fide retail sale in the industry.

(o) Hours Worked—In determining for the purposes of sections 6 and 7 the hours for which an employee is employed, there shall be excluded any time spent in changing clothes or washing at the beginning or end of each workday which was excluded from measured working time during the week involved by the express terms of or by custom or practice under a bona fide collective-bargaining agreement applicable to the particular employee.

(p) "American vessel" includes any vessel which is documented or numbered under the laws of the United States.

(q) "Secretary" means the Secretary of Labor.

(r) "Enterprise" means the related activities performed (either through unified operation or common control) by any person or persons for a common business purpose, and includes all such activities whether performed in one or more establishments or by one or more corporate or other organizational units including departments of an establishment operated through leasing arrangements, but shall not include the related activities performed for such enterprise by an independent contractor; *Provided*, That within the meaning of this subsection, a retail or service establishment which is under independent ownership shall not be deemed to be so operated or controlled as to be other than a separate and distinct enterprise by reason of any arrangement, which includes, but is not necessarily limited to, an agreement, (1) that it will sell, or sell only, certain goods specified by a particular manufacturer, distributor, or advertiser, or (2) that it will join with other such establishments in the same industry for the purpose of collective purchasing, or (3) that it will have the exclusive right to sell the goods or use the brand name of a manufacturer, distributor, or advertiser within a specified area, or by reason of the fact that it occupies premises leased to it by a person who also leases premises to other retail or service establishments. For purposes of this subsection, the activities performed by any person or persons—

    (1) in connection with the operation of a hospital, an institution primarily engaged in the care of the sick, the aged, the mentally ill or defective who reside on the premises of such institution, a school for mentally or physically handicapped or gifted children, a preschool, elementary or secondary school, or an institution of higher education (regardless of whether or not such hospital, institution, or school is public or private or operated for profit or not for profit), or

    (2) in connection with the operation of a street, suburban or interurban electric railway, or local trolley or motorbus carrier, if the rates and services of such railway or carrier are subject to regulation by a State or local agency (regardless of whether or not such railway or carrier is

public or private or operated for profit or not for profit), or

(3) in connection with the activities of a public agency,

shall be deemed to be activities performed for a business purpose.

(s) "Enterprise engaged in commerce or in the production of goods for commerce" means an enterprise which has employees engaged in commerce or the production of goods for commerce or employees handling, selling, or otherwise working on goods or materials that have been moved in or produced for commerce by any person, and which—

(1) during the period February 1, 1967, through January 31, 1969, is an enterprise whose annual gross volume of sales made or business done is not less than $500,000 (exclusive of excise taxes at the retail level which are separately stated) or is a gasoline service establishment whose annual gross volume of sales is not less than $250,000 (exclusive of excise taxes at the retail level which are separately stated), and beginning February 1, 1969, is an enterprise other than an enterprise which is comprised exclusively of retail or service establishments and which is described in paragraph (2), whose annual gross volume of sales made or business done is not less than $250,000 (exclusive of excise taxes at the retail level which are separately stated);

(2) is an enterprise which is comprised exclusively of one or more retail or service establishments, as defined in section 13(a)(2), and whose annual gross volume of sales made or business done is not less than $250,000 (exclusive of excise taxes at the retail level which are separately stated) beginning July 1, 1978, whose annual gross volume of sales made or business done is not less than $275,000 (exclusive of excise taxes at the retail level which are separately stated), beginning July 1, 1980, whose annual gross volume of sales made or business done is not less than $325,000 (exclusive of excise taxes at the retail level which are separately stated) and after December 31, 1981, whose annual gross volume of sales made or business done is not less than $362,500 (exclusive of excise taxes at the retail level which are separately stated); except that an employer who is required to pay the minimum wage on the day before the date of enactment of the Fair Labor Standards Amendments of 1977 and who would not be so required subsequent to enactment of the Fair Labor Standards Amendments of 1977 may not decrease the wages or increase the maximum hours required by this Act of any employee who received the minimum wage applicable during the time at which the employer was required to pay the minimum wage;

(3) is engaged in laundering, cleaning, or repairing clothing or fabrics;

(4) is engaged in the business of construction or reconstruction, or both;

(5) is engaged in the operation of a hospital, an institution primarily engaged in the care of the sick, the aged, the mentally ill or defective who reside on the premises of such institution, a school for mentally or physically handicapped or gifted children, a preschool, elementary or

secondary school, or an institution of higher education (regardless of whether or not such hospital, institution, or school is public or private or operated for profit or not for profit); or

(6) is an activity of a public agency. Any establishment which has as its only regular employee the owner thereof or the parent, spouse, child or other member of the immediate family of such owner shall not be considered to be an enterprise engaged in commerce or in the production of goods for commerce or a part of such an enterprise, and the sales of such establishment shall not be included for the purpose of determining the annual gross volume of sales of any enterprise for the purpose of this subsection. The employees of an enterprise which is a public agency shall for purposes of this subsection be deemed to be employees engaged in commerce, or in the production of goods for commerce, or employees handling, selling, or otherwise working on goods or materials that have been moved in or produced for commerce. Notwithstanding paragraph (2), an enterprise which is comprised of one or more retail or service establishments, which on June 30, 1978, was subject to section 6(a)(1), and which because of a change in the dollar volume standard in such paragraph prescribed by the Fair Labor Standards Amendments of 1977 is not subject to such section shall, if its annual gross volume of sales made or business done is not less than $250,000 (exclusive of excise taxes at the retail level which are separately stated), pay its employees not less than the minimum wage in effect under such section on the day before such change takes effect and shall pay its employees in accordance with section 7. A violation of the preceding sentence shall be considered a violation of section 6 or 7, as the case may be.

(t) "Tipped employee" means any employee engaged in an occupation in which he customarily and regularly receives more than $20 [$30 effective January 1, 1978] a month in tips.

(u) "Man-day" means any day during which an employee performs any agricultural labor for not less than one hour.

(v) "Elementary school" means a day or residential school which provides elementary education, as determined under State law.

(w) "Secondary school" means a day or residential school which provides secondary education, as determined under State law.

(x) "Public agency" means the Government of the United States; the government of a State or political subdivision thereof; any agency of the United States (including the United States Postal Service and Postal Rate Commission), a State, or a political subdivision of a State; or any interstate governmental agency.

§ 204. Administration

[Sec. 4] (a) There is hereby created in the Department of Labor a Wage and Hour Division which shall be under the direction of an Administrator to be known as the Administrator of the Wage and Hour Division (in this Act referred to as the "Administrator"). The Administrator shall be appointed by the President, by and with the advice and consent of the Senate.

(b) The Administrator may, subject to the civil service laws, appoint such employees as he deems necessary to carry out his functions and duties under this Act and shall fix their compensation in accordance with chapter 51 and subchapter III of chapter 53 of Title V. The Administrator may establish and utilize such regional, local or other agencies, and utilize such voluntary and uncompensated services, as may from time to time be needed. Attorneys appointed under this section may appear for and represent the Administrator in any litigation, but all such litigation shall be subject to the direction and control of the Attorney General. In the appointment, selection, classification, and promotion of officers and employees of the Administrator, no political test or qualification shall be permitted or given consideration, but all such appointments and promotions shall be given and made on the basis of merit and efficiency.

(c) The principal office of the Administrator shall be in the District of Columbia, but he or his duly authorized representative may exercise any or all of his powers in any place.

(d)(1) The Secretary shall submit annually in January a report to the Congress covering his activities for the preceding year and including such information, data, and recommendations for further legislation in connection with the matters covered by this Act as he may find advisable. Such report shall contain an evaluation and appraisal by the Secretary of the minimum wages and overtime coverage established by this Act, together with his recommendations to the Congress. In making such evaluation and appraisal, the Secretary shall take into consideration any changes which may have occurred in the cost of living and in productivity and the level of wages in manufacturing, the ability of employers to absorb wage increases, and such other factors as he may deem pertinent. Such report shall also include a summary of the special certificates issued under section 14(b).

(2) The Secretary shall conduct studies on the justification or lack thereof for each of the special exemptions set forth in section 13 of this Act, and the extent to which such exemptions apply to employees of establishments described in subsection (g) of such section and the economic effects of the application of such exemptions to such employees. The Secretary shall submit a report of his findings and recommendations to the Congress with respect to the studies conducted under this paragraph not later than January 1, 1976.

(3) The Secretary shall conduct a continuing study on means to prevent curtailment of employment opportunities for manpower groups which have had historically high incidences of unemployment (such as disadvantaged minorities, youth, elderly, and such other groups as the Secretary may designate). The first report of the results of such study

shall be transmitted to the Congress not later than one year after the effective date of the Fair Labor Standards Amendments of 1974. Subsequent reports on such study shall be transmitted to the Congress at two-year intervals after such effective date. Each such report shall include suggestions respecting the Secretary's authority under section 14 of this Act.

(e) Whenever the Secretary has reason to believe that in any industry under this Act the competition of foreign producers in United States markets or in markets abroad, or both, has resulted, or is likely to result, in increased unemployment in the United States, he shall undertake an investigation to gain full information with respect to the matter. If he determines such increased unemployment has in fact resulted, or is in fact likely to result, from such competition, he shall make a full and complete report of his findings and determinations to the President and to the Congress: *Provided,* That he may also include in such report information on the increased employment resulting from additional exports in any industry under this Act as he may determine to be pertinent to such report.

(f) The Secretary is authorized to enter into an agreement with the Librarian of Congress with respect to individuals employed in the Library of Congress to provide for the carrying out of the Secretary's functions under this Act with respect to such individuals. Notwithstanding any other provision of this Act, or any other law, the Civil Service Commission is authorized to administer the provisions of this Act with respect to any individual employed by the United States (other than an individual employed in the Library of Congress, United States Postal Service, Postal Rate Commission, or the Tennessee Valley Authority). Nothing in this subsection shall be construed to affect the right of an employee to bring an action for unpaid minimum wages, or unpaid overtime compensation, and liquidated damages under section 16(b) of this Act.

§ 205. Special industry committees for Puerto Rico and the Virgin Islands

[Sec. 5] (a) The Administrator shall as soon as practicable appoint a special industry committee to recommend the minimum rate or rates of wages to be paid under section 6 to employees in Puerto Rico or the Virgin Islands, engaged in commerce or in the production of goods for commerce, or employed in any enterprise engaged in commerce or in the production of goods for commerce, or the Administrator may appoint separate industry committees to recommend the minimum rate or rates of wages to be paid under section 6 to employees therein engaged in commerce or in the production of goods for commerce or employed in any enterprise engaged in commerce or in the production of goods for commerce in particular industries. An industry committee appointed under this subsection shall be composed of residents of such island or islands where the employees with respect to whom such committee was appointed are employed and residents of the United States outside of Puerto Rico and the Virgin Islands. In determining the minimum rate or rates of wages to be paid, and in determining classifications, such industry committees shall be subject to the provisions of section 8.

(b) An industry committee shall be appointed by the Administrator without regard to any other provisions of law regarding the appointment and compensation of employees of the United States. It shall include a number of disinterested persons representing the public, one of whom the Administrator shall designate as chairman, a like number of persons representing employees in the industry, and a like number representing employers in the industry. In the appointment of the persons representing each group, the Administrator shall give due regard to the geographical regions in which the industry is carried on.

(c) Two-thirds of the members of an industry committee shall constitute a quorum, and the decision of the committee shall require a vote of not less than a majority of all its members. Members of an industry committee shall receive as compensation for their services a reasonable per diem, which the Administrator shall by rules and regulations prescribe, for each day actually spent in the work of the committee, and shall in addition be reimbursed for their necessary traveling and other expenses. The Administrator shall furnish the committee with adequate legal, stenographic, clerical, and other assistance, and shall by rules and regulations prescribe the procedure to be followed by the committee.

(d) The Administrator shall submit to an industry committee from time to time such data as he may have available on the matters referred to it, and shall cause to be brought before it in connection with such matters any witnesses whom he deems material. An industry committee may summon other witnesses or call upon the Administrator to furnish additional information to aid it in its deliberations.

(e) The provisions of this section, section 6(c), and section 8 shall not apply with respect to the minimum wage rate of any employee employed in Puerto Rico or the Virgin Islands (1) by the United States or by the government of the Virgin Islands, (2) by an establishment which is a hotel, motel, or restaurant, or (3) by any other retail or service establishment which employs such employee primarily in connection with the preparation or offering of food or beverages for human consumption, either on the premises, or by such services as catering, banquet, box lunch, or curb or counter service, to the public, to employees, or to members or guests of members of clubs. The minimum wage rate of such an employee shall be determined under this Act in the same manner as the minimum wage rate for employees employed in a State of the United States is determined under this Act. As used in the preceding sentence, the term "State" does not include a territory or possession of the United States.

§ 206. Minimum wage

[Sec. 6] (a) Every employer shall pay to each of his employees who in any workweek is engaged in commerce or in the production of goods for commerce, or is employed in an enterprise engaged in commerce or in the production of goods for commerce, wages at the following rates:

(1) not less than $2.65 an hour during the year beginning January 1, 1978, not less than $2.90 an hour during the year beginning January 1, 1979; not less than $3.10 an hour during the year beginning January 1, 1980; and not less than $3.35 an hour after December 31, 1980, except as otherwise provided in this section;

(2) if such employee is a home worker in Puerto Rico or the Virgin Islands, not less than the minimum piece rate prescribed by regulation or order; or, if no such minimum piece rate is in effect, any piece rate adopted by such employer which shall yield, to the proportion or class of employees prescribed by regulation or order, not less than the applicable minimum hourly wage rate. Such minimum piece rates or employer piece rates shall be commensurate with, and shall be paid in lieu of, the minimum hourly wage rate applicable under the provisions of this section. The Administrator, or his authorized representative, shall have power to make such regulations or orders as are necessary or appropriate to carry out any of the provisions of this paragraph, including the power, without limiting the generality of the foregoing, to define any operation or occupation which is performed by such home work employees in Puerto Rico or the Virgin Islands; to establish minimum piece rates for any operation or occupation so defined; to prescribe the methods and procedure for ascertaining and promulgating minimum piece rates; to prescribe standards for employer piece rates, including the proportion or class of employees who shall receive not less than the minimum hourly wage rate; to define the term "home worker"; and to prescribe the conditions under which employers, agents, contractors, and subcontractors shall cause goods to be produced by home workers;

(3) if such employee is employed in American Samoa, in lieu of the rate or rates provided by this subsection or subsection (b), not less than the applicable rate established by the Secretary of Labor in accordance with recommendations of a special industry committee or committees which he shall appoint in the same manner and pursuant to the same provisions as are applicable to the special industry committees provided for Puerto Rico and the Virgin Islands by this Act as amended from time to time. Each such committee shall have the same powers and duties and shall apply the same standards with respect to the

application of the provisions of this Act to employees employed in American Samoa as pertain to special industry committees established under section 5 with respect to employees employed in Puerto Rico or the Virgin Islands. The minimum wage rate thus established shall not exceed the rates prescribed in paragraph (1) of this subsection;

(4) if such employee is employed as a seaman on an American vessel, not less than the rate which will provide to the employee, for the period covered by the wage payment, wages equal to compensation at the hourly rate prescribed by paragraph (1) of this subsection for all hours during such period when he was actually on duty (including periods aboard ship when the employee was on watch or was, at the direction of a superior officer, performing work or standing by, but not including off-duty periods which are provided pursuant to the employment agreement); or

(5) if such employee is employed in agriculture, not less than the minimum wage in effect under paragraph (1) after December 31, 1977.

(b) Every employer shall pay to each of his employees (other than an employee to whom subsection (a)(5) applies) who in any workweek is engaged in commerce or in the production of goods for commerce, or is employed in an enterprise engaged in commerce or in the production of goods for commerce, and who in such workweek is brought within the purview of this section by the amendments made to this Act by the Fair Labor Standards Amendments of 1966, title IX of the Education Amendments of 1972, or the Fair Labor Standards Amendments of 1974, wages at the following rate: Effective after December 31, 1977, not less than the minimum wage rate in effect under subsection (a)(1).

(c)(1) The rate or rates provided by subsection (a)(1) of this section shall be superseded in the case of any employee in Puerto Rico or the Virgin Islands only for so long as and insofar as such employee is covered by a wage order, (A) heretofore or hereafter issued by the Secretary pursuant to the recommendations of a special industry committee appointed pursuant to section 5, and (B) which prescribes the wage order rate which is less than the wage rate in effect under subsection (a)(1).

(2)(A) Each wage order rate under a wage order described in paragraph (1) which on December 31, 1977, is at least $2 an hour shall, except as provided in paragraph (3), be increased—

(i) effective January 1, 1978, by $0.25 an hour or by such greater amount as may be recommended by a special industry committee under section 8,

(ii) effective January 1, 1979, and January 1, of each succeeding year, by $0.30 an hour or by such greater amount as may be so recommended by such special industry committee.

(B) Each wage order rate under a wage order described in paragraph (1) which on December 31, 1977, is less than $2 an hour shall, except as provided in paragraph (3), be increased—

   (i) effective January 1, 1978, by $0.20 an hour or by such greater amount as may be recommended by a special industry committee under section 8,

   (ii) effective January 1, 1979, and January 1 of each succeeding year—

     (I) until such wage order rate is not less than $2.30 an hour, by $0.25 an hour or by such greater amount as may be so recommended by a special industry committee, and

     (II) if such wage order rate is not less than $2.30 an hour, by $0.30 an hour or by such greater amount as may be so recommended by a special industry committee.

(C) In the case of any employee in agriculture who is covered by a wage order issued by the Secretary pursuant to the recommendation of a special industry committee appointed pursuant to section 5, to whom the rate or rates prescribed by section (a)(5) of this section would otherwise apply, and whose hourly wage is increased above the wage rate prescribed by such wage order by a subsidy (or income supplement) paid, in whole or in part, by the government of Puerto Rico, the applicable increases prescribed by subparagraph (A) or (B) shall be applied to the sum of the wage rate in effect under such wage order and the amount by which the employee's hourly wage is increased by the subsidy (or income supplement) above the wage rate in effect under such wage order.

(3) If the wage rate of an employee is to be increased under this subsection to a wage rate which equals or is greater than the wage rate under subsection (a)(1) which, but for paragraph (1) of this subsection, would be applicable to such employee, this subsection shall be inapplicable to such employee and the applicable rate under subsection (a)(1) shall apply to such employee.

(4) Each minimum wage rate prescribed by or under paragraph (2) shall be in effect unless such minimum wage rate has been superseded by a wage order (issued by the Secretary pursuant to the recommendation of a special industry committee convened under section 8) fixing a higher minimum wage rate.

(d)(1) No employer having employees subject to any provisions of this section shall discriminate, within any establishment in which such employees are employed, between employees on the basis of sex by paying wages to employees in such establishment at a rate less than the rate at which he pays wages to employees of the opposite sex in such establishment for equal work on jobs the performance of which requires equal skill, effort, and responsibility, and which are performed under similar working conditions, except where such payment is made pursuant to (i) a seniority system; (ii) a merit system; (iii) a system which measures earnings by quantity or quality of production; or (iv) a differential based on any other factor other than sex:

Provided, That an employer who is paying a wage rate differential in violation of this subsection shall not, in order to comply with the provisions of this subsection, reduce the wage rate of any employee.

(2) No labor organization or its agents, representing employees of an employer having employees subject to any provisions of this section shall cause or attempt to cause such an employer to discriminate against an employee in violation of paragraph (1) of this subsection.

(3) For purposes of administration and enforcement, any amounts owing to any employee which have been withheld in violation of this subsection shall be deemed to be unpaid minimum wages or unpaid overtime compensation under this Act.

(4) As used in this subsection, the term "labor organization" means any organization of any kind, or any agency or employee representation committee or plan, in which employees participate and which exists for the purpose, in whole or in part, of dealing with employers concerning grievances, labor disputes, wages, rates of pay, hours of employment, or conditions of work.

(e)(1) Notwithstanding the provisions of section 13 of this Act (except subsections (a)(1) and (f) thereof), every employer providing any contract services (other than linen supply services) under a contract with the United States or any subcontract thereunder shall pay to each of his employees whose rate of pay is not governed by the Service Contract Act of 1965 (41 U.S.C. 351–357) or to whom subsection (a)(1) of this section is not applicable, wages at rates not less than the rates provided for in subsection (b) of this section.

(2) Notwithstanding the provisions of section 13 of this Act (except subsections (a)(1) and (f) thereof) and the provisions of the Service Contract Act of 1965, every employer in an establishment providing linen supply services to the United States under a contract with the United States or any subcontract thereunder shall pay to each of his employees in such establishment wages at rates not less than those prescribed in subsection (b), except that if more than 50 per centum of the gross annual dollar volume of sales made or business done by such establishment is derived from providing such linen supply services under any such contracts or subcontracts, such employer shall pay to each of his employees in such establishment wages at rates not less than those prescribed in subsection (a)(1) of this section.

(f) Any employee—(1) who in any workweek is employed in domestic service in a household shall be paid wages at a rate not less than the wage rate in effect under section 6(b) unless such employee's compensation for such service would not because of section 209(g) of the Social Security Act constitute wages for the purposes of title II of such Act, or

(2) who in any workweek—

(A) is employed in domestic service in one or more households, and

(B) is so employed for more than 8 hours in the aggregate,

shall be paid wages for such employment in such workweek at a rate not less than the wage rate in effect under section 6(b).

§ 207. Maximum hours

[Sec. 7] (a)(1) Except as otherwise provided in this section, no employer shall employ any of his employees who in any workweek is engaged in commerce or in the production of goods for commerce, or is employed in an enterprise engaged in commerce or in the production of goods for commerce, for a workweek longer than forty hours unless such employee receives compensation for his employment in excess of the hours above specified at a rate not less than one and one-half times the regular rate at which he is employed.

(2) No employer shall employ any of his employees who in any workweek is engaged in commerce or in the production of goods for commerce, or is employed in an enterprise engaged in commerce or in the production of goods for commerce, and who in such workweek is brought within the purview of this subsection by the amendments made to this Act by the Fair Labor Standards Amendments of 1966—

(A) for a workweek longer than forty-four hours during the first year from the effective date of the Fair Labor Standards Amendments of 1966,

(B) for a workweek longer than forty-two hours during the second year from such date, or

(C) for a workweek longer than forty hours after the expiration of the second year from such date,

unless such employee receives compensation for his employment in excess of the hours above specified at a rate not less than one and one-half times the regular rate at which he is employed.

(b) No employer shall be deemed to have violated subsection (a) of this section by employing any employee for a workweek in excess of that specified in such subsection without paying the compensation for overtime employment prescribed therein if such employee is so employed—

(1) in pursuance of an agreement, made as a result of collective bargaining by representatives of employees certified as bona fide by the National Labor Relations Board, which provides that no employee shall be employed more than one thousand and forty hours during any period of twenty-six consecutive weeks; or

(2) in pursuance of an agreement, made as a result of collective bargaining by representatives of employees certified as bona fide by the National Labor Relations Board, which provides that during a specified period of fifty-two consecutive weeks the employee shall be employed not more than two thousand two hundred and forty hours and shall be guaranteed not less than one thousand eight hundred and

forty hours (or not less than forty-six weeks at the normal number of hours worked per week, but not less than thirty hours per week) and not more than two thousand and eighty hours of employment for which he shall receive compensation for all hours guaranteed or worked at rates not less than those applicable under the agreement to the work performed and for all hours in excess of the guaranty which are also in excess of the maximum workweek applicable to such employee under subsection (a) or two thousand and eighty in such period at rates not less than one and one-half times the regular rate at which he is employed; or

(3) by an independently owned and controlled local enterprise (including an enterprise with more than one bulk storage establishment) engaged in the wholesale or bulk distribution of petroleum products if—

(A) the annual gross volume of sales of such enterprise is less than $1,000,000 exclusive of excise taxes,

(B) more than 75 per centum of such enterprise's annual dollar volume of sales is made within the State in which such enterprise is located, and

(C) not more than 25 per centum of the annual dollar volume of sales of such enterprise is to customers who are engaged in the bulk distribution of such products for resale,

and such employee receives compensation for employment in excess of forty hours in any workweek at a rate not less than one and one-half times the minimum wage rate applicable to him under section 6,

and if such employee receives compensation for employment in excess of twelve hours in any workday, or for employment in excess of fifty-six hours in any workweek, as the case may be, at a rate not less than one and one-half times the regular rate at which he is employed.

(c) [Repealed.]

(d) [Repealed.]

(e) As used in this section the "regular rate" at which an employee is employed shall be deemed to include all remuneration for employment paid to, or on behalf of, the employee, but shall not be deemed to include—

(1) sums paid as gifts; payments in the nature of gifts made at Christmas time or on other special occasions, as a reward for service, the amounts of which are not measured by or dependent on hours worked, production, or efficiency;

(2) payments made for occasional periods when no work is performed due to vacation, holiday, illness, failure of the employer to provide sufficient work, or other similar cause; reasonable payments for traveling expenses, or other expenses, incurred by an employee in the furtherance of his employer's interests and properly reimbursable by the employer; and other similar payments to an employee which are not made as compensation for his hours of employment;

(3) sums paid in recognition of services performed during a given period if

either, (a) both the fact that payment is to be made and the amount of the payment are determined at the sole discretion of the employer at or near the end of the period and not pursuant to any prior contract, agreement, or promise causing the employee to expect such payments regularly; or (b) the payments are made pursuant to a bona fide profit-sharing plan or trust, or bona fide thrift or savings plan, meeting the requirements of the Administrator set forth in appropriate regulations which he shall issue, having due regard, among other relevant factors, to the extent to which the amounts paid to the employee are determined without regard to hours of work, production, or efficiency; or (c) the payments are talent fees (as such talent fees are defined and delimited by regulations of the Administrator) paid to performers, including announcers, on radio and television programs;

(4) contributions irrevocably made by an employer to a trustee or third person pursuant to a bona fide plan for providing old-age, retirement, life, accident, or health insurance or similar benefits for employees;

(5) extra compensation provided by a premium rate paid for certain hours worked by the employee in any day or workweek because such hours are hours worked in excess of eight in a day or in excess of the maximum workweek applicable to such employee under subsection (a) or in excess of the employee's normal working hours or regular working hours, as the case may be;

(6) extra compensation provided by a premium rate paid for work by the employee on Saturdays, Sundays, holidays, or regular days of rest, or on the sixth or seventh day of the workweek, where such premium rate is not less than one and one-half times the rate established in good faith for like work performed in nonovertime hours on other days; or

(7) extra compensation provided by a premium rate paid to the employee, in pursuance of an applicable employment contract or collective-bargaining agreement, for work outside of the hours established in good faith by the contract or agreement as the basic, normal, or regular workday (not exceeding eight hours) or workweek (not exceeding the maximum workweek applicable to such employee under subsection (a)) of this section, where such premium rate is not less than one and one-half times the rate established in good faith by the contract or agreement for like work performed during such workday or workweek.

(f) No employer shall be deemed to have violated subsection (a) of this section by employing any employee for a workweek in excess of the maximum workweek applicable to such employee under subsection (a) if such employee is employed pursuant to a bona fide individual contract, or pursuant to an agreement made as a result of collective bargaining by representatives of employees, if the duties of such employee necessitate irregular hours of work, and the contract or agreement (1) specifies a regular rate of pay not less than the minimum hourly rate provided in subsection (a) or (b) of section 6 (whichever may be applicable) and compensation at not less than one and one-half times such rate for all hours worked in excess of such maximum workweek and (2) provides a weekly guaranty of pay for not more than sixty hours based on the rates so specified.

(g) No employer shall be deemed to have violated subsection (a) of this section by employing any employee for a workweek in excess of the maximum workweek applicable to such employee under such subsection if, pursuant to an agreement or understanding arrived at between the employer and the employee before performance of the work, the amount paid to the employee for the number of hours worked by him in such workweek in excess of the maximum workweek applicable to such employee under such subsection—

(1) in the case of an employee employed at piece rates, is computed at piece rates not less than one and one-half times the bona fide piece rates applicable to the same work when performed during nonovertime hours; or

(2) in the case of an employee performing two or more kinds of work for which different hourly or piece rates have been established, is computed at rates not less than one and one-half times such bona fide rates applicable to the same work when performed during nonovertime hours; or

(3) is computed at a rate not less than one and one-half times the rate established by such agreement or understanding as the basic rate to be used in computing overtime compensation thereunder: *Provided,* That the rate so established shall be authorized by regulation by the Administrator as being substantially equivalent to the average hourly earnings of the employee, exclusive of overtime premiums, in the particular work over a representative period of time;

and if (1) the employee's average hourly earnings for the workweek exclusive of payments described in paragraphs (1) through (7) of subsection (e) of this section are not less than the minimum hourly rate required by applicable law, and (ii) extra overtime compensation is properly computed and paid on other forms of additional pay required to be included in computing the regular rate.

(h) Extra compensation paid as described in paragraphs (5), (6), and (7) of subsection (e) of this section shall be creditable toward overtime compensation payable pursuant to this section.

(i) No employer shall be deemed to have violated subsection (a) of this section by employing any employee of a retail or service establishment for a workweek in excess of the applicable workweek specified therein, if (1) the regular rate of pay of such employee is in excess of one and one-half times the minimum hourly rate applicable to him under section 206 of this title, and (2) more than half his compensation for a representative period (not less than one month) represents commissions on goods or services. In determining the proportion of compensation representing commissions, all earnings resulting from the application of a bona fide commission rate shall be deemed commissions on goods or services without regard to whether the computed commissions exceed the draw or guarantee.

(j) No employer engaged in the operation of a hospital or an establishment which is an institution primarily engaged in the care of the sick, the aged, or the mentally ill or defective who reside on the premises shall be deemed to have violated subsection (a) of this section if, pursuant to an agreement or understanding arrived at between the employer and the employee before performance of the work, a work period of fourteen consecutive days is accepted in lieu of the workweek of seven consecutive days for purposes of overtime computation and if, for his employment in excess of eight hours in any workday and in excess of eighty hours in such fourteen-day period, the employee receives compensation at a rate not less than one and one-half times the regular rate at which he is employed.

(k) No public agency shall be deemed to have violated subsection (a) of this section with respect to the employment of any employee in fire protection activities or any employee in law enforcement activities (including security personnel in correctional institutions) if—

(1) in a work period of 28 consecutive days the employee receives for tours of duty which in the aggregate exceed the lesser of (A) 216 hours or (B) the average number of hours (as determined by the Secretary pursuant to section 6(c)(3) of the Fair Labor Standards Amendments of 1974) in tours of duty of employees engaged in such activities in work periods of 28 consecutive days in calendar year 1975; or

(2) in the case of such an employee to whom a work period of at least 7 but less than 28 days applies, in his work period the employee receives for tours of duty which in the aggregate exceed a number of hours which bears the same ratio to the number of consecutive days in his work period as 216 hours (or if lower, the number of hours referred to in clause (B) of paragraph (1)) bears to 28 days,

compensation at a rate not less than one and one-half times the regular rate at which he is employed.

(l) No employer shall employ any employee in domestic service in one or more households for a workweek longer than forty hours unless such employee receives compensation for such employment in accordance with subsection (a) of this section.

(m) For a period or periods of not more than fourteen workweeks in the aggregate in any calendar year, any employer may employ any employee for a workweek in excess of that specified in subsection (a) of this section without paying the compensation for overtime employment prescribed in such subsection, if such employee—

(1) is employed by such employer—

(A) to provide services (including stripping and grading) necessary and incidental to the sale at auction of green leaf tobacco of type 11, 12, 13, 14, 21, 22, 23, 24, 31, 35, 36, or 37 (as such types are defined by the Secretary of Agriculture), or in auction sale, buying, handling, stemming, redrying, packing, and storing of such tobacco,

    (B) in auction sale, buying, handling, sorting, grading, packing, or storing green leaf tobacco of type 32 (as such type is defined by the Secretary of Agriculture), or

    (C) in auction sale, buying, handling, stripping, sorting, grading, sizing, packing, or stemming prior to packing, of perishable cigar leaf tobacco of type 41, 42, 43, 44, 45, 46, 51, 52, 53, 54, 55, 61, or 62 (as such types are defined by the Secretary of Agriculture); and

  (2) receives for—

    (A) such employment by such employer which is in excess of ten hours in any workday, and

    (B) such employment by such employer which is in excess of forty-eight hours in any workweek,

  compensation at a rate not less than one and one-half times the regular rate at which he is employed.

An employer who receives an exemption under this subsection shall not be eligible for any other exemption under this section.

  (n) In the case of an employee of an employer engaged in the business of operating a street, suburban or interurban electric railway, or local trolley or motorbus carrier (regardless of whether or not such railway or carrier is public or private or operated for profit or not for profit), in determining the hours of employment of such an employee to which the rate prescribed by subsection (a) applies there shall be excluded the hours such employee was employed in charter activities by such employer if (1) the employee's employment in such activities was pursuant to an agreement or understanding with his employer arrived at before engaging in such employment, and (2) if employment in such activities is not part of such employee's regular employment.

  (o)(1) Employees of a public agency which is a State, a political subdivision of a State, or an interstate governmental agency may receive, in accordance with this subsection and in lieu of overtime compensation, compensatory time off at a rate not less than one and one-half hours for each hour of employment for which overtime compensation is required by this section.

  (2) A public agency may provide compensatory time under paragraph (1) only—

    (A) pursuant to—

      (i) applicable provisions of a collective bargaining agreement, memorandum of understanding, or any other agreement between the public agency and representatives of such employees; or

      (ii) in the case of employees not covered by subclause (i), an agreement or understanding arrived at between the employer and employee before the performance of the work; and

(B) if the employee has not accrued compensatory time in excess of the limit applicable to the employee prescribed by paragraph (3).

In the case of employees described in clause (A)(ii) hired prior to April 15, 1986, the regular practice in effect on April 15, 1986, with respect to compensatory time off for such employees in lieu of the receipt of overtime compensation, shall constitute an agreement or understanding under such clause (A)(ii). Except as provided in the previous sentence, the provision of compensatory time off to such employees for hours worked after April 14, 1986, shall be in accordance with this subsection.

(3)(A) If the work of an employee for which compensatory time may be provided included work in a public safety activity, an emergency response activity, or a seasonal activity, the employee engaged in such work may accrue not more than 480 hours of compensatory time for hours worked after April 15, 1986. If such work was any other work, the employee engaged in such work may accrue not more than 240 hours of compensatory time for hours worked after April 15, 1986. Any such employee who, after April 15, 1986, has accrued 480 or 240 hours, as the case may be, of compensatory time off shall, for additional overtime hours of work, be paid overtime compensation.

(B) If compensation is paid to an employee for accrued compensatory time off, such compensation shall be paid at the regular rate earned by the employee at the time the employee receives such payment.

(4) An employee who has accrued compensatory time off authorized to be provided under paragraph (1) shall, upon termination of employment, be paid for the unused compensatory time at a rate of compensation not less than—

(A) the average regular rate received by such employee during the last 3 years of the employee's employment, or

(B) the final regular rate received by such employee, whichever is higher.

(5) An employee of a public agency which is a State, political subdivision of a State, or an interstate governmental agency—

(A) who has accrued compensatory time off authorized to be provided under paragraph (1), and

(B) who has requested the use of such compensatory time,

shall be permitted by the employee's employer to use such time within a reasonable period after making the request if the use of the compensatory time does not unduly disrupt the operations of the public agency.

(6) For purposes of this subsection—

(A) the term "overtime compensation" means the compensation required by subsection (a), and

    (B) the terms "compensatory time" and "compensatory time off" mean hours during which an employee is not working, which are not counted as hours worked during the applicable workweek or other work period for purposes of overtime compensation, and for which the employee is compensated at the employee's regular rate.

(p)(1) If an individual who is employed by a State, political subdivision of a State, or an interstate governmental agency in fire protection or law enforcement activities (including activities of security personnel in correctional institutions) and who, solely at such individual's option, agrees to be employed on a special detail by a separate or independent employer in fire protection, law enforcement, or related activities, the hours such individual was employed by such separate and independent employer shall be excluded by the public agency employing such individual in the calculation of the hours for which the employee is entitled to overtime compensation under this section if the public agency—

    (A) requires that its employees engaged in fire protection, law enforcement, or security activities be hired by a separate and independent employer to perform the special detail,

    (B) facilitates the employment of such employees by a separate and independent employer, or

    (C) otherwise affects the condition of employment of such employees by a separate and independent employer.

(2) If an employee of a public agency which is a State, political subdivision of a State, or an interstate governmental agency undertakes, on an occasional or sporadic basis and solely at the employee's option, part-time employment for the public agency which is in a different capacity from any capacity in which the employee is regularly employed with the public agency, the hours such employee was employed in performing the different employment shall be excluded by the public agency in the calculation of the hours for which the employee is entitled to overtime compensation under this section.

(3) If an individual who is employed by any capacity by a public agency which is a State, political subdivision of a State, or an interstate governmental agency, agrees, with the approval of the public agency and solely at the option of such individual, to substitute during scheduled work hours for another individual who is employed by such agency in the same capacity, the hours such employee worked as a substitute shall be excluded by the public agency in the calculation of the hours for which the employee is entitled to overtime compensation under this section.

§ 208. Wage orders in Puerto Rico and the Virgin Islands

[Sec. 8] (a) The policy of this Act with respect to industries or enterprises in Puerto Rico and the Virgin Islands engaged in commerce or in the production of goods for commerce is to reach as rapidly as is economically feasible without substantially curtailing employment the objective of the minimum wage rate which would apply in each such industry under paragraph (1) or (5) of section 6(a) but for section 6(c). The Secretary shall, from time to time, convene an industry committee or committees, appointed pursuant to section 5, and any such industry committee—

(1) shall, from time to time, recommend the minimum wage rates to be paid by employers who are in Puerto Rico, in the Virgin Islands, or in both places and who but for section 6(c) would be subject to the minimum wage requirements of section 6(a)(1), and

(2) may, from time to time, recommend increases in the incremental increases authorized by section 6(c)(2).

(b) Upon the convening of any such industry committee, the Administrator shall refer to it the question of the minimum wage rates to be fixed for such industry. The industry committee shall investigate conditions in the industry and the committee, or any authorized subcommittee thereof, shall after due notice hear such witnesses and receive such evidence as may be necessary or appropriate to enable the committee to perform its duties and functions under this Act. The committee shall recommend to the Administrator the highest minimum wage rates for the industry which it determines, having due regard to economic and competitive conditions, will not substantially curtail employment in the industry and will not give any industry in Puerto Rico or in the Virgin Islands a competitive advantage over any industry in the United States outside of Puerto Rico and the Virgin Islands; except that the committee shall recommend to the Secretary the minimum wage rate prescribed in section 6(a) or 6(b), which would be applicable but for section 6(c), unless there is substantial documentary evidence, including pertinent unabridged profit and loss statements and balance sheets for a representative period of years or in the case of employees of public agencies other appropriate information, in the record which establishes that the industry, or a predominant portion thereof, is unable to pay that wage.

(c) The industry committee shall recommend such reasonable classifications within any industry as it determines to be necessary for the purpose of fixing for each classification within such industry the highest minimum wage rate (not in excess of that in effect under paragraph (1) or (5) of section 6(a) (as the case may be)) which (1) will not substantially curtail employment in such classification and (2) will not give a competitive advantage to any group in the industry, and shall recommend for each classification in the industry the highest minimum-wage rate which the committee determines will not substantially curtail employment in such classification. In determining whether such classification should be made in any industry, in making such classifications, and in determining the minimum wage rates for such classifications, no classification shall be made, and no minimum wage rate shall be fixed, solely on a regional basis, but the industry committee shall consider among other relevant factors the following:

(1) competitive conditions as affected by transportation, living, and production costs;

(2) the wages established for work of like or comparable character by collective labor agreements negotiated between employers and employees by representatives of their own choosing; and

(3) the wages paid for work of like or comparable character by employers who voluntarily maintain minimum-wage standards in the industry.

No classification shall be made under this section on the basis of age or sex.

(d) The industry committee shall file with the Secretary a report containing its findings of fact and recommendation with respect to the matters referred to it. Upon the filing of such report, the Secretary shall publish such recommendations in the Federal Register and shall provide by order that the recommendations contained in such report shall take effect upon the expiration of 15 days after the date of such publication.

(e) Orders issued under this section shall define the industries and classifications therein to which they are to apply, and shall contain such terms and conditions as the Secretary finds necessary to carry out the purposes of such orders, to prevent the circumvention or evasion thereof, and to safeguard the minimum wage rates established therein.

(f) Due notice of any hearing provided for in this section shall be given by publication in the Federal Register and by such other means as the Secretary deems reasonably calculated to give general notice to interested persons.

§ 209. Attendance of witnesses

[Sec. 9] For the purpose of any hearing or investigation provided for in this Act, the provisions of sections 9 and 10 (relating to the attendance of witnesses and the production of books, papers, and documents) of the Federal Trade Commission Act of September 16, 1914, as amended (U.S.C., 1934 edition, title 15, secs. 49 and 50), are hereby made applicable to the jurisdiction, powers, and duties of the Administrator, the Secretary of Labor, and the industry committees.

§ 210. Court review of wage orders in Puerto Rico and the Virgin Islands

[Sec. 10] (a) Any person aggrieved by an order of the Secretary issued under section 8 may obtain a review of such order in the United States Court of Appeals for any circuit wherein such person resides or has his principal place of business, or in the United States Court of Appeals for the District of Columbia, by filing in such court, within 60 days after the entry of such order a written petition praying that the order of the Secretary be modified or set aside in whole or in part. A copy of such petition shall forthwith be transmitted by the clerk of the court to the Secretary, and thereupon the Secretary shall file in the court the record of the industry committee upon which the order complained of was entered, as provided in Section 2112 of Title 28, United States Code. Upon the filing of such petition such court shall have exclusive jurisdiction to affirm, modify (including provision for the payment of an appropriate minimum wage rate), or set aside such order in whole or in part, so far as it is applicable to the petitioner. The review by the court shall be limited to questions of law, and findings of fact by such industry committee when supported by substantial evidence shall be conclusive. No objection to the order of the Secretary shall be considered by the court unless such objection shall have been urged before such industry committee or unless there were reasonable grounds for failure so to do. If application is made to the court for leave to adduce additional evidence, and it is shown to the satisfaction of the court that such additional evidence may materially affect the result of the proceeding and that there were reasonable grounds for failure to adduce such evidence in the proceedings before such industry committee, the court may order such additional evidence to be taken before an industry committee and to be adduced upon the hearing in such manner and upon such terms and conditions as to the court may seem proper. Such industry committee may modify the initial findings by reason of the additional evidence so taken, and shall file with the court such modified or new findings which if supported by substantial evidence shall be conclusive, and shall also file its recommendation, if any, for the modification or setting aside of the original order. The judgment and decree of the court shall be final, subject to review by the Supreme Court of the United States upon certiorari or certification as provided in section 1254 of title 28 of the United States Code.

(b) The commencement of proceedings under subsection (a) shall not, unless specifically ordered by the court, operate as a stay of the Secretary's order. The court shall not grant any stay of the order unless the person complaining of such order shall file in court an undertaking with a surety or sureties satisfactory to the court for the payment to the employees affected by the order, in the event such order is affirmed, of the amount by which the compensation such employees are entitled to receive under the order exceeds the compensation they actually receive while such stay is in effect.

§ 211.   Collection of data

[Sec. 11] (a) The Administrator or his designated representatives may investigate and gather data regarding the wages, hours, and other conditions and practices of employment in any industry subject to this Act, and may enter and inspect such places and such records (and make such transcriptions thereof), question such employees, and investigate such facts, conditions, practices, or matters as he may deem necessary or appropriate to determine whether any person has violated any provision of this Act, or which may aid in the enforcement of the provisions of this Act. Except as provided in section 12 and in subsection (b) of this section, the Administrator shall utilize the bureaus and divisions of the Department of Labor for all the investigations and inspections necessary under this section. Except as provided in section 12, the Secretary of Labor shall bring all actions under section 17 to restrain violations of this Act.

(b) With the consent and cooperation of State agencies charged with the administration of State labor laws, the Administrator and the Secretary of Labor may, for the purpose of carrying out their respective functions and duties under this Act, utilize the service of State and local agencies and their employees and, notwithstanding any other provision of law, may reimburse such State and local agencies and their employees for services rendered for such purposes.

(c) Every employer subject to any provision of this Act or of any order issued under this Act shall make, keep, and preserve such records of the persons employed by him and of the wages, hours, and other conditions and practices of employment maintained by him, and shall preserve such records for such periods of time, and shall make such reports therefrom to the Administrator as he shall prescribe by regulation or order as necessary or appropriate for the enforcement of the provisions of this Act or the regulations or orders thereunder. The employer of an employee who performs substitute work described in section (p)(3) may not be required under this subsection to keep a record of the hours of the substitute work.

(d) The Administrator is authorized to make such regulations and orders regulating, restricting, or prohibiting industrial homework as are necessary or appropriate to prevent the circumvention or evasion of and to safeguard the minimum wage rate prescribed in this Act, and all existing regulations or orders of the Administrator relating to industrial homework are hereby continued in full force and effect.

§ 212.   Child labor provisions

[Sec. 12] (a) No producer, manufacturer, or dealer shall ship or deliver for shipment in commerce any goods produced in an establishment situated in the United States in or about which within thirty days prior to the removal of such goods therefrom any oppressive child labor has been employed: *Provided*, That any such shipment or delivery for shipment or sale of such goods by a purchaser who acquired them in good faith in reliance on written assurance from the producer, manufacturer, or dealer that the goods were produced in compliance with the requirements of this section, and who acquired such goods for value without notice of any such violation, shall not be deemed prohibited by this subsection: *And provided further*, That a prosecution and conviction of a defendant for the shipment or delivery for shipment of any goods under the conditions herein prohibited shall be a bar to any further prosecution against the same defendant for shipments or deliveries for shipment of any such goods before the beginning of said prosecution.

(b) The Secretary of Labor, or any of his authorized representatives, shall make all investigations and inspections under section 11(a) with respect to the employment of minors, and, subject to the direction and control of the Attorney-General, shall bring all actions under section 17 to enjoin any act or practice which is unlawful by reason of the existence of oppressive child labor, and shall administer all other provisions of this Act relating to oppressive child labor.

(c) No employer shall employ any oppressive child labor in commerce or in the production of goods for commerce or in any enterprise engaged in commerce or in the production of goods for commerce.

(d) In order to carry out the objectives of this section, the Secretary may by regulation require employers to obtain from any employee proof of age.

§ 213. Exemptions

[Sec. 13] (a) The provisions of sections 6 (except section 6(d) in the case of paragraph (1) of this subsection) and 7 shall not apply with respect to—
  (1) any employee employed in a bona fide executive, administrative, or professional capacity (including any employee employed in the capacity of academic administrative personnel or teacher in elementary or secondary schools), or in the capacity of outside salesman (as such terms are defined and delimited from time to time by regulations of the Secretary, subject to the provisions of the Administrative Procedure Act, except that an employee of a retail or service establishment shall not be excluded from the definition of employee in a bona fide executive or administrative capacity because of the number of hours in his workweek which he devotes to activities not directly or closely related to the performance of executive or administrative activities, if less than 40 per centum of his hours worked in the workweek are devoted to such activities); or
  (2) any employee employed by any retail or service establishment (except an establishment or employee engaged in laundering, cleaning, or repairing clothing or fabrics or an establishment engaged in the operation of a hospital, institution, or school described in section 3(s)(5)), if more than 50 per centum of such establishment's annual dollar volume of sales of goods or services is made within the State in which the establishment is located, and such establishment is not in an enterprise described in section 3(s). A "retail or service establishment" shall mean an establishment 75 per centum of whose annual dollar volume of sales of goods or services (or of both) is not for resale and is recognized as retail sales or services in the particular industry; or

(3) any employee employed by an establishment which is an amusement or recreational establishment, organized camp, or religious or non-profit educational conference center, if (A) it does not operate for more than seven months in any calendar year, or (B) during the preceding calendar year, its average receipts for any six months of such year were not more than 33 1/3 per centum of its average receipts for the other six months of such year, except that the exemption from sections 6 and 7 provided by this paragraph does not apply with respect to any employee of a private entity engaged in providing services or facilities (other than in the case of the exemption from section 6, a private entity engaged in providing services and facilities directly related to skiing) in a national park or a national forest, or on land in the national wildlife refuge system, under a contract with the Secretary of the Interior or the Secretary of Agriculture; or

(4) any employee employed by an establishment which qualifies as an exempt retail establishment under clause (2) of this subsection and is recognized as a retail establishment in the particular industry notwithstanding that such establishment makes or processes at the retail establishment the goods that it sells: *Provided,* That more than 85 per centum of such establishment's annual dollar volume of sales of goods so made or processed is made within the State in which the establishment is located; or

(5) any employee employed in the catching, taking, propagating, harvesting, cultivating, or farming of any kind of fish, shellfish, crustacea, sponges, seaweeds, or other aquatic forms of animal and vegetable life, or in the first processing, canning or packing such marine products at sea as an incident to, or in conjunction with, such fishing operations, including the going to and returning from work and loading and unloading when performed by any such employee; or

(6) any employee in agriculture (A) if such employee is employed by an employer who did not, during any calendar quarter during the preceding calendar year, use more than five hundred man-days of agricultural labor, (B) if such employee is the parent, spouse, child, or other member of his employer's immediate family, (C) if such employee (i) is employed as a hand harvest laborer and is paid on a piece rate basis in an operation which has been, and is customarily and generally recognized as having been, paid on a piece rate basis in the region of employment, (ii) commutes daily from his permanent residence to the farm on which he is so employed, and (iii) has been employed in agriculture less than thirteen weeks during the preceding calendar year, (D) if such employee (other than an employee described in clause (C) of this subsection) (i) is sixteen years of age or under and is employed as a hand harvest laborer, is paid on a piece rate basis in an operation which has been, and is customarily and generally recognized as having been, paid on a piece rate basis in the region of employment,

(ii) is employed on the same farm as his parent or person standing in the place of his parent, and (iii) is paid at the same piece rate as employees over age sixteen are paid on the same farm, or (E) if such employee is principally engaged in the range production of livestock; or

(7) any employee to the extent that such employee is exempted by regulations, orders, or certificates of the Secretary issued under section 14; or

(8) any employee employed in connection with the publication of any weekly, semiweekly, or daily newspaper with a circulation of less than four thousand the major part of which circulation is within the county where published or counties contiguous thereto; or

(9) [Repealed.]

(10) any switchboard operator employed by an independently owned public telephone company which has not more than seven hundred and fifty stations; or

(11) [Repealed.]

(12) any employee employed as a seaman on a vessel other than an American vessel; or

(13) [Repealed.]

(14) [Repealed.]

(15) any employee employed on a casual basis in domestic service employment to provide babysitting services or any employee employed in domestic service employment to provide companionship services for individuals who (because of age or infirmity) are unable to care for themselves (as such terms are defined and delimited by regulations of the Secretary).

(b) The provisions of section 7 shall not apply with respect to

(1) any employee with respect to whom the Secretary of Transportation has power to establish qualifications and maximum hours of service pursuant to the provisions of section 204 of the Motor Carrier Act, 1935; or

(2) any employee of an employer engaged in the operation of a common carrier by rail and subject to the provisions of Part I of the Interstate Commerce Act; or

(3) any employee of a carrier by air subject to the provisions of title II of the Railway Labor Act, or

(4) [Repealed.]

(5) any individual employed as an outside buyer of poultry, eggs, cream, or milk, in their raw or natural state; or

(6) any employee employed as a seaman; or

(7) [Repealed.]

(8) [Repealed.]

(9) any employee employed as an announcer, news editor, or chief engineer by a radio or television station the major studio of which is

located (A) in a city or town of one hundred thousand population or less, according to the latest available decennial census figures as compiled by the Bureau of the Census, except where such city or town is part of a standard metropolitan statistical area, as defined and designated by the Office of Management and Budget, which has a total population in excess of one hundred thousand, or (B) in a city or town of twenty-five thousand population or less, which is part of such an area but is at least 40 airline miles from the principal city in such area; or

(10)(A) any salesman, partsman, or mechanic primarily engaged in selling or servicing automobiles, trucks, or farm implements, if he is employed by a nonmanufacturing establishment primarily engaged in the business of selling such vehicles or implements to ultimate purchasers; or

(B) any salesman primarily engaged in selling trailers, boats, or aircraft, if he is employed by a nonmanufacturing establishment primarily engaged in the business of selling trailers, boats, or aircraft to ultimate purchasers; or

(11) any employee employed as a driver or driver's helper making local deliveries, who is compensated for such employment on the basis of trip rates, or other delivery payment plan, if the Secretary shall find that such plan has the general purpose and effect of reducing hours worked by such employees to, or below, the maximum workweek applicable to them under section 7(a); or

(12) any employee employed in agriculture or in connection with the operation or maintenance of ditches, canals, reservoirs, or waterways, not owned or operated for profit, or operated on a sharecrop basis, and which are used exclusively for supply and storing of water for agricultural purposes; or

(13) any employee with respect to his employment in agriculture by a farmer, notwithstanding other employment of such employee in connection with livestock auction operations in which such farmer is engaged as an adjunct to the raising of livestock, either on his own account or in conjunction with other farmers, if such employee (A) is primarily employed during his workweek in agriculture by such farmer, and (B) is paid for his employment in connection with such livestock auction operation at a wage rate not less than that prescribed by section 6(a)(1); or

(14) any employee employed within the area of production (as defined by the Secretary) by an establishment commonly recognized as a country elevator, including such an establishment which sells products and services used in the operation of a farm, if no more than five employees are employed in the establishment in such operations; or

(15) any employee engaged in the processing of maple sap into sugar (other than refined sugar) or syrup; or

(16) any employee engaged (A) in the transportation and preparation for transportation of fruits or vegetables, whether or not performed by the farmer, from the farm to a place of first processing or first marketing within the same State, or (B) in transportation, whether or not performed by the farmer, between the farm and any point within the same State of persons employed or to be employed in the harvesting of fruits or vegetables; or

(17) any driver employed by an employer engaged in the business of operating taxicabs; or

(18) [Repealed.]

(19) [Repealed.]

(20) any employee of a public agency who in any workweek is employed in fire protection activities or any employee of a public agency who in any workweek is employed in law enforcement activities (including security personnel in correctional institutions), if the public agency employs during the workweek less than 5 employees in fire protection or law enforcement activities, as the case may be; or

(21) any employee who is employed in domestic service in a household and who resides in such household; or

(22) [Repealed.]

(23) [Repealed.]

(24) any employee who is employed with his spouse by a nonprofit educational institution to serve as the parents of children—

(A) who are orphans or one of whose natural parents is deceased, or

(B) who are enrolled in such institution and reside in residential facilities of the institution, while such children are in residence at such institution, if such employee and his spouse reside in such facilities, receive, without cost, board and lodging from such institution, and are together compensated, on a cash basis, at an annual rate of not less than $10,000; or

(25) [Repealed.]

(26) [Repealed.]

(27) any employee employed by an establishment which is a motion picture theater; or

(28) any employee employed in planting or tending trees, cruising, surveying, or felling timber, or in preparing or transporting logs or other forestry products to the mill, processing plant, railroad, or other transportation terminal, if the number of employees employed by his employer in such forestry or lumbering operations does not exceed eight; or

(29) any employee of an amusement or recreational establishment located in a national park or national forest or on land in the National Wildlife Refuge System if such employee (A) is an employee of a private entity engaged in providing services or facilities in a national park or national forest, or on land in the National Wildlife Refuge

System, under a contract with the Secretary of the Interior or the Secretary of Agriculture, and (B) receives compensation for employment in excess of fifty-six hours in any workweek at a rate not less than one and one-half times the regular rate at which he is employed.

(c)(1) Except as provided in paragraph (2) or (4), the provisions of section 12 relating to child labor shall not apply to any employee employed in agriculture outside of school hours for the school district where such employee is living while he is so employed, if such employee—

(A) is less than twelve years of age and (i) is employed by his parent, or by a person standing in the place of his parent, on a farm owned or operated by such parent or person, or (ii) is employed, with the consent of his parent or person standing in the place of his parent, on a farm, none of the employees of which are (because of section 13(a)(6)(A)) required to be paid at the wage rate prescribed by section 6(a)(5),

(B) is twelve years or thirteen years of age and (i) such employment is with the consent of his parent or person standing in the place of his parent, or (ii) his parent or such person is employed on the same farm as such employee, or

(C) is fourteen years of age or older.

(2) The provisions of section 12 relating to child labor shall apply to an employee below the age of sixteen employed in agriculture in an occupation that the Secretary of Labor finds and declares to be particularly hazardous for the employment of children below the age of sixteen, except where such employee is employed by his parent or by a person standing in the place of his parent on a farm owned or operated by such parent or person.

(3) The provisions of section 12 relating to child labor shall not apply to any child employed as an actor or performer in motion pictures or theatrical productions, or in radio or television productions.

(4)(A) An employer or group of employers may apply to the Secretary for a waiver of the application of section 12 to the employment for not more than eight weeks in any calendar year of individuals who are less than twelve years of age, but not less than ten years of age, as hand harvest laborers in an agricultural operation which has been, and is customarily and generally recognized as being, paid on a piece rate basis in the region in which such individuals would be employed. The Secretary may not grant such a waiver unless he finds, based on objective data submitted by the applicant, that—

(i) the crop to be harvested is one with a particularly short harvesting season and the application of section 12 would cause severe economic disruption in the industry of the employer or group of employers applying for the waiver;

(ii) the employment of the individuals to whom the waiver would apply would not be deleterious to their health or well-being;

    (iii) the level and type of pesticides and other chemicals used would not have an adverse effect on the health or well-being of the individuals to whom the waiver would apply;

    (iv) individuals aged twelve and above are not available for such employment; and

    (v) the industry of such employer or group of employers has traditionally and substantially employed individuals under twelve years of age without displacing substantial job opportunities for individuals over sixteen years of age.

  (B) Any waiver granted by the Secretary under subparagraph (A) shall require that—

    (i) the individuals employed under such waiver be employed outside of school hours for the school district where they are living while so employed;

    (ii) such individuals while so employed commute daily from their permanent residence to the farm on which they are so employed; and

    (iii) such individuals be employed under such waiver (I) for not more than eight weeks between June 1 and October 15 of any calendar year, and (II) in accordance with such other terms and conditions as the Secretary shall prescribe for such individuals' protection.

  (d) The provisions of sections 6, 7, and 12 shall not apply with respect to any employee engaged in the delivery of newspapers to the consumer or to any homeworker engaged in the making of wreaths composed principally of natural holly, pine, cedar, or other evergreens (including the harvesting of the evergreens or other forest products used in making such wreaths).

  (e) The provisions of section 7 shall not apply with respect to employees for whom the Secretary of Labor is authorized to establish minimum wage rates as provided in section 6(a)(3), except with respect to employees for whom such rates are in effect; and with respect to such employees the Secretary may make rules and regulations providing reasonable limitations and allowing reasonable variations, tolerances, and exemptions to and from any or all of the provisions of section 7 if he shall find, after a public hearing on the matter, and taking into account the factors set forth in section 6(a)(3), that economic conditions warrant such action.

  (f) The provisions of Sections 6, 7, 11, and 12 shall not apply with respect to any employee whose services during the workweek are performed in a workplace within a foreign country or within territory under the jurisdiction of the United States other than the following: a State of the United States; the District of Columbia; Puerto Rico; the Virgin Islands; outer Continental Shelf lands defined in the Outer Continental Shelf Lands Act (Ch. 345, 67 Stat. 462); American Samoa; Guam; Wake Island; Eniwetok Atoll; Kwajalein Atoll; and Johnston Island.

  (g) The exemption from section 6 provided by paragraphs (2) and (6) of subsection (a) of this section shall not apply with respect to any employee employed by an establishment (1) which controls, is controlled by, or is under common control with, another establishment the activities of which are not related for a common business purpose to, but materially support, the activities of the establishment employing such employee; and (2) whose annual gross volume of sales made or business done, when combined with the annual gross volume of sales made or business done by each establishment which controls, is controlled by, or is under common control with, the establishment employing such employee, exceeds $10,000,000 (exclusive of excise taxes at the retail level which are separately stated), except that the exemption from section 6 provided by paragraph (2) of subsection (a) of this section shall apply with respect to any establishment described in this subsection which has an annual dollar volume of sales which would permit it to qualify for the exemption provided in paragraph (2) of subsection (a) if it were in an enterprise described in section 3(s).

(h) The provisions of section 7 shall not apply for a period or periods of not more than fourteen workweeks in the aggregate in any calendar year to any employee who—

(1) is employed by such employer—

    (A) exclusively to provide services necessary and incidental to the ginning of cotton in an establishment primarily engaged in the ginning of cotton;

    (B) exclusively to provide services necessary and incidental to the receiving, handling, and storing of raw cotton and the compressing of raw cotton when performed at a cotton warehouse or compress-warehouse facility, other than one operated in conjunction with a cotton mill, primarily engaged in storing and compressing;

    (C) exclusively to provide services necessary and incidental to the receiving, handling, storing, and processing of cottonseed in an establishment primarily engaged in the receiving, handling, storing, and processing of cottonseed; or

    (D) exclusively to provide services necessary and incidental to the processing of sugar cane or sugar beets in an establishment primarily engaged in the processing of sugar cane or sugar beets; and

(2) receives for—

    (A) such employment by such employer which is in excess of ten hours in any workday, and

    (B) such employment by such employer which is in excess of forty-eight hours in any workweek,

compensation at a rate not less than one and one-half times the regular rate at which he is employed.

Any employer who receives an exemption under this subsection shall not be eligible for any other exemption under this section or section 7.

(i) The provisions of section 7 shall not apply for a period or periods of not more than fourteen workweeks in the aggregate in any period of fifty-two consecutive weeks to any employee who—

(1) is engaged in the ginning of cotton for market in any place of employment located in a county where cotton is grown in commercial quantities; and

(2) receives for any such employment during such workweeks—

(A) in excess of ten hours in any workday, and

(B) in excess of forty-eight hours in any workweek,

compensation at a rate not less than one and one-half times the regular rate at which he is employed. No week included in any fifty-two week period for purposes of the preceding sentence may be included for such purposes in any other fifty-two week period.

(j) The provisions of section 7 shall not apply for a period or periods of not more than fourteen workweeks in the aggregate in any period of fifty-two consecutive weeks to any employee who—

(1) is engaged in the processing of sugar beets, sugar beet molasses, or sugar cane into sugar (other than refined sugar) or syrup; and

(2) receives for any such employment during such workweeks—

(A) in excess of ten hours in any workday, and

(B) in excess of forty-eight hours in any workweek,

compensation at a rate not less than one and one-half times the regular rate at which he is employed. No week included in any fifty-two week period for purposes of the preceding sentence may be included for such purposes in any other fifty-two week period.

§ 214. Employment under special certifications

[Sec. 14] (a) The Secretary, to the extent necessary in order to prevent curtailment of opportunities for employment, shall by regulations or by orders provide for the employment of learners, of apprentices, and of messengers employed primarily in delivering letters and messages, under special certificates issued pursuant to regulations of the Secretary, at such wages lower than the minimum wage applicable under section 6 and subject to such limitations as to time, number, proportion, and length of service as the Secretary shall prescribe.

(b)(1)(A) The Secretary, to the extent necessary in order to prevent curtailment of opportunities for employment, shall by special certificate issued under a regulation or order provide, in accordance with subparagraph (B), for the employment, at a wage rate not less than 85 per centum of the otherwise applicable wage rate in effect under section 6 or not less than $1.60 an hour, whichever is the higher (or in the case of employment in Puerto Rico or the Virgin Islands not described in section 5(e), at a wage rate not less than 85 per centum of the otherwise applicable wage rate in effect under section 6(c)), of fulltime students (regardless of age but in compliance with applicable child labor laws) in retail or service establishments.

(B) Except as provided in paragraph (4)(B), during any month in which fulltime students are to be employed in any retail or service establishment under certificates issued under this subsection the proportion of student hours of employment to the total hours of employment of all employees, in such establishment may not exceed—

(i) in the case of a retail or service establishment whose employees (other than employees engaged in commerce or in the production of goods for commerce) were covered by this Act before the effective date of the Fair Labor Standards Amendments of 1974—

(I) the proportion of student hours of employment to the total hours of employment of all employees in such establishment for the corresponding month of the immediately preceding twelve-month period,

(II) the maximum proportion for any corresponding month of student hours of employment to the total hours of employment of all employees in such establishment applicable to the issuance of certificates under this section at any time before the effective date of the Fair Labor Standards Amendments of 1974 for the employment of students by such employer, or

(III) a proportion equal to one-tenth of the total hours of employment of all employees in such establishment,
    whichever is greater;

(ii) in the case of retail or service establishment whose employees (other than employees engaged in commerce or in the production of goods for commerce) are covered for the first time on or after the effective date of the Fair Labor Standards Amendments of 1974—

(I) the proportion of hours of employment of students in such establishment to the total hours of employment of all employees in such establishment for the corresponding month of the twelve-month period immediately prior to the effective date of such Amendments,

(II) the proportion of student hours of employment to the total hours of employment of all employees in such establishment for the corresponding month of the immediately preceding twelve-month period, or

(III) a proportion equal to one-tenth of the total hours of employment of all employees in such establishment, whichever is greater; or

(iii) in the case of a retail or service establishment for which records of student hours worked are not available, the proportion of student hours of employment to the total hours of employment of all employees based on the practice during the immediately preceding twelve-month period in (I) similar establishments of the same employer in the same general metropolitan area in which such establishment is located, (II) similar establishments of the same or nearby communities if such establishment is not in a metropolitan area, or (III) other establishments of the same general character operating in the community or the nearest comparable community.

For purpose of clauses (i), (ii), and (iii) of this subparagraph, the term "student hours of employment" means hours during which students are employed in a retail or service establishment under certificates issued under this subsection.

(2) The Secretary, to the extent necessary in order to prevent curtailment of opportunities for employment, shall by special certificate issued under a regulation or order provide for the employment, at a wage rate not less than 85 per centum of the wage rate in effect under section 6(a)(5) or not less than $1.30 an hour, whichever is the higher (or in the case of employment in Puerto Rico or the Virgin Islands not described in section 5(e), at a wage rate not less than 85 per centum of the wage rate in effect under section 6(c)), of full-time students (regardless of age but in compliance with applicable child labor laws) in any occupation in agriculture.

(3) The Secretary, to the extent necessary in order to prevent curtailment of opportunities for employment, shall by special certificate issued under a regulation or order provide for the employment by an institution of higher education, at a wage rate not less than 85 per centum of the otherwise applicable wage rate in effect under section 6 or not less than $1.60 an hour, whichever is the higher (or in the case of employment in Puerto Rico or the Virgin Islands not described in section 5(e), at a wage rate not less than 85 per centum of the wage rate in effect under section 6(c)), of fulltime students (regardless of age but in compliance with applicable child labor laws) who are enrolled in such institution. The Secretary shall by regulation prescribe standards and requirements to insure that this paragraph will not create a substantial probability of reducing the full-time employment opportunities of persons other than those to whom the minimum wage rate authorized by this paragraph is applicable.

(4)(A) A special certificate issued under paragraph (1), (2), or (3) shall provide that the student or students for whom it is issued shall, except during vacation periods, be employed on a part-time basis and not in excess of twenty hours in any workweek.

(B) If the issuance of a special certificate under paragraph (1) or (2) for an employer will cause the number of students employed by such employer under special certificates issued under this subsection to exceed six, the Secretary may not issue such a special certificate for the employment of a student by such employer unless the Secretary finds employment of such student will not create a substantial probability of reducing the full-time employment opportunities of persons other than those employed under special certificates issued under this subsection. If the issuance of a special certificate under paragraph (1) or (2) for an employer will not cause the number of students employed by such employer under special certificates issued under this subsection to exceed six—

(i) the Secretary may issue a special certificate under paragraph (1) or (2) for the employment of a student by such employer if such employer certifies to the Secretary that the employment of such student will not reduce the full-time employment opportunities of persons other than those employed under special certificates issued under this subsection, and

(ii) in the case of an employer which is a retail or service establishment, subparagraph (B) of paragraph (1) shall not apply with respect to the issuance of special certificates for such employer under such paragraph. The requirement of this subparagraph shall not apply in the case of the issuance of special certificates under paragraph (3) for the employment of full-time students by institutions of higher education; except that if the Secretary determines that an institution of higher education is employing students under certificates issued under paragraph (3) but in violation of the requirements of that paragraph or of regulations issued thereunder, the requirements of this subparagraph shall apply with respect to the issuance of special certificates under paragraph (3) for the employment of students by such institutions.

(C) No special certificate may be issued under this subsection unless the employer for whom the certificate is to be issued provides evidence satisfactory to the Secretary of the student status of the employees to be employed under such special certificate.

(D) To minimize paperwork and encourage small business concerns to employ students under special certificates issued under paragraphs (1) and (2), the Secretary shall, by regulation or order, prescribe a simplified application form to be used by employers in applying for such a certificate for the employment of not more than six full-time students. Such an application shall require only—

(i) a listing of the name, address, and business of the applicant employer,

(ii) a listing of the date the applicant began business, and

(iii) the certification that the employment of such full-time students will not reduce the full-time employment opportunities of persons other than persons employed under special certificates.

(c)(1) The Secretary, to the extent necessary to prevent curtailment of opportunities for employment, shall by regulation or order provide for the employment, under special certificates of individuals (including individuals employed in agriculture) whose earning or productive capacity is impaired by age, physical or mental deficiency, or injury, at wages which are—

(A) lower than the minimum wage applicable under section 6,

(B) commensurate with those paid to nonhandicapped workers, employed in the vicinity in which the individuals under the certificates are employed, for essentially the same type, quality, and quantity of work, and

(C) related to the individual's productivity.

(2) The Secretary shall not issue a certificate under paragraph (1) unless the employer provides written assurances to the Secretary that—

(A) in the case of individuals paid on an hourly rate basis, wages paid in accordance with paragraph (1) will be reviewed by the employer at periodic intervals at least once every six months, and

(B) wages paid in accordance with paragraph (1) will be adjusted by the employer at periodic intervals, at least once each year, to reflect changes in the prevailing wage paid to experienced nonhandicapped individuals employed in the locality for essentially the same type of work.

(3) Notwithstanding paragraph (1), no employer shall be permitted to reduce the hourly wage rate prescribed by certificate under this subsection in effect on June 1, 1986, of any handicapped individual for a period of two years from such date without prior authorization of the Secretary.

(4) Nothing in this subsection shall be construed to prohibit an employer from maintaining or establishing work activities centers to provide therapeutic activities for handicapped clients.

(5)(A) Notwithstanding any other provision of this subsection, any employee receiving a special minimum wage at a rate specified pursuant to this subsection or the parent or guardian of such an employee may petition the Secretary to obtain a review of such special minimum wage rate. An employee or the employee's parent or guardian may file such a petition for and in behalf of the employee or in behalf of the employee and other employees similarly situated. No employee may be a party to any such action unless the employee or the employee's parent or guardian gives consent in writing to become such a party and such consent is filed with the Secretary.

(B) Upon receipt of a petition filed in accordance with subparagraph

(A), the Secretary within ten days shall assign the petition to an administrative law judge appointed pursuant to section 3105 of title 5, United States Code. The administrative law judge shall conduct a hearing on the record in accordance with section 554 of title 5, United States Code, with respect to such petition within thirty days after assignment.

(C) In any such proceeding, the employer shall have the burden of demonstrating that the special minimum wage rate is justified as necessary in order to prevent curtailment of opportunities for employment.

(D) In determining whether any special minimum wage rate is justified pursuant to subparagraph (C), the administrative law judge shall consider—

   (i) the productivity of the employee or employees identified in the petition and the conditions under which such productivity was measured; and

   (ii) the productivity of other employees performing work of essentially the same type and quality for other employers in the same vicinity.

(E) The administrative law judge shall issue a decision within thirty days after the hearing provided for in subparagraph (B). Such action shall be deemed to be a final agency action unless within thirty days the Secretary grants a request to review the decision of the administrative law judge. Either the petitioner or the employer may request review by the Secretary within fifteen days of the date of issuance of the decision by the administrative law judge.

(F) The Secretary, within thirty days after receiving a request for review, shall review the record and either adopt the decision of the administrative law judge or issue exceptions. The decision of the administrative law judge, together with any exceptions, shall be deemed to be a final agency action.

(G) A final agency action shall be subject to judicial review pursuant to chapter 7 of title 5, United States Code. An action seeking such review shall be brought within thirty days of a final agency action described in subparagraph (F).

   (d) The Secretary may by regulation or order provide that sections 6 and 7 shall not apply with respect to the employment by an elementary or secondary school of its students if such employment constitutes, as determined under regulations prescribed by the Secretary, an integral part of the regular education program provided by such school and such employment is in accordance with applicable child labor laws.

§ 215. Prohibited acts; prima facie evidence

[Sec. 15] (a) After the expiration of one hundred and twenty days from the date of enactment of this Act, it shall be unlawful for any person—

(1) to transport, offer for transportation, ship, deliver, or sell in commerce, or to ship, deliver, or sell with knowledge that shipment or delivery or sale thereof in commerce is intended, any goods in the production of which any employee was employed in violation of section 6 or section 7, or in violation of any regulation or order of the Secretary of Labor issued under section 14; except that no provision of this Act shall impose any liability upon any common carrier for the transportation in commerce in the regular course of its business of any goods not produced by such common carrier, and no provision of this Act shall excuse any common carrier from its obligation to accept any goods for transportation; and except that any such transportation, offer, shipment, delivery, or sale of such goods by a purchaser who acquired them in good faith in reliance on written assurance from the producer that the goods were produced in compliance with the requirements of the Act, and who acquired such goods for value without notice of any such violation, shall not be deemed unlawful;

(2) to violate any of the provisions of section 6 or section 7, or any of the provisions of any regulation or order of the Secretary issued under section 14;

(3) to discharge or in any other manner discriminate against any employee because such employee has filed any complaint or instituted or caused to be instituted any proceeding under or related to this Act, or has testified or is about to testify in any such proceeding or has served or is about to serve on an industry committee;

(4) to violate any of the provisions of section 12;

(5) to violate any of the provisions of section 11(c), or any regulation or order made or continued in effect under the provisions of section 11(d), or to make any statement, report, or record filed or kept pursuant to the provisions of such section or of any regulation or order thereunder, knowing such statement, report, or record to be false in a material respect.

(b) For the purpose of subsection (a)(1) proof that any employee was employed in any place of employment where goods shipped or sold in commerce were produced, within ninety days prior to the removal of the goods from such place of employment, shall be prima facie evidence that such employee was engaged in the production of such goods.

§ 216. Penalties

[Sec. 16] (a) Any person who willfully violates any of the provisions of section 15 shall upon conviction thereof be subject to a fine of not more than $10,000, or to imprisonment for not more than six months, or both. No person shall be imprisoned under this subsection except for an offense committed after the conviction of such person for a prior offense under this subsection.

(b) Any employer who violates the provisions of section 6 or section 7 of this Act shall be liable to the employee or employees affected in the amount of their unpaid minimum wages, or their unpaid overtime compensation, as the case may be, and in an additional equal amount as liquidated damages. Any employer who violates the provisions of section 15(a)(3) of this Act shall be liable for such legal or equitable relief as may be appropriate to effectuate the purposes of section 15(a)(3), including without limitation employment, reinstatement, promotion and the payment of wages lost, and an additional equal amount as liquidated damages. An action to recover the liability prescribed in either of the preceding sentences may be maintained against any employer (including a public agency) in any Federal or state court of competent jurisdiction by any one or more employees for and in behalf of himself or themselves and other employees similarly situated. No employee shall be a party plaintiff to any such action unless he gives his consent in writing to become such a party and such consent is filed in the court in which such action is brought. The court in such action shall, in addition to any judgment awarded to the plaintiff or plaintiffs, allow a reasonable attorney's fee to be paid by the defendant and costs of the action. The right provided by this subsection to bring an action by or on behalf of any employee, and the right of any employee to become a party plaintiff to any such action, shall terminate upon the filing of a complaint by the Secretary of Labor in an action under section 17 in which (1) restraint is sought of any further delay in the payment of unpaid minimum wages, or the amount of unpaid overtime compensation, as the case may be, owing to such employee under section 6 or section 7 of this Act by an employer liable therefor under the provisions of this subsection or (2) legal or equitable relief is sought as a result of alleged violations of section 15(a)(3).

(c) The Secretary is authorized to supervise the payment of the unpaid minimum wages or the unpaid overtime compensation owing to any employee or employees under section 6 or 7 of this Act, and the agreement of any employee to accept such payment shall upon payment in full constitute a waiver by such employee of any right he may have under subsection (b) of this section to such unpaid minimum wages or unpaid overtime compensation and an additional equal amount as liquidated damages. The Secretary may bring an action in any court of competent jurisdiction to recover the amount of the unpaid minimum wages or overtime compensation and an equal amount as liquidated damages. The right provided by subsection (b) to bring an action by or on behalf of any employee to recover the liability specified in the first sentence of such subsection and of any employee to become a party plaintiff to any such action shall terminate upon the filing of a complaint by the Secretary in an action under this subsection in which a recovery is sought of unpaid minimum wages or unpaid overtime compensation under sections 6 and 7 or liquidated or other damages provided by this subsection owing to such employee by an employer liable under the provisions of subsection (b), unless such action is dismissed without prejudice on motion of the Secretary. Any sums thus recovered by the Secretary of Labor on behalf of an employee pursuant to this subsection shall be held in a special deposit account and shall be paid, on order of the Secretary of Labor, directly to the employee or employees affected. Any such sums not paid to an employee because of inability to do so within a period of three years shall be covered into the Treasury of the United States as miscellaneous receipts. In determining when an action is commenced by the Secretary of Labor under this subsection for the purposes of the statutes of limitations provided in section 6(a) of the Portal-to-Portal Act of 1947, it shall be considered to be commenced in the case of any individual claimant on the date when the complaint is filed if he is specifically named as a party plaintiff in the complaint, or if his name did not so appear, on the subsequent date on which his name is added as a party plaintiff in such action.

(d) In any action or proceeding commenced prior to, on, or after the date of enactment of this subsection, no employer shall be subject to any liability or punishment under this Act or the Portal-to-Portal Act of 1947 on account of his failure to comply with any provision or provisions of such Acts (1) with respect to work heretofore or hereafter performed in a workplace to which the exemption in Section 13(f) is applicable, (2) with respect to work performed in Guam, the Canal Zone or Wake Island before the effective date of this amendment of subsection (d), or (3) with respect to work performed in a possession named in Section 6(a)(3) at any time prior to the establishment by the Secretary, as provided therein, of a minimum wage rate applicable to such work.

(e) Any person who violates the provisions of section 12, relating to child labor, or any regulation issued under that section, shall be subject to a civil penalty of not to exceed $1,000 for each such violation. In determining the amount of such penalty, the appropriateness of such penalty to the size of the business of the person charged and the gravity of the violation shall be considered. The amount of such penalty, when finally determined, may be—

(1) deducted from any sums owing by the United States to the person charged;

(2) recovered in a civil action brought by the Secretary in any court of competent jurisdiction, in which litigation the Secretary shall be represented by the Solicitor of Labor; or

(3) ordered by the court, in an action brought for a violation of section 15(a)(4), to be paid to the Secretary.

Any administrative determination by the Secretary of the amount of such penalty shall be final, unless within fifteen days after receipt of notice thereof by certified mail the person charged with the violation takes exception to the determination that the violations for which the penalty is imposed occurred, in which event final determination of the penalty shall be made in an administrative proceeding after opportunity for hearing in accordance with section 554 of title 5, United States Code, and regulations to be promulgated by the Secretary. Sums collected as penalties pursuant to this section shall be applied toward reimbursement of the costs of determining the violations and assessing and collecting such penalties, in accordance with the provisions of section 9(a) of this title.

§ 217. Injunction proceedings

[Sec. 17] The district courts, together with the United States District Court for the District of the Canal Zone, the District Court of the Virgin Islands, and the District Court of Guam shall have jurisdiction, for cause shown, to restrain violations of section 15, including in the case of violations of section 15(a)(2) the restraint of any withholding of payment of minimum wages or overtime compensation found by the court to be due to employees under this Act (except sums which employees are barred from recovering, at the time of the commencement of the action to restrain the violations, by virtue of the provisions of section 6 of the Portal-to-Portal Act of 1947).

§ 218. Relation to other laws

[Sec. 18] (a) No provision of this Act or of any order thereunder shall excuse noncompliance with any Federal or State law or municipal ordinance establishing a minimum wage higher than the minimum wage established under this Act or a maximum workweek lower than the maximum workweek established under this Act, and no provision of this Act relating to the employment of child labor shall justify noncompliance with any Federal or State law or municipal ordinance establishing a higher standard than the standard established under this Act. No provision of this Act shall justify any employer in reducing a wage paid by him which is in excess of the applicable minimum wage under this Act, or justify any employer in increasing hours of employment maintained by him which are shorter than the maximum hours applicable under this Act.

(b) Notwithstanding any other provision of this chapter (other than section 13(f)) or any other law—

(1) any Federal employee in the Canal Zone engaged in employment of the kind described in section 5102(c)(7) of Title 5 or

(2) any employee employed in a nonappropriated fund instrumentality under the jurisdiction of the Armed Forces,

shall have his basic compensation fixed or adjusted at a wage rate that is not less than the appropriate wage rate provided for in section 6(a)(1) of this Act (except that the wage rate provided for in section 6(b) shall apply to any employee who performed services during the workweek in a work place within the Canal Zone), and shall have his overtime compensation set at an hourly rate not less than the overtime rate provided for in section 7(a)(1) of this Act.

§ 219. Separability of provisions

[Sec. 19] If any provision of this Act or the application of such provision to any person or circumstance is held invalid, the remainder of the Act and the application of such provision to other persons or circumstances shall not be affected thereby.

FLSA Amendments — Unincorporated

(P.L. 99-150, approved November 13, 1985, effective April 15, 1986)

[Sec. 2.] Compensatory time

* * *

(b) A collective bargaining agreement which is in effect on April 15, 1986, and which permits compensatory time off in lieu of overtime compensation shall remain in effect until its expiration date unless otherwise modified, except that compensatory time shall be provided after April 14, 1986, in accordance with section 7(o) of the Fair Labor Standards Act of 1938 (as added by subsection (a) of this Act.)

(c)(1) No state, political subdivision of a State, or interstate governmental agency shall be liable under section 16 of the Fair Labor Standards Act of 1938 for a violation of section 6 (in the case of a territory or possession of the United States), 7, or 11(c) (as it relates to section 7) of such Act occurring before April 15, 1986, with respect to any employee of the State, political subdivision, or agency who would not have been covered by such Act under the Secretary of Labor's special enforcement policy on January 1, 1985, and published in sections 775.2 and 775.4 of title 29 of the Code of Federal Regulations.

(2) A State, political subdivision of a State, or interstate governmental agency may defer until August 1, 1986, the payment of monetary overtime compensation under section 7 of the Fair Labor Standards Act of 1938 for hours worked after April 14, 1986.

* * *

[Sec. 4.] Volunteers

(c) If, before April 15, 1986, the practice of a public agency was to treat certain individuals as volunteers, such individuals shall until April 15, 1986, be considered, for purposes of the Fair Labor Standards Act of 1938, as volunteers and not as employees. No public agency which is a State, a

250

political subdivision of a State, or an interstate governmental agency shall be liable for a violation of section 6 occurring before April 15, 1986, with respect to services deemed by that agency to have been performed for it by an individual on a voluntary basis.

* * *

[Sec. 7.] Effect of Amendments

The amendments made by this Act shall not affect whether a public agency which is a State, political subdivision of a State, or an interstate governmental agency is liable under section 16 of the Fair Labor Standards Act of 1938 for a violation of section 6, 7, or 11 of such Act occurring before April 15, 1986, with respect to any employee of such public agency who would have been covered by such Act under the Secretary of Labor's special enforcement policy on January 1, 1985, and published in section 775.3 of title 29 of the Code of Federal Regulations.

[Sec. 8.] Discrimination

A public agency which is a State, political subdivision of a State, or an interstate governmental agency and which discriminates or has discriminated against an employee with respect to the employee's wages or other terms or conditions of employment because on or after February 19, 1985, the employee asserted coverage under section 7 of the Fair Labor Standards Act of 1938 shall be held to have violated section 15(a)(3) of such Act. The protection against discrimination afforded by the preceding sentence shall be available after August 1, 1986, only for an employee who takes an action described in section 15(a)(3) of such Act.

(P.L. 95-151, effective November 1, 1977)

§ 206(e)(2)(a). Minimum Wage Study Commission [defunct]

[Sec. 2] (e)(1) There is established the Minimum Wage Study Commission (hereinafter in this subsection referred to as the "Commission") which shall conduct a study of the Fair Labor Standards Act of 1938 and the social, political, and economic ramifications of the minimum wage, overtime, and other requirements of that Act. Such study shall include but not be limited to—

> (A) the beneficial effects of the minimum wage, including its effect in ameliorating poverty among working citizens;

(B) the inflationary impact (if any) of increases in the minimum wage prescribed by that Act;

(C) the effect (if any) such increases have on wages paid employees at a rate in excess of the rate prescribed by that Act;

(D) the economic consequence (if any) of authorizing an automatic increase in the rate prescribed in that Act on the basis of an increase in a wage, price, or other index;

(E) the employment and unemployment effects (if any) of providing a different minimum wage rate for youth, and the employment and unemployment effects (if any) on handicapped and aged individuals of an increase in such rate and of providing a different minimum wage rate for such individuals;

(F) the effect (if any) of the full-time student certification program on employment and unemployment;

(G) the employment and unemployment effects (if any) of the minimum wage;

(H) the exemptions from the minimum wage and overtime requirements of the Act;

(I) the relationship (if any) between the Federal minimum wage rates and public assistance programs, including the extent to which employees at such rates are also eligible to receive food stamps and other public assistance;

(J) the overall level of noncompliance with that Act; and

(K) the demographic profile of minimum wage workers.

(2) The Commission shall conduct a study concerning the extent to which the exemptions from the minimum wage and overtime requirements of the Fair Labor Standards Act of 1938 may apply to employees of conglomerates, and shall make a report, within one year after the date of the appointment of the members of the Commission, of the results of such study. For the purposes of this paragraph a "conglomerate" means an establishment (A) which controls, is controlled by, or is under common control with, another establishment the activities of which are not related for a common business purpose to the activities of the establishment employing such employees and (B) whose annual gross volume of sales made or business done, when combined with the annual gross volume of sales made or business done by each establishment which controls, is controlled by, or is under common control with, the establishment employing such employee, exceeds $100,000,000 (exclusive of excise taxes at the retail level which are separately stated). The report shall include an analysis of the effects of eliminating the exemptions from the minimum wage and overtime requirements of such Act that may currently apply to the employees of such conglomerates.

(3) The Commission shall make a report of the results of the study conducted pursuant to paragraph (1) thirty-six months after the date

of the appointment of the members of the Commission. The report shall include such recommendations for legislation as the Commission determines are appropriate. The Commission may make interim or additional reports which it determines are appropriate. Each report shall be made to the President and to the Congress. The Commission shall cease to exist thirty days after the submission of the report required by this paragraph.

(4)(A) The Commission shall consist of eight members as follows:

    (i) Two members appointed by the Secretary of Labor.

    (ii) Two members appointed by the Secretary of Commerce.

    (iii) Two members appointed by the Secretary of Agriculture.

    (iv) Two members appointed by the Secretary of Health and Human Services.

The appointments authorized under this paragraph shall be made within 180 days after the date of enactment of this subsection.

(B) The Chairperson shall be selected by the members of the Commission. Any vacancy in the Commission shall not affect its powers and shall be filled in the same manner in which the original appointment was made.

(C)(i) Except as provided in clause (ii), members of the Commission who are officers or employees of the Federal Government shall serve without compensation. Other members, while engaged in the activities of the Commission, shall be paid at a rate equal to the per diem equivalent of the annual rate payable for grade GS-18 of the General Schedule under section 5332 of title 5, United States Code.

    (ii) While away from their homes or regular places of business in the performance of services for the Commission, members of the Commission shall be allowed travel expenses, including per diem in lieu of subsistence, in the same manner as persons employed intermittently in the Government service are allowed expenses under section 5703 of title 5 of the United States Code.

(5)(A) The Commission may prescribe such rules as may be necessary to carry out its duties under this subsection.

(B) The Commission may hold such hearings, sit and act at such times and places, take such testimony, and receive such evidence as it deems advisable.

(C) Upon request of the Commission, the head of any Federal department or agency is authorized to detail, on a reimbursable basis, any of the personnel of such department or agency to the Commission to assist it in carrying out its duties under this subsection.

(D) The Department of Labor shall furnish such professional, technical, and research assistance as required by the Commission.

(E) The Administrator of General Services shall provide to the Commission on a reimbursable basis such administrative support services as the Commission may request to carry out its duties under this subsection.

(F) The Commission may secure directly from any department or agency of the United States such information as the Commission may require to carry out its duties under this subsection. Upon request of the Commission, the head of any such department or agency shall furnish such information to the Commission.

(G) The Commission may use the United States mails in the same manner and upon the same conditions as other departments and agencies of the United States.

(6)(A) The Chairperson may appoint an executive director of the Commission who shall perform such duties as the Chairperson may prescribe.

(B) With approval of the Chairperson, the executive director may appoint and fix the pay of such clerical personnel as are necessary for the Commission to carry out its duties.

(C) The executive director and staff shall be appointed without regard to the provisions of title 5, United States Code, governing appointments in the competitive service, and shall be paid without regard to the provisions of chapter 51 and subchapter III of chapter 53 of such title relating to classification and General Schedule pay rates but at rates not in excess of the annual rate payable for grade GS-18 of the General Schedule under section 5332 of such title.

(D) The executive director, with the concurrence of the Chairperson, may obtain temporary and intermittent services of experts and consultants in accordance with the provisions of section 3109 of title 5, United States Code.

Portal-To-Portal Act of 1947

(P.L. 49, approved May 14, 1947; as last amended by P.L. 93–259,
effective May 1, 1974)

§ 251.   Congressional findings and declaration of policy

[Sec. 1] (a) The Congress hereby finds that the Fair Labor Standards Act
of 1938, as amended, has been interpreted judicially in disregard of long-
established customs, practices, and contracts between employers and employees, thereby creating wholly unexpected liabilities, immense in amount and
retroactive in operation, upon employers with the results that, if said Act as
so interpreted or claims arising under such interpretations were permitted to
stand, (1) the payment of such liabilities would bring about financial ruin of
many employers and seriously impair the capital resources of many others,
thereby resulting in the reduction of industrial operations, halting of expan-
sion and development, curtailing employment, and the earning power of
employees; (2) the credit of many employers would be seriously impaired;
(3) there would be created both an extended and continuous uncertainty on
the part of industry, both employer and employee, as to the financial
condition of productive establishments and a gross inequality of competitive
conditions between employers and between industries; (4) employees would
receive windfall payments, including liquidated damages, of sums for activities performed by them without any expectation of reward beyond that
included in their agreed rates of pay; (5) there would occur the promotion of
increasing demands for payment to employees for engaging in activities no
compensation for which had been contemplated by either the employer or
employee at the time they were engaged in; (6) voluntary collective bargaining would be interfered with and industrial disputes between employees and
employers and between employees and employees would be created; (7) the
courts of the country would be burdened with excessive and needless
litigation and champertous practices would be encouraged; (8) the Public
Treasury would be deprived of large sums of revenues and public finances
would be seriously deranged by claims against the Public Treasury for
refunds of taxes already paid; (9) the cost to the Government of goods and
services heretofore and hereafter purchased by its various departments and

255

agencies would be unreasonably increased and the Public Treasury would be seriously affected by consequent increased cost of war contracts; and (10) serious and adverse effects upon the revenues of Federal, State, and local governments would occur.

The Congress further finds that all of the foregoing constitutes a substanial burden on commerce and a substantial obstruction to the free flow of goods in commerce.

The Congress, therefore, further finds and declares that it is in the national public interest and for the general welfare, essential to national defense, and necessary to aid, protect, and foster commerce, that this Act be enacted.

The Congress further finds that the varying and extended periods of time for which, under the laws of the several States, potential retroactive liability may be imposed upon employers, have given and will give rise to great difficulties in the sound and orderly conduct of business and industry.

The Congress further finds and declares that all of the results which have arisen or may rise under the Fair Labor Standards Act of 1938, as amended, as aforesaid, may (except as to liability for liquidated damages) arise with respect to the Walsh-Healey and Bacon-Davis Acts and that it is, therefore, in the national public interest and for the general welfare, essential to national defense, and necessary to aid, protect, and foster commerce, that this Act shall apply to the Walsh-Healey Act and the Bacon-Davis Act.

(b) It is hereby declared to be the policy of the Congress in order to meet the existing emergency and to correct existing evils (1) to relieve and protect interstate commerce from practices which burden and obstruct it; (2) to protect the right of collective bargaining; and (3) to define and limit the jurisdiction of the courts.

§ 252. Relief from certain existing claims under the Fair Labor Standards Act of 1938, the Walsh-Healey Act, and the Bacon-Davis Act

[Sec. 2] (a) No employer shall be subject to any liability or punishment under the Fair Labor Standards Act of 1938, as amended, the Walsh-Healey Act, or the Bacon-Davis Act (in any action or proceeding commenced prior to or on or after the date of the enactment of this Act), on account of the failure of such employer to pay an employee minimum wages, or to pay an employee overtime compensation, for or on account of any activity of an employee engaged in prior to the date of the enactment of this Act, except an activity which was compensated by either—

(1) an express provision of a written or nonwritten contract in effect, at the time of such activity, between such employee, his agent, or collective-bargaining representative and his employer; or

(2) a custom or practice in effect, at the time of such activity, at the establishment or other place where such employee was employed,

covering such activity, not inconsistent with a written or nonwritten contract, in effect at the time of such activity, between such employee, his agent, or collective-bargaining representative and his employer.

(b) For the purposes of subsection (a), an activity shall be considered as compensable under such contract provision or such custom or practice only when it was engaged in during the portion of the day with respect to which it was so made compensable.

(c) In the application of the minimum wage and overtime compensation provisions of the Fair Labor Standards Act of 1938, as amended, of the Walsh-Healey Act, or of the Bacon-Davis Act, in determining the time for which an employer employed an employee there shall be counted all that time, but only that time, during which the employee engaged in activities which were compensable within the meaning of subsections (a) and (b) of this section.

(d) No court of the United States, of any State, Territory, or possession of the United States, or of the District of Columbia, shall have jurisdiction of any action or proceeding, whether instituted prior to or on or after the date of the enactment of this Act, to enforce liability or impose punishment for or on account of the failure of the employer to pay minimum wages or overtime compensation under the Fair Labor Standards Act of 1938, as amended, under the Walsh-Healey Act, or under the Bacon-Davis Act, to the extent that such action or proceeding seeks to enforce any liability or impose any punishment with respect to an activity which was not compensable under subsections (a) and (b) of this section.

(e) No cause of action based on unpaid minimum wages, unpaid overtime compensation, or liquidated damages, under the Fair Labor Standards Act of 1938, as amended, the Walsh-Healey Act, or the Bacon-Davis Act, which accrued prior to the date of the enactment of this Act, or any interest in such cause of action, shall hereafter be assignable, in whole or in part, to the extent that such cause of action is based on an activity which was not compensable within the meaning of subsections (a) and (b).

§ 253. Compromise and waiver

[Sec. 3] (a) Any cause of action under the Fair Labor Standards Act of 1938, as amended, the Walsh-Healey Act, or the Bacon-Davis Act, which accrued prior to the date of the enactment of this Act, or any action (whether instituted prior to or on or after the date of the enactment of this Act) to enforce such a cause of action, may hereafter be compromised in whole or in part, if there exists a bona fide dispute as to the amount payable by the employer to his employee; except that no such action or cause of action may be so compromised to the extent that such compromise is based on an hourly wage rate less than the minimum required under such Act, or on a payment for overtime at a rate less than one and one-half times such minimum hourly wage rate.

(b) Any employee may hereafter waive his right under the Fair Labor Standards Act of 1938, as amended, to liquidated damages, in whole or in part, with respect to activities engaged in prior to the date of the enactment of this Act.

(c) Any such compromise or waiver, in the absence of fraud or duress, shall, according to the terms thereof, be a complete satisfaction of such cause of action and a complete bar to any action based on such cause of action.

(d) The provisions of this section shall also be applicable to any compromise or waiver heretofore so made or given.

(e) As used in this section, the term "compromise" includes "adjustment", "settlement", and "release".

§ 254. Relief from liability and punishment under the Fair Labor Standards Act of 1938, the Walsh-Healey Act, and the Bacon-Davis Act

[Sec. 4] (a) Except as provided in subsection (b), no employer shall be subject to any liability or punishment under the Fair Labor Standards Act of 1938, as amended, the Walsh-Healey Act, or the Bacon-Davis Act, on account of the failure of such employer to pay an employee minimum wages, or to pay an employee overtime compensation, for or on account of any of the following activities of such employee engaged in on or after the date of the enactment of this Act—

(1) walking, riding, or traveling to and from the actual place of performance of the principal activity or activities which such employee is employed to perform, and

(2) activities which are preliminary to or postliminary to said principal activity or activities,

which occur either prior to the time on any particular workday at which such employee commences, or subsequent to the time on any particular workday at which he ceases, such principal activity or activities.

(b) Notwithstanding the provisions of subsection (a) which relieve an employer from liability and punishment with respect to an activity, the employer shall not be so relieved if such activity is compensable by either—

(1) an express provision of a written or nonwritten contract in effect, at the time of such activity, between such employee, his agent, or collective-bargaining representative and his employer; or

(2) a custom or practice in effect, at the time of such activity, at the establishment or other place where such employee is employed, covering such activity, not inconsistent with a written or nonwritten contract, in effect at the time of such activity, between such employee, his agent, or collective-bargaining representative and his employer.

(c) For the purposes of subsection (b), an activity shall be considered as compensable under such contract provision or such custom or practice only when it is engaged in during the portion of the day with respect to which it is so made compensable.

(d) In the application of the minimum wage and overtime compensation provisions of the Fair Labor Standards Act of 1938, as amended, of the Walsh-Healey Act, or of the Bacon-Davis Act, in determining the time for which an employer employs an employee with respect to walking, riding, traveling, or other preliminary or postliminary activities described in subsection (a) of this section, there shall be counted all that time, but only that time, during which the employee engages in any such activity which is compensable within the meaning of subsections (b) and (c) of this section.

[Sec. 5] [Deleted.]

§ 255. Statute of limitations

[Sec. 6] Any action commenced on or after the date of the enactment of this Act to enforce any cause of action for unpaid minimum wages, unpaid overtime compensation, or liquidated damages, under the Fair Labor Standards Act of 1938, as amended, the Walsh-Healey Act, or the Bacon-Davis Act—

(a) if the cause of action accrues on or after the date of the enactment of this Act—may be commenced within two years after the cause of action accrued, and every such action shall be forever barred unless commenced within two years after the cause of action accrued, except that a cause of action arising out of a willful violation may be commenced within three years after the cause of action accrued;

(b) if the cause of action accrued prior to the date of the enactment of this Act—may be commenced within whichever of the following periods is the shorter: (1) two years after the cause of action accrued, or (2) the period prescribed by the applicable State statute of limitations; and, except as provided in paragraph (c), every such action shall be forever barred unless commenced within the shorter of such two periods;

(c) if the cause of action accrued prior to the date of the enactment of this Act, the action shall not be barred by paragraph (b) if it is commenced within one hundred and twenty days after the date of the enactment of this Act unless at the time commenced it is barred by an applicable State statute of limitations;

(d) with respect to any cause of action brought under section 16(b) of the Fair Labor Standards Act of 1938 against a State or a political subdivision of a State in a district court of the United States on or before April 18, 1973, the running of the statutory periods of limitation shall be deemed suspended during the period beginning with the commencement of any such action and ending one hundred and eighty days after the effective date of the Fair Labor Standards Amendments of 1974, except that such suspension shall not be applicable if in such action judgment has been entered for the defendant on the grounds other than State immunity from Federal jurisdiction.

§ 256. Determination of commencement of future actions

[Sec. 7] In determining when an action is commenced for the purposes of section 6, an action commenced on or after the date of the enactment of this Act under the Fair Labor Standards Act of 1938, as amended, the Walsh-Healey Act, or the Bacon-Davis Act, shall be considered to be commenced on the date when the complaint is filed; except that in the case of a collective or class action instituted under the Fair Labor Standards Act of 1938, as amended, or the Bacon-Davis Act, it shall be considered to be commenced in the case of any individual claimant—

(a) on the date when the complaint is filed, if he is specifically named as a party plaintiff in the complaint and his written consent to become a party plaintiff is filed on such date in the court in which the action is brought; or

(b) if such written consent was not so filed or if his name did not so appear—on the subsequent date on which such written consent is filed in the court in which the action was commenced.

§ 257. Pending collective and representative actions

[Sec. 8] The statute of limitations prescribed in section 6(b) shall also be applicable (in the case of a collective or representative action commenced prior to the date of the enactment of this Act under the Fair Labor Standards Act of 1938, as amended) to an individual claimant who has not been specifically named as a party plaintiff to the action prior to the expiration of one hundred and twenty days after the date of the enactment of this Act. In the application of such statute of limitations such action shall be considered to have been commenced as to him when, and only when, his written consent to become a party plaintiff to the action is filed in the court in which the action was brought.

§ 258. Reliance on past administrative rulings, etc.

[Sec. 9] In any action or proceeding commenced prior to or on or after the date of the enactment of this Act based on any act or omission prior to the date of the enactment of this Act, no employer shall be subject to any liability or punishment for or on account of the failure of the employer to pay minimum wages or overtime compensation under the Fair Labor Standards Act of 1938, as amended, the Walsh-Healey Act, or the Bacon-Davis Act, if he pleads and proves that the act or omission complained of was in good faith in conformity with and in reliance on any administrative regulation, order, ruling, approval, or interpretation, of any agency of the United States, or any administrative practice or enforcement policy of any such agency with respect to the class of employers to which he belonged. Such a defense, if established, shall be a bar to the action or proceeding, notwithstanding that after such act or omission, such administrative regulation, order, ruling, approval, interpretation, practice, or enforcement policy is modified or rescinded or is determined by judicial authority to be invalid or of no legal effect.

§ 259.   Reliance in future on administrative rulings, etc.

[Sec. 10] (a) In any action or proceeding based on any act or omission on or after the date of the enactment of this Act, no employer shall be subject to any liability or punishment for or on account of the failure of the employer to pay minimum wages or overtime compensation under the Fair Labor Standards Act of 1938, as amended, the Walsh-Healey Act, or the Bacon-Davis Act, if he pleads and proves that the act or omission complained of was in good faith in conformity with and in reliance on any written administrative regulation, order, ruling, approval, or interpretation, of the agency of the United States specified in subsection (b) of this section, or any administrative practice or enforcement policy of such agency with respect to the class of employers to which he belonged. Such a defense, if established, shall be a bar to the action or proceeding, notwithstanding that after such act or omission, such administrative regulation, order, ruling, approval, interpretation, practice, or enforcement policy is modified or rescinded or is determined by judicial authority to be invalid or of no legal effect.

(b) The agency referred to in subsection (a) shall be—
(1) In the case of the Fair Labor Standards Act of 1938, as amended—the Administrator of the Wage and Hour Division of the Department of Labor;
(2) In the case of the Walsh-Healey Act—the Secretary of Labor, or any Federal officer utilized by him in the administration of such Act; and
(3) In the case of the Bacon-Davis Act—the Secretary of Labor.

§ 260.   Liquidated damages

[Sec. 11] In any action commenced prior to or on or after the date of the enactment of this Act to recover unpaid minimum wages, unpaid overtime compensation, or liquidated damages, under the Fair Labor Standards Act of 1938, as amended, if the employer shows to the satisfaction of the court that the act or omission giving rise to such action was in good faith and that he had reasonable grounds for believing that his act or omission was not a violation of the Fair Labor Standards Act of 1938, as amended, the court may, in its sound discretion, award no liquidated damages or award any amount thereof not to exceed the amount specified in section 16 of such Act.

§ 261. Applicability of "area of production" regulations

[Sec. 12] No employer shall be subject to any liability or punishment under the Fair Labor Standards Act of 1938, as amended, on account of the failure of such employer to pay an employee minimum wages, or to pay an employee overtime compensation, for or on account of an activity engaged in by such employee prior to December 26, 1946, if such employer—

(1) was not so subject by reason of the definition of an "area of production", by a regulation of the Administrator of the Wage and Hour Division of the Department of Labor, which regulation was applicable at the time of performance of the activity even though at that time the regulation was invalid; or

(2) would not have been so subject if the regulation signed on December 18, 1946 (Federal Register, Vol. 11, p. 14648) had been in force on or after October 24, 1938.

§ 262. Definitions

[Sec. 13] (a) When the terms "employer", "employee", and "wage" are used in this Act in relation to the Fair Labor Standards Act of 1938, as amended, they shall have the same meaning as when used in such Act of 1938.

(b) When the term "employer" is used in this Act in relation to the Walsh-Healey Act or Bacon-Davis Act it shall mean the contractor or subcontractor covered by such Act.

(c) When the term "employee" is used in this Act in relation to the Walsh-Healey Act or the Bacon-Davis Act it shall mean any individual employed by the contractor or subcontractor covered by such Act in the performance of his contract or subcontract.

(d) The term "Walsh-Healey Act" means the Act entitled "An Act to provide conditions for the purchase of supplies and the making of contracts by the United States, and for other purposes", approved June 30, 1936 (49 Stat. 2036), as amended; and the term "Bacon-Davis Act" means the Act entitled "An Act to amend the Act approved March 3, 1931, relating to the rate of wages for laborers and mechanics employed by contractors and subcontractors on public buildings", approved August 30, 1935 (49 Stat. 1011), as amended.

(e) As used in section 6 the term "State" means any State of the United States or the District of Columbia or any Territory or possession of the United States.

Equal Pay Act of 1963

(P.L. 88–38, approved June 10, 1963, effective June 11, 1964; amending P.L. 75–718, effective October 24, 1938)

§ 206(d)(1).   Prohibition of sex discrimination

[Sec. 2] (d)(1) No employer having employees subject to any provisions of this section shall discriminate, within any establishment in which such employees are employed, between employees on the basis of sex by paying wages to employees in such establishment at a rate less than the rate at which he pays wages to employees of the opposite sex in such establishment for equal work on jobs the performance of which requires equal skill, effort, and responsibility, and which are performed under similar working conditions, except where such payment is made pursuant to (i) a seniority system; (ii) a merit system; (iii) a system which measures earnings by quantity or quality of production; or (iv) a differential based on any other factor other than sex: *Provided*, That an employer who is paying a wage rate differential in violation of this subsection shall not, in order to comply with the provisions of this subsection, reduce the wage rate of any employee.

(2) No labor organization, or its agents, representing employees of an employer having employees subject to any provisions of this section shall cause or attempt to cause such an employer to discriminate against an employee in violation of paragraph (1) of this subsection.

(3) For purposes of administration and enforcement, any amounts owing to any employee which have been withheld in violation of this subsection shall be deemed to be unpaid minimum wages or unpaid overtime compensation under this Act.

(4) As used in this subsection, the term "labor organization" means any organization of any kind, or any agency or employee representation committee or plan, in which employees participate and which exists for the purpose, in whole or in part, of dealing with employers concerning grievances, labor disputes, wages, rate of pay, hours of employment, or conditions of work.

6

Government Contract Laws

Davis-Bacon Act

(P.L. 403, approved March 3, 1931; as last amended by P.L. 88–349, effective September 30, 1964)

§ 276a.   Rate of wages for laborers and mechanics

[Sec. 1] (a) The advertised specifications for every contract in excess of $2,000, to which the United States or the District of Columbia is a party, for construction, alteration, and/or repair, including painting and decorating, of public buildings or public works of the United States or the District of Columbia within the geographical limits of the States of the Union or the District of Columbia, and which requires or involves the employment of mechanics and/or laborers shall contain a provision stating the minimum wages to be paid various classes of laborers and mechanics which shall be based upon the wages that will be determined by the Secretary of Labor to be prevailing for the corresponding classes of laborers and mechanics employed on projects of a character similar to the contract work in the city, town, village, or other civil subdivision of the State in which the work is to be performed, or in the District of Columbia if the work is to be performed there; and every contract based upon these specifications shall contain a stipulation that the contractor or his subcontractor shall pay all mechanics and laborers employed directly upon the site of the work, unconditionally and not less often than once a week, and without subsequent deduction or rebate on any account, the full amounts accrued at time of payment, computed at wage rates not less than those stated in the advertised specifications, regardless of any contractual relationship which may be alleged to exist between the contractor or subcontractor and such laborers and mechanics, and that the scale of wages to be paid shall be posted by the contractor in a prominent and easily accessible place at the site of work; and further stipulation that there may be withheld from the contractor so much of accrued payments as may be considered necessary by the contracting officer to pay to laborers and mechanics employed by the contractor or any subcontractor on the work the difference between the rates of wages required by the contract to be paid laborers and mechanics on the work and the rates of wages received by such laborers and mechanics and not refunded to the contractor, subcontractors, or their agents.

(b) As used in this Act the term "wages", "scale of wages", "wage rates", "minimum wages", and "prevailing wages" shall include—
  (1) the basic hourly rate of pay; and
  (2) the amount of—
    (A) the rate of contribution irrevocably made by a contractor or subcontractor to a trustee or to a third person pursuant to a fund, plan, or program; and
    (B) the rate of costs to the contractor or subcontractor which may be reasonably anticipated in providing benefits to laborers and mechanics pursuant to an enforcible commitment to carry out a financially responsible plan or program which was communicated in writing to the laborers and mechanics affected,

for medical or hospital care, pensions on retirement or death, compensation for injuries or illness resulting from occupational activity, or insurance to provide any of the foregoing, for unemployment benefits, life insurance, disability and sickness insurance, or accident insurance, for vacation and holiday pay, for defraying costs of apprenticeship or other similar programs, or for other bona fide fringe benefits, but only where the contractor or subcontractor is not required by other Federal, State, or local law to provide any of such benefits:

Provided, That the obligation of a contractor or subcontractor to make payment in accordance with the prevailing wage determinations of the Secretary of Labor, insofar as this Act and other Acts incorporating this Act by reference are concerned may be discharged by the making of payments in cash, by the making of contributions of a type referred to in paragraph (2)(A), or by the assumption of an enforcible commitment to bear the costs of a plan or program of a type referred to in paragraph (2)(B), or any combination thereof, where the aggregate of any such payments, contributions, and costs is not less than the rate of pay described in paragraph (1) plus the amount referred to in paragraph (2).

In determining the overtime pay to which the laborer or mechanic is entitled under any Federal law, his regular or basic hourly rate of pay (or other alternative rate upon which premium rate of overtime compensation is computed) shall be deemed to be the rate computed under paragraph (1), except that where the amount of payments, contributions, or costs incurred with respect to him exceeds the prevailing wage applicable to him under this Act, such regular or basic hourly rate of pay (or such other alternative rate) shall be arrived at by deducting from the amount of payments, contributions or costs actually incurred with respect to him, the amount of contributions or costs of the types described in paragraph (2) actually incurred with respect to him, or the amount determined under paragraph (2) but not actually paid, whichever amount is the greater.

§ 276a–1. Termination of work on failure to pay agreed wages; completion of work by Government

[Sec. 2] Every contract within the scope of this Act shall contain the further provision that in the event it is found by the contracting officer that any laborer or mechanic employed by the contractor or any subcontractor directly on the site of the work covered by the contract has been or is being paid a rate of wages less than the rate of wages required by the contract to be paid as aforesaid, the Government may, by written notice to the contractor, terminate his right to proceed with the work or such part of the work as to which there has been a failure to pay said required wages and to prosecute the work to completion by contract or otherwise, and the contractor and his sureties shall be liable to the Government for any excess costs occasioned the Government thereby.

§ 276a–2. Payment of wages by Comptroller General from withheld payments; listing contractors violating contracts

[Sec. 3] (a) The Comptroller General of the United States is hereby authorized and directed to pay directly to laborers and mechanics from any accrued payments withheld under the terms of the contract any wages found to be due laborers and mechanics pursuant to this Act; and the Comptroller General of the United States is further authorized and is directed to distribute a list to all departments of the Government giving the names of persons or firms whom he has found to have disregarded their obligations to employees and subcontractors. No contract shall be awarded to the persons or firms appearing on this list or to any firm, corporation, partnership, or association in which such persons or firms have an interest until three years have elapsed from the date of publication of the list containing the names of such persons or firms.

(b) If the accrued payments withheld under the terms of the contract, as aforesaid, are insufficient to reimburse all the laborers and mechanics with respect to whom there has been a failure to pay the wages required pursuant to this Act, such laborers and mechanics shall have the right of action and/or of intervention against the contractor and his sureties conferred by law upon persons furnishing labor or materials, and in such proceedings it shall be no defense that such laborers and mechanics accepted or agreed to accept less than the required rate of wages or voluntarily made refunds.

§ 276a–3. Effect on other Federal laws

[Sec. 4] Sections 276a to 276a-5 of this title shall not be construed to supersede or impair any authority otherwise granted by Federal law to provide for the establishment of specific wage rates.

§ 276a–4. Effective date of sections 276a to 276a–5

[Sec. 5] Sections 276a to 276a-5 of this title shall take effect thirty days after August 30, 1935, but shall not affect any contract then existing or any contract that may thereafter be entered into pursuant to invitation for bids that are outstanding on August 30, 1935.

§ 276a–5. Suspension of sections 276a to 276a–5 during emergency

[Sec. 6] In the event of a national emergency the President is authorized to suspend the provisions of Sections 276a to 276a-5 of this title.

* * *

§ 276a–7. Application of sections 276a to 276a–5 to contracts entered into without regard to section 5 of title 41

The fact that any contract authorized by any Act is entered into without regard to Section 5 of Title 41, or upon a cost-plus-a-fixed-fee basis or otherwise without advertising for proposals, shall not be construed to render inapplicable the provisions of Sections 276a to 276a-5 of this title, if such Act would otherwise be applicable to such contract.

Walsh-Healey Public Contracts Act

(P.L. 846, approved June 30, 1936; as last amended by P.L. 99–145, effective January 1, 1986)

§ 35. Contracts for materials, etc., exceeding $10,000; representations and stipulations

[Sec. 1] In any contract made and entered into by any executive department, independent establishment, or other agency or instrumentality of the United States, or by the District of Columbia, or by any corporation all the stock of which is beneficially owned by the United States (all the foregoing being hereinafter designated as agencies of the United States), for the manufacture or furnishing of materials, supplies, articles, and equipment in any amount exceeding $10,000, there shall be included the following representations and stipulations:

(a) That the contractor is the manufacturer of a regular dealer in the materials, supplies, articles, or equipment to be manufactured or used in the performance of the contract;

(b) That all persons employed by the contractor in the manufacture or furnishing of the materials, supplies, articles, or equipment used in the performance of the contract will be paid, without subsequent deduction or rebate on any account, not less than the minimum wages as determined by the Secretary of Labor to be the prevailing minimum wages for persons employed on similar work or in the particular or similar industries or groups of industries currently operating in the locality in which the materials, supplies, articles, or equipment are to be manufactured or furnished under said contract;

(c) That no person employed by the contractor in the manufacture or furnishing of the materials, supplies, articles, or equipment used in the performance of the contract shall be permitted to work in excess of forty hours in any one week: *Provided*, That the provisions of this subsection shall not apply to any employer who shall have entered into an agreement with his employees pursuant to the provisions of paragraphs (1) or (2) of subsection (b) of section 7 of an Act entitled "Fair Labor Standards Act of 1938";

(d) That no male person under sixteen years of age and no female person under eighteen years of age and no convict labor will be employed by the contractor in the manufacture or production or furnishing of any of the materials, supplies, articles, or equipment included in such contract, except that this section, or any other law or Executive order containing similar prohibitions against purchase of goods by the Federal Government, shall not apply to convict labor which satisfies the conditions of section 1761(c) of title 18; and

(e) That no part of such contract will be performed nor will any of the materials, supplies, articles, or equipment to be manufactured or furnished under said contract be manufactured or fabricated in any plants, factories, buildings, or surroundings or under working conditions which are unsanitary or hazardous or dangerous to the health and safety of employees engaged in the performance of said contract. Compliance with the safety, sanitary, and factory inspection laws of the State in which the work or part thereof is to be performed shall be prima-facie evidence of compliance with this subsection.

§ 36. Same; liability for contract breach; cancellation; completion by Government agency; employee's wages

[Sec. 2] Any breach or violation of any of the representations and stipulations in any contract for the purposes set forth in section 1 hereof shall render the party responsible therefor liable to the United States of America for liquidated damages, in addition to damages for any other breach of such contract, the sum of $10 per day for each male person under sixteen years of age or each female person under eighteen years of age, or each convict laborer knowingly employed in the performance of such contract, and a sum equal to the amount of any deductions, rebates, refunds, or underpayment of wages due to any employee engaged in the performance of such contract; and, in addition the agency of the United States entering into such contract shall have the right to cancel same and to make open-market purchases or enter into other contracts for the completion of the original contract, charging any additional cost to the original contractor. Any sums of money due to the United States of America by reason of any violation of any of the representations and stipulations of said contract set forth in section 1 hereof may be withheld from any amounts due on any such contracts or may be recovered in suits brought in the name of the United States of America by the Attorney General thereof. All sums withheld or recovered as deductions, rebates, refunds, or underpayments of wages shall be held in a special deposit account and shall be paid, on order of the Secretary of Labor, directly to the employees who have been paid less than minimum rates of pay as set forth in such contracts and on whose account such sums were withheld or recovered: *Provided*, That no claims by employees for such payments shall be entertained unless made within one year from the date of actual notice to the contractor of the withholding or recovery of such sums by the United States of America.

§ 37. Same; distribution of list of persons breaching contract; future contracts prohibited

[Sec. 3] The Comptroller General is authorized and directed to distribute a list to all agencies of the United States containing the names of persons or firms found by the Secretary of Labor to have breached any of the agreements or representations required by this Act. Unless the Secretary of Labor otherwise recommends no contracts shall be awarded to such persons or firms or to any firm, corporation, partnership, or association in which such persons or firms have a controlling interest until three years have elapsed from the date the Secretary of Labor determines such breach to have occurred.

§ 38. Same; administration of provisions; officers and employees; appointment; investigations; rules and regulations

[Sec. 4] The Secretary of Labor is authorized and directed to administer the provisions of this Act and to utilize such Federal officers and employees and, with the consent of the State, such State and local officers and employees as he may find necessary to assist in the administration of said sections and to prescribe rules and regulations with respect thereto. The Secretary shall appoint, subject to chapter 51 and subchapter III of chapter 53 of title 5, an administrative officer, and such attorneys and experts, and other employees with regard to existing laws applicable to the employment and compensation of officers and employees of the United States, as he may from time to time find necessary for the administration of this Act. The Secretary of Labor or his authorized representatives shall have power to make investigations and findings as herein provided, and prosecute any inquiry necessary to his functions in any part of the United States. The Secretary of Labor shall have authority from time to time to make, amend, and rescind such rules and regulations as may be necessary to carry out the provisions of this Act.

§ 39. Same; hearings on provisions by Secretary of Labor; witness fees; failure to obey order; punishment

[Sec. 5] Upon his own motion or on application of any person affected by any ruling of any agency of the United States in relation to any proposal or contract involving any of the provisions of this Act, and on complaint of a breach or violation of any representation or stipulation as provided in said sections, the Secretary of Labor, or an impartial representative designated by him, shall have the power to hold hearings and to issue orders requiring the attendance and testimony of witnesses and the production of evidence under oath. Witnesses shall be paid the same fees and mileage that are paid witnesses in the courts of the United States. In case of contumacy, failure, or refusal of any person to obey such an order, any District Court of the United States or of any Territory or possession within the jurisdiction of which the inquiry is carried on, or within the jurisdiction of which said person who is guilty of contumacy, failure, or refusal is found, or resides or transacts business, upon the application by the Secretary of Labor or representative designated by him, shall have jurisdiction to issue to such person an order requiring such person to appear before him or representative designed by him, to produce evidence if, as, and when so ordered, and to give testimony relating to the matter under investigation or in question; and any failure to obey such order of the court may be punished by said court as a contempt thereof; and shall make findings of fact after notice and hearing, which findings shall be conclusive upon all agencies of the United States, and if supported by the preponderance of the evidence, shall be conclusive in any court of the United States; and the Secretary of Labor or authorized representative shall have the power, and is authorized, to make such decisions, based upon findings of fact, as are deemed to be necessary to enforce the provisions of sections 35 to 45 of this Act.

§ 40. Same; exceptions; modification of contracts; variations; overtime; suspension of representations and stipulations

[Sec. 6] Upon a written finding by the head of the contracting agency or department that the inclusion in the proposal or contract of the representations or stipulations set forth in section 1 of this title will seriously impair the conduct of Government business, the Secretary of Labor shall make exceptions in specific cases or otherwise when justice or public interest will be served thereby. Upon the joint recommendation of the contracting agency and the contractor, the Secretary of Labor may modify the terms of an existing contract respecting minimum rates of pay and maximum hours of labor as he may find necessary and proper in the public interest or to prevent injustice and undue hardship. The Secretary of Labor may provide reasonable limitations and may make rules and regulations allowing reasonable variations, tolerances, and exemptions to and from any or all provisions of this Act respecting minimum rates of pay and maximum hours of labor or the extent of the application of this Act to contractors, as hereinbefore described. Whenever the Secretary of Labor shall permit an increase in the maximum hours of labor stipulated in the contract, he shall set a rate of pay for any overtime, which rate shall be not less than one and one-half times the basic hourly rate received by any employee affected: *Provided,* That whenever in his judgment such course is in the public interest, the President is authorized to suspend any or all of the representations and stipulations contained in section 1 of this Act.

§ 41. Same; "person" defined

[Sec. 7] Whenever used in this Act, the word "person" includes one or more individuals, partnerships, associations, corporations, legal representatives, trustees, trustees in bankruptcy, or receivers.

§ 42. Same; effect of sections 35-45 on other laws

[Sec. 8] The provisions of this Act shall not be construed to modify or amend Title III of the act entitled "An Act making appropriations for the Treasury and Post Office Departments for the fiscal year ending June 30, 1934, and for other purposes", approved May 3, 1933 (commonly known as the Buy American Act), nor shall the provisions of this Act be construed to modify or amend the Act entitled "An Act relating to the rate of wages for laborers and mechanics employed on public buildings of the United States and the District of Columbia by contractors and subcontractors, and for other purposes", approved March 3, 1931 (commonly known as the Bacon-Davis Act), as amended from time to time, nor the labor provisions of Title II of the National Industrial Recovery Act, approved June 16, 1933, as extended, or of section 7 of the Emergency Relief Appropriation Act, approved April 8, 1935; nor shall the provisions of this Act be construed to modify or amend chapter 307 and section 4162 of title 18.

§ 43. Same; sections 35-45 not applicable to certain contracts

[Sec. 9] This Act shall not apply to purchases of such materials, supplies, articles, or equipment as may usually be bought in the open market; nor shall they apply to perishables, including dairy, livestock and nursery products, or to agricultural or farm products processed for first sale by the original producers; nor to any contracts made by the Secretary of Agriculture for the purchase of agricultural commodities or the products thereof. Nothing in said sections shall be construed to apply to carriage of freight or personnel by vessel, airplane, bus, truck, express, or railway line where published tariff rates are in effect or to common carriers subject to the Communications Act of 1934.

§ 43a. Applicability of Administrative Procedure Act; wage determination; administrative review; judicial review

[Sec. 10] (a) Notwithstanding any provision of the Administrative Procedure Act, such Act shall be applicable in the administration of sections 1 to 5 and 7 to 9 of this Act.

(b) All wage determinations under section 1 of this Act shall be made on the record after opportunity for a hearing. Review of any such wage determination, or of the applicability of any such wage determination, may be had within ninety days after such determination is made in the manner provided in chapter 7 of title 5 by any person adversely affected or aggrieved thereby, who shall be deemed to include any manufacturer of, or regular dealer in, materials, supplies, articles or equipment purchased or to be purchased by the Government from any source, who is in any industry to which such wage determination is applicable.

(c) Notwithstanding the inclusion of any stipulations required by any provision of this Act in any contract subject to this Act, any interested person shall have the right of judicial review of any legal question which might otherwise be raised, including, but not limited to, wage determinations and the interpretation of the terms "locality", "regular dealer", "manufacturer", and "open market".

§ 44. Separability of Walsh-Healey provisions

[Sec. 11] If any provision of this Act, or the application thereof to any persons or circumstances, is held invalid, the remainder of the Act, and the application of such provisions to other persons or circumstances, shall not be affected thereby.

§ 45. Same; effective date; exception as to representations with respect to minimum wages

[Sec. 12] This Act shall apply to all contracts entered into pursuant to invitations for bids issued on or after ninety days from the effective date of this Act: *Provided, however,* That the provisions requiring the inclusion of representations with respect to minimum wages shall apply only to purchases or contracts relating to such industries as have been the subject matter of a determination by the Secretary of Labor.

McNamara-O'Hara Service Contract Act

(P.L. 89–286, approved October 22, 1965; as last amended by P.L. 94–489, October 13, 1976)

§ 351. Required contract provisions; minimum wages

[Sec. 2] (a) Every contract (and any bid specification therefor) entered into by the United States or the District of Columbia in excess of $2,500, except as provided in section 7 of this Act, whether negotiated or advertised, the principal purpose of which is to furnish services in the United States through the use of service employees shall contain the following:

(1) A provision specifying the minimum monetary wages to be paid the various classes of service employees in the performance of the contract or any subcontract thereunder, as determined by the Secretary, or his authorized representative, in accordance with prevailing rates for such employees in the locality, or, where a collective-bargaining agreement covers any such service employees, in accordance with the rates for such employees provided for in such agreement, including prospective wage increases provided for in such agreement as a result of arm's length negotiations. In no case shall such wages be lower than the minimum specified in subsection (b) of this section.

(2) A provision specifying the fringe benefits to be furnished in the various classes of service employees, engaged in the performance of the contract or any subcontract thereunder, as determined by the Secretary or his authorized representative to be prevailing for such employees in the locality, or, where a collective-bargaining agreement covers any such service employees, to be provided for in such agreement, including prospective fringe benefits increases provided for in such agreement as a result of arm's-length negotiations. Such fringe benefits shall include medical or hospital care, pensions on retirement or death, compensation for injuries or illness resulting from occupational activity, or insurance to provide any of the foregoing, unemployment benefits, life insurance, disability and sickness insurance, accident insurance, vacation and holiday pay, costs of apprenticeship or other similar programs and other bona fide fringe benefits not otherwise

required by Federal, State, or local law to be provided by the contractor or subcontractor. The obligation under this subparagraph may be discharged by furnishing any equivalent combinations of fringe benefits or by making equivalent or differential payments in cash under rules and regulations established by the Secretary.

(3) A provision that no part of the services covered by this chapter will be performed in buildings or surroundings or under working conditions, provided by or under the control or supervision of the contractor or any subcontractor, which are unsanitary or hazardous or dangerous to the health or safety of service employees engaged to furnish the services.

(4) A provision that on the date a service employee commences work on a contract to which this chapter applies, the contractor or subcontractor will deliver to the employee a notice of the compensation required under paragraphs (1) and (2) of this subsection, on a form prepared by the Federal agency, or will post a notice of the required compensation in a prominent place at the worksite.

(5) A statement of the rates that would be paid by the Federal agency to the various classes of service employees if section 5341 or section 5332 of title 5 were applicable to them. The Secretary shall give due consideration to such rates in making the wage and fringe benefit determinations specified in this section.

(b)(1) No contractor who enters into any contract with the Federal Government the principal purpose of which is to furnish services through the use of service employees and no subcontractor thereunder shall pay any of his employees engaged in performing work on such contracts less than the minimum wage specified under section 206(a)(1) of the Fair Labor Standards Act of 1938, as amended.

(2) The provisions of sections 3, 4, and 5 of this Act shall be applicable to violations of this subsection.

§ 352. Violations

[Sec. 3] (a) Any violation of any of the contract stipulations required by section 2(a)(1) or (2) or of section 2(b) of this title shall render the party responsible therefor liable for a sum equal to the amount of any deductions, rebates, refunds, or underpayment of compensation due to any employee engaged in the performance of such contract. So much of the accrued payment due on the contract or any other contract between the same contractor and the Federal Government may be withheld as is necessary to pay such employees. Such withheld sums shall be held in a deposit fund. On order of the Secretary, any compensation which the head of the Federal agency or the Secretary has found to be due pursuant to this chapter shall be paid directly to the underpaid employees from any accrued payments withheld under this chapter.

(b) In accordance with regulations prescribed pursuant to section 4 of this Act, the Federal agency head or the Secretary is hereby authorized to carry out the provisions of this section.

(c) In addition, when a violation is found of any contract stipulation, the contract is subject upon written notice to cancellation by the contracting agency. Whereupon, the United States may enter into other contracts or arrangements for the completion of the original contract, charging any additional cost to the original contractor.

§ 353. Law governing authority of Secretary

[Sec. 4] (a) Sections 38 and 39 of this title shall govern the Secretary's authority to enforce this chapter, make rules, regulations, issue orders, hold hearings, and make decisions based upon findings of fact, and take other appropriate action hereunder.

(b) The Secretary may provide such reasonable limitations and may make such rules and regulations allowing reasonable variation, tolerances, and exemptions to and from any or all provisions of this Act (other than 10), but only in special circumstances where he determines that such limitation, variation, tolerance, or exemption is necessary and proper in the public interest or to avoid the serious impairment of government business, and is in accord with the remedial purpose of this Act to protect prevailing labor standards.

(c) No contractor or subcontractor under a contract, which succeeds a contract subject to this chapter and under which substantially the same services are furnished, shall pay any service employee under such contract less than the wages and fringe benefits, including accrued wages and fringe benefits, and any prospective increases in wages and fringe benefits provided for in a collective-bargaining agreement as a result of arm's-length negotiations, to which such service employees would have been entitled if they were employed under the predecessor contract: *Provided*, That in any of the foregoing circumstances such obligations shall not apply if the Secretary finds after a hearing in accordance with regulations adopted by the Secretary that such wages and fringe benefits are substantially at variance with those which prevail for services of a character similar in the locality.

(d) Subject to limitations in annual appropriation Acts but notwithstanding any other provision of law, contracts to which this Act applies may, if authorized by the Secretary, be for any term of years not exceeding five, if each such contract provides for the periodic adjustment of wages and fringe benefits pursuant to future determinations, issued in the manner prescribed in section 2 of this Act no less often than once every two years during the term of the contract, covering the various classes of service employees.

§ 354. List of violators; prohibition of contract award to firms appearing on list; actions to recover underpayments; payment of sums recovered

[Sec. 5] (a) The Comptroller General is directed to distribute a list to all agencies of the Government giving the names of persons or firms that the Federal agencies or the Secretary have found to have violated this chapter. Unless the Secretary otherwise recommends because of unusual circumstances, no contract of the United States shall be awarded to the persons or firms appearing on this list or to any firm, corporation, partnership, or association in which such persons or firms have a substantial interest until three years have elapsed from the date of publication of the list containing the name of such persons or firms. Where the Secretary does not otherwise recommend because of unusual circumstances, he shall, not later than ninety days after a hearing examiner has made a finding of a violation of this chapter, forward to the Comptroller General the name of the individual or firm found to have violated the provisions of this Act.

(b) If the accrued payments withheld under the terms of the contract are insufficient to reimburse all service employees with respect to whom there has been a failure to pay the compensation required pursuant to this chapter, the United States may bring action against the contractor, subcontractor, or any sureties in any court of competent jurisdiction to recover the remaining amount of underpayments. Any sums thus recovered by the United States shall be held in the deposit fund and shall be paid, on order of the Secretary, directly to the underpaid employee or employees. Any sum not paid to an employee because of inability to do so within three years shall be covered into the Treasury of the United States as miscellaneous receipts.

§ 355. Exclusion of fringe benefit payments in determining overtime pay

[Sec. 6] In determining any overtime pay to which such service employees are entitled under any Federal law, the regular or basic hourly rate of pay of such an employee shall not include any fringe benefit payments computed hereunder which are excluded from the regular rate under the Fair Labor Standards Act [29 U.S.C. 201 et seq.] by provisions of section 7(d) thereof [29 U.S.C. 207(d)].

§ 356. Exemptions

[Sec. 7] This chapter shall not apply to—
(1) any contract of the United States or District of Columbia for construction, alteration and/or repair, including painting and decorating of public buildings or public works;

(2) any work required to be done in accordance with the provisions of the Walsh-Healey Public Contracts Act [41 U.S.C. 35 et seq.];

(3) any contract for the carriage of freight or personnel by vessel, airplane, bus, truck, express, railway line or oil or gas pipeline where published tariff rates are in effect;

(4) any contract for the furnishing of services by radio, telephone, telegraph, or cable companies, subject to the Communications Act of 1934 [47 U.S.C. 151 et seq.];

(5) any contract for public utility services including electric light and power, water, steam, and gas;

(6) any employment contract providing for direct services to a Federal agency by an individual or individuals; and

(7) any contract with the United States Postal Service, the principal purpose of which is the operation of postal contract stations.

§ 357. Definitions

[Sec. 8] For the purposes of this Act—

(a) "Secretary" means Secretary of Labor.

(b) The term "service employee" means any person engaged in the performance of a contract entered into by the United States and not exempted under section 356 of this title, whether negotiated or advertised, the principal purpose of which is to furnish services in the United States (other than any person employed in a bona fide executive, administrative, or professional capacity, as those terms are defined in part 541 of Title 29, Code of Federal Regulations, as of July 30, 1976, and any subsequent revision of those regulations); and shall include all such persons regardless of any contractual relationship that may be alleged to exist between a contractor or subcontractor and such persons.

(c) The term "compensation" means any of the payments or fringe benefits described in section 2 of this title.

(d) The term "United States" when used in a geographical sense shall include any State of the United States, the District of Columbia, Puerto Rico, the Virgin Islands, Outer Continental Shelf lands as defined in the Outer Continental Shelf Lands Act, American Samoa, Guam, Wake Island, Eniwetok Atoll, Kwajalein Atoll, Johnston Island, and Canton Island, but shall not include any other territory under the jurisdiction of the United States or any United States base or possession within a foreign country.

§ 358. Wage and fringe benefit determinations of Secretary

[Sec. 10] It is the intent of the Congress that determinations of minimum monetary wages and fringe benefits for the various classes of service employees under the provisions of paragraphs (1) and (2) of section 351 [So in original. Probably should be "section 351(a)".] of this title should be made with respect to all contracts subject to this chapter, as soon as it is administratively feasible to do so. In any event, the Secretary shall make such determinations with respect to at least the following contracts subject to this chapter which are entered into during the applicable fiscal year:

(1) For the fiscal year ending June 30, 1973, all contracts under which more than twenty-five service employees are to be employed.

(2) For the fiscal year ending June 30, 1974, all contracts under which more than twenty service employees are to be employed.

(3) For the fiscal year ending June 30, 1975, all contracts under which more than fifteen service employees are to be employed.

(4) For the fiscal year ending June 30, 1976, all contracts under which more than ten service employees are to be employed.

(5) On or after July 1, 1976, all contracts under which more than five service employees are to be employed.

Contract Work Hours and Safety Standards Act

(Title I of P.L. 87-581, approved August 13, 1962; as last amended by P.L. 99-145, effective January 1, 1986)

§ 327. "Secretary" defined

[Sec. 101] As used herein, the term "Secretary" means the Secretary of Labor, United States Department of Labor.

§ 328. Forty hour week; overtime compensation; contractual conditions; liability of employers for violation; withholding funds to satisfy liabilities of employers

[Sec. 102] (a) Notwithstanding any other provision of law, the wages of every laborer and mechanic employed by any contractor or subcontractor in his performance of work on any contract of the character specified in section 103 shall be computed on the basis of a standard workweek of forty hours, and work in excess of such standard workweek shall be permitted subject to provisions of this section. For each workweek in which any such laborer or mechanic is so employed such wages shall include compensation, at a rate not less than one and one-half times the basic rate of pay, for all hours worked in excess of forty hours in the workweek.

(b) The following provisions shall be a condition of every contract of the character specified in section 103 and of any obligation of the United States, any territory, or the District of Columbia in connection therewith:

(1) No contractor or subcontractor contracting for any part of the contract work which may require or involve the employment of laborers or mechanics shall require or permit any laborer or mechanic, in any workweek in which he is employed on such work, to work in excess of forty hours in such workweek except in accordance with the provisions of this subchapter; and

(2) In the event of violation of the provisions of paragraph (1), the contractor and any subcontractor responsible therefor shall be liable to such affected employee for his unpaid wages and shall, in addition, be

liable to the United States (or, in the case of work done under contract for the District of Columbia or a territory, to such District or to such territory) for liquidated damages as provided therein. Such liquidated damages shall be computed, with respect to each individual employed as a laborer or mechanic in violation of any provision of this subchapter, in the sum of $10 for each calendar day on which such individual was required or permitted to work in excess of the standard workweek of forty hours without payment of the overtime wages required by this subchapter. The governmental agency for which the contract work is done or by which financial assistance for the work is provided may withhold, or cause to be withheld, subject to the provisions of section 104, from any moneys payable on account of work performed by a contractor or subcontractor, such sums as may be administratively be determined to be necessary to satisfy any liabilities of such contractor or subcontractor for unpaid wages and liquidated damages as herein provided.

§ 329. Contracts subject to this subchapter; workers covered; exceptions

[Sec. 103] (a) The provisions of this Act shall apply, except as otherwise provided, to any contract which may require or involve the employment of laborers or mechanics upon a public work of the United States, of any territory, or of the District of Columbia, and to any other contract which may require or involve the employment of laborers or mechanics if such contract is one (1) to which the United States or any agency or instrumentality thereof, any territory, or the District of Columbia is a party, or (2) which is made for or on behalf of the United States, any agency or instrumentality thereof, any territory, or the District of Columbia or (3) which is a contract for work financed in whole or in part by loans or grants from, or loans insured or guaranteed by, the United States or any agency or instrumentality thereof under any statute of the United States providing wage standards for such work: *Provided,* That the provisions of section 102 shall not apply to work where the assistance from the United States or any agency or instrumentality as set forth above is only in that nature of a loan guarantee, or insurance. Except as otherwise expressly provided, the provisions of this Act shall apply to all laborers and mechanics, including watchmen and guards, employed by any contractor or subcontractor in the performance of any part of the work contemplated by any such contract, and for purposes of this Act, laborers and mechanics shall include workmen performing services in connection with dredging or rock excavation in any river or harbor of the United States or of any territory or of the District of Columbia, but shall not include any employee employed as a seaman.

(b) This Act shall not apply to contracts for transportation by land, air, or water, or for the transmission of intelligence, or for the purchase of supplies or materials or articles ordinarily available in the open market. This Act shall not apply with respect to any work required to be done in accordance with the provisions of the Walsh-Healey Public Contracts Act.

§ 330. Report of violations and withholding of funds for unpaid wages and liquidated damages

[Sec. 104] (a) Any officer or person designated as inspector of the work to be performed under any contract of the character specified in section 103, or to aid in the enforcement or fulfillment thereof shall, upon observation or investigation, forthwith report to the proper officer of the United States, of any territory or possession, or of the District of Columbia, all violations of the provisions of this subchapter occurring in the performance of such work, together with the name of each laborer or mechanic who was required or permitted to work in violation of such provisions and the day or days of such violation. The amount of unpaid wages and liquidated damages owing under the provisions of this subchapter shall be administratively determined and the officer or person whose duty it is to approve the payment of moneys by the United States, the territory, or the District of Columbia in connection with the performance of the contract work shall direct the amount of such liquidated damages to be withheld for the use and benefit of the United States, said territory, or said District, and shall direct the amount of such unpaid wages to be withheld for the use and benefit of the laborers and mechanics who were not compensated as required under the provisions of this subchapter. The Comptroller General of the United States is authorized and directed to pay directly to such laborers and mechanics, from the sums withheld on account of underpayments of wages, the respective amounts administratively determined to be due, if the funds withheld are adequate, and, if not, an equitable proportion of such amounts.

(b) If the accrued payments withheld under the terms of the contracts, as aforesaid, are insufficient to reimburse all the laborers and mechanics with respect to whom there has been a failure to pay the wages required pursuant to this subchapter, such laborers and mechanics shall, in the case of a department or agency of the Federal Government, have the rights of action and/or of intervention against the contractor and his sureties conferred by law upon persons furnishing labor or materials, and in such proceedings it shall be no defense that such laborers and mechanics accepted or agreed to accept less than the required rate of wages or voluntarily made refunds.

(c) Any contractor or subcontractor aggrieved by the withholding of a sum as liquidated damages as provided in this subchapter shall have the right, within sixty days thereafter, to appeal to the head of the agency of the United States or of the territory for which the contract work is done or by which financial assistance for the work is provided, or to the Mayor of the District of Columbia in the case of liquidated damages withheld for the use and benefit of said District. Such agency head or Mayor, as the case may be, shall have authority to review the administrative determination of liquidated damages and to issue a final order affirming such determination; or, if it is found that the sum determined is incorrect or that the contractor or subcontractor violated the provisions of this Act inadvertently notwithstanding the exercise of due care on his part and that of his agents, recommendations may be made to the Secretary that an appropriate adjustment in liquidated damages be made, or that the contractor or subcontractor be relieved of liability for such liquidated damages. The Secretary shall review all pertinent facts in the matter and may conduct such investigations as he deems necessary, so as to affirm or reject the recommendation. The decision of the Secretary shall be final. In all such cases in which a contractor or subcontractor may be aggrieved by a final order for the withholding of liquidated damages as hereinbefore provided, such contractor or subcontractor may, within sixty days after such final order, file a claim in the United States Claims Court: *Provided, however,* That final orders of the agency head, the Mayor of the District of Columbia or the Secretary, as the case may be, shall be conclusive with respect to findings of fact if such findings are supported by substantial evidence.

(d) Reorganization Plan Numbered 14 of 1950 (64 Stat. 1267) shall be applicable with respect to the provisions of this Act, and section 276c of this title shall be applicable with respect to those contractors and subcontractors referred to therein who are engaged in the performance of contracts subject to the provisions of this Act.

§ 331. Limitations, variations, tolerances, and exemptions

[Sec. 105] The Secretary may provide such reasonable limitations and may make such rules and regulations allowing reasonable variations, tolerances, and exemptions to and from any or all provisions of this subchapter as he may find necessary and proper in the public interest to prevent injustice or undue hardship or to avoid serious impairment of the conduct of Government business.

§ 332. Violations; penalties

[Sec. 106] Any contractor or subcontractor whose duty it shall be to employ, direct, or control any labor or mechanic employed in the performance of any work contemplated by any contract to which this Act applies, who shall intentionally violate any provision of this Act, shall be deemed guilty of a misdemeanor, and for each and every such offense shall, upon conviction, be punished by a fine of not to exceed $1,000 or by imprisonment for not more than six months, or by both such fine and imprisonment, in the discretion of the court having jurisdiction thereof.

§ 333. Health and safety standards in building trades and construction industry

[Sec. 107] (a) It shall be a condition of each contract which is entered into under legislation subject to Reorganization Plan Numbered 14 of 1950 (64 Stat. 1267), and is for construction, alteration, and/or repair, including painting and decorating, that no contractor or subcontractor contracting for any part of the contract work shall require any laborer or mechanic employed in the performance of the contract to work in surroundings or under working conditions which are unsanitary, hazardous, or dangerous to his health or safety, as determined under construction safety and health standards promulgated by the Secretary by regulation based on proceedings pursuant to section 553 of Title 5, provided that such proceedings include a hearing of the nature authorized by said section. In formulating such standards, the Secretary shall consult with the Advisory Committee created by subsection (e) of this section.

(b) The Secretary is authorized to make such inspections, hold such hearings, issue such orders, and make such decisions based on findings of fact, as are deemed necessary to gain compliance with this section and any health and safety standard promulgated by the Secretary under subsection (a) of this section, and for such purposes the Secretary and the United States district courts shall have the authority and jurisdiction provided by sections 38 and 39 of Title 41. In the event that the Secretary of Labor determines noncompliance under the provisions of this section after an opportunity for an adjudicatory hearing by the Secretary of any condition of a contract of a type described in clause (1) or (2) of section 103(a) of this Act, the governmental agency for which the contract work is done shall have the right to cancel the contract, and to enter into other contracts for the completion of the contract work, charging any additional cost to the original contractor. In the event of noncompliance, as determined by the Secretary after an opportunity for an adjudicatory hearing by the Secretary, of any condition of a contract of a type described in clause (3) of section 103(a) of this Act, the governmental agency by which financial guarantee, assistance, or insurance for the contract work is provided shall have the right to withhold any such assistance attributable to the performance of the contract. Section 104 shall not apply to the enforcement of this section.

(c) The United States district courts shall have jurisdiction for cause shown, in any actions brought by the Secretary, to enforce compliance with the construction safety and health standard promulgated by the Secretary under subsection (a) of this section.

(d)(1) If the Secretary determines on the record after an opportunity for an agency hearing that, by repeated willful or grossly negligent violations of this subchapter, a contractor or subcontractor has demonstrated that the provisions of subsections (b) and (c) of this section are not effective to protect the safety and health of his employees, the Secretary shall make a finding to that effect and shall, not sooner than thirty days after giving notice of the findings to all interested persons, transmit the name of such contractor or subcontractor to the Comptroller General.

(2) The Comptroller General shall distribute each name so transmitted to him to all agencies of the Government. Unless the Secretary otherwise recommends, no contract subject to this section shall be awarded to such contractor or subcontractor or to any person in which such contractor or subcontractor has a substantial interest until three years have elapsed from the date the name is transmitted to the Comptroller General. If, before the end of such three-year period, the Secretary, after affording interested persons due notice and opportunity for hearing, is satisfied that a contractor or subcontractor whose name he has transmitted to the Comptroller General will thereafter comply responsibly with the requirements of this section, he shall terminate the application of the preceding sentence to such contractor or subcontractor (and to any person in which the contractor or subcontractor has a substantial interest); and when the Comptroller General is informed of the Secretary's action he shall inform all agencies of the Government thereof.

(3) Any person aggrieved by the Secretary's action under subsections (b) or (d) of this section may, within sixty days after receiving notice thereof, file with the appropriate United States court of appeals a petition for review of such action. A copy of the petition shall be forthwith transmitted by the clerk of the court to the Secretary, who shall thereupon file in the court the record upon which he based his action, as provided in section 2112 of Title 28. The findings of fact by the Secretary, if supported by substantial evidence shall be final. The court shall have power to make and enter a decree enforcing, modifying, and enforcing as so modified, or setting aside in whole or in part, the order of the Secretary or the appropriate Government agency. The judgment of the court shall be subject to review by the Supreme Court of the United States upon certiorari or certification as provided in section 1254 of Title 28.

(e)(1) The Secretary shall establish in the Department of Labor an Advisory Committee on Construction Safety and Health (hereinafter referred to as the "Advisory Committee") consisting of nine members appointed, without regard to the civil service laws, by the Secretary. The Secretary shall appoint one such member as Chairman. Three members of the Advisory Committee shall be persons representative of contractors to whom this section applies, three members shall be persons representative of employees primarily in the building trades and construction industry engaged in carrying out contracts to which this section applies, and three public representatives who shall be selected on the basis of their professional and technical competence and experience in the construction health and safety field.

(2) The Advisory Committee shall advise the Secretary in the formulation of construction safety and health standards and other regulations, and with respect to policy matters arising in the administration of this section. The Secretary may appoint such special advisory and technical experts or consultants as may be necessary to carry out the functions of the Advisory Committee.

(3) Members of the Advisory Committee shall, while serving on the business of the Advisory Committee, be entitled to receive compensation at rates fixed by the Secretary, but not exceeding $100 per day, including traveltime; and while so serving away from their homes or regular places of business, they may be allowed travel expenses, including per diem in lieu of subsistence, as authorized by section 5703 of Title 5 for persons in the Government service employed intermittently.

(f) The Secretary shall provide for the establishment and supervision of programs for the education and training of employers and employees in the recognition, avoidance, and prevention of unsafe working conditions in employments covered by this Act, and to collect such reports and data and to consult with and advise employers as to the best means of preventing injuries.

7

Occupational Safety Laws

Occupational Safety and Health Act of 1970

(P.L. 91–596, December 29, 1970, effective April 28, 1971; as last amended by P.L. 98–620, November 8, 1984)

§ 651. Congressional statement of findings and declaration of purpose and policy

[Sec. (2)] (a) The Congress finds that personal injuries and illnesses arising out of work situations impose a substantial burden upon, and are a hindrance to, interstate commerce in terms of lost production, wage loss, medical expenses, and disability compensation payments.

(b) The Congress declares it to be its purpose and policy, through the exercise of its powers to regulate commerce among the several States and with foreign nations and to provide for the general welfare, to assure so far as possible every working man and woman in the Nation safe and healthful working conditions and to preserve our human resources—

(1) by encouraging employers and employees in their efforts to reduce the number of occupational safety and health hazards at their places of employment, and to stimulate employers and employees to institute new and to perfect existing programs for providing safe and healthful working conditions;

(2) by providing that employers and employees have separate but dependent responsibilities and rights with respect to achieving safe and healthful working conditions;

(3) by authorizing the Secretary of Labor to set mandatory occupational safety and health standards applicable to businesses affecting interstate commerce, and by creating an Occupational Safety and Health Review Commission for carrying out adjudicatory functions under the Act;

(4) by building upon advances already made through employer and employee initiative for providing safe and healthful working conditions;

(5) by providing for research in the field of occupational safety and health, including the psychological factors involved, and by developing innovative methods, techniques, and approaches for dealing with occupational safety and health problems;

(6) by exploring ways to discover latent diseases, establishing causal connections between diseases and work in environmental conditions, and conducting other research relating to health problems, in recognition of the fact that occupational health standards present problems often different from those involved in occupational safety;

(7) by providing medical criteria which will assure insofar as practicable that no employee will suffer diminished health, functional capacity, or life expectancy as a result of his work experience;

(8) by providing for training programs to increase the number and competence of personnel engaged in the field of occupational safety and health;

(9) by providing for the development and promulgation of occupational safety and health standards;

(10) by providing an effective enforcement program which shall include a prohibition against giving advance notice of any inspection and sanctions for any individual violating this prohibition;

(11) by encouraging the States to assume the fullest responsibility for the administration and enforcement of their occupational safety and health laws by providing grants to the States to assist in identifying their needs and responsibilities in the area of occupational safety and health, to develop plans in accordance with the provisions of this Act, to improve the administration and enforcement of State occupational safety and health laws, and to conduct experimental and demonstration projects in connection therewith;

(12) by providing for appropriate reporting procedures with respect to occupational safety and health which procedures will help achieve the objectives of this Act and accurately describe the nature of the occupational safety and health problems;

(13) by encouraging joint labor-management efforts to reduce injuries and disease arising out of employment.

§ 652. Definitions

[Sec. 3] For the purposes of this Act—

(1) The term "Secretary" means the Secretary of Labor,

(2) The term "Commission" means the Occupational Safety and Health Review Commission established under this Act.

(3) The term "commerce" means trade, traffic, commerce, transportation, or communication among the several States, or between a State and any place outside thereof, or within the District of Columbia, or a possession of the United States (other than the Trust Territory of the Pacific Islands), or between points in the same State but through a point outside thereof.

(4) The term "person" means one or more individuals, partnerships, associations, corporations, business trusts, legal representatives, or any organized group of persons.

(5) The term "employer" means a person engaged in a business affecting commerce who has employees, but does not include the United States or any State or political subdivision of a State.

(6) The term "employee" means an employee of an employer who is employed in a business of his employer which affects commerce.

(7) The term "State" includes a State of the United States, the District of Columbia, Puerto Rico, the Virgin Islands, American Samoa, Guam, and the Trust Territory of the Pacific Islands.

(8) The term "occupational safety and health standard" means a standard which requires conditions, or the adoption or use of one or more practices, means, methods, operations, or processes, reasonably necessary or appropriate to provide safe or healthful employment and places of employment.

(9) The term "national consensus standard" means any occupational safety and health standard or modification thereof which (1), has been adopted and promulgated by a nationally recognized standards-producing organization under procedures whereby it can be determined by the Secretary that persons interested and affected by the scope or provisions of the standard have reached substantial agreement on its adoption, (2) was formulated in a manner which afforded an opportunity for diverse views to be considered and (3) has been designated as such a standard by the Secretary, after consultation with other appropriate Federal agencies.

(10) The term "established Federal standard" means any operative occupational safety and health standard established by any agency of the United States and presently in effect, or contained in any Act of Congress in force on the date of enactment of this Act.

(11) The term "Committee" means the National Advisory Committee on Occupational Safety and Health established under this Act.

(12) The term "Director" means the Director of the National Institute for Occupational Safety and Health.

(13) The term "Institute" means the National Institute for Occupational Safety and Health established under this Act.

(14) The term "Workmen's Compensation Commission" means the National Commission on State Workmen's Compensation Laws established under this Act.

§ 653. Geographic applicability; judicial enforcement; applicability to existing standards; report to Congress on duplication and coordination of Federal laws; workmen's compensation law or common law or statutory rights, duties, or liabilities of employers and employees unaffected

[Sec. 4] (a) This Act shall apply with respect to employment performed in a workplace in a State, the District of Columbia, the Commonwealth of

Puerto Rico, the Virgin Islands, American Samoa, Guam, the Trust Territory of the Pacific Islands, Wake Island, Outer Continental Shelf lands defined in the Outer Continental Shelf Lands Act, Johnston Island, and the Canal Zone. The Secretary of the Interior shall, by regulation, provide for judicial enforcement of this Act by the courts established for areas in which there are no United States district courts having jurisdiction.

(b)(1) Nothing in this Act shall apply to working conditions of employees with respect to which other Federal agencies, and State agencies acting under section 274 of the Atomic Energy Act of 1954, as amended (42 U.S.C. 2021), exercise statutory authority to prescribe or enforce standards or regulations affecting occupational safety or health.

(2) The safety and health standards promulgated under the Act of June 30, 1936, commonly known as the Walsh-Healey Act (41 U.S.C. 35 et seq.), the Service Contract Act of 1965 (41 U.S.C. 351 et seq.), Public Law 91–54, Act of August 9, 1969 (40 U.S.C. 333), Public Law 85–742, Act of August 23, 1958 (33 U.S.C. 941), and the National Foundation on Arts and Humanities Act (20 U.S.C. 951 et seq.) are superseded on the effective date of corresponding standards, promulgated under this Act, which are determined by the Secretary to be more effective. Standards issued under the laws listed in this paragraph and in effect on or after the effective date of this Act shall be deemed to be occupational safety and health standards issued under this Act, as well as under such other Acts.

(3) The Secretary shall, within three years after the effective date of this Act, report to the Congress his recommendations for legislation to avoid unnecessary duplication and to achieve coordination between this Act and other Federal laws.

(4) Nothing in this Act shall be construed to supersede or in any manner affect any workmen's compensation law or to enlarge or diminish or affect in any other manner the common law or statutory rights, duties, or liabilities of employers and employees under any law with respect to injuries, diseases, or death of employees arising out of, or in the course of, employment.

§ 654. Duties of employers and employees

[Sec. 5] (a) Each employer—
(1) Shall furnish to each of his employees employment and a place of employment which are free from recognized hazards that are causing or are likely to cause death or serious physical harm to his employees;
(2) shall comply with occupational safety and health standards promulgated under this Act.

(b) Each employee shall comply with occupational safety and health standards and all rules, regulations, and orders issued pursuant to this Act which are applicable to his own actions and conduct.

§ 655. Standards

[Sec. 6] (a) Without regard to chapter 5 of title 5, United States Code, or to the other subsections of this section, the Secretary shall, as soon as practicable during the period beginning with the effective date of this Act and ending two years after such date, by rule promulgate as an occupational safety or health standard any national consensus standard, and any established Federal standard, unless he determines that the promulgation of such a standard would not result in improved safety or health for specifically designated employees. In the event of conflict among any such standards, the Secretary shall promulgate the standard which assures the greatest protection of the safety or health of the affected employees.

(b) The Secretary may by rule promulgate, modify, or revoke any occupational safety or health standard in the following manner:

(1) Whenever the Secretary, upon the basis of information submitted to him in writing by an interested person, a representative of any organization of employers or employees, a nationally recognized standards-producing organization, the Secretary of Health and Human Services, the National Institute for Occupational Safety and Health, or a State or political subdivision, or on the basis of information developed by the Secretary or otherwise available to him, determines that a rule should be promulgated in order to serve the objectives of this Act, the Secretary may request the recommendations of an advisory committee appointed under section 7 of this Act. The Secretary shall provide such an advisory committee with any proposals of his own or of the Secretary of Health and Human Services, together with all pertinent factual information developed by the Secretary or the Secretary of Health and Human Services, or otherwise available, including the results of research, demonstrations, and experiments. An advisory committee shall submit to the Secretary its recommendations regarding the rule to be promulgated within ninety days from the date of its appointment or within such longer or shorter period as may be prescribed by the Secretary, but in no event for a period which is longer than two hundred and seventy days.

(2) The Secretary shall publish a proposed rule promulgating, modifying, or revoking an occupational safety or health standard in the Federal Register and shall afford interested persons a period of thirty days after publication to submit written data or comments. Where an advisory committee is appointed and the Secretary determines that a rule should be issued, he shall publish the proposed rule within sixty days after the submission of the advisory committee's recommendations or the expiration of the period prescribed by the Secretary for such submission.

(3) On or before the last day of the period provided for the submission of written data or comments under paragraph (2), any interested person may file with the Secretary written objections to the proposed rule,

stating the grounds therefor and requesting a public hearing on such objections. Within thirty days after the last day for filing such objections, the Secretary shall publish in the Federal Register a notice specifying the occupational safety or health standard to which objections have been filed and a hearing requested, and specifying a time and place for such hearing.

(4) Within sixty days after the expiration of the period provided for the submission of written data or comments under paragraph (2), or within sixty days after the completion of any hearing held under paragraph (3), the Secretary shall issue a rule promulgating, modifying, or revoking an occupational safety or health standard or make a determination that a rule should not be issued. Such a rule may contain a provision delaying its effective date for such period (not in excess of ninety days) as the Secretary determines may be necessary to insure that affected employers and employees will be informed of the existence of the standard and of its terms and that employers affected are given an opportunity to familiarize themselves and their employees with the existence of the requirements of the standard.

(5) The Secretary, in promulgating standards dealing with toxic materials or harmful physical agents under this subsection, shall set the standard which most adequately assures, to the extent feasible, on the basis of the best available evidence, that no employee will suffer material impairment of health or functional capacity even if such employee has regular exposure to the hazard dealt with by such standard for the period of his working life. Development of standards under this subsection shall be based upon research, demonstrations, experiments, and such other information as may be appropriate. In addition to the attainment of the highest degree of health and safety protection for the employee, other considerations shall be the latest available scientific data in the field, the feasibility of the standards, and experience gained under this and other health and safety laws. Whenever practicable, the standard promulgated shall be expressed in terms of objective criteria and of the performance desired.

(6)(A) Any employer may apply to the Secretary for a temporary order granting a variance from a standard or any provision thereof promulgated under this section. Such temporary order shall be granted only if the employer files an application which meets the requirements of clause (B) and establishes that (i) he is unable to comply with a standard by its effective date because of unavailability of professional or technical personnel or of materials and equipment needed to come into compliance with the standard or because necessary construction or alteration of facilities cannot be completed by the effective date, (ii) he is taking all available steps to safeguard his employees against the hazards covered by the standard, and (iii) he has an effective program for coming into compliance with the standard as quickly as practicable. Any temporary order issued under this paragraph shall prescribe the practices, means, methods, operations, and processes which the employer must adopt and use while the order is in effect and state in detail his program for coming into compliance with the standard. Such a temporary order may be granted only after notice to employees and an opportunity for a hearing: *Provided*, That the Secretary may issue one interim order to be effective until a decision is made on the basis of the hearing. No temporary order may be in effect for longer than the period needed by the employer to achieve compliance with the standard or one year, whichever is shorter, except that such an order may be renewed not more than twice (I) so long as the requirements of this paragraph are met and (II) if an application for renewal is filed at least 90 days prior to the expiration date of the order. No interim renewal of an order may remain in effect for longer than 180 days.

(B) An application for a temporary order under this paragraph (6) shall contain:

    (i) a specification of the standard or portion thereof from which the employer seeks a variance,

    (ii) a representation by the employer, supported by representations from qualified persons having firsthand knowledge of the facts represented, that he is unable to comply with the standard or portion thereof and a detailed statement of the reasons therefor,

    (iii) a statement of the steps he has taken and will take (with specific dates) to protect employees against the hazard covered by the standard,

    (iv) a statement of when he expects to be able to comply with the standards and what steps he has taken and what steps he will take (with dates specified) to come into compliance with the standard, and

    (v) a certification that he has informed his employees of the application by giving a copy thereof to their authorized representative, posting a statement giving a summary of the application and specifying where a copy may be examined at the place or places where notices to employees are normally posted, and by other appropriate means.

A description of how employees have been informed shall be contained in the certification. The information to employees shall also inform them of their right to petition the Secretary for a hearing.

(C) The Secretary is authorized to grant a variance from any standard or portion thereof whenever he determines, or the Secretary of Health and Human Services certifies, that such variance is necessary to permit an employer to participate in an experiment approved by him or the Secretary of Health and Human Services designed to demonstrate or validate new and improved techniques to safeguard the health or safety of workers.

(7) Any standard promulgated under this subsection shall prescribe the use of labels or other appropriate forms of warning as are necessary to insure that employees are apprised of all hazards to which they are exposed, relevant symptoms and appropriate emergency treatment, and proper conditions and precautions of safe use or exposure. Where appropriate, such standard shall also prescribe suitable protective equipment and control or technological procedures to be used in connection with such hazards and shall provide for monitoring or measuring employee exposure at such locations and intervals, and in such manner as may be necessary for the protection of employees. In addition, where appropriate, any such standard shall prescribe the type and frequency of medical examinations or other tests which shall be made available, by the employer or at his cost, to employees exposed to such hazards in order to most effectively determine whether the health of such employees is adversely affected by such exposure. In the event such medical examinations are in the nature of research, as determined by the Secretary of Health and Human Services, such examinations may be furnished at the expense of the Secretary of Health and Human Services. The results of such examinations or tests shall be furnished only to the Secretary or the Secretary of Health and Human Services, and, at the request of the employee, to his physician. The Secretary, in consultation with the Secretary of Health and Human Services, may by rule promulgated pursuant to section 553 of title 5, United States Code, make appropriate modifications in the foregoing requirements relating to the use of labels or other forms of warning, monitoring or measuring, and medical examinations, as may be warranted by experience, information, or medical or technological developments acquired subsequent to the promulgation of the relevant standard.

(8) Whenever a rule promulgated by the Secretary differs substantially from an existing national consensus standard, the Secretary shall, at the same time, publish in the Federal Register a statement of the reasons why the rule as adopted will better effectuate the purposes of this Act than the national consensus standard.

(c)(1) The Secretary shall provide, without regard to the requirements of chapter 5 of title 5, United States Code, for an emergency temporary standard to take immediate effect upon publication in the Federal Register if he determines (A) that employees are exposed to grave danger from exposure to substances or agents determined to be toxic or physically harmful or from new hazards, and (B) that such emergency standard is necessary to protect employees from such danger.

(2) Such standard shall be effective until superseded by a standard promulgated in accordance with the procedures prescribed in para-

graph (3) of this subsection.

(3) Upon publication of such standard in the Federal Register the Secretary shall commence a proceeding in accordance with section 6(b) of this Act, and the standard as published shall also serve as a proposed rule for the proceeding. The Secretary shall promulgate a standard under this paragraph no later than six months after publication of the emergency standard as provided in paragraph (2) of this subsection.

(d) Any affected employer may apply to the Secretary for a rule or order for a variance from a standard promulgated under this section. Affected employees shall be given notice of each such application and an opportunity to participate in a hearing. The Secretary shall issue such rule or order if he determines on the record, after opportunity for an inspection where appropriate and a hearing, that the proponent of the variance has demonstrated by a preponderance of the evidence that the conditions, practices, means, methods, operations, or processes used or proposed to be used by an employer will provide employment and places of employment to his employees which are as safe and healthful as those which would prevail if he complied with the standard. The rule or order so issued shall prescribe the conditions the employer must maintain, and the practices, means, methods, operations, and processes which he must adopt and utilize to the extent they differ from the standard in question. Such a rule or order may be modified or revoked upon application by an employer, employees, or by the Secretary on his own motion, in the manner prescribed for its issuance under this subsection at any time after six months from its issuance.

(e) Whenever the Secretary promulgates any standard, makes any rule, order, or decision, grants any exemption or extension of time, or compromises, mitigates, or settles any penalty assessed under this Act, he shall include a statement of the reasons for such action, which shall be published in the Federal Register.

(f) Any person who may be adversely affected by a standard issued under this section may at any time prior to the sixtieth day after such standard is promulgated file a petition challenging the validity of such standard with the United States court of appeals for the circuit wherein such person resides or has his principal place of business, for a judicial review of such standard. A copy of the petition shall be forthwith transmitted by the clerk of the court to the Secretary. The filing of such petition shall not, unless otherwise ordered by the court, operate as a stay of the standard. The determinations of the Secretary shall be conclusive if supported by substantial evidence in the record considered as a whole.

(g) In determining the priority for establishing standards under this section, the Secretary shall give due regard to the urgency of the need for mandatory safety and health standards for particular industries, trades, crafts, occupations, businesses, workplaces or work environments. The Secretary shall also give due regard to the recommendations of the Secretary of Health and Human Services regarding the need for mandatory standards in determining the priority for establishing such standards.

§ 656. Administration

[Sec. 7] (a)(1) There is hereby established a National Advisory Committee on Occupational Safety and Health consisting of twelve members appointed by the Secretary, four of whom are to be designated by the Secretary of Health and Human Services, without regard to the provisions of title 5, United States Code, governing appointments in the competitive service, and composed of representatives of management, labor, occupational safety and occupational health professions, and of the public. The Secretary shall designate one of the public members as Chairman. The members shall be selected upon the basis of their experience and competence in the field of occupational safety and health.

    (2) The Committee shall advise, consult with, and make recommendations to the Secretary and the Secretary of Health and Human Services on matters relating to the administration of the Act. The Committee shall hold no fewer than two meetings during each calendar year. All meetings of the Committee shall be open to the public and a transcript shall be kept and made available for public inspection.

    (3) The members of the Committee shall be compensated in accordance with the provisions of section 3109 of title 5, United States Code.

    (4) The Secretary shall furnish to the Committee an executive secretary and such secretarial, clerical, and other services as are deemed necessary to the conduct of its business.

    (b) An advisory committee may be appointed by the Secretary to assist him in his standard-setting functions under section 6 of this Act. Each such committee shall consist of not more than fifteen members and shall include as a member one or more designees of the Secretary of Health and Human Services, and shall include among its members an equal number of persons qualified by experience and affiliation to present the viewpoint of the employers involved, and of persons similarly qualified to present the viewpoint of the workers involved, as well as one or more representatives of health and safety agencies of the States. An advisory committee may also include such other persons as the Secretary may appoint who are qualified by knowledge and experience to make a useful contribution to the work of such committee, including one or more representatives of professional organizations of technicians or professionals specializing in occupational safety or health, and one or more representatives of nationally recognized standards-producing organizations, but the number of persons so appointed to any such advisory committee shall not exceed the number appointed to such committee as representatives of Federal and State agencies. Persons appointed to advisory committees from private life shall be compensated in the same manner as consultants or experts under section 3109 of title 5, United States Code. The Secretary shall pay to any State which is the employer of a member of such a committee who is a representative of the health or safety agency of that State, reimbursement sufficient to cover the actual cost to the State resulting from such representative's membership on such committee. Any meeting of such committee shall be open to the public and an accurate record shall be kept and made available to the public. No member of such committee (other than representatives of employers and employees) shall have an economic interest in any proposed rule.

(c) In carrying out his responsibilities under this Act, the Secretary is authorized to—

(1) use, with the consent of any Federal agency, the services, facilities, and personnel of such agency, with or without reimbursement, and with the consent of any State or political subdivision thereof, accept and use the services, facilities, and personnel of any agency of such State or subdivision with reimbursement; and

(2) employ experts and consultants or organizations thereof as authorized by section 3109 of title 5, United States Code, except that contracts for such employment may be renewed annually; compensate individuals so employed at rates not in excess of the rate specified at the time of service for grade GS-18 under section 5332 of title 5, United States Code, including traveltime, and allow them while away from their homes or regular places of business travel expenses (including per diem in lieu of subsistence) as authorized by section 5703 of title 5, United States Code, for persons in the Government service employed intermittently, while so employed.

§ 657. Inspections, investigations, and recordkeeping

[Sec. 8] (a) In order to carry out the purposes of this Act, the Secretary, upon presenting appropriate credentials to the owner, operator, or agency in charge, is authorized—

(1) to enter without delay and at reasonable times any factory, plant, establishment, construction site, or other area, workplace or environment where work is performed by an employee of an employer; and

(2) to inspect and investigate during regular working hours and at other reasonable times, and within reasonable limits and in a reasonable manner, any such place of employment and all pertinent conditions, structures, machines, apparatus, devices, equipment, and materials therein, and to question privately any such employer, owner, operator, agent or employee.

(b) In making his inspections and investigations under this Act the Secretary may require the attendance and testimony of witnesses and the production of evidence under oath. Witnesses shall be paid the same fees and mileage that are paid witnesses in the courts of the United States. In case of a contumacy, failure, or refusal of any person to obey such an order, any district court of the United States or the United States courts of any territory or possession, within the jurisdiction of which such person is found, or resides or transacts business, upon the application by the Secretary, shall have jurisdiction to issue to such person an order requiring such person to appear to produce evidence if, as, and when so ordered, and to give testimony relating to the matter under investigation or in question, and any failure to obey such order of the court may be punished by said court as a contempt thereof.

(c)(1) Each employer shall make, keep and preserve, and make available to the Secretary or the Secretary of Health and Human Services such records regarding his activities relating to this Act as the Secretary, in cooperation with the Secretary of Health and Human Services, may prescribe by regulation as necessary or appropriate for the enforcement of this Act or for developing information regarding the causes and prevention of occupational accidents and illnesses. In order to carry out the provisions of this paragraph such regulations may include provisions requiring employers to conduct periodic inspections. The Secretary shall also issue regulations requiring that employers, through posting of notices or other appropriate means, keep their employees informed of their protections and obligations under this Act, including the provisions of applicable standards.

(2) The Secretary, in cooperation with the Secretary of Health and Human Services, shall prescribe regulations requiring employers to maintain accurate records of, and to make periodic reports on, work-related deaths, injuries and illness other than minor injuries requiring only first aid treatment and which do not involve medical treatment, loss of consciousness, restriction of work or motion, or transfer to another job.

(3) The Secretary, in cooperation with the Secretary of Health and Human Services, shall issue regulations requiring employers to maintain accurate records of employee exposures to potentially toxic materials or harmful physical agents which are required to be monitored or measured under section 6. Such regulations shall provide employees or their representatives with an opportunity to observe such monitoring or measuring, and to have access to the records thereof. Such regulations shall also make appropriate provision for each employee or former employee to have access to such records as will indicate his own exposure to toxic materials or harmful physical agents. Each employer shall promptly notify any employee who has been or is being exposed to toxic materials or harmful physical agents in concentrations or at levels which exceed those prescribed by an applicable occupational safety and health standard promulgated under section 6, and shall inform any employee who is being thus exposed of the corrective action being taken.

(d) Any information obtained by the Secretary, the Secretary of Health and Human Services, or a State agency under this Act shall be obtained with a minimum burden upon employers, especially those operating small businesses. Unnecessary duplication of efforts in obtaining information shall be reduced to the maximum extent feasible.

(e) Subject to regulations issued by the Secretary, a representative of the employer and a representative authorized by his employees shall be given an opportunity to accompany the Secretary or his authorized representative during the physical inspection of any workplace under subsection (a) for the purpose of aiding such inspection. Where there is no authorized employee representative, the Secretary or his authorized representative shall consult with a reasonable number of employees concerning matters of health and safety in the workplace.

(f)(1) Any employees or representative of employees who believe that a violation of a safety or health standard exists that threatens physical harm, or that an imminent danger exists, may request an inspection by giving notice to the Secretary or his authorized representative of such violation or danger. Any such notice shall be reduced to writing, shall set forth with reasonable particularity the grounds for the notice, and shall be signed by the employees or representative of employees, and a copy shall be provided the employer or his agent no later than at the time of inspection, except that, upon the request of the person giving such notice, his name and the names of individual employees referred to therein shall not appear in such copy or on any record published, released, or made available pursuant to subsection (g) of this section. If upon receipt of such notification the Secretary determines there are reasonable grounds to believe that such violation or danger exists, he shall make a special inspection in accordance with the provisions of this section as soon as practicable, to determine if such violation or danger exists. If the Secretary determines there are no reasonable grounds to believe that a violation or danger exists he shall notify the employees or representative of the employees in writing of such determination.

(2) Prior to or during any inspection of a workplace, any employees or representative of employees employed in such workplace may notify the Secretary or any representative of the Secretary responsible for conducting the inspection, in writing, of any violation of this Act which they have reason to believe exists in such workplace. The Secretary shall, by regulation, establish procedures for informal review of any refusal by a representative of the Secretary to issue a citation with respect to any such alleged violation and shall furnish the employees or representative of employees requesting such review a written statement of the reasons for the Secretary's final disposition of the case.

(g)(1) The Secretary and Secretary of Health and Human Services are authorized to compile, analyze, and publish, either in summary or detailed form, all reports or information obtained under this section.

(2) The Secretary and the Secretary of Health and Human Services shall each prescribe such rules and regulations as he may deem necessary to carry out their responsibilities under this Act, including rules and regulations dealing with the inspection of an employer's establishment.

§ 658. Citations

[Sec. 9] (a) If, upon inspection or investigation, the Secretary or his authorized representative believes that an employer has violated a requirement of section 5 of this Act, of any standard, rule or order promulgated pursuant to section 6 of this Act, or of any regulations prescribed pursuant to this Act, he shall with reasonable promptness issue a citation to the employer. Each citation shall be in writing and shall describe with particularity the nature of the violation, including a reference to the provision of the Act, standard, rule, regulation, or order alleged to have been violated. In addition, the citation shall fix a reasonable time for the abatement of the violation. The Secretary may prescribe procedures for the issuance of a notice in lieu of a citation with respect to de minimis violations which have no direct or immediate relationship to safety or health.

(b) Each citation issued under this section, or a copy or copies thereof, shall be prominently posted, as prescribed in regulations issued by the Secretary, at or near each place a violation referred to in the citation occurred.

(c) No citation may be issued under this section after the expiration of six months following the occurrence of any violation.

§ 659. Enforcement procedures

[Sec. 10] (a) If, after an inspection or investigation, the Secretary issues a citation under section 9(a), he shall, within a reasonable time after the termination of such inspection or investigation, notify the employer by certified mail of the penalty, if any, proposed to be assessed under section 17 and that the employer has fifteen working days within which to notify the Secretary that he wishes to contest the citation or proposed assessment of penalty. If, within fifteen working days from the receipt of the notice issued by the Secretary the employer fails to notify the Secretary that he intends to contest the citation or proposed assessment of penalty, and no notice is filed by any employee or representative of employees under subsection (c) within such time, the citation and the assessment, as proposed, shall be deemed a final order of the Commission and not subject to review by any court or agency.

(b) If the Secretary has reason to believe that an employer has failed to correct a violation for which a citation has been issued within the period permitted for its correction (which period shall not begin to run until the entry of a final order by the Commission in the case of any review proceedings under this section initiated by the employer in good faith and not solely for delay or avoidance of penalties), the Secretary shall notify the employer by certified mail of such failure and of the penalty proposed to be assessed under section 17 by reason of such failure, and that the employer has fifteen working days within which to notify the Secretary that he wishes to contest the Secretary's notification or the proposed assessment of penalty. If, within fifteen working days from the receipt of notification issued by the Secretary, the employer fails to notify the Secretary that he intends to contest the notification or proposed assessment of penalty, the notification and assessment, as proposed, shall be deemed a final order of the Commission and not subject to review by any court or agency.

(c) If an employer notifies the Secretary that he intends to contest a citation issued under section 9(a) or notification issued under subsection (a) or (b) of this section, or if, within fifteen working days of the issuance of a citation under section 9(a), any employee or representative of employees files a notice with the Secretary alleging that the period of time fixed in the citation for the abatement of the violation is unreasonable, the Secretary shall immediately advise the Commission of such notification, and the Commission shall afford an opportunity for a hearing (in accordance with section 554 of title 5, United States Code, but without regard to subsection (a)(3) of such section). The Commission shall thereafter issue an order, based on findings of fact, affirming, modifying, or vacating the Secretary's citation or proposed penalty, or directing other appropriate relief, and such order shall become final thirty days after its issuance. Upon a showing by an employer of a good faith effort to comply with the abatement requirements of a citation, and that abatement has not been completed because of factors beyond his reasonable control, the Secretary, after an opportunity for a hearing as provided in this subsection, shall issue an order affirming or modifying the abatement requirements in such citation. The rules of procedure prescribed by the Commission shall provide affected employees or representatives of affected employees an opportunity to participate as parties to hearings under this subsection.

§ 660. Judicial review

[Sec. 11] (a) Any person adversely affected or aggrieved by an order of the Commission issued under subsection (c) of section 10 may obtain a review of such order in any United States court of appeals for the circuit in which the violation is alleged to have occurred or where the employer has its principal office, or in the Court of Appeals for the District of Columbia Circuit, by filing in such court within sixty days following the issuance of such order a written petition praying that the order be modified or set aside. A copy of such petition shall be forthwith transmitted by the clerk of the court to the Commission and to the other parties, and thereupon the Commission shall file in the court the record in the proceeding as provided in section 2112 of title 28, United States Code. Upon such filing, the court shall have jurisdiction of the proceeding and of the question determined therein, and shall have power to grant such temporary relief or restraining order as it deems just and proper, and to make and enter upon the pleadings, testimony, and proceedings set forth in such record a decree affirming, modifying, or setting aside in whole or in part, the order of the Commission and enforcing the same to the extent that such order is affirmed or modified. The commencement of proceedings under this subsection shall not, unless ordered by the court, operate as a stay of the order of the Commission. No objection that has not been urged before the Commission shall be considered by the court, unless the failure or neglect to urge the objection shall be excused because of extraordinary circumstances. The findings of the Commission with respect to questions of fact, if supported by substantial evidence on the record considered as a whole, shall be conclusive. If any party shall apply to the court for leave to adduce additional evidence and shall show to the satisfaction of the court that such additional evidence is material and that there were reasonable grounds for the failure to adduce such evidence in the hearing before the Commission, the court may order such additional evidence to be taken before the Commission and to be made a part of the record. The Commission may modify its findings as to the facts, or make new findings, by reason of additional evidence so taken and filed, and it shall file such modified or new findings, which findings with respect to questions of fact, if supported by substantial evidence on the record considered as a whole, shall be conclusive, and its recommendations, if any, for the modification or setting aside of its original order. Upon the filing of the record with it, the jurisdiction of the court shall be exclusive and its judgment and decree shall be final, except that the same shall be subject to review by the Supreme Court of the United States, as provided in section 1254 of title 28, United States Code.

(b) The Secretary may also obtain review or enforcement of any final order of the Commission by filing a petition for such relief in the United States court of appeals for the circuit in which the alleged violation occurred or in which the employer has its principal office, and the provisions of subsection (a) shall govern such proceedings to the extent applicable. If no petition for review, as provided in subsection (a), is filed within sixty days after service of the Commission's order, the Commission's findings of fact and order shall be conclusive in connection with any petition for enforcement which is filed by the Secretary after the expiration of such sixty-day period. In any such case, as well as in the case of a noncontested citation or notification by the Secretary which has become a final order of the Commission under subsection (a) or (b) of section 10, the clerk of the court, unless otherwise ordered by the court, shall forthwith enter a decree enforcing the order and shall transmit a copy of such decree to the Secretary and the employer named in the petition. In any contempt proceeding brought to enforce a decree of a court of appeals entered pursuant to this subsection or subsection (a), the court of appeals may assess the penalties provided in section 17, in addition to invoking any other available remedies.

(c)(1) No person shall discharge or in any manner discriminate against any employee because such employee has filed any complaint or instituted or caused to be instituted any proceeding under or related to this Act or has testified or is about to testify in any such proceeding or because of the exercise by such employee on behalf of himself or others of any right afforded by this Act.

(2) Any employee who believes that he has been discharged or otherwise discriminated against by any person in violation of this subsection may, within thirty days after such violation occurs, file a complaint with the Secretary alleging such discrimination. Upon receipt of such complaint, the Secretary shall cause such investigation to be made as he deems appropriate. If upon such investigation, the Secretary determines that the provisions of this subsection have been violated, he shall bring an action in any appropriate United States district court against such person. In any such action the United States district courts shall have jurisdiction, for cause shown to restrain violations of paragraph (1) of this subsection and order all appropriate relief including rehiring or reinstatement of the employee to his former position with back pay.

(3) Within 90 days of the receipt of a complaint filed under this subsection the Secretary shall notify the complainant of his determination under paragraph 2 of this subsection.

§ 661. Occupational Safety and Health Review Commission

[Sec. 12] (a) The Occupational Safety and Health Review Commission is hereby established. The Commission shall be composed of three members who shall be appointed by the President, by and with the advice and consent of the Senate, from among persons who by reason of training, education, or experience are qualified to carry out the functions of the Commission under this Act. The President shall designate one of the members of the Commission to serve as Chairman.

(b) The terms of members of the Commission shall be six years except that (1) the members of the Commission first taking office shall serve, as designated by the President at the time of appointment, one for a term of two years, one for a term of four years, and one for a term of six years, and (2) a vacancy caused by the death, resignation, or removal of a member prior to the expiration of the term for which he was appointed shall be filled only for the remainder of such unexpired term. A member of the Commission may be removed by the President for inefficiency, neglect of duty, or malfeasance in office.

(c) [Omitted.]

(d) The principal office of the Commission shall be in the District of Columbia. Whenever the Commission deems that the convenience of the public or of the parties may be promoted, or delay or expense may be minimized, it may hold hearings or conduct other proceedings at any other place.

(e) The Chairman shall be responsible on behalf of the Commission for the administrative operations of the Commission and shall appoint such administrative law judges and other employees as he deems necessary to assist in the performance of the Commission's functions and to fix their compensation in accordance with the provisions of chapter 51 and subchapter III of chapter 53 of title 5, United States Code, relating to classification and General Schedule pay rates: *Provided,* That assignment, removal and compensation of administrative law judges shall be in accordance with sections 3105, 3344, 5372, and 7521 of title 5, United States Code.

(f) For the purpose of carrying out its functions under this Act, two members of the Commission shall constitute a quorum and official action can be taken only on the affirmative vote of at least two members.

(g) Every official act of the Commission shall be entered of record, and its hearings and records shall be open to the public. The Commission is authorized to make such rules as are necessary for the orderly transaction of its proceedings. Unless the Commission has adopted a different rule, its proceedings shall be in accordance with the Federal Rules of Civil Procedure.

(h) The Commission may order testimony to be taken by deposition in any proceedings pending before it at any state of such proceeding. Any person may be compelled to appear and depose, and to produce books, papers, or documents, in the same manner as witnesses may be compelled to appear and testify and produce like documentary evidence before the Commission. Witnesses whose depositions are taken under this subsection, and the persons taking such depositions, shall be entitled to the same fees as are paid for like services in the courts of the United States.

(i) For the purpose of any proceeding before the Commission, the provisions of section 11 of the National Labor Relations Act (29 U.S.C. 161) are hereby made applicable to the jurisdiction and powers of the Commission.

(j) An administrative law judge appointed by the Commission shall hear, and make a determination upon, any proceeding instituted before the Commission and any motion in connection therewith, assigned to such administrative law judge by the Chairman of the Commission, and shall make a report of any such determination which constitutes his final disposition of the proceedings. The report of the administrative law judge shall become the final order of the Commission within thirty days after such report by the administrative law judge, unless within such period any Commission member has directed that such report shall be reviewed by the Commission.

(k) Except as otherwise provided in this Act, the administrative law judges shall be subject to the laws governing employees in the classified civil service, except, that appointments shall be made without regard to section 5108 of title 5, United States Code. Each administrative law judge shall receive compensation at a rate not less than that prescribed for GS-16 under section 5332 of title 5, United States Code.

§ 662. Injunction proceedings

[Sec. 13] (a) The United States district courts shall have jurisdiction, upon petition of the Secretary, to restrain any conditions or practices in any place of employment which are such that a danger exists which could reasonably be expected to cause death or serious physical harm immediately or before the imminence of such danger can be eliminated through the enforcement procedures otherwise provided by this Act. Any order issued under this section may require such steps to be taken as may be necessary to avoid, correct, or remove such imminent danger and prohibit the employment or presence of any individual in locations or under conditions where such imminent danger exists, except individuals whose presence is necessary to avoid, correct, or remove such imminent danger or to maintain the capacity of a continuous process operation to resume normal operations without a complete cessation of operations, or where a cessation of operations is necessary, to permit such to be accomplished in a safe and orderly manner.

(b) Upon the filing of any such petition the district court shall have jurisdiction to grant such injunctive relief or temporary restraining order pending the outcome of an enforcement proceeding pursuant to this Act. The proceeding shall be as provided by Rule 65 of the Federal Rules, Civil Procedure, except that no temporary restraining order issued without notice shall be effective for a period longer than five days.

(c) Whenever and as soon as an inspector concludes that conditions or practices described in subsection (a) exist in any place of employment, he shall inform the affected employees and employers of the danger and that he is recommending to the Secretary that relief be sought.

(d) If the Secretary arbitrarily or capriciously fails to seek relief under this section, any employee who may be injured by reason of such failure, or the representative of such employees, might bring an action against the Secretary in the United States district court for the district in which the imminent danger is alleged to exist or the employer has its principal office, or for the

District of Columbia, for a writ of mandamus to compel the Secretary to seek such an order and for such further relief as may be appropriate.

§ 663. Representation in civil litigation

[Sec. 14] Except as provided in section 518(a) of title 28, United States Code, relating to litigation before the Supreme Court, the Solicitor of Labor may appear for and represent the Secretary in any civil litigation brought under this Act but all such litigation shall be subject to the direction and control of the Attorney General.

§ 664. Disclosure of trade secrets; protective orders

[Sec. 15] All information reported to or otherwise obtained by the Secretary or his representative in connection with any inspection or proceeding under this Act which contains or which might reveal a trade secret referred to in section 1905 of title 18 of the United States Code shall be considered confidential for the purpose of that section, except that such information may be disclosed to other officers or employees concerned with carrying out this Act or when relevant in any proceeding under this Act. In any such proceeding the Secretary, the Commission, or the court shall issue such orders as may be appropriate to protect the confidentiality of trade secrets.

§ 665. Variations, tolerances, and exemptions from required provisions; procedures; duration

[Sec. 16] The Secretary, on the record, after notice and opportunity for a hearing may provide such reasonable limitations and may make such rules and regulations allowing reasonable variations, tolerances, and exemptions to and from any or all provisions of this Act as he may find necessary and proper to avoid serious impairment of the national defense. Such action shall not be in effect for more than six months without notification to affected employees and an opportunity being afforded for a hearing.

§ 666. Civil and criminal penalties

[Sec. 17] (a) Any employer who willfully or repeatedly violates the requirements of section 5 of this Act, any standard, rule, or order promulgated pursuant to section 6 of this Act, or regulations prescribed pursuant to this Act, may be assessed a civil penalty of not more than $10,000 for each violation.

(b) Any employer who has received a citation for a serious violation of the requirements of section 5 of this Act, of any standard, rule, or order promulgated pursuant to section 6 of this Act, or of any regulations prescribed pursuant to this Act, shall be assessed a civil penalty of up to $1,000 for each such violation.

(c) Any employer who has received a citation for a violation of the requirements of section 5 of this Act, of any standard, rule, or order promulgated pursuant to section 6 of this Act, or of regulations prescribed pursuant to this Act, and such violation is specifically determined not to be of a serious nature, may be assessed a civil penalty of up to $1,000 for each such violation.

(d) Any employer who fails to correct a violation for which a citation has been issued under section 9(a) within the period permitted for its correction (which period shall not begin to run until the date of the final order of the Commission in the case of any review proceeding under section 10 initiated by the employer in good faith and not solely for delay or avoidance of penalties), may be assessed a civil penalty of not more than $1,000 for each day during which such failure or violation continues.

(e) Any employer who willfully violates any standard, rule, or order promulgated pursuant to section 6 of this Act, or of any regulations prescribed pursuant to this Act, and that violation caused death to any employee, shall, upon conviction, be punished by a fine of not more than $10,000 or by imprisonment for not more than six months, or by both; except that if the conviction is for a violation committed after a first conviction of such person, punishment shall be by a fine of not more than $20,000 or by imprisonment for not more than one year, or by both.

(f) Any person who gives advance notice of any inspection to be conducted under this Act, without authority from the Secretary or his designees, shall, upon conviction, be punished by a fine of not more than $1,000 or by imprisonment for not more than six months, or by both.

(g) Whoever knowingly makes any false statement, representation, or certification in any application, record, report, plan, or other document filed or required to be maintained pursuant to this Act shall, upon conviction, be punished by a fine of not more than $10,000, or by imprisonment for not more than six months, or by both.

(h) [Omitted.]

(i) Any employer who violates any of the posting requirements, as prescribed under the provisions of this Act, shall be assessed a civil penalty of up to $1,000 for each violation.

(j) The Commission shall have authority to assess all civil penalties provided in this section, giving due consideration to the appropriateness of the penalty with respect to the size of the business of the employer being charged, the gravity of the violation, the good faith of the employer, and the history of previous violations.

(k) For purposes of this section, a serious violation shall be deemed to exist in a place of employment if there is a substantial probability that death or serious physical harm could result from a condition which exists, or from one or more practices, means, methods, operations, or processes which have been adopted or are in use, in such place of employment unless the employer did not, and could not with the exercise of reasonable diligence, know of the presence of the violation.

(l) Civil penalties owed under this Act shall be paid to the Secretary for deposit into the Treasury of the United States and shall accrue to the United States and may be recovered in a civil action in the name of the United States brought in the United States district court for the district where the violation is alleged to have occurred or where the employer has its principal office.

§ 667. State jurisdiction and plans

[Sec. 18] (a) Nothing in this Act shall prevent any State agency or court from asserting jurisdiction under State law over any occupational safety or health issue with respect to which no standard is in effect under section 6.

(b) Any State which, at any time, desires to assume responsibility for development and enforcement therein of occupational safety and health standards relating to any occupational safety or health issue with respect to which a Federal standard has been promulgated under section 6 shall submit a State plan for the development of such standards and their enforcement.

(c) The Secretary shall approve the plan submitted by a State under subsection (b), or any modification thereof, if such plan in his judgment—

(1) designates a State agency or agencies as the agency or agencies responsible for administering the plan throughout the State,

(2) provides for the development and enforcement of safety and health standards relating to one or more safety or health issues, which standards (and the enforcement of which standards) are or will be at least as effective in providing safe and healthful employment and places of employment as the standards promulgated under section 6 which relate to the same issues, and which standards, when applicable to products which are distributed or used in interstate commerce, are required by compelling local conditions and do not unduly burden interstate commerce,

(3) provides for a right of entry and inspection of all work-places subject to the Act which is at least as effective as that provided in section 8, and includes a prohibition on advance notice of inspections,

(4) contains satisfactory assurances that such agency or agencies have or will have the legal authority and qualified personnel necessary for the enforcement of such standards,

(5) gives satisfactory assurances that such State will devote adequate funds to the administration and enforcement of such standards,

(6) contains satisfactory assurances that such State will, to the extent permitted by its law, establish and maintain an effective and comprehensive occupational safety and health program applicable to all employees of public agencies of the State and its political subdivisions, which program is as effective as the standards contained in an approved plan,

(7) requires employers in the State to make reports to the Secretary in the same manner and to the same extent as if the plan were not in effect, and

(8) provides that the State agency will make such reports to the Secretary in such form and containing such information, as the Secretary shall from time to time require.

(d) If the Secretary rejects a plan submitted under subsection (b), he shall afford the State submitting the plan due notice and opportunity for a hearing before so doing.

(e) After the Secretary approves a State plan submitted under subsection (b), he may, but shall not be required to, exercise his authority under sections 8, 9, 13, and 17 with respect to comparable standards promulgated under section 6, for the period specified in the next sentence. The Secretary may exercise the authority referred to above until he determines, on the basis of actual operations under the State plan, that the criteria set forth in subsection (c) are being applied, but he shall not make such determination for at least three years after the plan's approval under subsection (c). Upon making the determination referred to in the preceding sentence, the provisions of sections 5(a)(2), 8 (except for the purpose of carrying out subsection (f) of this section), 9, 10, 13, and 17, and standards promulgated under section 6 of this Act, shall not apply with respect to any occupational safety or health issues covered under the plan, but the Secretary may retain jurisdiction under the above provisions in any proceeding commenced under section 9 or 10 before the date of determination.

(f) The Secretary shall, on the basis of reports submitted by the State agency and his own inspections make a continuing evaluation of the manner in which each State having a plan approved under this section is carrying out such plan. Whenever the Secretary finds, after affording due notice and opportunity for a hearing, that in the administration of the State plan there is a failure to comply substantially with any provision of the State plan (or any assurance contained therein), he shall notify the State agency of his withdrawal of approval of such plan and upon receipt of such notice such plan shall cease to be in effect, but the State may retain jurisdiction in any case commenced before the withdrawal of the plan in order to enforce standards under the plan whenever the issues involved do not relate to the reasons for the withdrawal of the plan.

(g) The State may obtain a review of a decision of the Secretary withdrawing approval of or rejecting its plan by the United States court of appeals for the circuit in which the State is located by filing in such court within thirty days following receipt of notice of such decision a petition to modify or set aside in whole or in part the action of the Secretary. A copy of such petition shall forthwith be served upon the Secretary, and thereupon the Secretary shall certify and file in the court the record upon which the decision complained of was issued as provided in section 2112 of title 28, United States Code. Unless the court finds that the Secretary's decision in rejecting a proposed State plan or withdrawing his approval of such a plan is not supported by substantial evidence the court shall affirm the Secretary's decision. The judgment of the court shall be subject to review by the Supreme Court of the United States upon certiorari or certification as provided in section 1254 of title 28, United States Code.

(h) The Secretary may enter into an agreement with a State under which the State will be permitted to continue to enforce one or more occupational health and safety standards in effect in such State until final action is taken by the Secretary with respect to a plan submitted by a State under subsection (b) of this section, or two years from the date of enactment of this Act, whichever is earlier.

§ 668.   Programs of Federal agencies

[Sec. 19] (a) It shall be the responsibility of the head of each Federal agency to establish and maintain an effective and comprehensive occupational safety and health program which is consistent with the standards promulgated under section 6. The head of each agency shall (after consultation with representatives of the employees thereof)—

(1) provide safe and healthful places and conditions of employment, consistent with the standards set under section 6;

(2) acquire, maintain, and require the use of safety equipment, personal protective equipment, and devices reasonably necessary to protect employees;

(3) keep adequate records of all occupational accidents and illnesses for proper evaluation and necessary corrective action;

(4) consult with the Secretary with regard to the adequacy as to form and content of records kept pursuant to subsection (a)(3) of this section; and

(5) make an annual report to the Secretary with respect to occupational accidents and injuries and the agency's program under this section. Such report shall include any report submitted under section 7902 (e)(2) of title 5, United States Code.

(b) The Secretary shall report to the President a summary or digest of reports submitted to him under subsection (a)(5) of this section, together with his evaluations of and recommendations derived from such reports. The President shall transmit annually to the Senate and the House of Representatives a report of the activities of Federal agencies under this section.

(c) [Omitted.]

(d) The Secretary shall have access to records and reports kept and filed by Federal agencies pursuant to subsections (a)(3) and (5) of this section unless those records and reports are specifically required by Executive order to be kept secret in the interest of the national defense or foreign policy, in which case the Secretary shall have access to such information as will not jeopardize national defense or foreign policy.

§ 669. Research and related activities

[Sec. 20] (a)(1) The Secretary of Health and Human Services, after consultation with the Secretary and with other appropriate Federal departments or agencies, shall conduct (directly or by grants or contracts) research, experiments, and demonstrations relating to occupational safety and health, including studies of psychological factors involved, and relating to innovative methods, techniques, and approaches for dealing with occupational safety and health problems.

(2) The Secretary of Health and Human Services shall from time to time consult with the Secretary in order to develop specific plans for such research, demonstrations, and experiments as are necessary to produce criteria, including criteria identifying toxic substances, enabling the Secretary to meet his responsibility for the formulation of safety and health standards under this Act; and the Secretary of Health and Human Services, on the basis of such research, demonstrations, and experiments and any other information available to him, shall develop and publish at least annually such criteria as will effectuate the purposes of this Act.

(3) The Secretary of Health and Human Services, on the basis of such research, demonstrations, and experiments, and any other information available to him, shall develop criteria dealing with toxic materials and harmful physical agents and substances which will describe exposure levels that are safe for various periods of employment, including but not limited to the exposure levels at which no employee will suffer impaired health or functional capacities or diminished life expectancy as a result of his work experience.

(4) The Secretary of Health and Human Services shall also conduct special research, experiments, and demonstrations relating to occupational safety and health as are necessary to explore new problems, including those created by new technology in occupational safety and health, which may require ameliorative action beyond that which is otherwise provided for in the operating provisions of this Act. The Secretary of Health and Human Services shall also conduct research into the motivational and behavioral factors relating to the field of occupational safety and health.

(5) The Secretary of Health and Human Services, in order to comply with his responsibilities under paragraph (2), and in order to develop needed information regarding potentially toxic substances or harmful physical agents, may prescribe regulations requiring employers to measure, record, and make reports on the exposure of employees to substances or physical agents which the Secretary of Health and Human Services, reasonably believes may endanger the health or safety of employees. The Secretary of Health and Human Services also is authorized to establish such programs of medical examinations and tests as may be necessary for determining the incidence of occupational illnesses and the susceptibility of employees to such illnesses. Nothing in this or any other provision of this Act shall be deemed to authorize or require medical examination, immunization, or treatment for those who object thereto on religious grounds, except where such is necessary for the protection of the health or safety of others. Upon the request of any employer who is required to measure and record exposure of employees to substances or physical agents as provided under this subsection, the Secretary of Health and Human Services shall furnish full financial or other assistance to such employer for the purpose of defraying any additional expense incurred by him in carrying out the measuring and recording as provided in this subsection.

(6) The Secretary of Health and Human Services shall publish within six months of the enactment of this Act and thereafter as needed but at least annually a list of all known toxic substances by generic family or other useful grouping, and the concentrations at which such toxicity is known to occur. He shall determine following a written request by any employer or authorized representative of employees, specifying with reasonable particularity the grounds on which the request is made, whether any substance normally found in the place of employment has potentially toxic effects in such concentrations as used or found; and shall submit such determination both to employers and affected employees as soon as possible. If the Secretary of Health and Human Services determines that any substance is potentially toxic at the concentrations in which it is used or found in a place of employment, and such substance is not covered by an occupational safety or health standard promulgated under section 6, the Secretary of Health and Human Services shall immediately submit such determination to the Secretary, together with all pertinent criteria.

(7) Within two years of enactment of this Act, and annually thereafter the Secretary of Health and Human Services shall conduct and publish industrywide studies of the effect of chronic or low-level exposure to industrial materials, processes, and stresses on the potential for illness, disease, or loss of functional capacity in aging adults.

(b) The Secretary of Health and Human Services is authorized to make inspections and question employers and employees as provided in section 8 of this Act in order to carry out his functions and responsibilities under this section.

(c) The Secretary is authorized to enter into contracts, agreements, or other arrangements with appropriate public agencies or private organizations for the purpose of conducting studies relating to his responsibilities under this Act. In carrying out his responsibilities under this subsection, the Secretary shall cooperate with the Secretary of Health and Human Services in order to avoid any duplication of efforts under this section.

(d) Information obtained by the Secretary and the Secretary of Health and Human Services under this section shall be disseminated by the Secretary to employers and employees and organizations thereof.

(e) The functions of the Secretary of Health and Human Services under this Act shall, to the extent feasible, be delegated to the Director of the National Institute for Occupational Safety and Health established by section 22 of this Act.

§ 670. Training and employee education

[Sec. 21] (a) The Secretary of Health and Human Services, after consultation with the Secretary and with other appropriate Federal departments and agencies, shall conduct, directly or by grants or contracts (1) education programs to provide an adequate supply of qualified personnel to carry out the purposes of this Act, and (2) informational programs on the importance of and proper use of adequate safety and health equipment.

(b) The Secretary is also authorized to conduct, directly or by grants or contracts, short-term training of personnel engaged in work related to his responsibilities under this Act.

(c) The Secretary, in consultation with the Secretary of Health and Human Services, shall (1) provide for the establishment and supervision of programs for the education and training of employers and employees in the recognition, avoidance, and prevention of unsafe or unhealthful working conditions in employments covered by this Act, and (2) consult with and advise employers and employees, and organizations representing employers and employees as to effective means of preventing occupational injuries and illness.

§ 671. National Institute for Occupational Safety and Health

[Sec. 22] (a) It is the purpose of this section to establish a National Institute for Occupational Safety and Health in the Department of Health and Human Services in order to carry out the policy set forth in section 2 of this Act and to perform the functions of the Secretary of Health and Human Services under sections 20 and 21 of this Act.

(b) There is hereby established in the Department of Health and Human Services a National Institute for Occupational Safety and Health. The Institute shall be headed by a Director who shall be appointed by the Secretary of Health and Human Services, and who shall serve for a term of six years unless previously removed by the Secretary of Health and Human Services.

(c) The Institute is authorized to—

(1) develop and establish recommended occupational safety and health standards; and

(2) perform all functions of the Secretary of Health and Human Services under sections 20 and 21 of this Act.

(d) Upon his own initiative, or upon the request of the Secretary or the Secretary of Health and Human Services, the Director is authorized (1) to conduct such research and experimental programs as he determines are necessary for the development of criteria for new and improved occupational safety and health standards, and (2) after consideration of the results of such research and experimental programs make recommendations concerning new or improved occupational safety and health standards. Any occupational safety and health standard recommended pursuant to this section shall immediately be forwarded to the Secretary of Labor, and to the Secretary of Health and Human Services.

(e) In addition to any authority vested in the Institute by other provisions of this section, the Director, in carrying out the functions of the Institute, is authorized to—

(1) prescribe such regulations as he deems necessary governing the manner in which its functions shall be carried out;

(2) receive money and other property donated, bequeathed, or devised, without condition or restriction other than that it be used for the purposes of the Institute and to use, sell, or otherwise dispose of such property for the purpose of carrying out its functions;

(3) receive (and use, sell, or otherwise dispose of, in accordance with paragraph (2)), money and other property donated, bequeathed, and devised to the Institute with a condition or restriction, including a condition that the Institute use other funds of the Institute for the purposes of the gift;

(4) in accordance with the civil service laws, appoint and fix the compensation of such personnel as may be necessary to carry out the provisions of this section;

(5) obtain the services of experts and consultants in accordance with the provisions of section 3109 of title 5, United States Code;

(6) accept and utilize the services of voluntary and noncompensated personnel and reimburse them for travel expenses, including per diem, as authorized by section 5703 of title 5, United States Code;

(7) enter into contracts, grants or other arrangements, or modifications thereof to carry out the provisions of this section, and such contracts or

modifications thereof may be entered into without performance or other bonds, and without regard to section 3709 of the Revised Statutes, as amended (41 U.S.C. 5), or any other provision of law relating to competitive bidding;

(8) make advance, progress, and other payments which the Director deems necessary under this title without regard to the provisions of section 3324(a) and (b) of title 31, United States Code; and

(9) make other necessary expenditures.

(f) The Director shall submit to the Secretary of Health and Human Services, to the President, and to the Congress an annual report of the operations of the Institute under this Act, which shall include a detailed statement of all private and public funds received and expended by it, and such recommendations as he deems appropriate.

§ 672. Grants to states

[Sec. 23] (a) The Secretary is authorized, during the fiscal year ending June 30, 1971, and the two succeeding fiscal years, to make grants to the States which have designated a State agency under section 18 to assist them—

(1) in identifying their needs and responsibilities in the area of occupational safety and health,

(2) in developing State plants under section 18, or

(3) in developing plans for—

(A) establishing systems for the collection of information concerning the nature and frequency of occupational injuries and diseases;

(B) increasing the expertise and enforcement capabilities of their personnel engaged in occupational safety and health programs; or

(C) otherwise improving the administration and enforcement of State occupational safety and health laws, including standards thereunder, consistent with the objectives of this Act.

(b) The Secretary is authorized, during the fiscal year ending June 30, 1971, and the two succeeding fiscal years, to make grants to the States for experimental and demonstration projects consistent with the objectives set forth in subsection (a) of this section.

(c) The Governor of the State shall designate the appropriate State agency for receipt of any grant made by the Secretary under this section.

(d) Any State agency designated by the Governor of the State desiring a grant under this section shall submit an application therefor to the Secretary.

(e) The Secretary shall review the application, and shall, after consultation with the Secretary of Health and Human Services, approve or reject such application.

(f) The Federal share for each State grant under subsection (a) or (b) of this section may not exceed 90 per centum of the total cost of the application.

In the event the Federal share for all States under either such subsection is not the same, the differences among the States shall be established on the basis of objective criteria.

(g) The Secretary is authorized to make grants to the States to assist them in administering and enforcing programs for occupational safety and health contained in State plans approved by the Secretary pursuant to section 18 of this Act. The Federal share for each State grant under this subsection may not exceed 50 per centum of the total cost to the State of such a program. The last sentence of subsection (f) shall be applicable in determining the Federal share under this subsection.

(h) Prior to June 30, 1973, the Secretary shall, after consultation with the Secretary of Health and Human Services, transmit a report to the President and to the Congress, describing the experience under the grant programs authorized by this section and making any recommendations he may deem appropriate.

§ 673. Statistics

[Sec. 24] (a) In order to further the purposes of this Act, the Secretary, in consultation with the Secretary of Health and Human Services, shall develop and maintain an effective program of collection, compilation, and analysis of occupational safety and health statistics. Such program may cover all employments whether or not subject to any other provisions of this Act but shall not cover employments excluded by section 4 of the Act. The Secretary shall compile accurate statistics on work injuries and illnesses which shall include all disabling, serious, or significant injuries and illnesses, whether or not involving loss of time from work, other than minor injuries requiring only first aid treatment and which do not involve medical treatment, loss of consciousness, restriction of work or motion, or transfer to another job.

(b) To carry out his duties under subsection (a) of this section, the Secretary may—

(1) promote, encourage, or directly engage in programs of studies, information and communication concerning occupational safety and health statistics;

(2) make grants to States or political subdivisions thereof in order to assist them in developing and administering programs dealing with occupational safety and health statistics; and

(3) arrange, through grants or contracts, for the conduct of such research and investigations as give promise of furthering the objectives of this section.

(c) The Federal share for each grant under subsection (b) of this section may be up to 50 per centum of the State's total cost.

(d) The Secretary may, with the consent of any State or political subdivision thereof, accept and use the services, facilities, and employees of the agencies of such State or political subdivision, with or without reimbursement, in order to assist him in carrying out his functions under this section.

(e) On the basis of the records made and kept pursuant to section 8(c) of this Act, employers shall file such reports with the Secretary as he shall prescribe by regulation, as necessary to carry out his functions under this Act.

(f) Agreements between the Department of Labor and States pertaining to the collection of occupational safety and health statistics already in effect on the effective date of this Act shall remain in effect until superseded by grants or contracts made under this Act.

§ 674. Audit of grant recipient; maintenance of records; contents of records; access to books, etc.

[Sec. 25] (a) Each recipient of a grant under this Act shall keep such records as the Secretary or the Secretary of Health and Human Services shall prescribe, including records which fully disclose the amount and disposition by such recipient of the proceeds of such grant, the total cost of the project or undertaking in connection with which such grant is made or used, and the amount of that portion of the cost of the project or undertaking supplied by other sources, and such other records as will facilitate an effective audit.

(b) The Secretary or the Secretary of Health and Human Services, and the Comptroller General of the United States, or any of their duly authorized representatives, shall have access for the purpose of audit and examination to any books, documents, papers, and records of the recipients of any grant under this Act that are pertinent to any such grant.

§ 675. Annual reports by Secretary of Labor and Secretary of Health and Human Services; contents

[Sec. 26] Within one hundred and twenty days following the convening of each regular session of Congress, the Secretary and the Secretary of Health and Human Services shall each prepare and submit to the President for transmittal to the Congress a report upon the subject matter of this Act, the progress toward achievement of the purpose of this Act, the needs and requirements in the field of occupational safety and health, and any other relevant information. Such reports shall include information regarding occupational safety and health standards, and criteria for such standards, developed during the preceding year; evaluation of standards and criteria previously developed under this Act, defining areas of emphasis for new criteria and standards; an evaluation of the degree of observance of applicable occupational safety and health standards, and a summary of inspection and enforcement activity undertaken; analysis and evaluation of research activities for which results have been obtained under governmental and nongovernmental sponsorship; an analysis of major occupational diseases; evaluation of available control and measurement technology for hazards for which standards or criteria have been developed during the preceding year; description of cooperative efforts undertaken between Government agencies and other interested parties in the implementation of this Act during the preceding year; a progress report on the development of an adequate supply of trained manpower in the field of occupational safety and health, including estimates of future needs and the efforts being made by Government and others to meet those needs; listing of all toxic substances in industrial usage for which labeling requirements, criteria, or standards have not yet been established; and such recommendations for additional legislation as are deemed necessary to protect the safety and health of the worker and improve the administration of this Act.

§ 676.   [Omitted.]

§ 677.   Separability of provisions

[Sec. 32] If any provision of this Act, or the application of such provision to any person or circumstance, shall be held invalid, the remainder of this Act, or the application of such provision to persons or circumstances other than those as to which it is held invalid, shall not be affected thereby.

§ 678.   Authorization of appropriations

[Sec. 33] There are authorized to be appropriated to carry out this Act for each fiscal year such sums as the Congress shall deem necessary.

8

Alien Employment Laws

Immigration and Nationality Act (1952)

(Act of June 27, 1952, ch. 477, 66 Stat. 163, as last amended by P.L. 99–603, enacted November 6, 1986)

Subchapter I. General Provisions

§ 1101. Definitions

[Sec. 101] (a) As used in this chapter—

* * *

(15) The term "immigrant" means every alien except an alien who is within one of the following classes of nonimmigrant aliens—

* * *

(H) an alien having a residence in a foreign country which he has no intention of abandoning (i) who is of distinguished merit and ability and who is coming temporarily to the United States to perform services of an exceptional nature requiring such merit and ability, and who, in the case of a graduate of a medical school coming to the United States to perform services as a member of the medical profession, is coming pursuant to an invitation from a public or nonprofit private educational or research institution or agency in the United States to teach or conduct research, or both, at or for such institution or agency; or (ii) who is coming temporarily to the United States (a) to perform agricultural labor or services, as defined by the Secretary of Labor in regulations and including agricultural labor defined in section 3121(g) of the Internal Revenue Code of 1954 and agriculture as defined in section 3(f) of the Fair Labor Standards Act of 1938 (29 U.S.C. 203(f)), of a temporary or seasonal nature, or (b) to perform other temporary service or labor if unemployed persons capable of performing such service or labor cannot be found in this country, but this clause shall not apply to graduates of medical schools coming to the United States to perform services as members of the medical profession; or (iii) who is coming temporarily to the United States as a trainee, other than to receive graduate medical education or training; and the alien spouse and minor children of any such alien specified in this paragraph if accompanying him or following to join him;

* * *

Subchapter II. Immigration

Part I. Selection System

§ 1158.   Special agricultural workers

[Sec. 210] (a)(1) The Attorney General shall adjust the status of an alien to that of an alien lawfully admitted for temporary residence if the Attorney General determines that the alien meets the following requirements:

(A) The alien must apply for such adjustment during the 18-month period beginning on the first day of the seventh month that begins after the date of enactment of this section.

(B) The alien must establish that he has—
   (i) resided in the United States, and
   (ii) performed seasonal agricultural services in the United States for at least 90 man-days,

   during the 12-month period ending on May 1, 1986. For purposes of the previous sentence, performance of seasonal agricultural services in the United States for more than one employer on any one day shall be counted as performance of services for only 1 man-day.

(C) The alien must establish that he is admissible to the United States as an immigrant, except as otherwise provided under subsection (c)(2).

(2) The Attorney General shall adjust the status of any alien provided lawful temporary resident status under paragraph (1) to that of an alien lawfully admitted for permanent residence on the following date:

(A) Subject to the numerical limitation established under subparagraph (C), in the case of an alien who has established, at the time of application for temporary residence under paragraph (1), that the alien performed seasonal agricultural services in the United States for at least 90 man-days during each of the 12-month periods ending on May 1, 1984, 1985, and 1986, the adjustment shall occur on the first day after the end of the one-year period that begins on the later of (I) the date the alien was granted such temporary resident status, or (II) the day after the last day of the application period described in paragraph (1)(A).

(B) In the case of aliens to which subparagraph (A) does not apply, the adjustment shall occur on the day after the last day of the two-year period that begins on the later of (I) the date the alien was granted such temporary resident status, or (II) the day after the last day of the application period described in paragraph (1)(A).

(C) Subparagraph (A) shall not apply to more than 350,000 aliens. If more than 350,000 aliens meet the requirements of such subparagraph, such subparagraph shall apply to the 350,000 aliens whose applications for adjustment were first filed under paragraph (1) and subparagraph (B) shall apply to the remaining aliens.

(3) During the period of temporary resident status granted an alien under paragraph (1), the Attorney General may terminate such status only upon a determination under this Act that the alien is deportable.

(4) During the period an alien is in lawful temporary resident status granted under this subsection, the alien has the right to travel abroad (including commutation from a residence abroad) and shall be granted authorization to engage in employment in the United States and shall be provided an "employment authorized" endorsement or other appropriate work permit, in the same manner as for aliens lawfully admitted for permanent residence.

(5) Except as otherwise provided in this subsection, an alien who acquires the status of an alien lawfully admitted for temporary residence under paragraph (1), such status not having changed, is considered to be an alien lawfully admitted for permanent residence (as described in section 101(a)(20)), other than under any provision of the immigration laws.

(b)(1)(A) The Attorney General shall provide that application for adjustment of status under subsection (a) may be filed—

(i) with the Attorney General, or

(ii) with a designated entity (designated under paragraph (2)), but only if the applicant consents to the forwarding of the application to the Attorney General.

(B) The Attorney General, in cooperation with the Secretary of State, shall provide a procedure whereby an alien may apply for adjustment of status under subsection (a)(1) at an appropriate consular office outside the United States. If the alien otherwise qualifies for such adjustment, the Attorney General shall provide such documentation of authorization to enter the United States and to have the alien's status adjusted upon entry as may be necessary to carry out the provisions of this section.

(2) For purposes of receiving applications under this section, the Attorney General—

    (A) shall designate qualified voluntary organizations and other qualified State, local, community, farm labor organizations, and associations of agricultural employers, and

    (B) may designate such other persons as the Attorney General determines are qualified and have substantial experience, demonstrated competence, and traditional long-term involvement in the preparation and submittal of applications for adjustment of status under section 209 or 245, Public Law 89–732, or Public Law 95–145.

(3)(A) An alien may establish that he meets the requirement of subsection (a)(1)(B)(ii) through government employment records, records supplied by employers or collective bargaining organizations, and such other reliable documentation as the alien may provide. The Attorney General shall establish special procedures to credit properly work in cases in which an alien was employed under an assumed name.

    (B)(i) An alien applying for adjustment of status under subsection (a)(1) has the burden of proving by a preponderance of the evidence that the alien has worked the requisite number of mandays (as required under subsection (a)(1)(B)(ii).

    (ii) If an employer or farm labor contractor employing such an alien has kept proper and adequate records respecting such employment, the alien's burden of proof under clause (i) may be met by securing timely production of those records under regulations to be promulgated by the Attorney General.

    (iii) An alien can meet such burden of proof if the alien establishes that the alien has in fact performed the work described in subsection (a)(1)(B)(ii) by producing sufficient evidence to show the extent of that employment as a matter of just and reasonable inference. In such a case, the burden then shifts to the Attorney General to disprove the alien's evidence with a showing which negates the reasonableness of the inference to be drawn from the evidence.

* * *

(d)(1) The Attorney General shall provide that in the case of an alien who is apprehended before the beginning of the application period described in subsection (a)(1) and who can establish a nonfrivolous case of eligibility to have his status adjusted under subsection (a) (but for the fact that he may not apply for such adjustment until the beginning of such period), until the alien has had the opportunity during the first 30 days of the application period to complete the filing of an application for adjustment, the alien—

    (A) may not be excluded or deported, and

    (B) shall be granted authorization to engage in employment in the

United States and be provided an "employment authorized" endorsement or other appropriate work permit.

(2) The Attorney General shall provide that in the case of an alien who presents a nonfrivolous application for adjustment of status under subsection (a) during the application period, and until a final determination on the application has been made in accordance with this section, the alien—

(A) may not be excluded or deported, and

(B) shall be granted authorization to engage in employment in the United States and be provided an "employment authorized" endorsement or other appropriate work permit.

* * *

(h) In this section, the term "seasonal agricultural services" means the performance of field work related to planting, cultural practices, cultivating, growing and harvesting of fruits and vegetables of every kind and other perishable commodities, as defined in regulations by the Secretary of Agriculture.

§ 1158a. Determination of agricultural labor shortages and admission of additional special agricultural workers

[Sec. 210A] (a)(1) Before the beginning of each fiscal year (beginning with fiscal year 1990 and ending with fiscal year 1993), the Secretaries of Labor and Agriculture (in this section referred to as the "Secretaries") shall jointly determine the number (if any) of additional aliens who should be admitted to the United States or who should otherwise acquire the status of aliens lawfully admitted for temporary residence under this section during the fiscal year to meet a shortage of workers to perform seasonal agricultural services in the United States during the year. Such number is, in this section, referred to as the "shortage number."

(2) The shortage number is—

(A) the anticipated need for special agricultural workers (as determined under paragraph (4)) for the fiscal year, minus

(B) the supply of such workers (as determined under paragraph (5)) for that year,

divided by the factor (determined under paragraph (6)) for man-days per worker.

(3) In determining the shortage number, the Secretaries may not determine that there is a shortage unless, after considering all of the criteria set forth in paragraphs (4) and (5), the Secretaries determine that there will not be sufficient able, willing, and qualified workers available to perform seasonal agricultural services required in the fiscal year involved.

(4) For purposes of paragraph (2)(A), the anticipated need for special

agricultural workers for a fiscal year is determined as follows:

(A) The Secretaries shall jointly estimate, using statistically valid methods, the number of man-days of labor performed in seasonal agricultural services in the United States in the previous fiscal year.

(B) The Secretaries shall jointly—

   (i) increase such number by the number of man-days of labor in seasonal agricultural services in the United States that would have been needed in the previous fiscal year to avoid any crop damage or other loss that resulted from the unavailability of labor, and

   (ii) adjust such number to take into account the protected growth or contraction in the requirements for seasonal agricultural services as a result of—

      (I) growth or contraction in the seasonal agriculture industry, and

      (II) the use of technologies and personnel practices that affect the need for, and retention of, workers to perform such services.

(5) For purposes of paragraph (2)(B), the anticipated supply of special agricultural workers for a fiscal year is determined as follows:

(A) The Secretaries shall use the number estimated under paragraph (4)(A).

(B) The Secretaries shall jointly—

   (i) decrease such number by the number of man-days of labor in seasonal agricultural services in the United States that will be lost due to retirement and movement of workers out of performance of seasonal agricultural services, and

   (ii) increase such number by the number of additional man-days of labor in seasonal agricultural services in the United States that can reasonably be expected to result from the availability of able, willing, qualified, and unemployed special agricultural workers, rural low skill, or manual, laborers, and domestic agricultural workers.

(C) In making the adjustment under subparagraph (B)(ii), the Secretaries shall consider—

   (i) the effect, if any, that improvements in wages and working conditions offered by employers will have on the availability of workers to perform seasonal agricultural services, taking into account the adverse effect, if any, of such improvements in wages and working conditions on the economic competitiveness of the perishable agricultural industry,

   (ii) the effect, if any, of enhanced recruitment efforts by the employers of such workers and government employment services in the traditional and expected areas of supply of such workers, and

    (iii) the number of able, willing, and qualified individuals who apply for employment opportunities in seasonal agricultural services listed with offices of government employment services.

(D) Nothing in this subsection shall be deemed to require any individual employer to pay any specified level of wages, to provide any specified working conditions, or to provide for any specified recruitment of workers.

(6)(A) For fiscal year 1990—

    (i) Subject to clause (ii), for purposes of paragraph (2) the factor under this paragraph is the average number, as estimated by the Director of the Bureau of the Census under subsection (b)(3)(A)(ii), of man-days of seasonal agricultural services performed in the United States in fiscal year 1989 by special agricultural workers whose status is adjusted under section 210 and who performed seasonal agricultural services in the United States at any time during the fiscal year.

    (ii) If the Director determines that—

        (I) the information reported under subsection (b)(2)(A) is not adequate to make a reasonable estimate of the average number described in clause (i), but

       (II) the inadequacy of the information is not due to the refusal or failure of employers to report the information required under subsection (b)(2)(A),

    the factor under this paragraph is 90.

(B) For purposes of paragraph (2) for fiscal year 1991, the factor under this paragraph is the average number, as estimated by the Director of the Bureau of the Census under subsection (b)(3)(A)(ii), of man-days of seasonal agricultural services performed in the United States in fiscal year 1990 by special agricultural workers who obtained lawful temporary resident status under this section.

(C) For purposes of paragraph (2) for fiscal years 1992 and 1993, the factor under this paragraph is the average number, as estimated by the Director of the Bureau of the Census under subsection (b)(3)(A)(ii), of man-days of seasonal agricultural services performed in the United States in each of the two previous fiscal years by special agricultural workers who obtained lawful temporary resident status under this section during either of such fiscal years.

(7)(A) After the beginning of a fiscal year, a group or association representing employers (and potential employers) of individuals who perform seasonal agricultural services may request the Secretaries to increase the shortage number for the fiscal year based upon a showing that extraordinary, unusual, and unforeseen circumstances have resulted in a significant increase in the shortage number due to (i) a significant increase in the need for special agricultural workers in the year, (ii) a significant decrease in the availability of able, willing, and qualified workers to perform seasonal agricultural services, or (iii) a significant decrease (below the factor used for purposes of paragraph (6)) in the number of man-days of seasonal agricultural services performed by aliens who were recently admitted (or whose status was recently adjusted) under this section.

(B) Not later than 3 days after the date the Secretaries receive a request under subparagraph (A), the Secretaries shall provide for notice in the Federal Register of the substance of the request and shall provide an opportunity for interested parties to submit information to the Secretaries on a timely basis respecting the request.

(C) The Secretaries, not later than 21 days after the date of the receipt of such a request and after consideration of any information submitted on a timely basis with respect to the request, shall make and publish in the Federal Register their determination on the request. The request shall be granted, and the shortage number for the fiscal year shall be increased, to the extent that the Secretaries determine that such an increase is justified based upon the showing and circumstances described in subparagraph (A) and that such an increase takes into account reasonable recruitment efforts having been undertaken.

(8)(A) After the beginning of a fiscal year, a group of special agricultural workers may request the Secretaries to decrease the number of man-days required under subparagraphs (A) and (B) of subsection (d)(2) with respect to the fiscal year based upon a showing that extraordinary, unusual, and unforeseen circumstances have resulted in a significant decrease in the shortage number due to (i) a significant decrease in the need for special agricultural workers in the year, (ii) a significant increase in the availability of able, willing, and qualified workers to perform seasonal agricultural services, or (iii) a significant increase (above the factor used for purposes of paragraph (6)) in the number of man-days of seasonal agricultural services performed by aliens who were recently admitted (or whose status was recently adjusted) under this section.

(B) Not later than 3 days after the date the Secretaries receive a request under subparagraph (A), the Secretaries shall provide for notice in the Federal Register of the substance of the request and shall provide an opportunity for interested parties to submit information to the Secretaries on a timely basis respecting the request.

(C) The Secretaries, before the end of the fiscal year involved and after consideration of any information submitted on a timely basis with respect to the request, shall make and publish in the Federal Register their determination on the request. The request shall be granted, and the number of man-days specified in subparagraphs (A) and (B) of subsection (d)(2) for the fiscal year shall be reduced by the same proportion as the Secretaries determine that a decrease in the shortage number is justified based upon the showing and circumstances described in subparagraph (A).

(b)(1)(A) The numerical limitation on the number of aliens who may be admitted under subsection (c)(1) or who otherwise may acquire lawful temporary residence under such subsection for fiscal year 1990 is—

> (i) 95 percent of the number of individuals whose status was adjusted under section 210(a), minus
>
> (ii) the number estimated under paragraph (3)(A)(i) for the previous fiscal year 1989 (as adjusted in accordance with subparagraph (C)).

(B) The numerical limitation on the number of aliens who may be admitted under subsection (c)(1) or who otherwise may acquire lawful temporary residence under such subsection for fiscal year 1991, 1992, or 1993 is—

> (i) 90 percent of the number described in this clause for the previous fiscal year (or, for fiscal year 1991, the number described in subparagraph (A)(i)), minus—
>
> (ii) the number estimated under paragraph (3)(A)(i) for the previous fiscal year (as adjusted in accordance with subparagraph (C)).

(C) The number used under subparagraph (A)(ii) or (B)(ii) (as the case may be) shall be increased or decreased to reflect any numerical increase or decrease, respectively, in the number of aliens admitted to perform temporary seasonal agricultural services (as defined in subsection (g)(2)) under section 101(a)(15)(H)(ii)(a) in the fiscal year compared to such number in the previous fiscal year.

(2) In the case of a person or entity who employs, during a fiscal year (beginning with fiscal year 1989 and ending with fiscal year 1992) in seasonal agricultural services, a special agricultural worker—

(A) whose status was adjusted under section 210, the person or entity shall furnish an official designated by the Secretaries with a certificate (at such time, in such form, and containing such information as the Secretaries establish, after consultation with the Attorney General and the Director of the Bureau of the Census) of the number of man-days of employment performed by the alien in seasonal agricultural services during the fiscal year, or

(B) who was admitted or whose status was adjusted under this section, the person or entity shall furnish the alien and an official designated by the Secretaries with a certificate (at such time, in such form, and containing such information as the Secretaries establish, after consultation with the Attorney General and the Director of the Bureau of the Census) of the number of man-days of employment performed by the alien in seasonal agricultural services during the fiscal year.

(3)(A) The Director of the Bureau of the Census shall, before the end of each fiscal year (beginning with fiscal year 1989 and ending with fiscal year 1992), estimate—

(i) the number of special agricultural workers who have performed seasonal agricultural services in the United States at any time during the fiscal year, and

(ii) for purposes of subsection (a)(5), the average number of man-days of such services certain of such workers have performed in the United States during the fiscal year.

(B) The official designated by the Secretaries under paragraph (2) shall furnish to the Director, in such form and manner as the Director specifies, information contained in the certifications furnished to the official under paragraph (2).

(C) The Director shall base the estimates under subparagraph (A) on the information furnished under subparagraph (B), but shall take into account (to the extent feasible) the underreporting or duplicate reporting of special agricultural workers who have performed seasonal agricultural services at any time during the fiscal year. The Director shall periodically conduct appropriate surveys, of agricultural employers and others, to ascertain the extent of such underreporting or duplicate reporting.

(D) The Director shall annually prepare and report to the Congress information on the estimates made under this paragraph.

(c)(1) For each fiscal year (beginning with fiscal year 1990 and ending with fiscal year 1993), the Attorney General shall provide for the admission for lawful temporary resident status, or for the adjustment of status to lawful temporary resident status, of a number of aliens equal to the shortage number (if any, determined under subsection (a)) for the fiscal year, or, if less, the numerical limitation established under subsection (b)(1) for the fiscal year. No such alien shall be admitted who is not admissible to the United States as an immigrant, except as otherwise provided under subsection (e).

(2) The Attorney General shall, in consultation with the Secretary of State, provide such process as may be appropriate for aliens to petition for immigrant visas or to adjust status to become aliens lawfully admitted for temporary residence under this subsection. No alien may be issued a visa as an alien to be admitted under this subsection or may have the alien's status adjusted under this subsection unless the alien has had a petition approved under this paragraph.

(d)(1) The Attorney General shall adjust the status of any alien provided lawful temporary resident status under subsection (c) to that of an alien lawfully admitted for permanent residence at the end of the 3-year period that begins on the date the alien was granted such temporary resident status.

(2) During the period of temporary resident status granted an alien under subsection (c), the Attorney General may terminate such status only upon a determination under this Act that the alien is deportable.

(3) During the period an alien is in lawful temporary resident status granted under this section, the alien has the right to travel abroad (including commutation from a residence abroad) and shall be granted authorization to engage in employment in the United States and shall be provided an "employment authorized" endorsement or other appropriate work permit, in the same manner as for aliens lawfully admitted for permanent residence.

(4) Except as otherwise provided in this subsection, an alien who acquires the status of an alien lawfully admitted for temporary residence under subsection (c), such status not having changed, is considered to be an alien lawfully admitted for permanent residence (as described in section 101(a)(20)), other than under any provision of the immigration laws.

(5)(A) In order to meet the requirement of this paragraph (for purposes of this subsection and section 241(a)(20)), an alien, who has obtained the status of an alien lawfully admitted for temporary residence under this section, must establish to the Attorney General that the alien has performed 90 man-days of seasonal agricultural services—

(i) during the one-year period beginning on the date the alien obtained such status,

(ii) during the one-year period beginning one year after the date the alien obtained such status, and

(iii) during the one-year period beginning two years after the date the alien obtained such status.

(B) Notwithstanding any provision in title III, an alien admitted under this section may not be naturalized as a citizen of the United States under that title unless the alien has performed 90 man-days of seasonal agricultural services in each of five fiscal years (not including any fiscal year before the fiscal year in which the alien was admitted under this section).

(C) In meeting the requirements of subparagraphs (A) and (B), an alien may submit such documentation as may be submitted under section 210(b)(3).

(D) The number of man-days specified in subparagraphs (A) and (B) are subject to adjustment under subsection (a)(8).

(6) The provisions of section 245A(h) (other than paragraph (1)(A)(iii)) shall apply to an alien who has obtained the status of an alien lawfully admitted for temporary residence under this section, during the five-

year period beginning on the date the alien obtained such status, in the same manner as they apply to an alien granted lawful temporary residence under section 245A; except that, for purposes of this paragraph, assistance furnished under the Legal Services Corporation Act (42 U.S.C. 2996 et seq.) or under title V of the Housing Act of 1949 (42 U.S.C. 1471 et seq.) shall not be construed to be financial assistance described in section 245A(h)(1)(A)(i).

(e) In the determination of an alien's admissibility under subsection (c)(1)—

(1) The provisions of paragraphs (14), (20), (21), (25), and (32) of section 212(a) shall not apply.

(2)(A) Except as provided in subparagraph (B), the Attorney General may waive any other provision of section 212(a) in the case of individual aliens for humanitarian purposes, to assure family unity, or when it is otherwise in the public interest.

(B) The following provisions of section 212(a) may not be waived by the Attorney General under subparagraph (A):

    (i) Paragraphs (9) and (10) (relating to criminals).

    (ii) Paragraph (23) (relating to drug offenses), except for so much of such paragraph as relates to a single offense of simple possession of 30 grams or less of marihuana.

    (iii) Paragraphs (27), (28), and (29) (relating to national security and members of certain organizations).

    (iv) Paragraph (33) (relating to those who assisted in the Nazi persecutions).

(C) An alien is not ineligible for adjustment of status under this section due to being inadmissible under section 212(a)(15) if the alien demonstrates a history of employment in the United States evidencing self-support without reliance on public cash assistance.

(3) The alien shall be required, at the alien's expense, to undergo such a medical examination (including a determination of immunization status) as is appropriate and conforms to generally accepted professional standards of medical practice.

(f)(1) If a person employs an alien, who was admitted or whose status is adjusted under subsection (c), in the performance of seasonal agricultural services and provides transportation arrangements or assistance for such workers, the employer must provide the same transportation arrangements or assistance (generally comparable in expense and scope) for other individuals employed in the performance of seasonal agricultural services.

(2) A farm labor contractor, agricultural employer, or agricultural association who is an exempt person (as defined in paragraph (5)) shall not knowingly provide false or misleading information to an alien who was admitted or whose status was adjusted under subsection (c) concerning the terms, conditions, or existence of agricultural employment (described in subsection (a), (b), or (c) of section 301 of MASAWPA).

(3) In the case of an exempt person and with respect to aliens who have been admitted or whose status has been adjusted under subsection (c), the provisions of section 505 of MASAWPA shall apply to any proceeding under or related to (and rights and protections afforded by) this section in the same manner as they apply to proceedings under or related to (and rights and protections afforded by) MASAWPA.

(4) If a person or entity—
   (A) fails to furnish a certificate required under subsection (b)(2) or furnishes false statement of a material fact in such a certificate,
   (B) violates paragraph (1) or (2), or
   (C) violates the provisions of section 505(a) of MASAWPA (as they apply under paragraph (3)),
the person or entity is subject to a civil money penalty under section 503 of MASAWPA in the same manner as if the person or entity had committed a violation of MASAWPA.

(5) In this subsection:
   (A) MASAWPA.—The term "MASAWPA" means the Migrant and Seasonal Agricultural Worker Protection Act (Public Law 97–470).
   (B) The term "exempt person" means a person or entity who would be subject to the provisions of MASAWPA but for paragraph (1) or (2), or both, of section 4(a) of MASAWPA.

(g) In this section:

(1) The term "special agricultural worker" means an individual, regardless of present status, whose status was at any time adjusted under section 210 or who at any time was admitted or had the individual's status adjusted under subsection (c).

(2) The term "seasonal agricultural services" has the meaning given such term in section 210(h).

(3) The term "Director" refers to the Director of the Bureau of the Census.

(4) The term "man-day" means, with respect to seasonal agricultural services, the performance during a calendar day of at least 4 hours of seasonal agricultural services.

Part II. Admission Qualifications for Aliens

§ 1186. Admission of temporary H-2A workers

[Sec. 216] (a)(1) A petition to import an alien as an H-2A worker (as defined in subsection (i)(2)) may not be approved by the Attorney General unless the petitioner has applied to the Secretary of Labor for a certification that—

(A) there are not sufficient workers who are able, willing, and qualified, and who will be available at the time and place needed, to perform the labor or services involved in the petition, and

(B) the employment of the alien in such labor or services will not adversely affect the wages, and working conditions of workers in the United States similarly employed.

(2) The Secretary of Labor may require by regulation, as a condition of issuing the certification, the payment of a fee to recover the reasonable costs of processing applications for certification.

(b) The Secretary of Labor may not issue a certification under subsection (a) with respect to an employer if the conditions described in that subsection are not met or if any of the following conditions are met:

(1) There is a strike or lockout in the course of a labor dispute which, under the regulations, precludes such certification.

(2)(A) The employer during the previous two-year period employed H-2A workers and the Secretary of Labor has determined, after notice and opportunity for a hearing, that the employer at any time during that period substantially violated a material term or condition of the labor certification with respect to the employment of domestic or nonimmigrant workers.

(B) No employer may be denied certification under subparagraph (A) for more than three years for any violation described in such subparagraph.

(3) The employer has not provided the Secretary with satisfactory assurances that if the employment for which the certification is sought is not covered by State workers' compensation law, the employer will provide, at no cost to the worker, insurance covering injury and disease arising out of and in the course of the worker's employment which will provide benefits at least equal to those provided under the State workers' compensation law for comparable employment.

(4) The Secretary determines that the employer has not made positive recruitment efforts within a multi-state region of traditional or expected labor supply where the Secretary finds that there are a significant number of qualified United States workers who, if recruited, would be willing to make themselves available for work at the time and place needed. Positive recruitment under this paragraph is in addition to, and shall be conducted within the same time period as, the circulation through the interstate employment service system of the employer's job offer. The obligation to engage in positive recruitment under this paragraph shall terminate on the date the H-2A workers depart for the employer's place of employment.

(c) The following rules shall apply in the case of the filing and consideration of an application for a labor certification under this section:

(1) The Secretary of Labor may not require that the application be filed more than 60 days before the first date the employer requires the labor

or services of the H-2A worker.

(2)(A) The employer shall be notified in writing within seven days of the date of filing if the application does not meet the standards (other than that described in subsection (a)(1)(A)) for approval.

(B) If the application does not meet such standards, the notice shall include the reasons therefor and the Secretary shall provide an opportunity for the prompt resubmission of a modified application.

(3)(A) The Secretary of Labor shall make, not later than 20 days before the date such labor or services are first required to be performed, the certification described in subsection (a)(1) if—

    (i) the employer has complied with the criteria for certification (including criteria for the recruitment of eligible individuals as prescribed by the Secretary), and

    (ii) the employer does not actually have, or has not been provided with referrals of, qualified eligible individuals who have indicated their availability to perform such labor or services on the terms and conditions of a job offer which meets the requirements of the Secretary.

In considering the question of whether a specific qualification is appropriate in a job offer, the Secretary shall apply the normal and accepted qualifications required by non-H-2A-employers in the same or comparable occupations and crops.

(B)(i) For a period of 3 years subsequent to the effective date of this section, labor certifications shall remain effective only if, from the time the foreign worker departs for the employer's place of employment, the employer will provide employment to any qualified United States worker who applies to the employer until 50 percent of the period of the work contract, under which the foreign worker who is in the job was hired, has elapsed. In addition, the employer will offer to provide benefits, wages, and working conditions required pursuant to this section and regulations.

    (ii) The requirement of clause (i) shall not apply to any employer who—

      (I) did not, during any calendar quarter during the preceding calendar year, use more than 500 man-days of agricultural labor, as defined in section 3(u) of the Fair Labor Standards Act of 1938 (29 U.S.C. 203(u)),

      (II) is not a member of an association which has petitioned for certification under this section for its members, and

      (III) has not otherwise associated with other employers who are petitioning for temporary foreign workers under this section.

    (iii) Six months before the end of the 3-year period described in clause (i), the Secretary of Labor shall consider the findings of the report mandated by section 403(a)(4)(D) of the Immigration Reform and Control Act of 1986 as well as other relevant materials, including evidence of benefits to United States workers and costs to employers, addressing the advisability of continuing a policy which requires an employer, as a condition for certification under this section, to continue to accept qualified, eligible United States workers for employment after the date the H-2A workers depart for work with the employer. The Secretary's review of such findings and materials shall lead to the issuance of findings in furtherance of the Congressional policy that aliens not be admitted under this section unless there are not sufficient workers in the United States who are able, willing, and qualified to perform the labor or service needed and that the employment of the aliens in such labor or services will not aversely affect the wages and working conditions of workers in the United States similarly employed. In the absence of the enactment of Federal legislation prior to three months before the end of the 3-year period described in clause (i) which addresses the subject matter of this subparagraph, the Secretary shall immediately publish the findings required by this clause, and shall promulgate, on an interim or final basis, regulations based on his findings which shall be effective no later than three years from the effective date of this section.

(iv) In complying with clause (i) of this subparagraph, an association shall be allowed to refer or transfer workers among its members: *Provided*, That for purposes of this section an association acting as an agent for its members shall not be considered a joint employer merely because of such referral or transfer.

(v) United States workers referred or transferred pursuant to clause (iv) of this subparagraph shall not be treated disparately.

(vi) An employer shall not be liable for payments under section 655.202(b)(6) of title 20, Code of Federal Regulations (or any successor regulation) with respect to an H-2A worker who is displaced due to compliance with the requirement of this subparagraph, if the Secretary of Labor certifies that the H-2A worker was displaced because of the employer's compliance with clause (i) of this subparagraph.

(vii)(I) No person or entity shall willfully and knowingly withhold domestic workers prior to the arrival of H-2A workers in order to force the hiring of domestic workers under clause (i).

(II) Upon the receipt of a complaint by an employer that a

violation of subclause (I) has occurred the Secretary shall immediately investigate. He shall within 36 hours of the receipt of the complaint issue findings concerning the alleged violation. Where the Secretary finds that a violation has occurred, he shall immediately suspend the application of clause (i) of this subparagraph with respect to that certification for that date of need.

(4) Employers shall furnish housing in accordance with regulations. The employer shall be permitted at the employer's option to provide housing meeting applicable Federal standards for temporary labor camps or to secure housing which meets the local standards for rental and/or public accommodations or other substantially similar class of habitation: *Provided*, That in the absence of applicable local standards, State standards for rental and/or public accommodations or other substantially similar class of habitation shall be met: *Provided further*, That in the absence of applicable local or State standards, Federal temporary labor camp standards shall apply: *Provided further*, That the Secretary of Labor shall issue regulations which address the specific requirements of housing for employees principally engaged in the range production of livestock: *Provided further*, That when it is the prevailing practice in the area and occupation of intended employment to provide family housing, family housing shall be provided to workers with families who request it: *And provided further*, That nothing in this paragraph shall require an employer to provide or secure housing for workers who are not entitled to it under the temporary labor certification regulations in effect on June 1, 1986.

(d)(1) A petition to import an alien as a temporary agricultural worker, and an application for a labor certification with respect to such a worker, may be filed by an association of agricultural producers which use agricultural services.

(2) If an association is a joint or sole employer of temporary agricultural workers, the certifications granted under this section to the association may be used for the certified job opportunities of any of its producer members and such workers may be transferred among its producer members to perform agricultural services of a temporary or seasonal nature for which the certifications were granted.

(3)(A) If an individual producer member of a joint employer association is determined to have committed an act that under subsection (b)(2) results in the denial of certification with respect to the member, the denial shall apply only to that member of the association unless the Secretary determines that the association or other member participated in, had knowledge of, or reason to know of, the violation.

(B)(i) If an association representing agricultural producers as a joint employer is determined to have committed an act that under subsection (b)(2) results in the denial of certification with respect to the association, the denial shall apply only to the association and does not apply to any individual producer member of the association unless the Secretary determines that the member participated in, had knowledge of, or reason to know of, the violation.

(ii) If an association of agricultural producers certified as a sole employer is determined to have committed an act that under subsection (b)(2) results in the denial of certification with respect to the association, no individual producer member of such association may be the beneficiary of the services of temporary alien agricultural workers admitted under this section in the commodity and occupation in which such aliens were employed by the association which was denied certification during the period such denial is in force, unless such producer member employs such aliens in the commodity and occupation in question directly or through an association which is a joint employer of such workers with the producer member.

(e)(1) Regulations shall provide for an expedited procedure for the review of a denial of certification under subsection (a)(1) or a revocation of such a certification or, at the applicant's request, for a de novo administrative hearing respecting the denial or revocation.

(2) The Secretary of Labor shall expeditiously, but in no case later than 72 hours after the time a new determination is requested, make a new determination on the request for certification in the case of an H-2A worker if able, willing, and qualified eligible individuals are not actually available at the time such labor or services are required and a certification was denied in whole or in part because of the availability of qualified workers. If the employer asserts that any eligible individual who has been referred is not able, willing, or qualified, the burden of proof is on the employer to establish that the individual referred is not able, willing, or qualified because of employment-related reasons.

(f) An alien may not be admitted to the United States as a temporary agricultural worker if the alien was admitted to the United States as such a worker within the previous five-year period and the alien during that period violated a term or condition of such previous admission.

(g)(1) There are authorized to be appropriated for each fiscal year, beginning with fiscal year 1987, $10,000,000 for the purposes—

(A) of recruiting domestic workers for temporary labor and services which might otherwise be performed by nonimmigrants described in section 101(a)(15)(H)(ii)(a), and

(B) of monitoring terms and conditions under which such nonimmigrants (and domestic workers employed by the same employers) are employed in the United States.

(2) The Secretary of Labor is authorized to take such actions, including

imposing appropriate penalties and seeking appropriate injunctive relief and specific performance of contractual obligations, as may be necessary to assure employer compliance with terms and conditions of employment under this section.

(3) There are authorized to be appropriated for each fiscal year, beginning with fiscal year 1987, such sums as may be necessary for the purpose of enabling the Secretary of Labor to make determinations and certifications under this section and under section 212(a)(14).

(4) There are authorized to be appropriated for each fiscal year, beginning with fiscal year 1987, such sums as may be necessary for the purposes of enabling the Secretary of Agriculture to carry out the Secretary's duties and responsibilities under this section.

(h)(1) The Attorney General shall provide for such endorsement of entry and exit documents of nonimmigrants described in section 101(a)(15)(H)(ii) as may be necessary to carry out this section and to provide notice for purposes of section 274A.

(2) The provisions of subsections (a) and (c) of section 214 and the provisions of this section preempt any State or local law regulating admissibility of nonimmigrant workers.

(i) For purposes of this section:

(1) The term "eligible individual" means, with respect to employment, an individual who is not an unauthorized alien (as defined in section 274A(h)) with respect to that employment.

(2) The term "H-2A worker" means a nonimmigrant described in section 101(a)(15)(H)(ii)(a).

Part V. Deportation; Adjustment of Status

§ 1255. Adjustment of status of nonimmigrant inspected and admitted or paroled into United States

[Sec. 245] (a) The status of an alien who was inspected and admitted or paroled into the United States may be adjusted by the Attorney General, in his discretion and under such regulations as he may prescribe, to that of an alien lawfully admitted for permanent residence if (1) the alien makes an application for such adjustment, (2) the alien is eligible to receive an immigrant visa and is admissible to the United States for permanent residence, and (3) an immigrant visa is immediately available to him at the time his application is filed.

(b) Upon the approval of an application for adjustment made under subsection (a) of this section, the Attorney General shall record the alien's lawful admission for permanent residence as of the date the order of the Attorney General approving the application for the adjustment of status is made, and the Secretary of State shall reduce by one the number of the preference or nonpreference visas authorized to be issued under sections 1152(e) or 1153(a) of this title within the class to which the alien is chargeable for the fiscal year then current.

(c) The provisions of this section shall not be applicable to (1) an alien crewman; (2) an alien (other than an immediate relative as defined in section 1151(b) of this title or a special immigrant described in section 1101(a)(27)(H) of this title) who hereafter continues in or accepts unauthorized employment prior to filing an application for adjustment of status or who is not in legal immigration status on the date of filing the application for adjustment of status or who has failed (other than through no fault of his own for technical reasons) to maintain continuously a legal status since entry into the United States; or (3) any alien admitted in transit without visa under section 1182(d)(4)(C) of this title.

* * *

§ 1255a. Adjustment of status of certain entrants before January 1, 1982, to that of person admitted for lawful residence

[Sec. 245A] (a) The Attorney General shall adjust the status of an alien to that of an alien lawfully admitted for temporary residence if the alien meets the following requirements:

(1)(A) Except as provided in subparagraph (B), the alien must apply for such adjustment during the 12-month period beginning on a date (not later than 180 days after November 6, 1986) designated by the Attorney General.

(B) An alien who, at any time during the first 11 months of the 12-month period described in subparagraph (A), is the subject of an order to show cause issued under section 242, must make application under this section not later than the end of the 30-day period beginning either on the first day of such 18-month period or on the date of the issuance of such order, whichever day is later.

(C) Each application under this subsection shall contain such information as the Attorney General may require, including information on living relatives of the applicant with respect to whom a petition for preference or other status may be filed by the applicant at any later date under section 204(a).

(2)(A) The alien must establish that he entered the United States before January 1, 1982, and that he has resided continuously in the United States in an unlawful status since such date and through the date the application is filed under this subsection.

(B) In the case of an alien who entered the United States as a nonimmigrant before January 1, 1982, the alien must establish that the alien's period of authorized stay as a nonimmigrant expired before such date through the passage of time or the alien's unlawful status was known to the Government as of such date.

(C) If the alien was at any time a nonimmigrant exchange alien (as defined in section 101(a)(15)(J)), the alien must establish that the alien was not subject to the two-year foreign residence requirement of section 212(e) or has fulfilled that requirement or received a waiver thereof.

(3)(A) The alien must establish that the alien has been continuously physically present in the United States since November 6, 1986.

(B) An alien shall not be considered to have failed to maintain continous physical presence in the United States for purposes of subparagraph (A) by virtue of brief, casual, and innocent absences from the United States.

(C) Nothing in this section shall be construed as authorizing an alien to apply for admission to, or to be admitted to, the United States in order to apply for adjustment of status under this subsection.

(4) The alien must establish that he—

(A) is admissible to the United States as an immigrant, except as otherwise provided under subsection (d)(2),

(B) has not been convicted of any felony or of three or more misdemeanors committed in the United States,

(C) has not assisted in the persecution of any person or persons on account of race, religion, nationality, membership in a particular social group, or political opinion, and

(D) is registered or registering under the Military Selective Service Act, if the alien is required to be so registered under that Act.

For purposes of this subsection, an alien in the status of a Cuban and Haitian entrant described in paragraph (1) or (2)(A) of section 501(e) of Public Law 96–422 [8 U.S.C. § 1522] shall be considered to have entered the United States and to be in an unlawful status in the United States.

(b) * * *

(3) During the period an alien is in lawful temporary resident status granted under subsection (a)—

* * *

(B) The Attorney General shall grant the alien authorization to engage in employment in the United States and provide to that alien an "employment authorized" endorsement or other appropriate work permit.

* * *

(e)(1) The Attorney General shall provide that in the case of an alien who is apprehended before the beginning of the application period described in subsection (a)(1)(A) and who can establish a prima facie case of eligibility to have his status adjusted under subsection (a) (but for the fact that he may not apply for such adjustment until the beginning of such period), until the alien has had the opportunity during the first 30 days of the application period to complete the filing of an application for adjustment, the alien—

(A) may not be deported, and

(B) shall be granted authorization to engage in employment in the United States and be provided an "employment authorized" endorsement or other appropriate work permit.

(2) The Attorney General shall provide that in the case of an alien who presents a prima facie application for adjustment of status under subsection (a) during the application period, and until a final determination on the application has been made in accordance with this section, the alien—

(A) may not be deported, and

(B) shall be granted authorization to engage in employment in the United States and be provided an "employment authorized" endorsement or other appropriate work permit.

Part VIII. General Penalty Provisions

§ 1324. Bringing in and harboring certain aliens

[Sec. 274] (a)(1) Any person who—

(A) knowing that a person is an alien, brings to or attempts to bring to the United States in any manner whatsoever such person at a place other than a designated port of entry or place other than as designated by the Commissioner, regardless of whether such alien has received prior official authorization to come to, enter, or reside in the United States and regardless of any future official action which may be taken with respect to such alien;

(B) knowing or in reckless disregard of the fact that an alien has come to, entered, or remains in the United States in violation of law, transports, or moves or attempts to transport or move such alien within the United States by means of transportation or otherwise, in furtherance of such violation of law;

(C) knowing or in reckless disregard of the fact that an alien has come to, entered, or remains in the United States in violation of law, conceals, harbors, or shields from detection, or attempts to conceal, harbor, or shield from detection, such alien in any place, including any building or any means of transportation; or

(D) encourages or induces an alien to come to, enter, or reside in the United States, knowing or in reckless disregard of the fact that such coming to, entry, or residence is or will be in violation of law,

shall be fined in accordance with title 18, United States Code, imprisoned not more than five years, or both, for each alien in respect to whom any violation of this subsection occurs.

(2) Any person who, knowing or in reckless disregard of the fact that an alien has not received prior official authorization to come to, enter, or reside in the United States, brings to or attempts to bring to the United States in any manner whatsoever, such alien, regardless of any official action which may later be taken with respect to such alien shall, for each transaction constituting a violation of this paragraph, regardless of the number of aliens involved—

(A) be fined in accordance with title 18, United States Code, or imprisoned not more than one year, or both; or

(B) in the case of—

(i) a second or subsequent offense,

(ii) an offense done for the purpose of commercial advantage or private financial gain, or

(iii) an offense in which the alien is not upon arrival immediately brought and presented to an appropriate immigration officer at a designated port of entry,

be fined in accordance with title 18, United States Code, or imprisoned not more than five years, or both.

* * *

§ 1324a. Unlawful employment of aliens

[Sec. 274A] (a)(1) It is unlawful for a person or other entity to hire, or to recruit or refer for a fee, for employment in the United States—

(A) an alien knowing the alien is an unauthorized alien (as defined in subsection (h)(3)) with respect to such employment, or

(B) an individual without complying with the requirements of subsection (b).

(2) It is unlawful for a person or other entity, after hiring an alien for employment in accordance with paragraph (1), to continue to employ the alien in the United States knowing the alien is (or has become) an unauthorized alien with respect to such employment.

(3) A person or entity that establishes that it has complied in good faith with the requirements of subsection (b) with respect to the hiring, recruiting, or referral for employment of an alien in the United States

has established an affirmative defense that the person or entity has not violated paragraph (1)(A) with respect to such hiring, recruiting, or referral.

(4) For purposes of this section, a person or other entity who uses a contract, subcontract, or exchange, entered into, renegotiated, or extended after the date of the enactment of this section, to obtain the labor of an alien in the United States knowing that the alien is an unauthorized alien (as defined in subsection (h)(3)) with respect to performing such labor, shall be considered to have hired the alien for employment in the United States in violation of paragraph (1)(A).

(5) For purposes of paragraphs (1)(B) and (3), a person or entity shall be deemed to have complied with the requirements of subsection (b) with respect to the hiring of an individual who was referred for such employment by a State employment agency (as defined by the Attorney General), if the person or entity has and retains (for the period and in the manner described in subsection (b)(3)) appropriate documentation of such referral by that agency, which documentation certifies that the agency has complied with the procedures specified in subsection (b) with respect to the individual's referral.

(b) The requirements referred to in paragraphs (1)(B) and (3) of subsection (a) are, in the case of a person or other entity hiring, recruiting, or referring an individual for employment in the United States, the requirements specified in the following three paragraphs:

(1)(A) The person or entity must attest, under penalty of perjury and on a form designated or established by the Attorney General by regulation, that it has verified that the individual is not an unauthorized alien by examining—

(i) a document described in subparagraph (B), or

(ii) a document described in subparagraph (C) and a document described in subparagraph (D).

A person or entity has complied with the requirement of this paragraph with respect to examination of a document if the document reasonably appears on its face to be genuine. If an individual provides a document or combination of documents that reasonably appears on its face to be genuine and that is sufficient to meet the requirements of such sentence, nothing in this paragraph shall be construed as requiring the person or entity to solicit the production of any other document or as requiring the individual to produce such a document.

(B) A document described in this subparagraph is an individual's—

(i) United States passport;

(ii) certificate of United States citizenship;

(iii) certificate of naturalization;

(iv) unexpired foreign passport, if the passport has an appropriate, unexpired endorsement of the Attorney General authorizing the individual's employment in the United States; or

(v) resident alien card or other alien registration card, if the card—

    (I) contains a photograph of the individual or such other personal identifying information relating to the individual as the Attorney General finds, by regulation, sufficient for purposes of this subsection, and

    (II) is evidence of authorization of employment in the United States.

(C) A document described in this subparagraph is an individual's—

    (i) social security account number card (other than such a card which specifies on the face that the issuance of the card does not authorize employment in the United States);

    (ii) certificate of birth in the United States or establishing United States nationality at birth, which certificate the Attorney General finds, by regulation, to be acceptable for purposes of this section; or

    (iii) other documentation evidencing authorization of employment in the United States which the Attorney General finds, by regulation, to be acceptable for purposes of this section.

(D) A document described in this subparagraph is an individual's—

    (i) driver's license or similar document issued for the purpose of identification by a State, if it contains a photograph of the individual or such other personal identifying information relating to the individual as the Attorney General finds, by regulation, sufficient for purposes of this section; or

    (ii) in the case of individuals under 16 years of age or in a State which does not provide for issuance of an identification document (other than a driver's license) referred to in clause (ii), documentation of personal identity of such other type as the Attorney General finds, by regulation, provides a reliable means of identification.

(2) The individual must attest, under penalty of perjury on the form designated or established for purposes of paragraph (1), that the individual is a citizen or national of the United States, an alien lawfully admitted for permanent residence, or an alien who is authorized under this Act or by the Attorney General to be hired, recruited, or referred for such employment.

(3) After completion of such form in accordance with paragraphs (1) and (2), the person or entity must retain the form and make it available for inspection by officers of the Service or the Department of Labor during a period beginning on the date of the hiring, recruiting, or referral of the individual and ending—

(A) in the case of the recruiting or referral for a fee (without hiring) of an individual, three years after the date of the recruiting or referral, and

    (B) in the case of the hiring of an individual—
       (i) three years after the date of such hiring, or
       (ii) one year after the date the individual's employment is terminated;
    whichever is later.

(4) Notwithstanding any other provision of law, the person or entity may copy a document presented by an individual pursuant to this subsection and may retain the copy, but only (except as otherwise permitted under law) for the purpose of complying with the requirements of this subsection.

(5) A form designated or established by the Attorney General under this subsection and any information contained in or appended to such form, may not be used for purposes other than for enforcement of this Act and sections 1001, 1028, 1546, and 1621 of title 18, United States Code.

(c) Nothing in this section shall be construed to authorize, directly or indirectly, the issuance or use of national identification cards or the establishment of a national identification card.

(d)(1)(A) The President shall provide for the monitoring and evaluation of the degree to which the employment verification system established under subsection (b) provides a secure system to determine employment eligibility in the United States and shall examine the suitability of existing Federal and State identification systems for use for this purpose.

    (B) To the extent that the system established under subsection (b) is found not to be a secure system to determine employment eligibility in the United States, the President shall, subject to paragraph (3) and taking into account the results of any demonstration projects conducted under paragraph (4), implement such changes in (including additions to) the requirements of subsection (b) as may be necessary to establish a secure system to determine employment eligibility in the United States. Such changes in the system may be implemented only if the changes conform to the requirements of paragraph (2).

(2) Any change the President proposes to implement under paragraph (1) in the verification system must be designed in a manner so the verification system, as so changed, meets the following requirements:
    (A) The system must be capable of reliably determining whether—
       (i) a person with the identity claimed by an employee or prospective employee is eligible to work, and
       (ii) the employee or prospective employee is claiming the identity of another individual.
    (B) If the system requires that a document be presented to or examined by an employer, the document must be in a form which is resistant to counterfeiting and tampering.

(C) Any personal information utilized by the system may not be made available to Government agencies, employers, and other persons except to the extent necessary to verify that an individual is not an unauthorized alien.

(D) The system must protect the privacy and security of personal information and identifiers utilized in the system.

(E) A verification that an employee or prospective employee is eligible to be employed in the United States may not be withheld or revoked under the system for any reason other than that the employee or prospective employee is an unauthorized alien.

(F) The system may not be used for law enforcement purposes, other than for enforcement of this Act or sections 1001, 1028, 1546, and 1621 of title 18, United States Code.

(G) If the system requires individuals to present a new card or other document (designed specifically for use for this purpose) at the time of hiring, recruitment, or referral, then such document may not be required to be presented for any purpose other than under this Act (or enforcement of sections 1001, 1028, 1546, and 1621 of title 18, United States Code) nor to be carried on one's person.

(3)(A) The President may not implement any change under paragraph (1) unless at least—

   (i) 60 days,

   (ii) one year, in the case of a major change described in subparagraph (D)(iii), or

   (iii) two years, in the case of a major change described in clause (i) or (ii) of subparagraph (D),

before the date of implementation of the change, the President has prepared and transmitted to the Committee on the Judiciary of the House of Representatives and to the Committee on the Judiciary of the Senate a written report setting forth the proposed change. If the President proposes to make any change regarding social security account number cards, the President shall transmit to the Committee on Ways and Means of the House of Representatives and to the Committee on Finance of the Senate a written report setting forth the proposed change. The President promptly shall cause to have printed in the Federal Register the substance of any major change (described in subparagraph (D)) proposed and reported to Congress.

(B) In any report under subparagraph (A) the President shall include recommendations for the establishment of civil and criminal sanctions for unauthorized use or disclosure of the information or identifiers contained in such system.

(C)(i) The Committees on the Judiciary of the House of Representatives and of the Senate shall cause to have printed in the Congressional Record the substance of any major change described in subparagraph (D), shall hold hearings respecting the feasibility and desirability of implementing such a change, and, within the two-year period before implementation, shall report to their respective Houses findings on whether or not such a change should be implemented.

(ii) No major change may be implemented unless the Congress specifically provides, in an appropriations or other Act, for funds for implementation of the change.

(D) As used in this paragraph, the term "major change" means a change which would—

(i) require an individual to present a new card or other document (designed specifically for use for this purpose) at the time of hiring, recruitment, or referral,

(ii) provide for a telephone verification system under which an employer, recruiter, or referrer must transmit to a Federal official information concerning the immigration status of prospective employees and the official transmits to the person, and the person must record, a verification code, or

(iii) require any change in any card used for accounting purposes under the Social Security Act, including any change requiring that the only social security account number cards which may be presented in order to comply with subsection (b)(1)(C)(i) are such cards as are in a counterfeit-resistant form consistent with the second sentence of section 205(c)(2)(D) of the Social Security Act.

(E) Any costs incurred in developing and implementing any change described in subparagraph (D)(iii) for purposes of this subsection shall not be paid for out of any trust fund established under the Social Security Act.

(4)(A) The President may undertake demonstration projects (consistent with paragraph (2)) of different changes in the requirements of subsection (b). No such project may extend over a period of longer than three years.

(B) The President shall report to the Congress on the results of demonstration projects conducted under this paragraph.

(e)(1) The Attorney General shall establish procedures—

(A) for individuals and entities to file written, signed complaints respecting potential violations of subsection (a),

(B) for the investigation of those complaints which, on their face, have a substantial probability of validity,

(C) for the investigation of such other violations of subsection (a) as the Attorney General determines to be appropriate, and

(D) for the designation in the Service of a unit which has, as its primary duty, the prosecution of cases of violations of subsection (a) under this subsection.

(2) In conducting investigations and hearings under this subsection—

(A) immigration officers and administrative law judges shall have reasonable access to examine evidence of any person or entity being investigated, and

(B) administrative law judges may, if necessary, compel by subpoena the attendance of witnesses and the production of evidence at any designated place or hearing.

In case of contumacy or refusal to obey a subpoena lawfully issued under this paragraph and upon application of the Attorney General, an appropriate district court of the United States may issue an order requiring compliance with such subpoena and any failure to obey such order may be punished by such court as a contempt thereof.

(3)(A) Before imposing an order described in paragraph (4) or (5) against a person or entity under this subsection for a violation of subsection (a), the Attorney General shall provide the person or entity with notice and, upon request made within a reasonable time (of not less than 30 days, as established by the Attorney General) of the date of the notice, a hearing respecting the violation.

(B) Any hearing so requested shall be conducted before an administrative law judge. The hearing shall be conducted in accordance with the requirements of section 554 of title 5, United States Code. The hearing shall be held at the nearest practicable place to the place where the person or entity resides or of the place where the alleged violation occurred. If no hearing is so requested, the Attorney General's imposition of the order shall constitute a final and unappealable order.

(C) If the administrative law judge determines, upon the preponderance of the evidence received, that a person or entity named in the complaint has violated subsection (a), the administrative law judge shall state his findings of fact and issue and cause to be served on such person or entity an order described in paragraph (4) or (5).

(4) With respect to a violation of subsection (a)(1)(A) or (a)(2), the order under this subsection—

(A) shall require the person or entity to cease and desist from such violations and to pay a civil penalty in an amount of—

(i) not less than $250 and not more than $2,000 for each unauthorized alien with respect to whom a violation of either such subsection occurred,

(ii) not less than $2,000 and not more than $5,000 for each such alien in the case of a person or entity previously subject to one order under this subparagraph, or

(iii) not less than $3,000 and not more than $10,000 for each such alien in the case of a person or entity previously subject to more than one order under this subparagraph; and

(B) may require the person or entity—

    (i) to comply with the requirements of subsection (b) (or subsection (d) if applicable) with respect to individuals hired (or recruited or referred for employment for a fee) during a period of up to three years, and

    (ii) to take such other remedial action as is appropriate.

In applying this subsection in the case of a person or entity composed of distinct, physically separate subdivisions each of which provides separately for the hiring, recruiting, or referring for employment, without reference to the practices of, and not under the control of or common control with, another subdivision, each such subdivision shall be considered a separate person or entity.

(5) With respect to a violation of subsection (a)(1)(B), the order under this subsection shall require the person or entity to pay a civil penalty in an amount of not less than $100 and not more than $1,000 for each individual with respect to whom such violation occurred. In determining the amount of the penalty, due consideration shall be given to the size of the business of the employer being charged, the good faith of the employer, the seriousness of the violation, whether or not the individual was an unauthorized alien, and the history of previous violations.

(6) The decision and order of an administrative law judge shall become the final agency decision and order of the Attorney General unless, within 30 days, the Attorney General modifies or vacates the decision and order, in which case the decision and order of the Attorney General shall become a final order under this subsection. The Attorney General may not delegate the Attorney General's authority under this paragraph to any entity which has review authority over immigration-related matters.

(7) A person or entity adversely affected by a final order respecting an assessment may, within 45 days after the date the final order is issued, file a petition in the Court of Appeals for the appropriate circuit for review of the order.

(8) If a person or entity fails to comply with a final order issued under this subsection against the person or entity, the Attorney General shall file a suit to seek compliance with the order in any appropriate district court of the United States. In any such suit, the validity and appropriateness of the final order shall not be subject to review.

(f)(1) Any person or entity which engages in a pattern or practice of violations of subsection (a)(1)(A) or (a)(2) shall be fined not more than $3,000 for each unauthorized alien with respect to whom such a violation occurs, imprisoned for not more than six months for the entire pattern or practice, or both, notwithstanding the provisions of any other Federal law relating to fine levels.

(2) Whenever the Attorney General has reasonable cause to believe that a person or entity is engaged in a pattern or practice of employment,

recruitment, or referral in violation of paragraph (1)(A) or (2) of subsection (a), the Attorney General may bring a civil action in the appropriate district court of the United States requesting such relief, including a permanent or temporary injunction, restraining order, or other order against the person or entity, as the Attorney General deems necessary.

(g)(1) It is unlawful for a person or other entity, in the hiring, recruiting, or referring for employment of any individual, to require the individual to post a bond or security, to pay or agree to pay an amount, or otherwise to provide a financial guarantee or indemnity, against any potential liability arising under this section relating to such hiring, recruiting, or referring of the individual.

    (2) Any person or entity which is determined, after notice and opportunity for an administrative hearing, to have violated paragraph (1) shall be subject to a civil penalty of $1,000 for each violation and to an administrative order requiring the return of any amounts received in violation of such paragraph to the employee or, if the employee cannot be located, to the general fund of the Treasury.

(h)(1) In providing documentation or endorsement of authorization of aliens (other than aliens lawfully admitted for permanent residence) authorized to be employed in the United States, the Attorney General shall provide that any limitations with respect to the period or type of employment or employer shall be conspicuously stated on the documentation or endorsement.

    (2) The provisions of this section preempt any State or local law imposing civil or criminal sanctions (other than through licensing and similar laws) upon those who employ, or recruit or refer for a fee for employment, unauthorized aliens.

    (3) As used in this section, the term "unauthorized alien" means, with respect to the employment of an alien at a particular time, that the alien is not at that time either (A) an alien lawfully admitted for permanent residence, or (B) authorized to be so employed by this Act or by the Attorney General.

(i)(1) During the six-month period beginning on the first day of the first month after the date of the enactment of this section—

    (A) The Attorney General, in cooperation with the Secretaries of Agriculture, Commerce, Health and Human Services, Labor, and the Treasury and the Administrator of the Small Business Administration, shall disseminate forms and information to employers, employment agencies, and organizations representing employees and provide for public education respecting the requirements of this section, and

    (B) the Attorney General shall not conduct any proceeding, nor issue any order, under this section on the basis of any violation alleged to have occurred during the period.

(2) In the case of a person or entity, in the first instance in which the Attorney General has reason to believe that the person or entity may have violated subsection (a) during the subsequent 12-month period, the Attorney General shall provide a citation to the person or entity indicating that such a violation or violations may have occurred and shall not conduct any proceeding, nor issue any order, under this section on the basis of such alleged violation or violations.

(3)(A) Except as provided in subparagraph (B), before the end of the application period (as defined in subparagraph (C)(i)), the Attorney General shall not conduct any proceeding, nor impose any penalty, under this section on the basis of any violation alleged to have occurred with respect to employment of an individual in seasonal agricultural services.

   (B)(i) During the application period, it is unlawful for a person or entity (including a farm labor contractor) or an agent of such a person or entity, to recruit an unauthorized alien (other than an alien described in clause (ii)) who is outside the United States to enter the United States to perform seasonal agricultural services.

    (ii) Clause (i) shall not apply to an alien who the person or entity reasonably believes meets the requirements of section 210(a)(2) of this Act (relating to performance of seasonal agricultural services).

    (iii) A person, entity, or agent that violates clause (i) shall be deemed to be subject to an order under this section in the same manner as if it had violated paragraph (1)(A), without regard to paragraph (2) of this subsection.

   (C) In this paragraph:

    (i) The term "application period" means the period described in section 210(a)(1).

    (ii) The term "seasonal agricultural services" has the meaning given such term in section 210(h).

(j)(1) Beginning one year after November 6, 1986, and at intervals of one year thereafter for a period of three years after such date, the Comptroller General of the United States shall prepare and transmit to the Congress and to the taskforce established under subsection (k) a report describing the results of a review of the implementation and enforcement of this section during the preceding twelve-month period, for the purpose of determining if—

   (A) such provisions have been carried out satisfactorily;

   (B) a pattern of discrimination has resulted against citizens or nationals of the United States or against eligible workers seeking employment; and

   (C) an unnecessary regulatory burden has been created for employers hiring such workers.

(2) In each report, the Comptroller General shall make a specific determi-

nation as to whether the implementation of that section has resulted in a pattern of discrimination in employment (against other than unauthorized aliens) on the basis of national origin.

(3) If the Comptroller General has determined that such a pattern of discrimination has resulted, the report—

(A) shall include a description of the scope of that discrimination, and

(B) may include recommendations for such legislation as may be appropriate to deter or remedy such discrimination.

(k)(1) The Attorney General, jointly with the Chairman of the Commission on Civil Rights and the Chairman of the Equal Employment Opportunity Commission, shall establish a taskforce to review each report of the Comptroller General transmitted under subsection (j)(1).

(2) If the report transmitted includes a determination that the implementation of this section has resulted in a pattern of discrimination in employment (against other than unauthorized aliens) on the basis of national origin, the taskforce shall, taking into consideration any recommendations in the report, report to Congress recommendations for such legislation as may be appropriate to deter or remedy such discrimination.

(3) The Committees on the Judiciary of the House of Representatives and of the Senate shall hold hearings respecting any report of the taskforce under paragraph (2) within 60 days after the date of receipt of the report.

(l)(1) The provisions of this section shall terminate 30 calendar days after receipt of the last report required to be transmitted under subsection (j), if—

(A) the Comptroller General determines, and so reports in such report, that a widespread pattern of discrimination has resulted against citizens or nationals of the United States or against eligible workers seeking employment solely from the implementation of this section; and

(B) there is enacted, within such period of 30 calendar days, a joint resolution stating in substance that the Congress approves the findings of the Comptroller General contained in such report.

* * *

§ 1324b. Unfair immigration-related employment practices

[Sec. 274B] (a)(1) It is an unfair immigration-related employment practice for a person or other entity to discriminate against any individual (other than an unauthorized alien) with respect to the hiring, or recruitment or referral for a fee, of the individual for employment or the discharging of the individual from employment—

    (A) because of such individual's national origin, or

    (B) in the case of a citizen or intending citizen (as defined in paragraph (3)), because of such individual's citizenship status.

(2) Paragraph (1) shall not apply to—

    (A) a person or other entity that employs three or fewer employees,

    (B) a person's or entity's discrimination because of an individual's national origin if the discrimination with respect to that person or entity and that individual is covered under section 703 of the Civil Rights Act of 1964, or

    (C) discrimination because of citizenship status which is otherwise required in order to comply with law, regulation, or executive order, or required by Federal, State, or local government contract, or which the Attorney General determines to be essential for an employer to do business with an agency or department of the Federal, State, or local government.

(3) As used in paragraph (1), the term "citizen or intending citizen" means an individual who—

    (A) is a citizen or national of the United States, or

    (B) is an alien who—

        (i) is lawfully admitted for permanent residence, is granted the status of an alien lawfully admitted for temporary residence under section 245A(a)(1), is admitted as a refugee under section 207, or is granted asylum under section 208, and

        (ii) evidences an intention to become a citizen of the United States through completing a declaration of intention to become a citizen;

but does not include (I) an alien who fails to apply for naturalization within six months of the date the alien first becomes eligible (by virtue of period of lawful permanent residence) to apply for naturalization or, if later, within six months after the date of the enactment of this section and (II) an alien who has applied on a timely basis, but has not been naturalized as a citizen within 2 years after the date of the application, unless the alien can establish that the alien is actively pursuing naturalization, except that time consumed in the Service's processing the application shall not be counted toward the 2-year period.

(4) Notwithstanding any other provision of this section, it is not an unfair immigration-related employment practice for a person or other entity to prefer to hire, recruit, or refer an individual who is a citizen or national of the United States over another individual who is an alien if the two individuals are equally qualified.

(b)(1) Except as provided in paragraph (2), any person alleging that the person is adversely affected directly by an unfair immigration-related employment practice (or a person on that person's behalf) or an officer of the Service alleging that an unfair immigration-related employment practice has occurred or is occurring may file a charge respecting such practice or violation with the Special Counsel (appointed under subsection (c)). Charges shall be in writing under oath or affirmation and shall contain such information as the Attorney General requires. The Special Counsel by certified mail shall serve a notice of the charge (including the date, place, and circumstances of the alleged unfair immigration-related employment practice) on the person or entity involved within 10 days.

(2) No charge may be filed respecting an unfair immigration-related employment practice described in subsection (a)(1)(A) if a charge with respect to that practice based on the same set of facts has been filed with the Equal Employment Opportunity Commission under title VII of the Civil Rights Act of 1964, unless the charge is dismissed as being outside the scope of such title. No charge respecting an employment practice may be filed with the Equal Employment Opportunity Commission under such title if a charge with respect to such practice based on the same set of facts has been filed under this subsection, unless the charge is dismissed under this section as being outside the scope of this section.

(c)(1) The President shall appoint, by and with the advice and consent of the Senate, a Special Counsel for Immigration-Related Unfair Employment Practices (hereinafter in this section referred to as the "Special Counsel") within the Department of Justice to serve for a term of four years. In the case of a vacancy in the office of the Special Counsel the President may designate the officer or employee who shall act as Special Counsel during such vacancy.

(2) The Special Counsel shall be responsible for investigation of charges and issuance of complaints under this section and in respect of the prosecution of all such complaints before administrative law judges and the exercise of certain functions under subsection (j)(1).

(3) The Special Counsel is entitled to receive compensation at a rate not to exceed the rate now or hereafter provided for grade GS-17 of the General Schedule, under section 5332 of title 5, United States Code.

(4) The Special Counsel, in accordance with regulations of the Attorney General, shall establish such regional offices as may be necessary to carry out his duties.

(d)(1) The Special Counsel shall investigate each charge received and, within 120 days of the date of the receipt of the charge, determine whether or not there is reasonable cause to believe that the charge is true and whether or not to bring a complaint with respect to the charge before an administrative law judge. The Special Counsel may, on his own initiative, conduct investigations respecting unfair immigration-related employment practices and, based on such an investigation and subject to paragraph (3), file a complaint before such a judge.

(2) If the Special Counsel, after receiving such a charge respecting an unfair immigration-related employment practice which alleges know-

ing and intentional discriminatory activity or a pattern or practice of discriminatory activity, has not filed a complaint before an administrative law judge with respect to such charge within such 120-day period, the person making the charge may (subject to paragraph (3)) file a complaint directly before such a judge.

(3) No complaint may be filed respecting any unfair immigration-related employment practice occurring more than 180 days prior to the date of the filing of the charge with the Special Counsel. This subparagraph shall not prevent the subsequent amending of a charge or complaint under subsection (e)(1).

(e)(1) Whenever a complaint is made that a person or entity has engaged in or is engaging in any such unfair immigration-related employment practice, an administrative law judge shall have power to issue and cause to be served upon such person or entity a copy of the complaint and a notice of hearing before the judge at a place therein fixed, not less than five days after the serving of the complaint. Any such complaint may be amended by the judge conducting the hearing, upon the motion of the party filing the complaint, in the judge's discretion at any time prior to the issuance of an order based thereon. The person or entity so complained of shall have the right to file an answer to the original or amended complaint and to appear in person or otherwise and give testimony at the place and time fixed in the complaint.

(2) Hearings on complaints under this subsection shall be considered before administrative law judges who are specially designated by the Attorney General as having special training respecting employment discrimination and, to the extent practicable, before such judges who only consider cases under this section.

(3) Any person filing a charge with the Special Counsel respecting an unfair immigration-related employment practice shall be considered a party to any complaint before an administrative law judge respecting such practice and any subsequent appeal respecting that complaint. In the discretion of the judge conducting the hearing, any other person may be allowed to intervene in the said proceeding and to present testimony.

(f)(1) The testimony taken by the administrative law judge shall be reduced to writing. Thereafter, the judge, in his discretion, upon notice may provide for the taking of further testimony or hear argument.

(2) In conducting investigations and hearings under this subsection and in accordance with regulations of the Attorney General, the Special Counsel and administrative law judges shall have reasonable access to examine evidence of any person or entity being investigated. The administrative law judges by subpoena may compel the attendance of witnesses and the production of evidence at any designated place or hearing. In case of contumacy or refusal to obey a subpoena lawfully issued under this paragraph and upon application of the administra-

tive law judge, an appropriate district court of the United States may issue an order requiring compliance with such subpoena and any failure to obey such order may be punished by such court as a contempt thereof.

(g)(1) The administrative law judge shall issue and cause to be served on the parties to the proceeding an order, which shall be final unless appealed as provided under subsection (i).

(2)(A) If, upon the preponderance of the evidence, an administrative law judge determines that any person or entity named in the complaint has engaged in or is engaging in any such unfair immigration-related employment practice, then the judge shall state his findings of fact and shall issue and cause to be served on such person or entity an order which requires such person or entity to cease and desist from such unfair immigration-related employment practice.

(B) Such an order also may require the person or entity—

    (i) to comply with the requirements of section 274A(b) with respect to individuals hired (or recruited or referred for employment for a fee) during a period of up to three years;

    (ii) to retain for the period referred to in clause (i) and only for purposes consistent with section 274(b)(5), the name and address of each individual who applies, in person or in writing, for hiring for an existing position, or for recruiting or referring for a fee, for employment in the United States;

    (iii) to hire individuals directly and adversely affected, with or without back pay; and

    (iv)(I) except as provided in subclause (II), to pay a civil penalty of not more than $1,000 for each individual discriminated against, and

    (II) in the case of a person or entity previously subject to such an order, to pay a civil penalty of not more than $2,000 for each individual discriminated against.

(C) In providing a remedy under subparagraph (B)(iii), back pay liability shall not accrue from a date more than two years prior to the date of the filing of a charge with an administrative law judge. Interim earnings or amounts earnable with reasonable diligence by the individual or individuals discriminated against shall operate to reduce the back pay otherwise allowable under such subparagraph. No order shall require the hiring of an individual as an employee or the payment to an individual of any back pay, if the individual was refused employment for any reason other than discrimination on account of national origin or citizenship status.

(D) In applying this subsection in the case of a person or entity composed of distinct, physically separate subdivisions each of which provides separately for the hiring, recruiting, or referring for employment, without reference to the practice of, and not under the control of or common control with, another subdivision, each such subdivision shall be considered a separate person or entity.

(3) If upon the preponderance of the evidence an administrative law judge determines that the person or entity named in the complaint has not engaged or is not engaging in any such unfair immigration-related employment practice, then the judge shall state his findings of fact and shall issue an order dismissing the complaint.

(h) In any complaint respecting an unfair immigration-related employment practice, an administrative law judge, in the judge's discretion, may allow a prevailing party, other than the United States, a reasonable attorney's fee, if the losing party's argument is without reasonable foundation in law and fact.

(i)(1) Not later than 60 days after the entry of such final order, any person aggrieved by such final order may seek a review of such order in the United States court of appeals for the circuit in which the violation is alleged to have occurred or in which the employer resides or transacts business.

(2) Upon the filing of the record with the court, the jurisdiction of the court shall be exclusive and its judgment shall be final, except that the same shall be subject to review by the Supreme Court of the United States upon writ of certiorari or certification as provided in section 1254 of title 28, United States Code.

(j)(1) If an order of the agency is not appealed under subsection (i)(1), the Special Counsel (or, if the Special Counsel fails to act, the person filing the charge) may petition the United States district court for the district in which a violation of the order is alleged to have occurred, or in which the respondent resides or transacts business, for the enforcement of the order of the administrative law judge, by filing in such court a written petition praying that such order be enforced.

(2) Upon the filing of such petition, the court shall have jurisdiction to make and enter a decree enforcing the order of the administrative law judge. In such a proceeding, the order of the administrative law judge shall not be subject to review.

(3) If, upon appeal of an order under subsection (i)(1), the United States court of appeals does not reverse such order, such court shall have the jurisdiction to make and enter a decree enforcing the order of the administrative law judge.

(4) In any judicial proceeding under subsection (i) or this subsection, the court, in its discretion, may allow a prevailing party, other than the United States, a reasonable attorney's fee as part of costs but only if the losing party's argument is without reasonable foundation in law and fact.

(k)(1) This section shall not apply to discrimination in hiring, recruiting, referring, or discharging of individuals occurring after the date of any termination of the provisions of section 274A, under subsection (1) of that section.

(2) The provisions of this section shall terminate 30 calendar days after receipt of the last report required to be transmitted under section 274A(j) if—

    (A) the Comptroller General determines, and so reports in such report that—

        (i) no significant discrimination has resulted, against citizens or nationals of the United States or against any eligible workers seeking employment, from the implementation of section 274A, or

        (ii) such section has created an unreasonable burden on employers hiring such workers; and

    (B) there has been enacted, within such period of 30 calendar days, a joint resolution stating in substance that the Congress approves the findings of the Comptroller General contained in such report.

* * *

Part IX. Miscellaneous

§ 1357. Powers of immigration officers and employees

[Sec. 287] (a) Any officer or employee of the Service authorized under regulations prescribed by the Attorney General shall have power without warrant—

(1) to interrogate any alien or person believed to be an alien as to his right to be or to remain in the United States;

(2) to arrest any alien who in his presence or view is entering or attempting to enter the United States in violation of any law or regulation made in pursuance of law regulating the admission, exclusion, or expulsion of aliens, or to arrest any alien in the United States, if he has reason to believe that the alien so arrested is in the United States in violation of any such law or regulation and is likely to escape before a warrant can be obtained for his arrest, but the alien arrested shall be taken without unnecessary delay for examination before an officer of the Service having authority to examine aliens as to their right to enter or remain in the United States;

(3) within a reasonable distance from any external boundary of the United States, to board and search for aliens any vessel within the territorial waters of the United States and any railway car, aircraft, conveyance, or vehicle, and within a distance of twenty-five miles from

any such external boundary to have access to private lands, but not dwellings, for the purpose of patrolling the border to prevent the illegal entry of aliens into the United States; and

(4) to make arrests for felonies which have been committed and which are cognizable under any law of the United States regulating the admission, exclusion, or expulsion of aliens, if he has reason to believe that the person so arrested is guilty of such felony and if there is likelihood of the person escaping before a warrant can be obtained for his arrest, but the person arrested shall be taken without unnecessary delay before the nearest available officer empowered to commit persons charged with offenses against the laws of the United States. Any such employee shall also have the power to execute any warrant or other process issued by any officer under any law regulating the admission, exclusion, or expulsion of aliens.

(b) Any officer or employee of the Service designated by the Attorney General, whether individually or as one of a class, shall have power and authority to administer oaths and to take and consider evidence concerning the privilege of any person to enter, reenter, pass through, or reside in the United States, or concerning any matter which is material or relevant to the enforcement of this chapter and the administration of the Service; and any person to whom such oath has been administered (or who has executed an unsworn declaration, certificate, verification, or statement under penalty of perjury as permitted under section 1746 of Title 28), under the provisions of this chapter, who shall knowingly or willfully give false evidence or swear (or subscribe under penalty of perjury as permitted under section 1746 of Title 28) to any false statement concerning any matter referred to in this subsection shall be guilty of perjury and shall be punished as provided by section 1621 of Title 18.

(c) Any officer or employee of the Service authorized and designated under regulations prescribed by the Attorney General, whether individually or as one of a class, shall have power to conduct a search, without warrant, of the person, and of the personal effects in the possession of any person seeking admission to the United States, concerning whom such officer or employee may have reasonable cause to suspect that grounds exist for exclusion from the United States under this chapter which would be disclosed by such search.

(d) [Added by P.L. 99–570] In the case of an alien who is arrested by a Federal, State, or local law enforcement official for a violation of any law relating to controlled substances, if the official (or another official)—

(1) has reason to believe that the alien may not have been lawfully admitted to the United States or otherwise is not lawfully present in the United States,

(2) expeditiously informs an appropriate officer or employee of the Service authorized and designated by the Attorney General of the arrest and of facts concerning the status of the alien, and

(3) requests the Service to determine promptly whether or not to issue a detainer to detain the alien, the officer or employee of the Service shall promptly determine whether or not to issue such a detainer. If such a detainer is issued and the alien is not otherwise detained by Federal, State, or local officials, the Attorney General shall effectively and expeditiously take custody of the alien.

(d) [Added by P.L. 99–603 without reference to above] Notwithstanding any other provision of this section other than paragraph (3) of subsection (a), an officer or employee of the Service may not enter without the consent of the owner (or agent thereof) or a properly executed warrant onto the premises of a farm or other outdoor agricultural operation for the purpose of interrogating a person believed to be an alien as to the person's right to be or to remain in the United States.

* * *

Title IV. Reports to Congress

§ 1364. Triennial comprehensive report on immigration

[Sec. 401] (a) The President shall transmit to the Congress, not later than January 1, 1989, and not later than January 1 of every third year thereafter, a comprehensive immigration-impact report.

(b) Each report shall include—

(1) the number and classification of aliens admitted (whether as immediate relatives, special immigrants, refugees, or under the preferences classifications, or as nonimmigrants), paroled, or granted asylum, during the relevant period;

(2) a reasonable estimate of the number of aliens who entered the United States during the period without visas or who became deportable during the period under section 241 of the Immigration and Nationality Act; and

(3) a description of the impact of admissions and other entries of immigrants, refugees, asylees, and parolees into the United States during the period on the economy, labor and housing markets, the educational system, social services, foreign policy, environmental quality and resources, the rate, size, and distribution of population growth in the United States, and the impact on specific States and local units of government of high rates of immigration resettlement.

(c) The information (referred to in subsection (b)) contained in each report shall be—

(1) described for the preceding three-year period, and

(2) projected for the succeeding five-year period, based on reasonable estimates substantiated by the best available evidence.

(d) The President also may include in such report any appropriate recommendations on changes in numerical limitations or other policies under title II of the Immigration and Nationality Act bearing on the admission and entry of such aliens to the United States.

Immigration Reform and Control Act of 1986 (Unincorporated)

(P.L. 99–603, approved November 6, 1986, amending Act of June 27, 1952, ch. 477, 66 Stat. 163, but unincorporated into original Act)

Title I. Control of Illegal Immigration

Part A. Employment

§ 101. Control of unlawful employment of aliens

(a) * * *

(a)(2) The Attorney General shall, not later than the first day of the seventh month beginning after the date of the enactment of this Act, first issue, on an interim or other basis, such regulations as may be necessary in order to implement this section.

    (3)(A) Section 274A(a)(1) of the Immigration and Nationality Act shall not apply to the hiring, or recruiting or referring of an individual for employment which has occurred before the date of the enactment of this Act.

    (B) Section 274A(a)(2) of the Immigration and Nationality Act shall not apply to continuing employment of an alien who was hired before the date of the enactment of this Act.

(b)(1) The Migrant and Seasonal Agricultural Worker Protection Act (Public Law 97-470) is amended—

    (A) by striking out "101(a)(15)(H)(ii)" in paragraphs (8)(B) and (10)(B) of section 3 (29 U.S.C. 1802) and inserting in lieu thereof "101(a)(15)(H)(ii)(a)";

    (B) in section 103(a) (29 U.S.C. 1813(a))—

        (i) by striking out "or" at the end of paragraph (4),

        (ii) by striking out the period at the end of paragraph (5) and inserting in lieu thereof "; or ", and

        (iii) by adding at the end the following new paragraph:

"(6) has been found to have violated paragraph (1) or (2) of section

274A(a) of the Immigration and Nationality Act.";

(C) by striking out section 106 (29 U.S.C. 1816) and the corresponding item in the table of contents; and

(D) by striking out "section 106" in section 501(b) (29 U.S.C.
1851(b)) and by inserting in lieu thereof "paragraph (1) or (2) of
section 274A(a) of the Immigration and Nationality Act".

(2) The amendments made by paragraph (1) shall apply to the employment, recruitment, referral, or utilization of the services of an
individual occurring on or after the first day of the seventh month
beginning after the date of the enactment of this Act.

* * *

(d)(1) The Attorney General, in consultation with the Secretary of Labor
and the Secretary of Health and Human Services, shall conduct a study for
use by the Department of Justice in determining employment eligibility of
aliens in the United States. Such study shall concentrate on those data bases
that are currently available to the Federal Government which through the
use of a telephone and computation capability could be used to verify
instantly the employment eligibility status of job applicants who are aliens.

(2) Such study shall be conducted in conjunction with any existing
Federal program which is designed for the purpose of providing
information on the resident or employment status of aliens for employers. The study shall include an analysis of costs and benefits which
shows the differences in costs and efficiency of having the Federal
Government or a contractor perform this service. Such comparisons
should include reference to such technical capabilities as processing
techniques and time, verification techniques and time, backup safeguards, and audit trail performance.

(3) Such study shall also concentrate on methods of phone verification
which demonstrate the best safety and service standards, the least
burden for the employer, the best capability for effective enforcement,
and procedures which are within the boundaries of the Privacy Act of
1974.

(4) Such study shall be conducted within twelve months of the date of
enactment of this Act.

(5) The Attorney General shall prepare and transmit to the Congress a
report—

(A) not later than six months after the date of enactment of this Act,
describing the status of such study; and

(B) not later than twelve months after such date, setting forth the
findings of such study.

(e) The Secretary of Health and Human Services, acting through the
Social Security Administration and in cooperation with the Attorney General
and the Secretary of Labor, shall conduct a study of the feasibility and costs
of establishing a social security number validation system to assist in
carrying out the purposes of section 274A of the Immigration and National-

ity Act, and of the privacy concerns that would be raised by the establishment of such a system. The Secretary shall submit to the Committees on Ways and Means and Judiciary of the House of Representatives and to the Committees on Finance and Judiciary of the Senate, within 2 years after the date of the enactment of this Act, a full and complete report on the results of the study together with such recommendations as may be appropriate.

(f)(1) The Comptroller General of the United States, upon consultation with the Attorney General and the Secretary of Health and Human Services as well as private sector representatives (including representatives of the financial, banking, and manufacturing industries), shall inquire into technological alternatives for producing and issuing social security account number cards that are more resistant to counterfeiting than social security account number cards being issued on the date of enactment of this Act by the Social Security Administration, including the use of encoded magnetic, optical, or active electronic media such as magnetic stripes, holograms, and integrated circuit chips. Such inquiry should focus on technologies that will help ensure the authenticity of the card, rather than the identity of the bearer.

(2) The Comptroller General of the United States shall explore additional actions that could be taken to reduce the potential for fraudulently obtaining and using social security account number cards.

(3) Not later than one year after the date of enactment of this Act, the Comptroller General of the United States shall prepare and transmit to the Committee on the Judiciary and the Committee on Ways and Means of the House of Representatives and the Committee on the Judiciary and the Committee on Finance of the Senate a report setting forth his findings and recommendations under this subsection.

§ 102. Unfair immigration-related employment practices

* * *

(b) Except as may be specifically provided in this section [8 U.S.C. 1324b], nothing in this section shall be construed to restrict the authority of the Equal Employment Opportunity Commission to investigate allegations, in writing and under oath or affirmation, of unlawful employment practices, as provided in section 706 of the Civil Rights Act of 1964 (42 U.S.C. 2000e-5), or any other authority provided therein.

Title III. Reform of Legal Immigration

Part A. Temporary Agricultural Workers

§ 301. H-2A agricultural workers

* * *

(d) The amendments made by this section apply to petitions and applications filed under sections 214(c) and 216 of the Immigration and Nationality Act on or after the first day of the seventh month beginning after the date of the enactment of this Act (hereinafter in this section referred to as the "effective date").

(e) The Attorney General, in consultation with the Secretary of Labor and the Secretary of Agriculture, shall approve all regulations to be issued implementing sections 101(a)(15)(H)(ii)(a) and 216 of the Immigration and Nationality Act. Notwithstanding any other provision of law, final regulations to implement such sections shall first be issued, on an interim or other basis, not later than the effective date.

§ 304. Commission on Agricultural Workers

(a)(1) There is established a Commission on Agricultural Workers (hereinafter in this section referred to as the "Commission"), to be composed of 12 members—
  (A) six to be appointed by the President,
  (B) three to be appointed by the Speaker of the House of Representatives, and
  (C) three to be appointed by the President pro tempore of the Senate.
(2) In making appointments under paragraph (1)(A), the President shall consult—
  (A) with the Attorney General in appointing two members,
  (B) with the Secretary of Labor in appointing two members, and
  (C) with the Secretary of Agriculture in appointing two members.
(3) A vacancy in the Commission shall be filled in the same manner in which the original appointment was made.
(4) Members shall be appointed to serve for the life of the Commission.
(b)(1) The Commission shall review the following:
  (A) The impact of the special agricultural worker provisions on the wages and working conditions of domestic farmworkers, on the adequacy of the supply of agricultural labor, and on the ability of agricultural workers to organize.
  (B) The extent to which aliens who have obtained lawful permanent or temporary resident status under the special agricultural worker provisions continue to perform seasonal agricultural services and the requirement that aliens who become special agricultural workers under section 210A of the Immigration and Nationality Act perform 90 man-days of seasonal agricultural services for certain periods in order to avoid deportation or to become naturalized.
  (C) The impact of the legalization program and the employers'

sanctions on the supply of agricultural labor.

(D) The extent to which the agricultural industry relies on the employment of a temporary workforce.

(E) The adequacy of the supply of agricultural labor in the United States and whether this supply needs to be further supplemented with foreign labor and the appropriateness of the numerical limitation on additional special agricultural workers imposed under section 210A(b) of the Immigration and Nationality Act.

(F) The extent of unemployment and underemployment of farmworkers who are United States citizens or aliens lawfully admitted for permanent residence.

(G) The extent to which the problems of agricultural employers in securing labor are related to the lack of modern labor-management techniques in agriculture.

(H) Whether certain geographic regions need special programs or provisions to meet their unique needs for agricultural labor.

(I) Impact of the special agricultural worker provisions on the ability of crops harvested in the United States to compete in international markets.

(2) The Commission shall conduct an overall evaluation of the special agricultural worker provisions, including the process for determining whether or not an agricultural labor shortage exists.

(c) The Commission shall report to the Congress not later than five years after the date of the enactment of this Act on its reviews under subsection (b). The Commission shall include in its report recommendations for appropriate changes that should be made in the special agricultural worker provisions.

(d)(1) Each member of the Commission who is not an officer or employee of the Federal Government is entitled to receive, subject to such amounts as are provided in advance in appropriations Acts, the daily equivalent of the minimum annual rate of basic pay in effect for grade GS-18 of the General Schedule for each day (including travel time) during which the member is engaged in the actual performance of duties of the Commission. Each member of the Commission who is such an officer or employee shall serve without additional pay.

(2) While away from their homes or regular places of business in the performance of services for the Commission, members of the Commission shall be allowed travel expenses, including per diem in lieu of subsistence.

(e)(1) Five members of the Commission shall constitute a quorum, but a lesser number may hold hearings.

(2) The Chairman and the Vice Chairman of the Commission shall be elected by the members of the Commission for the life of the Commission.

(3) The Commission shall meet at the call of the Chairman or a majority of its members.

(f)(1) The Chairman, in accordance with rules agreed upon by the Commission, may appoint and fix the compensation of a staff director and such other additional personnel as may be necessary to enable the Commission to carry out its functions, without regard to the laws, rules, and regulations governing appointment in the competitive service. Any Federal employee subject to those laws, rules, and regulations may be detailed to the Commission without reimbursement, and such detail shall be without interruption or loss of civil service status or privilege.

(2) The Commission may procure temporary and intermittent services under section 3109(b) of title 5, United States Code, but at rates for individuals not to exceed the daily equivalent of the minimum annual rate of basic pay payable for GS-18 of the General Schedule.

(g)(1) The Commission may for the purpose of carrying out this section, hold such hearings, sit and act at such times and places, take such testimony, and receive such evidence as the Commission considers appropriate.

(2) The Commission may secure directly from any department or agency of the United States information necessary to enable it to carry out this section. Upon request of the Chairman, the head of such department or agency shall furnish such information to the Commission.

(3) The Commission may accept, use, and dispose of gifts or donations of services or property.

(4) The Commission may use the United States mails in the same manner and under the same conditions as other departments and agencies of the United States.

(5) The Administrator of General Services shall provide to the Commission on a reimbursable basis such administrative support services as the Commission may request.

(h)(1) There are authorized to be appropriated such sums as may be necessary to carry out the purposes of this section.

(2) Notwithstanding any other provision of this section, the authority to make payments, or to enter into contracts, under this section shall be effective only to such extent, or in such amounts, as are provided in advance in appropriations Acts.

(i) The Commission shall cease to exist at the end of the 63-month period beginning with the month after the month in which this Act is enacted.

(j) In this section:

(1) The term "employer sanctions" means the provisions of section 274A of the Immigration and Nationality Act.

(2) The term "legalization program" refers to the provisions of section 245A of the Immigration and Nationality Act.

(3) The term "seasonal agricultural services" has the meaning given such term in section 210(h) of the Immigration and Nationality Act.

(4) The term "special agricultural worker provisions" refers to sections 210 and 210A of the Immigration and Nationality Act.

§ 305. Eligibility of H-2A agricultural workers for certain legal assistance

A nonimmigrant worker admitted to or permitted to remain in the United States under section 101(a)(15)(H)(ii)(a) of the Immigration and Nationality Act (8 U.S.C. 1101(a)(15)(H)(ii)(a)) for agricultural labor or service shall be considered to be an alien described in section 101(a)(20) of such Act (8 U.S.C. 1101(a)(20)) for purposes of establishing eligibility for legal assistance under the Legal Services Corporation Act (42 U.S.C. 2996 et seq.), but only with respect to legal assistance on matters relating to wages, housing, transportation, and other employment rights as provided in the worker's specific contract under which the nonimmigrant was admitted.

§ 402. Reports on unauthorized alien employment

The President shall transmit to Congress annual reports on the implementation of section 274A of the Immigration and Nationality Act (relating to unlawful employment of aliens) during the first three years after its implementation. Each report shall include—

(1) an analysis of the adequacy of the employment verification system provided under subsection (b) of that section;

(2) a description of the status of the development and implementation of changes in that system under subsection (d) of that section, including the results of any demonstration projects conducted under paragraph (4) of such subsection; and

(3) an analysis of the impact of the enforcement of that section on—

    (A) the employment, wages, and working conditions of United States workers and on the economy of the United States,

    (B) the number of aliens entering the United States illegally or who fail to maintain legal status after entry, and

    (C) the violation of terms and conditions of nonimmigrant visas by foreign visitors.

§ 403. Reports on H-2A program

(a) The President shall transmit to the Committees on the Judiciary of the Senate and of the House of Representatives reports on the implementation of the temporary agricultural worker (H-2A) program, which shall include—

(1) the number of foreign workers permitted to be employed under the program in each year;

(2) the compliance of employers and foreign workers with the terms and

conditions of the program;

(3) the impact of the program on the labor needs of the United States agricultural employers and on the wages and working conditions of United States agricultural workers; and

(4) recommendations for modifications of the program, including—

    (A) improving the timeliness of decisions regarding admission of temporary foreign workers under the program,

    (B) removing any economic disincentives to hiring United States citizens or permanent resident aliens for jobs for which temporary foreign workers have been requested,

    (C) improving cooperation among government agencies, employers, employer associations, workers, unions, and other worker associations to end the dependence of any industry on a constant supply of temporary foreign workers, and

    (D) the relative benefits to domestic workers and burdens upon employers of a policy which requires employers, as a condition for certification under the program, to continue to accept qualified Untied States workers for employment after the date the H-2A workers depart for work with the employer.

The recommendations under subparagraph (D) shall be made in furtherance of the congressional policy that aliens not be admitted under the H-2A program unless there are not sufficient workers in the United States who are able, willing, and qualified to perform the labor or services needed and that the employment of the alien in such labor or services will not adversely affect the wages and working conditions of workers in the United States similarly employed.

(b) A report on the H-2A temporary worker program under subsection (a) shall be submitted not later than two years after the date of the enactment of this Act, and every two years thereafter.

9

Agricultural Worker Laws

Migrant and Seasonal Agricultural Worker Act

**(P.L. 97–470, approved January 14, 1983; as last amended by
P.L. 99–603, approved November 6, 1986)**

§ 1801. Purpose

[Sec. 2] It is the purpose of this Act to remove the restraints on commerce caused by activities detrimental to migrant and seasonal agricultural workers; to require farm labor contractors to register under this Act; and to assure necessary protections for migrant and seasonal agricultural workers, agricultural associations, and agricultural employers.

§ 1802. Definitions

[Sec. 3] As used in this Act—
(1) The term "agricultural association" means any nonprofit or cooperative association of farmers, growers, or ranchers, incorporated or qualified under applicable State law, which recruits, solicits, hires, employs, furnishes, or transports any migrant or seasonal agricultural worker.
(2) The term "agricultural employer" means any person who owns or operates a farm, ranch, processing establishment, cannery, gin, packing shed or nursery, or who produces or conditions seed, and who either recruits, solicits, hires, employs, furnishes, or transports any migrant or seasonal agricultural worker.
(3) The term "agricultural employment" means employment in any service or activity included within the provisions of section 3(f) of the Fair Labor Standards Act of 1938 (29 U.S.C. 203(f)), or section 3121(g) of the Internal Revenue Code of 1954 (26 U.S.C. 3121(g)) and the handling, planting, drying, packing, packaging, processing, freezing, or grading prior to delivery for storage of any agricultural or horticultural commodity in its unmanufactured state.
(4) The term "day-haul operation" means the assembly of workers at a pick-up point waiting to be hired and employed, transportation of

379

such workers to agricultural employment, and the return of such workers to a drop-off point on the same day.

(5) The term "employ" has the meaning given such term under section 3(g) of the Fair Labor Standards Act of 1938 (29 U.S.C. 203(g)) for the purposes of implementing the requirements of that Act.

(6) The term "farm labor contracting activity" means recruiting, soliciting, hiring, employing, furnishing, or transporting any migrant or seasonal agricultural worker.

(7) The term "farm labor contractor" means any person, other than an agricultural employer, an agricultural association, or an employee of an agricultural employer or agricultural association, who, for any money or other valuable consideration paid or promised to be paid, performs any farm labor contracting activity.

(8)(A) Except as provided in subparagraph (B), the term "migrant agricultural worker" means an individual who is employed in agricultural employment of a seasonal or other temporary nature, and who is required to be absent overnight from his permanent place of residence.

(B) The term "migrant agricultural worker" does not include—

    (i) any immediate family member of an agricultural employer or a farm labor contractor; or

    (ii) any temporary nonimmigrant alien who is authorized to work in agricultural employment in the United States under sections 1101(a)(15)(H)(ii)(a) and 1184(c) of Title 8.

(9) The term "person" means any individual, partnership, association, joint stock company, trust, cooperative, or corporation.

(10)(A) Except as provided in subparagraph (B), the term "seasonal agricultural worker" means an individual who is employed in agricultural employment of a seasonal or other temporary nature and is not required to be absent overnight from his permanent place of residence—

    (i) when employed on a farm or ranch performing field work related to planting, cultivating, or harvesting operations; or

    (ii) when employed in canning, packing, ginning, seed conditioning or related research, or processing operations, and transported, or caused to be transported, to or from the place of employment by means of a day-haul operation.

(B) The term "seasonal agricultural worker" does not include—

    (i) any migrant agricultural worker;

    (ii) any immediate family member of an agricultural employer or a farm labor contractor; or

    (iii) any temporary nonimmigrant alien who is authorized to work in agricultural employment in the United States under sections 101(a)(15)(H)(ii)(a) and 1184(c) of Title 8.

(11) The term "Secretary" means the Secretary of Labor or the Secretary's authorized representative.

(12) The term "State" means any of the States of the United States, the District of Columbia, the Virgin Islands, the Commonwealth of Puerto Rico, and Guam.

§ 1803. Applicability of Act

[Sec. 4] (a) The following persons are not subject to this Act:

(1) Any individual who engages in a farm labor contracting activity on behalf of a farm, processing establishment, seed conditioning establishment, cannery, gin, packing shed, or nursery, which is owned or operated exclusively by such individual or an immediate family member of such individual, if such activities are performed only for such operation and exclusively by such individual or an immediate family member, but without regard to whether such individual has incorporated or otherwise organized for business purposes.

(2) Any person, other than a farm labor contractor, for whom the mandays exemption for agricultural labor provided under section 13(a)(6)(A) of the Fair Labor Standards Act of 1938 (29 U.S.C. 213(a)(6)(A)) is applicable.

(3)(A) Any common carrier which would be a farm labor contractor solely because the carrier is engaged in the farm labor contracting activity of transporting any migrant or seasonal agricultural worker.

    (B) Any labor organization, as defined in section 2(5) of the Labor Management Relations Act (29 U.S.C. 152(5)) (without regard to the exclusion of agricultural employees in that Act) or as defined under applicable State labor relations law.

    (C) Any nonprofit charitable organization or public or private nonprofit educational institution.

    (D) Any person who engages in any farm labor contracting activity solely within a twenty-five mile intrastate radius of such person's permanent place of residence and for not more than thirteen weeks per year.

    (E) Any custom combine, hay harvesting, or sheep shearing operation.

    (F) Any custom poultry harvesting, breeding, debeaking, desexing, or health service operation provided the employees of the operation are not regularly required to be away from their permanent place of residence other than during their normal working hours.

    (G)(i) Any person whose principal occupation or business is not agricultural employment, when supplying full-time students or other individuals whose principal occupation is not agricultural employment to detassel, rogue, or otherwise engage in the production of seed and to engage in related and incidental agricultural employment, unless such full-time students or other individuals are required to be away from their permanent place of residence overnight or there are individuals under eighteen years of age who are providing transportation on behalf of such person.

    (ii) Any person to the extent he is supplied with students or other individuals for agricultural employment in accordance with clause (i) of this subparagraph by a person who is exempt under such clause.

(H)(i) Any person whose principal occupation or business is not agricultural employment, when supplying full-time students or other individuals whose principal occupation is not agricultural employment to string or harvest shade grown tobacco and to engage in related and incidental agricultural employment, unless there are individuals under eighteen years of age who are providing transportation on behalf of such person.

    (ii) Any person to the extent he is supplied with students or other individuals for agricultural employment in accordance with clause (i) of this subparagraph by a person who is exempt under such clause.

(I) Any employee of any person described in subparagraphs (A) through (H) when performing farm labor contracting activities exclusively for such person.

(b) Subchapter I of this Act does not apply to any agricultural employer or agricultural association or to any employee of such an employer or association.

Subchapter I. Farm Labor Contractors

§ 1811. Certificate of registration required

[Sec. 101] (a) No person shall engage in any farm labor contracting activity, unless such person has a certificate of registration from the Secretary specifying which farm labor contracting activities such person is authorized to perform.

(b) A farm labor contractor shall not hire, employ, or use any individual to perform farm labor contracting activities unless such individual has a certificate of registration, or a certificate of registration as an employee of the farm labor contractor employer, which authorizes the activity for which such individual is hired, employed, or used. The farm labor contractor shall be held responsible for violations of this Act or any regulation under this Act by any employee regardless of whether the employee possesses a certificate of registration based on the contractor's certificate of registration.

(c) Each registered farm labor contractor and registered farm labor contractor employee shall carry at all times while engaging in farm labor contracting activities a certificate of registration and, upon request, shall exhibit that certificate to all persons with whom they intend to deal as a farm labor contractor or farm labor contractor employee.

(d) The facilities and the services authorized by the Act of June 6, 1933 (29 U.S.C. 49 et seq.), known as the Wagner-Peyser Act, shall be denied to any farm labor contractor upon refusal or failure to produce, when asked, a certificate of registration.

§ 1812. Issuance of certificate of registration

[Sec. 102] The Secretary, after appropriate investigation and approval, shall issue a certificate of registration (including a certificate of registration as an employee of a farm labor contractor) to any person who has filed with the Secretary a written application containing the following:

(1) a declaration, subscribed and sworn to by the applicant, stating the applicant's permanent place of residence, the farm labor contracting activities for which the certificate is requested, and such other relevant information as the Secretary may require;

(2) a statement identifying each vehicle to be used to transport any migrant or seasonal agricultural worker and, if the vehicle is or will be owned or controlled by the applicant, documentation showing that the applicant is in compliance with the requirements of section 401 with respect to each such vehicle;

(3) a statement identifying each facility or real property to be used to house any migrant agricultural worker and, if the facility or real property is or will be owned or controlled by the applicant, documentation showing that the applicant is in compliance with section 203 with respect to each such facility or real property;

(4) a set of fingerprints of the applicant; and

(5) a declaration, subscribed and sworn to by the applicant, consenting to the designation by a court of the Secretary as an agent available to accept service of summons in any action against the applicant, if the applicant has left the jurisdiction in which the action is commenced or otherwise has become unavailable to accept service.

§ 1813. Registration determinations

[Sec. 103] (a) In accordance with regulations, the Secretary may refuse to issue or renew, or may suspend or revoke, a certificate of registration (including a certificate of registration as an employee of a farm labor contractor) if the applicant or holder—

(1) has knowingly made any misrepresentation in the application for such certificate;

(2) is not the real party in interest in the application or certificate of registration and the real party in interest is a person who has been refused issuance or renewal of a certificate, has had a certificate suspended or revoked, or does not qualify under this section for a certificate;

(3) has failed to comply with this Act or any regulation under this Act;

(4) has failed—

(A) to pay any court judgment obtained by the Secretary or any other person under this Act or any regulation under this Act or under the Farm Labor Contractor Registration Act of 1963 [7 U.S.C. § 2041 et seq.] or any regulation under such Act, or

(B) to comply with any final order issued by the Secretary as a result of a violation of this Act or any regulation under this Act or a violation of the Farm Labor Contractor Registration Act of 1963 or any regulation under such Act;

(5) has been convicted within the preceding five years—

(A) of any crime under State or Federal law relating to gambling, or to the sale, distribution or possession of alcoholic beverages, in connection with or incident to any farm labor contracting activities; or

(B) of any felony under State or Federal law involving robbery, bribery, extortion, embezzlement, grand larceny, burglary, arson, violation of narcotics laws, murder, rape, assault with intent to kill, assault which inflicts grievous bodily injury, prostitution, peonage, or smuggling or harboring individuals who have entered the United States illegally; or

(6) has been found to have violated paragraph (1) or (2) of section 1324a(a) of Title 8.

(b)(1) The person who is refused the issuance or renewal of a certificate or whose certificate is suspended or revoked under subsection (a) shall be afforded an opportunity for agency hearing, upon request made within thirty days after the date of issuance of the notice of the refusal, suspension, or revocation. In such hearing, all issues shall be determined on the record pursuant to section 554 of title 5, United States Code. If no hearing is requested as herein provided, the refusal, suspension, or revocation shall constitute a final and unappealable order.

(2) If a hearing is requested, the initial agency decision shall be made by an administrative law judge, and such decision shall become the final order unless the Secretary modifies or vacates the decision. Notice of intent to modify or vacate the decision of the administrative law judge shall be issued to the parties within thirty days after the decision of the administrative law judge. A final order which takes effect under this paragraph shall be subject to review only as provided under subsection (c).

(c) Any person against whom an order has been entered after an agency hearing under this section may obtain review by the United States district court for any district in which he is located or the United States District Court for the District of Columbia by filing a notice of appeal in such court within thirty days from the date of such order, and simultaneously sending a copy of such notice by registered mail to the Secretary. The Secretary shall promptly certify and file in such court the record upon which the order was based. The findings of the Secretary shall be set aside only if found to be unsupported by substantial evidence as provided by section 706(2)(E) of title 5, United States Code. Any final decision, order, or judgment of such District Court concerning such review shall be subject to appeal as provided in chapter 83 of title 28, United States Code.

§ 1814. Transfer or assignment; expiration; renewal

[Sec. 104] (a) A certificate of registration may not be transferred or assigned.

(b)(1) Unless earlier suspended or revoked, a certificate shall expire twelve months from the date of issuance, except that (A) certificates issued under this Act during the period beginning December 1, 1982, and ending November 30, 1983, may be issued for a period of up to twenty-four months for the purpose of an orderly transition to registration under this Act, (B) a certificate may be temporarily extended by the filing of an application with the Secretary at least thirty days prior to its expiration date, and (C) the Secretary may renew a certificate for additional twelve-month periods or for periods in excess of twelve months but not in excess of twenty-four months.

(2) Eligibility for renewals for periods of more than twelve months shall be limited to farm labor contractors who have not been cited for a violation of this Act, or any regulation under this Act, or the Farm Labor Contractor Registration Act of 1963, or any regulation under such Act, during the preceding five years.

§ 1815. Notice of address change; amendment of certificate of registration

[Sec. 105] During the period for which the certificate of registration is in effect, each farm labor contractor shall—
(1) provide to the Secretary within thirty days a notice of each change of permanent place of residence; and
(2) apply to the Secretary to amend the certificate of registration whenever the farm labor contractor intends to—
(A) engage in another farm labor contracting activity,
(B) use, or cause to be used, another vehicle than that covered by the

certificate to transport any migrant or seasonal agricultural worker, or

(C) use, or cause to be used, another real property or facility to house any migrant agricultural worker than that covered by the certificate.

§ 1816. Prohibition against employing illegal aliens

[Sec. 106] [Repealed.]

Subchapter II. Migrant Agricultural Worker Protections

§ 1821. Information and recordkeeping requirements

[Sec. 201] (a) Each farm labor contractor, agricultural employer, and agricultural association which recruits any migrant agricultural worker shall ascertain and disclose in writing to each such worker who is recruited for employment the following information at the time of the worker's recruitment:

(1) the place of employment;

(2) the wage rates to be paid;

(3) the crops and kinds of activities on which the worker may be employed;

(4) the period of employment;

(5) the transportation, housing, and any other employee benefit to be provided, if any, and any costs to be charged for each of them;

(6) the existence of any strike or other concerted work stoppage, slow-down, or interruption of operations by employees at the place of employment; and

(7) the existence of any arrangements with any owner or agent of any establishment in the area of employment under which the farm labor contractor, the agricultural employer, or the agricultural association is to receive a commission or any other benefit resulting from any sales by such establishment to the workers.

(b) Each farm labor contractor, agricultural employer, and agricultural association which employs any migrant agricultural worker shall, at the place of employment, post in a conspicuous place a poster provided by the Secretary setting forth the rights and protections afforded such workers under this Act, including the right of a migrant agricultural worker to have, upon request, a written statement provided by the farm labor contractor, agricultural employer, or agricultural association, of the information described in subsection (a) of this section. Such employer shall provide upon request, a written statement of the information described in subsection (a) of this section.

(c) Each farm labor contractor, agricultural employer, and agricultural association which provides housing for any migrant agricultural worker shall post in a conspicuous place or present to such worker a statement of the terms and conditions, if any, of occupancy of such housing.

(d) Each farm labor contractor, agricultural employer, and agricultural association which employs any migrant agricultural worker shall—

(1) with respect to each such worker, make, keep, and preserve records for three years of the following information:

(A) the basis on which wages are paid;

(B) the number of piecework units earned, if paid on a piecework basis;

(C) the number of hours worked;

(D) the total pay period earnings;

(E) the specific sums withheld and the purpose of each sum withheld; and

(F) the net pay; and

(2) provide to each such worker for each pay period, an itemized written statement of the information required by paragraph (1) of this subsection.

(e) Each farm labor contractor shall provide to any other farm labor contractor, and to any agricultural employer and agricultural association to which such farm labor contractor has furnished migrant agricultural workers, copies of all records with respect to each such worker which such farm labor contractor is required to retain by subsection (d)(1) of this section. The recipient of such records shall keep them for a period of three years from the end of the period of employment.

(f) No farm labor contractor, agricultural employer, or agricultural association shall knowingly provide false or misleading information to any migrant agricultural worker concerning the terms, conditions, or existence of agricultural employment required to be disclosed by subsection (a), (b), (c), or (d) of this section.

(g) The information required to be disclosed by subsections (a) through (c) of this section to migrant agricultural workers shall be provided in written form. Such information shall be provided in English or, as necessary and reasonable, in Spanish or other language common to migrant agricultural workers who are not fluent or literate in English. The Department of Labor shall make forms available in English, Spanish, and other languages, as necessary, which may be used in providing workers with information required under this section.

§ 1822. Wages, supplies, and other working arrangements

[Sec. 202] (a) Each farm labor contractor, agricultural employer, and agricultural association which employs any migrant agricultural worker shall pay the wages owed to such worker when due.

(b) No farm labor contractor, agricultural employer, or agricultural association shall require any migrant agricultural worker to purchase any goods or services solely from such farm labor contractor, agricultural employer, or agricultural association.

(c) No farm labor contractor, agricultural employer, or agricultural association shall, without justification, violate the terms of any working arrangement made by that contractor, employer, or association with any migrant agricultural worker.

§ 1823. Safety and health of housing

[Sec. 203] (a) Except as provided in subsection (c) of this section, each person who owns or controls a facility or real property which is used as housing for migrant agricultural workers shall be responsible for ensuring that the facility or real property complies with substantive Federal and State safety and health standards applicable to that housing.

(b)(1) Except as provided in subsection (c) of this section and paragraph (2) of this subsection, no facility or real property may be occupied by any migrant agricultural worker unless either a State or local health authority or other appropriate agency has certified that the facility or property meets applicable safety and health standards. No person who owns or controls any such facility or property shall permit it to be occupied by any migrant agricultural worker unless a copy of the certification of occupancy is posted at the site. The receipt and posting of a certificate of occupancy does not relieve any person of responsibilities under subsection (a) of this section. Each such person shall retain the original certification for three years and shall make it available for inspection and review in accordance with section 512 [29 U.S.C. 1862].

(2) Notwithstanding paragraph (1) of this subsection, if a request for the inspection of a facility or real property is made to the appropriate State or local agency at least forty-five days prior to the date on which it is occupied by migrant agricultural workers and such agency has not conducted an inspection by such date, the facility or property may be so occupied.

(c) This section does not apply to any person who, in the ordinary course of that person's business, regularly provides housing on a commercial basis to the general public and who provides housing to migrant agricultural workers of the same character and on the same or comparable terms and conditions as is provided to the general public.

Subchapter III. Seasonal Agricultural Worker Protections

§ 1831. Information and recordkeeping requirements

[Sec. 301] (a)(1) Each farm labor contractor, agricultural employer, and agricultural association which recruits any seasonal agricultural worker (other than day-haul workers described in section 3(10)(A)(ii)) shall ascertain and, upon request, disclose in writing the following information when an offer of employment is made to such worker:

(A) the place of employment;

(B) the wage rates to be paid;

(C) the crops and kinds of activities on which the worker may be employed;

(D) the period of employment;

(E) the transportation and any other employee benefit to be provided, if any, and any costs to be charged for each of them;

(F) the existence of any strike or other concerted work stoppage, slowdown, or interruption of operations by employees at the place of employment; and

(G) the existence of any arrangements with any owner or agent of any establishment in the area of employment under which the farm labor contractor, the agricultural employer, or the agricultural association is to receive a commission or any other benefit resulting from any sales by such establishment to the workers.

(2) Each farm labor contractor, agricultural employer, and agricultural association which recruits seasonal agricultural workers through use of a day-haul operation described in section 1802(10)(A)(ii) of this title shall ascertain and disclose in writing to the worker at the place of recruitment the information described in paragraph (1).

(b) Each farm labor contractor, agricultural employer, and agricultural association which employs any seasonal agricultural worker shall, at the place of employment, post in a conspicuous place a poster provided by the Secretary setting forth the rights and protections afforded such workers under this Act, including the right of a seasonal agricultural worker to have, upon request, a written statement provided by the farm labor contractor, agricultural employer, or agricultural association, of the information described in subsection (a) of this section. Such employer shall provide, upon request, a written statement of the information described in subsection (a) of this section.

(c) Each farm labor contractor, agricultural employer, and agricultural association which employs any seasonal agricultural worker shall—

(1) with respect to each such worker, make, keep, and preserve records for three years of the following information:

(A) the basis on which wages are paid;

(B) the number of piecework units earned, if paid on a piecework basis;

(C) the number of hours worked;

(D) the total pay period earnings;

(E) the specific sums withheld and the purpose of each sum withheld; and

(F) the net pay; and

(2) provide to each such worker for each pay period, an itemized written statement of the information required by paragraph (1) of this subsection.

(d)(1) Each farm labor contractor shall provide to any other farm labor contractor and to any agricultural employer and agricultural association to which such farm labor contractor has furnished seasonal agricultural workers, copies of all records with respect to each such worker which such farm labor contractor is required to retain by subsection (c)(1). The recipient of these records shall keep them for a period of three years from the end of the period of employment.

(e) No farm labor contractor, agricultural employer, or agricultural association shall knowingly provide false or misleading information to any seasonal agricultural worker concerning the terms, conditions, or existence of agricultural employment required to be disclosed by subsection (a), (b), or (c).

(f) The information required to be disclosed by subsections (a) and (b) of this section to seasonal agricultural workers shall be provided in written form. Such information shall be provided in English, or as necessary and reasonable, in Spanish or other language common to seasonal agricultural workers who are not fluent or literate in English. The Department of Labor shall make forms available in English, Spanish, and other languages, as necessary, which may be used in providing workers with information required under this section.

§ 1832. Wages, supplies, and other working arrangements

[Sec. 302] (a) Each farm labor contractor, agricultural employer, and agricultural association which employs any seasonal agricultural worker shall pay the wages owed to such worker when due.

(b) No farm labor contractor, agricultural employer, or agricultural association shall require any seasonal agricultural worker to purchase any goods or services solely from such farm labor contractor, agricultural employer, or agricultural association.

(c) No farm labor contractor, agricultural employer, or agricultural association shall, without justification, violate the terms of any working arrangement made by that contractor, employer, or association with any seasonal agricultural worker.

Subchapter IV. Further Protections for Migrant and Seasonal Agricultural Workers

§ 1841. Motor vehicle safety

[Sec. 401] (a)(1) Except as provided in paragraph (2), this section applies to the transportation of any migrant or seasonal agricultural worker.

(2) This section does not apply to the transportation of any migrant or seasonal agricultural worker on a tractor, combine, harvester, picker, or other similar machinery and equipment while such worker is actually engaged in the planting, cultivating, or harvesting of any agricultural commodity or the care of livestock or poultry.

(b)(1) When using, or causing to be used, any vehicle for providing transportation to which this section applies, each agricultural employer, agricultural association, and farm labor contractor shall—

(A) ensure that such vehicle conforms to the standards prescribed by the Secretary under paragraph (2) of this subsection and other applicable Federal and State safety standards,

(B) ensure that each driver has a valid and appropriate license, as provided by State law, to operate the vehicle, and

(C) have an insurance policy or a liability bond that is in effect which insures the agricultural employer, the agricultural association, or the farm labor contractor against liability for damage to persons or property arising from the ownership, operation, or the causing to be operated, of any vehicle used to transport any migrant or seasonal agricultural worker.

(2)(A) For purposes of paragraph (1)(A), the Secretary shall prescribe such regulations as may be necessary to protect the health and safety of migrant and seasonal agricultural workers.

(B) To the extent consistent with the protection of the health and safety of migrant and seasonal agricultural workers, the Secretary shall, in promulgating regulations under subparagraph (A), consider, among other factors—

(i) the type of vehicle used,

(ii) the passenger capacity of the vehicle,

(iii) the distance which such workers will be carried in the vehicle,

(iv) the type of roads and highways on which such workers will be carried in the vehicle,

(v) the extent to which a proposed standard would cause an undue burden on agricultural employers, agricultural associations, or farm labor contractors.

(C) Standards prescribed by the Secretary under subparagraph (A) shall be in addition to, and shall not supersede or modify, any standard under part II of the Interstate Commerce Act (49 U.S.C. 301 et seq.), or any successor provision of subtitle IV of title 49, United States Code, or regulations issued thereunder, which is independently applicable to transportation to which this section applies. A violation of any such standard shall also constitute a violation under this Act.

(D) In the event that the Secretary fails for any reason to prescribe standards under subparagraph (A) by the effective date of this Act, the standards prescribed under section 3102 of Title 49, relating to the transportation of migrant workers, shall, for purposes of paragraph (1)(A), be deemed to be the standards prescribed by the Secretary under this paragraph, and shall, as appropriate, and reasonable in the circumstances, apply (i) without regard to the mileage and boundary line limitations contained in such section, and (ii) until superseded by standards actually prescribed by the Secretary in accordance with this paragraph.

(3) The level of the insurance required by paragraph (1)(C) shall be at least the amount currently required for common carriers of passengers under part II of the Interstate Commerce Act (49 U.S.C. 301 et seq.) and any successor provision of subtitle IV of title 49, United States Code, and regulations prescribed thereunder.

(c) If an agricultural employer, agricultural association, or farm labor contractor is the employer of any migrant or seasonal agricultural workers for purposes of a State workers' compensation law and such employer provides worker's compensation coverage for such worker in the case of bodily injury or death as provided by such State law, the following adjustments in the requirements of subsection (b)(1)(C) relating to having an insurance policy or liability bond apply:

(1) No insurance policy or liability bond shall be required of the employer, if such workers are transported only under circumstances for which there is coverage under such State law.

(2) An insurance policy or liability bond shall be required of the employer for circumstances under which coverage for the transportation of such workers is not provided under such State law.

(d) The Secretary shall, by regulations promulgated in accordance with section 1861 of this title not later than the effective date of this Act, prescribe the standards required for the purposes of implementing this section. Any subsequent revision of such standards shall also be accomplished by regulation promulgated in accordance with such section.

§ 1842.   Confirmation of registration

[Sec. 402] No person shall utilize the services of any farm labor contractor to supply any migrant or seasonal agricultural worker unless the person first takes reasonable steps to determine that the farm labor contractor possesses a certificate of registration which is valid and which authorizes the activity for which the contractor is utilized. In making that determination, the person may rely upon either possession of a certificate of registration, or confirmation of such registration by the Department of Labor. The Secretary shall maintain a central public registry of all persons issued a certificate of registration.

§ 1843.   Information on employment conditions

[Sec. 403] Each farm labor contractor, without regard to any other provisions of this Act, shall obtain at each place of employment and make available for inspection to every worker he furnishes for employment, a written statement of the conditions of such employment as described in sections 1821(b) and 1831(b) of this title.

§ 1844. Compliance with written agreements

[Sec. 404] (a) No farm labor contractor shall violate, without jurisdiction, the terms of any written agreements made with an agricultural employer or an agricultural association pertaining to any contracting activity or worker protection under this Act.

(b) Written agreements under this section do not relieve a person of any responsibility that such person would otherwise have under this Act.

Subchapter V. General Provisions

Part A. Enforcement Provisions

§ 1851. Criminal sanctions

[Sec. 501] (a) Any person who willfully and knowingly violates this Act or any regulation under this Act shall be fined not more than $1,000 or sentenced to prison for a term not to exceed one year, or both. Upon conviction for any subsequent violation of this Act, or any regulation under this Act, the defendant shall be fined not more than $10,000 or sentenced to prison for a term not to exceed three years, or both.

(b) If a farm labor contractor who commits a violation of paragraph (1) or (2) of section 1324a of Title 8 has been refused issuance or renewal of, or has failed to obtain, a certificate of registration or is a farm labor contractor whose certificate has been suspended or revoked, the contractor shall, upon conviction, be fined not more than $10,000 or sentenced to prison for a term not to exceed three years, or both.

§ 1852. Judicial enforcement

[Sec. 502] (a) The Secretary may petition any appropriate district court of the United States for temporary or permanent injunctive relief if the Secretary determines that this Act, or any regulation under this Act, has been violated.

(b) Except as provided in section 518(a) of title 28, United States Code, relating to litigation before the Supreme Court, the Solicitor of Labor may appear for and represent the Secretary in any civil litigation brought under this Act, but all such litigation shall be subject to the direction and control of the Attorney General.

§ 1853. Administrative sanctions

[Sec. 503] (a)(1) Subject to paragraph (2), any person who commits a violation of this Act or any regulation under this Act, may be assessed a civil money penalty of not more than $1,000 for each violation.

(2) In determining the amount of any penalty to be assessed under paragraph (1), the Secretary shall take into account (A) the previous record of the person in terms of compliance with this Act and with comparable requirements of the Farm Labor Contractor Registration Act of 1963, and with regulations promulgated under such Acts, and (B) the gravity of the violation.

(b)(1) The person assessed shall be afforded an opportunity for agency hearing, upon request made within thirty days after the date of issuance of the notice of assessment. In such hearing, all issues shall be determined on the record pursuant to section 554 of title 5, United States Code. If no hearing is requested as herein provided, the assessment shall constitute a final and unappealable order.

(2) If a hearing is requested, the initial agency decision shall be made by an administrative law judge, and such decision shall become the final order unless the Secretary modifies or vacates the decision. Notice of intent to modify or vacate the decision of the administrative law judge shall be issued to the parties within thirty days after the decision of the administrative law judge. A final order which takes effect under this paragraph shall be subject to review only as provided under subsection (c) of this section.

(c) Any person against whom an order imposing a civil money penalty has been entered after an agency hearing under this section may obtain review by the United States district court for any district in which he is located or the United States District Court for the District of Columbia by filing a notice of appeal in such court within thirty days from the date of such order, and simultaneously sending a copy of such notice by registered mail to the Secretary. The Secretary shall promptly certify and file in such court the record upon which the penalty was imposed. The findings of the Secretary shall be set aside only if found to be unsupported by substantial evidence as provided by section 706(2)(E) of title 5, United States Code. Any final decision, order, or judgment of such District Court concerning such review shall be subject to appeal as provided in chapter 83 of title 28, United States Code.

(d) If any person fails to pay an assessment after it has become a final and unappealable order, or after the court has entered final judgment in favor of the agency, the Secretary shall refer the matter to the Attorney General, who shall recover the amount assessed by action in the appropriate United States district court. In such action the validity and appropriateness of the final order imposing the penalty shall not be subject to review.

(e) All penalties collected under authority of this section shall be paid into the Treasury of the United States.

§ 1854. Private right of action

[Sec. 504] (a) Any person aggrieved by a violation of this Act or any regulation under this Act by a farm labor contractor, agricultural employer, agricultural association, or other person may file suit in any district court of the United States having jurisdiction of the parties, without respect to the amount in controversy and without regard to the citizenship of the parties and without regard to exhaustion of any alternative administrative remedies provided herein.

(b) Upon application by a complainant and in such circumstances as the court may deem just, the court may appoint an attorney for such complainant and may authorize the commencement of the action.

(c)(1) If the court finds that the respondent has intentionally violated any provision of this Act or any regulation under this Act, it may award damages up to and including an amount equal to the amount of actual damages, or statutory damages of up to $500 per plaintiff per violation, or other equitable relief, except that (A) multiple infractions of a single provision of this Act or of regulations under this Act shall constitute only one violation for purposes of determining the amount of statutory damages due a plaintiff; and (B) if such complaint is certified as a class action, the court shall award no more than the lesser of up to $500 per plaintiff per violation, or up to $500,000 or other equitable relief.

(2) In determining the amount of damages to be awarded under paragraph (1), the court is authorized to consider whether an attempt was made to resolve the issues in dispute before the resort to litigation.

(3) Any civil action brought under this section shall be subject to appeal as provided in chapter 83 of title 28, United States Code.

§ 1855. Discrimination prohibited

[Sec. 505] (a) No person shall intimidate, threaten, restrain, coerce, blacklist, discharge, charge, or in any manner discriminate against any migrant or seasonal agricultural worker because such worker has, with just cause, filed any complaint or instituted, or caused to be instituted, any proceeding under or related to this Act, or has testified or is about to testify in any such proceedings, or because of the exercise, with just cause, by such worker on behalf of himself or others of any right or protection afforded by this Act.

(b) A migrant or seasonal agricultural worker who believes, with just cause, that he has been discriminated against by any person in violation of this section may, within 180 days after such violation occurs, file a complaint with the Secretary alleging such discrimination. Upon receipt of such complaint, the Secretary shall cause such investigation to be made as he deems appropriate. If upon such investigation, the Secretary determines that the provisions of this section have been violated, the Secretary shall bring an action in any appropriate United States district court against such person. In any such action the United States district courts shall have jurisdiction, for cause shown, to restrain violation of subsection (a) and order all appropriate relief, including rehiring or reinstatement of the worker, with back pay, or damages.

§ 1856.   Waiver of rights

[Sec. 506] Agreements by employees purporting to waive or to modify their rights under this Act shall be void as contrary to public policy, except that a waiver or modification of rights in favor of the Secretary shall be valid for purposes of enforcement of this Act.

Part B. Administrative Provisions

§ 1861.   Rules and regulations

[Sec. 511] The Secretary may issue such rules and regulations as are necessary to carry out this Act, consistent with the requirements of chapter 5 of title 5, United States Code.

§ 1862.   Authority to obtain information

[Sec. 512] (a) To carry out this Act the Secretary, either pursuant to a complaint or otherwise, shall, as may be appropriate, investigate, and in connection therewith, enter and inspect such places (including housing and vehicles) and such records (and make transcriptions thereof), question such persons and gather such information to determine compliance with this Act, or regulations prescribed under this Act.

(b) The Secretary may issue subpoenas requiring the attendance and testimony of witnesses or the production of any evidence in connection with such investigations. The Secretary may administer oaths, examine witnesses, and receive evidence. For the purpose of any hearing or investigation provided for in this Act, the authority contained in sections 9 and 10 of the Federal Trade Commission Act (15 U.S.C. 49, 50), relating to the attendance of witnesses and the production of books, papers, and documents, shall be available to the Secretary. The Secretary shall conduct investigations in a manner which protects the confidentiality of any complainant or other party who provides information to the Secretary in good faith.

(c) It shall be a violation of this Act for any person to unlawfully resist, oppose, impede, intimidate, or interfere with any official of the Department of Labor assigned to perform an investigation, inspection, or law enforcement function pursuant to this Act during the performance of such duties.

§ 1863. Agreements with Federal and State agencies

[Sec. 513] (a) The Secretary may enter into agreements with Federal and State agencies (1) to use their facilities and services, (2) to delegate, subject to subsection (b), to Federal and State agencies such authority, other than rulemaking, as may be useful in carrying out this Act, and (3) to allocate or transfer funds to, or otherwise pay or reimburse, such agencies for expenses incurred pursuant to agreements under clause (1) or (2) of this section.

(b) Any delegation to a State agency pursuant to subsection (a)(2) shall be made only pursuant to a written State plan which—

(1) shall include a description of the functions to be performed, the methods of performing such functions, and the resources to be devoted to the performance of such functions; and

(2) provides assurances satisfactory to the Secretary that the State agency will comply with its description under paragraph (1) and that the State agency's performance of functions so delegated will be at least comparable to the performance of such functions by the Department of Labor.

Part C. Miscellaneous Provisions

§ 1871. State laws and regulations

[Sec. 521] This Act is intended to supplement State law, and compliance with this Act shall not excuse any person from compliance with appropriate State law and regulation.

§ 1872. Transition provision

[Sec. 522] The Secretary may deny a certificate of registration to any farm labor contractor, as defined in this Act, who has a judgment outstanding against him under the Farm Labor Contractor Registration Act of 1963 (7 U.S.C. 2041 et seq.), or is subject to a final order of the Secretary under that

Act assessing a civil money penalty which has not been paid. Any findings under the Farm Labor Contractor Registration Act of 1963 may also be applicable to determinations of willful and knowing violations under this Act.

Repealer

[Sec. 523] The Farm Labor Contractor Registration Act of 1963 (7 U.S.C. 2041 et seq.), is repealed.

Effective date

[Sec. 524] The provisions of this Act shall take effect ninety days from the date of enactment and shall be classified to title 29, United States Code.

10

Appendix

Appendix

The following regulations and official documents relating to labor and employment, not included in this book, may be found in Fair Employment Practice Manual *(FEPM)*, Labor Relations Reporter Expediter *(LRX)*, Individual Employment Rights Manual *(IERM)*, or Wages and Hours Manual *(WHM)*, all published by The Bureau of National Affairs, Inc., at the pages indicated.

Executive Orders

Number	Subject	Page
11141	Age discrimination	FEPM 401:615
		LRX 1845
11246	Nondiscrimination under federal contracts, as amended by EO 11375	FEPM 401:601
		LRX 2301
11478	Nondiscrimination in federal employment	FEPM 401:1101
		LRX 2311
11491	Labor-management relations in the federal service	LRX 1901
11521	Veterans readjustment appointments for veterans of the Vietnam era	LRX 2351
11625	Minority business enterprise	FEPM 401:2101
11701	Job listings for veterans	FEPM 401:531
		LRX 5835
11849	Establishing the collective bargaining committee in construction	LRX 4601
11935	Citizenship requirement in federal employment	FEPM 401:1105
12067	Equal employment opportunity	FEPM 401:91
12068	Functions of the Attorney General	FEPM 401:94
12125	Competitive status for handicapped federal cmployees	FEPM 401:1105

12138	Women's business enterprise	FEPM 401:2141
12171	Exclusions from the federal labor-management relations program	LRX 4439
12250	Leadership and coordination of non-discrimination laws	FEPM 401:2401
12391	National security exceptions to labor-management relations in the federal service	LRX 1915
12564	Drug-free federal workplace	LRX 4411
		IERM 595:501

Rules, Regulations, and Guidelines

Agency	Subject	Page
Education	Nondiscrimination by recipients of federal financial assistance	FEPM 401:2501
EEOC	Procedural regulations	FEPM 401:101
EEOC	Records and reports	FEPM 401:131
EEOC	Sex discrimination	FEPM 401:181
EEOC	Sexual harassment	FEPM 401:185
EEOC	Religious discrimination	FEPM 401:191
EEOC	National origin discrimination	FEPM 401:201
EEOC	EEO in the Federal Government	FEPM 401:291
EEOC	ADEA procedural regulations	FEPM 401:337
EEOC	ADEA records, reports, and exemptions	FEPM 401:341
EEOC	Equal Pay Act enforcement and record-keeping	WHM 95:601
EEOC	Equal Pay Act procedural regulations	FEPM 401:491
HHS	Age discrimination in federally funded programs	FEPM 401:379
HHS	Guidelines for preventing transmission of AIDS in the workplace	FEPM 401:2051
INS	Verification and antidiscrimination rules under the Immigration Reform and Control Act of 1986	FEPM 401:429 IERM 595:2201
Justice	Memorandum on application of Rehabilitation Act to persons with AIDS	FEPM 401:2021
Labor	Migrant and seasonal agricultural workers	LRX 8937 WHM 99:5507
Labor	Application of the Fair Labor Standards Act to employees of state and local governments	WHM 91:1143

Labor	Records to be kept by employers under FLSA	WHM 97:19
Labor	Regulations on handicapped discrimination in federally assisted programs	FEPM 401:541
NLRB	Statement of procedures, rules and regulations, series 8	LRX 4051
OFCCP	Affirmative action regulations for veterans	FEPM 401:901 FEPM 401:3001 FEPM 401:4001
OFCCP	Affirmative action regulations for handicapped workers	FEPM 401:921 FEPM 401:3021 FEPM 401:4001
OFCCP	Rules and regulations for federal contractors	FEPM 401:701 FEPM 401:2801 FEPM 401:4001